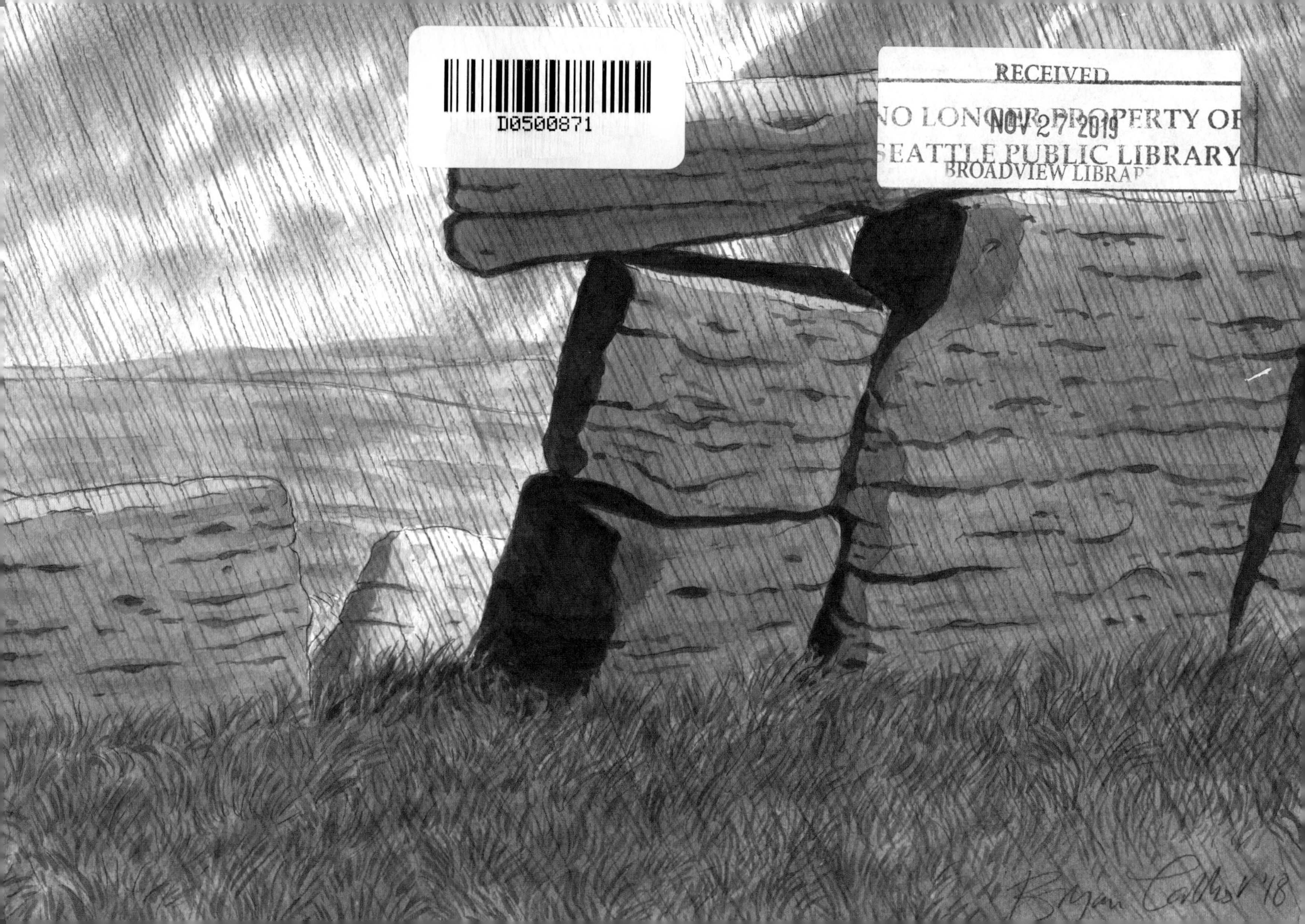
Bryan Talbot '18

RAIN

MARY M TALBOT
BRYAN TALBOT

DARK HORSE BOOKS · OREGON

Dedicated to our grandchildren: Tabitha, Madeline, Tyler, and Kalista.

"Our imagination is struck only by what is great; but the lover of natural philosophy should reflect equally on little things."
Alexander von Humboldt
Personal Narrative of Travels to the Equinoctial Regions of America, during the years 1799-1804 (1869) Vol. 2

With apologies to our old friend Stephen Gallagher for shamelessly lifting the title from his 1990 thriller, *Rain*.

Special thanks to Laura Atherton, Mike Atherton, Kate Charlesworth, Lawrence Dean, Dan Franklin, Friends of the Earth, Dr. Mel Gibson, Dr. Edward Hartley, Chris Warner, Tom and Mandy of *Two Tone Comics*, and the staff of *The White Lion*, Hebden Bridge.

The pictures in Mitch's living room are based on paintings by Louise Bourgeois. The one in Cathy's flat is based on an illustration of Wonder Woman by Trina Robbins. The book Aaron is reading from on pages 15 to 17 is Mark Avery's *Inglorious: Conflict in the Uplands*.

Supported using public funding by
ARTS COUNCIL ENGLAND
LOTTERY FUNDED

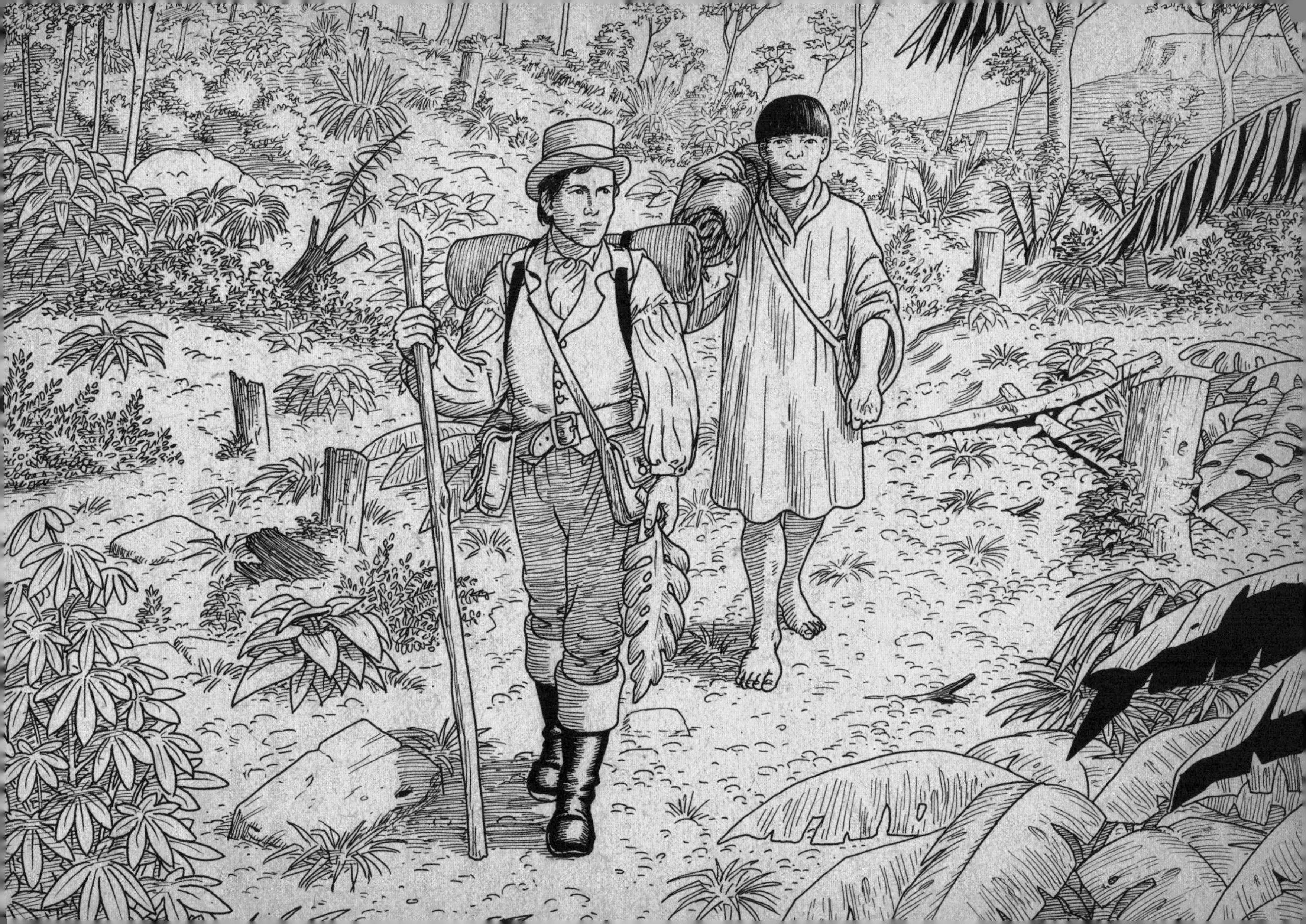

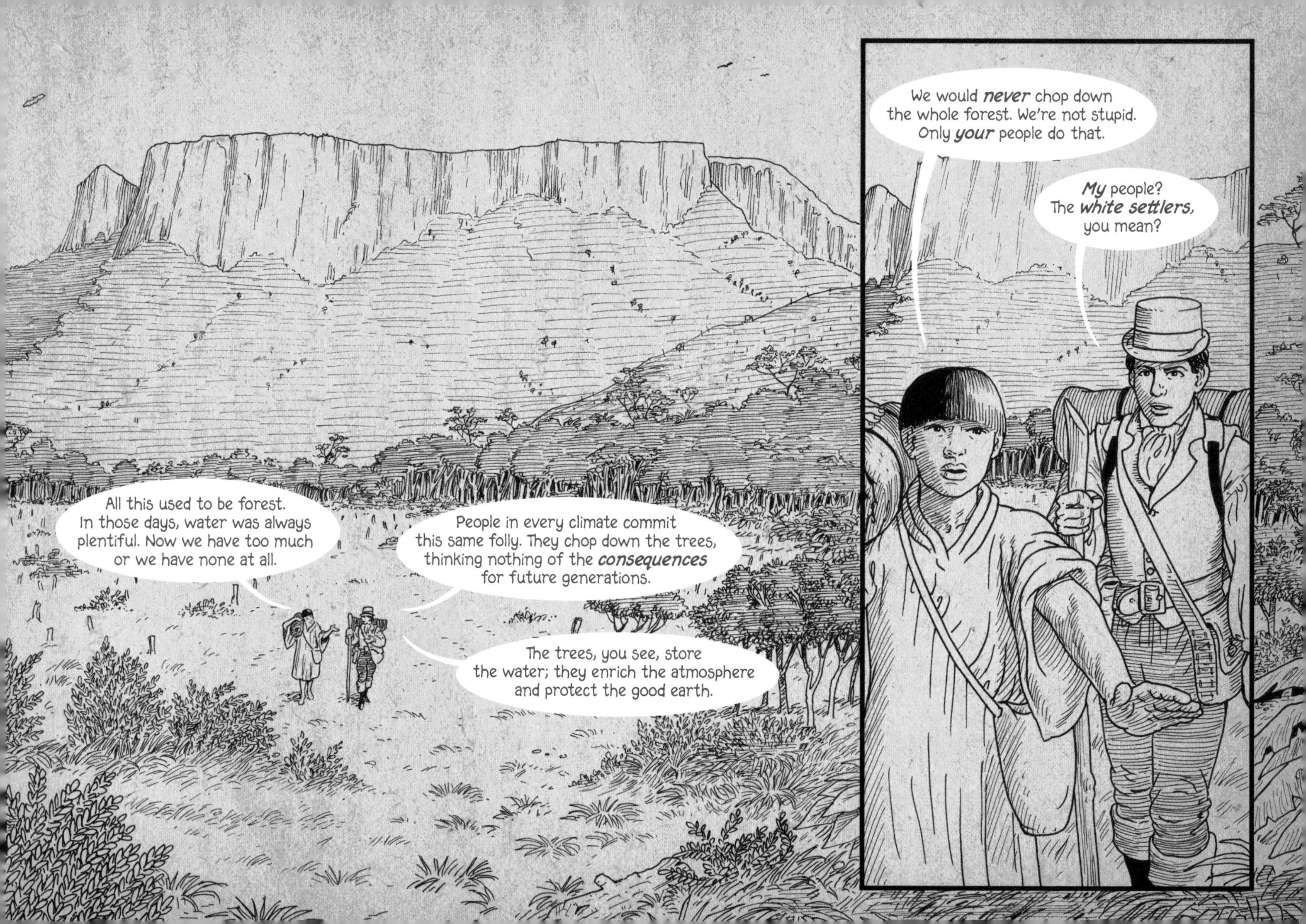

All this used to be forest. In those days, water was always plentiful. Now we have too much or we have none at all.
People in every climate commit this same folly. They chop down the trees, thinking nothing of the *consequences* for future generations.
The trees, you see, store the water; they enrich the atmosphere and protect the good earth.
We would *never* chop down the whole forest. We're not stupid. Only *your* people do that.
My people? The *white settlers*, you mean?

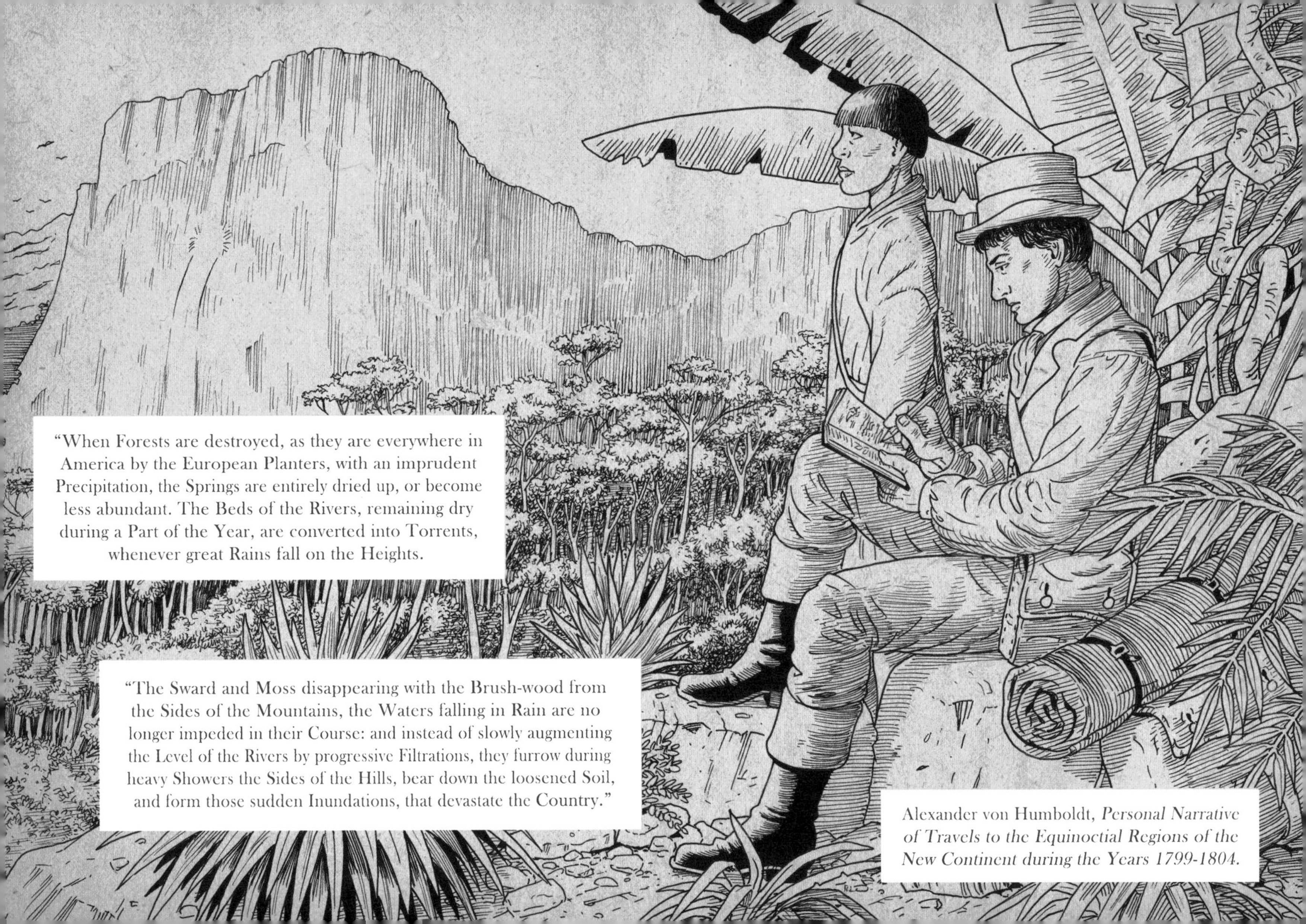
"When Forests are destroyed, as they are everywhere in America by the European Planters, with an imprudent Precipitation, the Springs are entirely dried up, or become less abundant. The Beds of the Rivers, remaining dry during a Part of the Year, are converted into Torrents, whenever great Rains fall on the Heights.
"The Sward and Moss disappearing with the Brush-wood from the Sides of the Mountains, the Waters falling in Rain are no longer impeded in their Course: and instead of slowly augmenting the Level of the Rivers by progressive Filtrations, they furrow during heavy Showers the Sides of the Hills, bear down the loosened Soil, and form those sudden Inundations, that devastate the Country."
Alexander von Humboldt, *Personal Narrative of Travels to the Equinoctial Regions of the New Continent during the Years 1799-1804.*

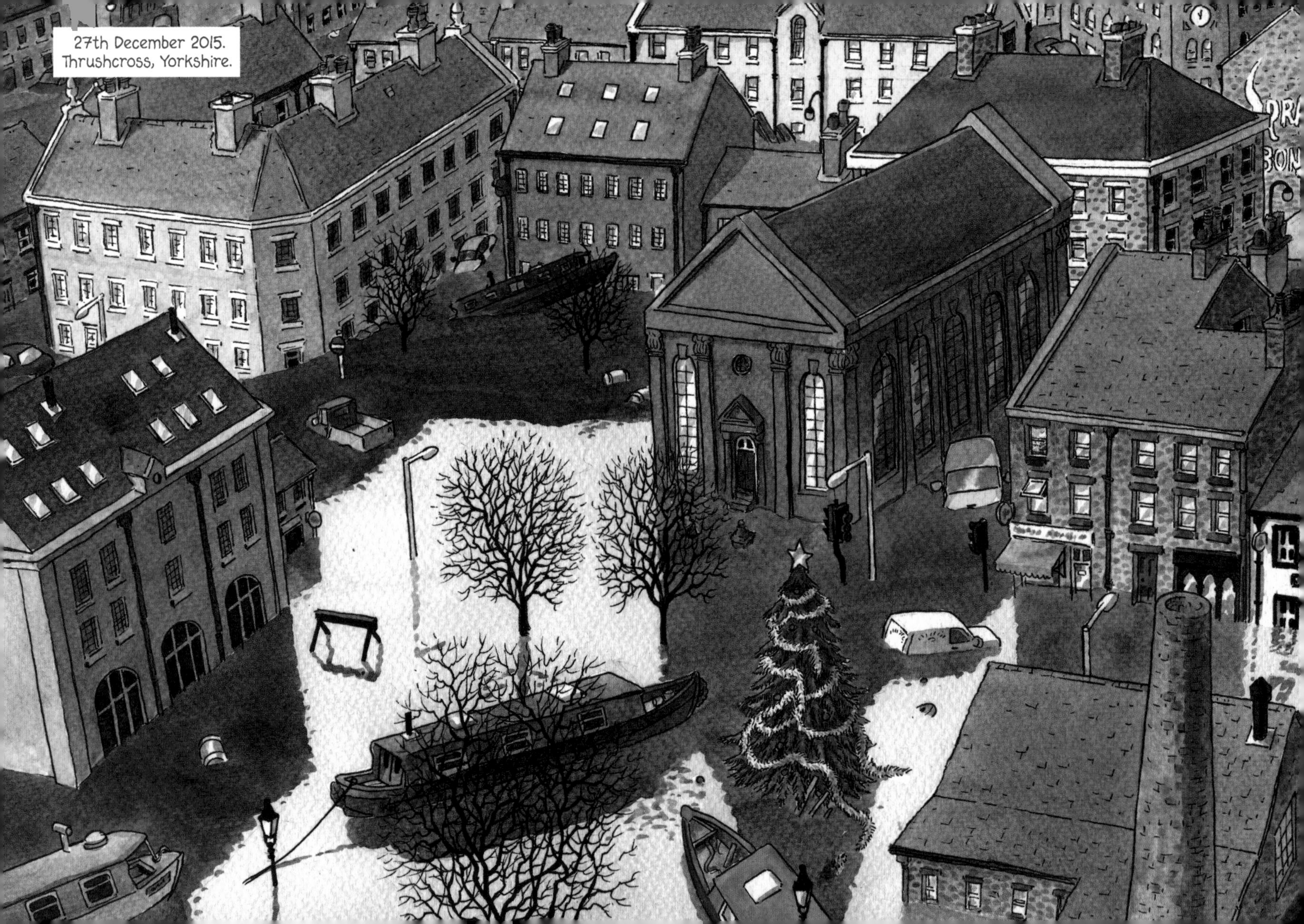
27th December 2015.
Thrushcross, Yorkshire.

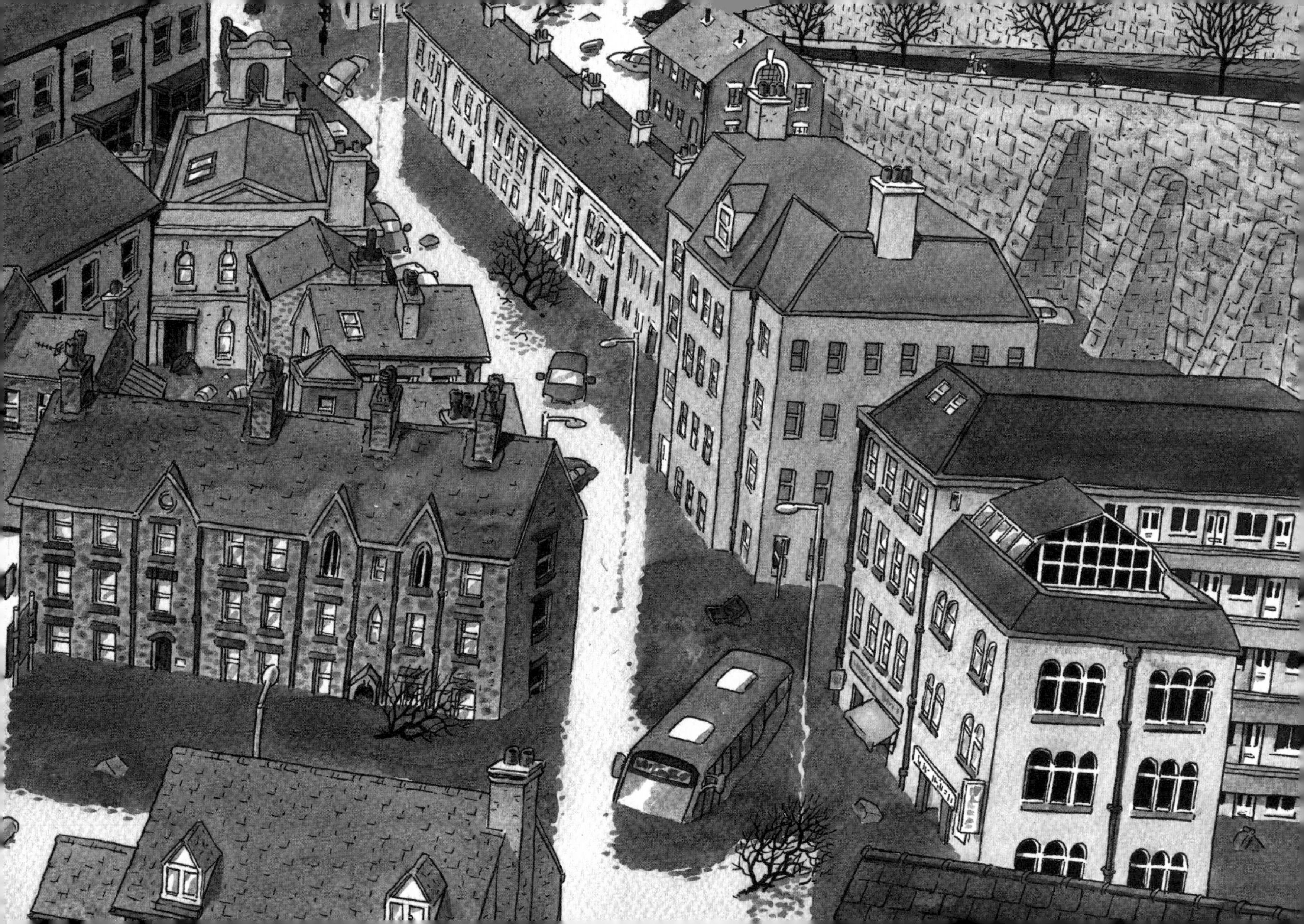

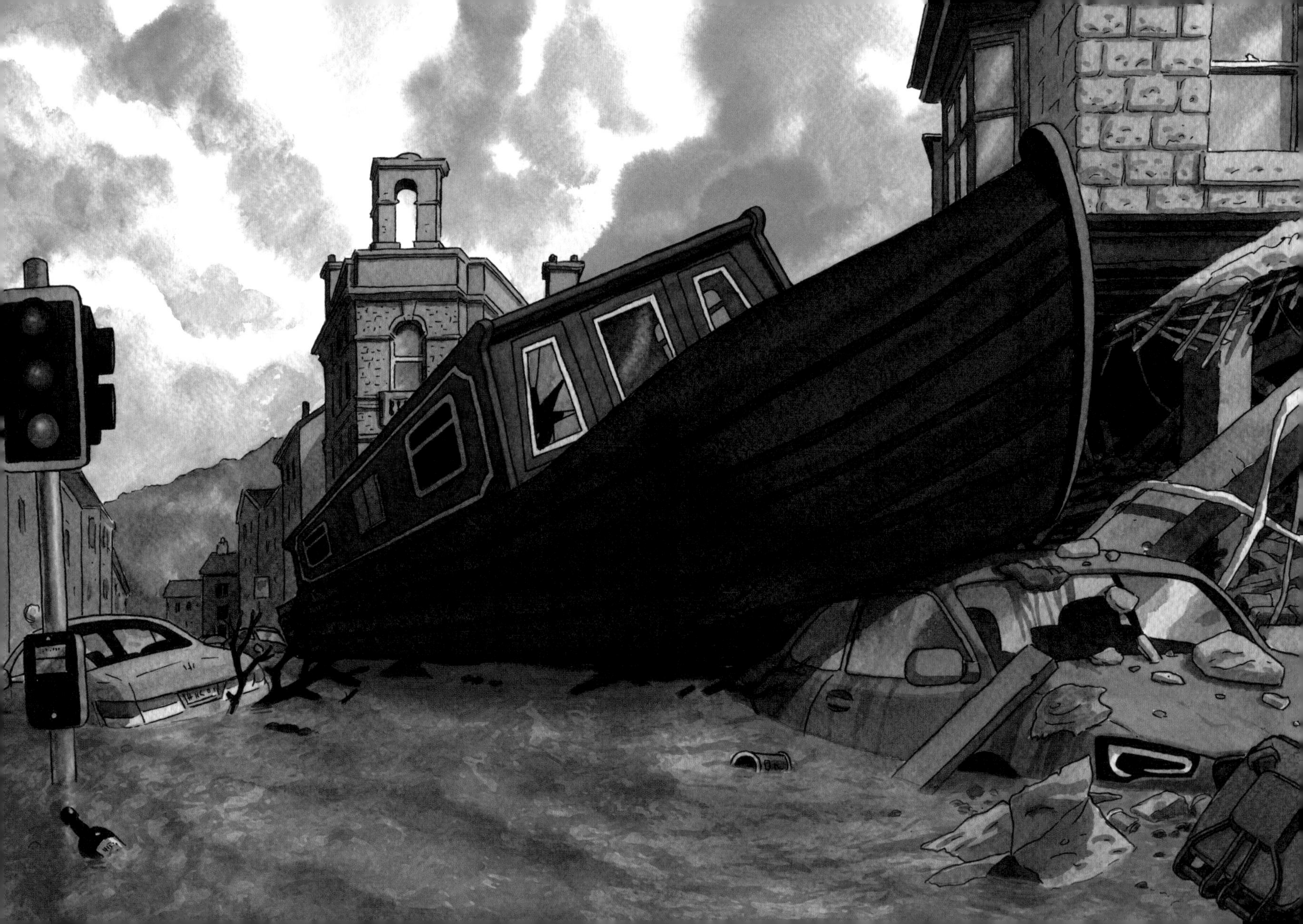

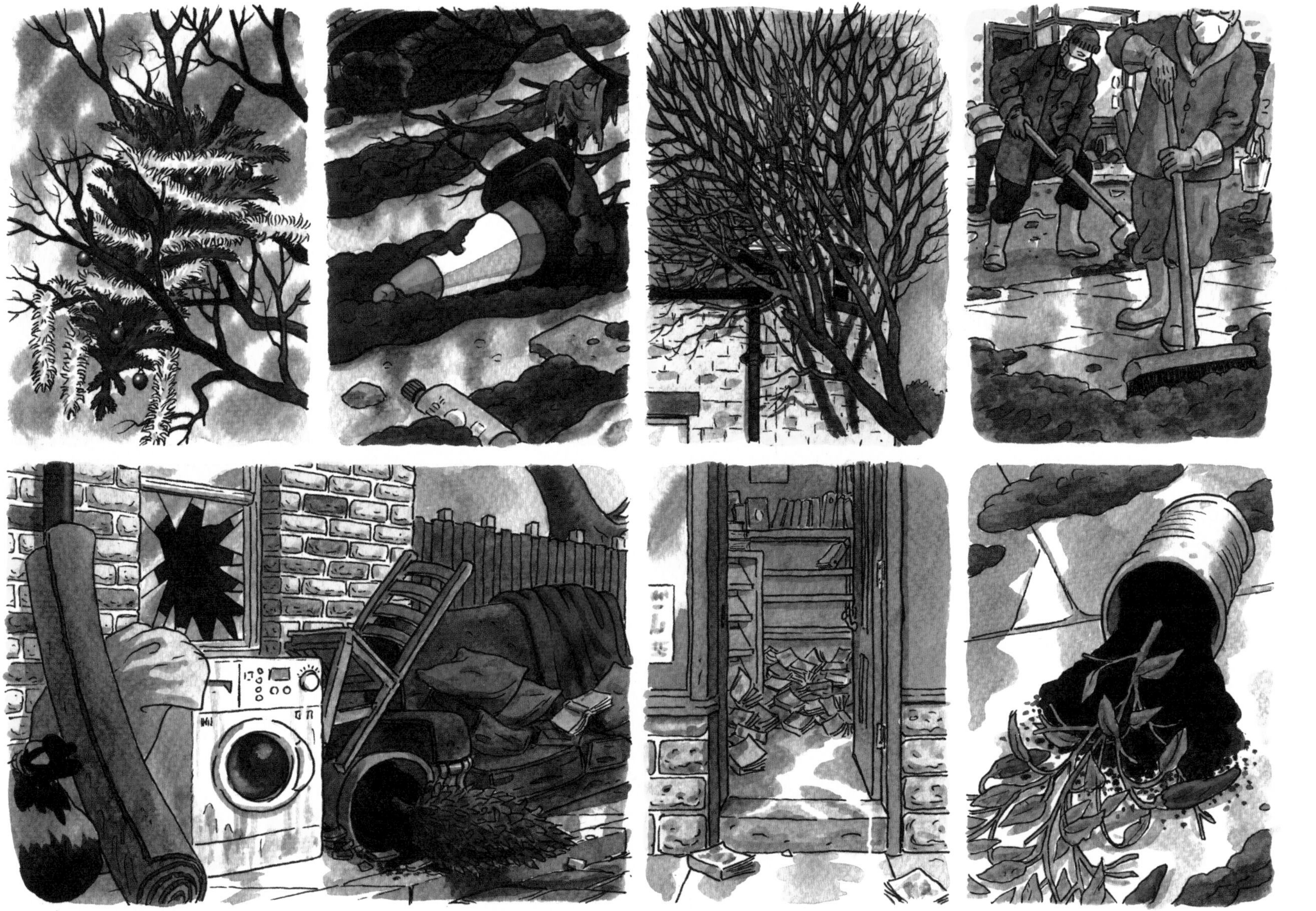

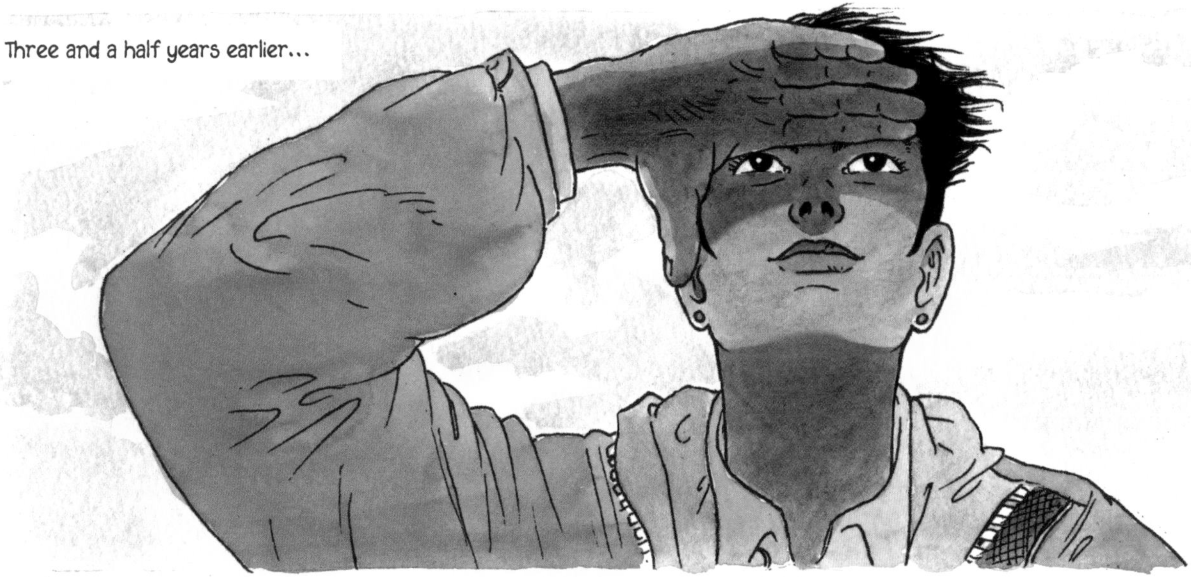
Three and a half years earlier...

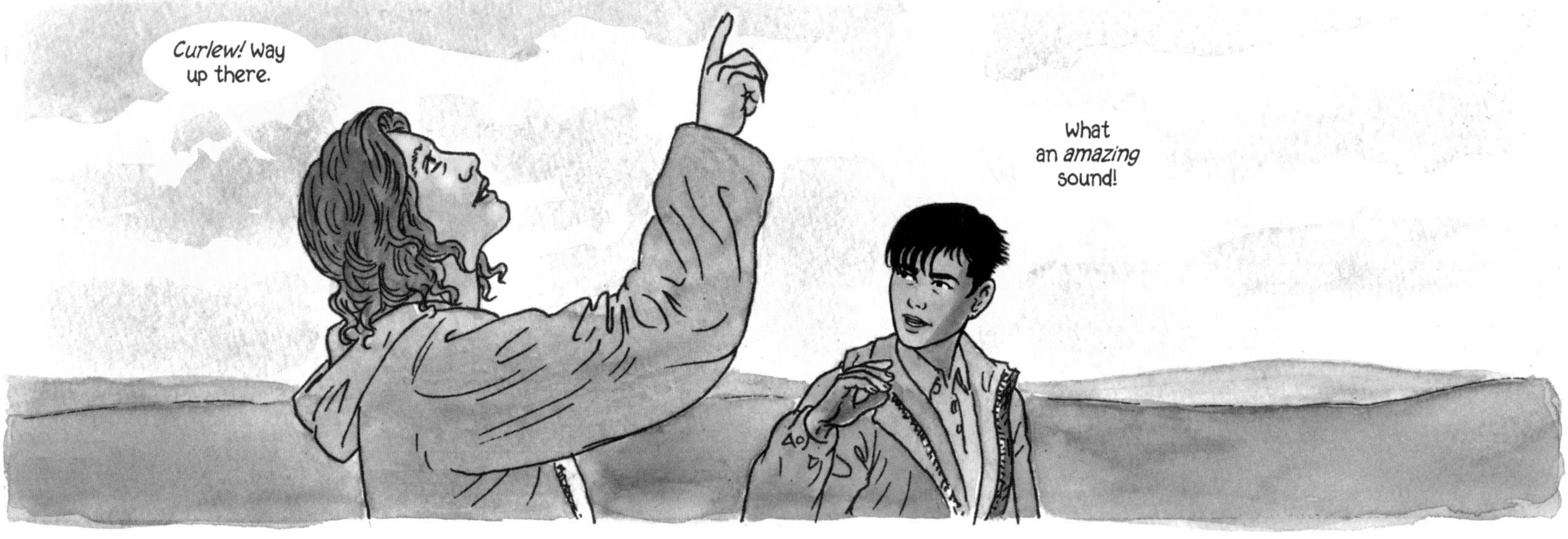
Curlew! Way up there.
What an *amazing* sound!

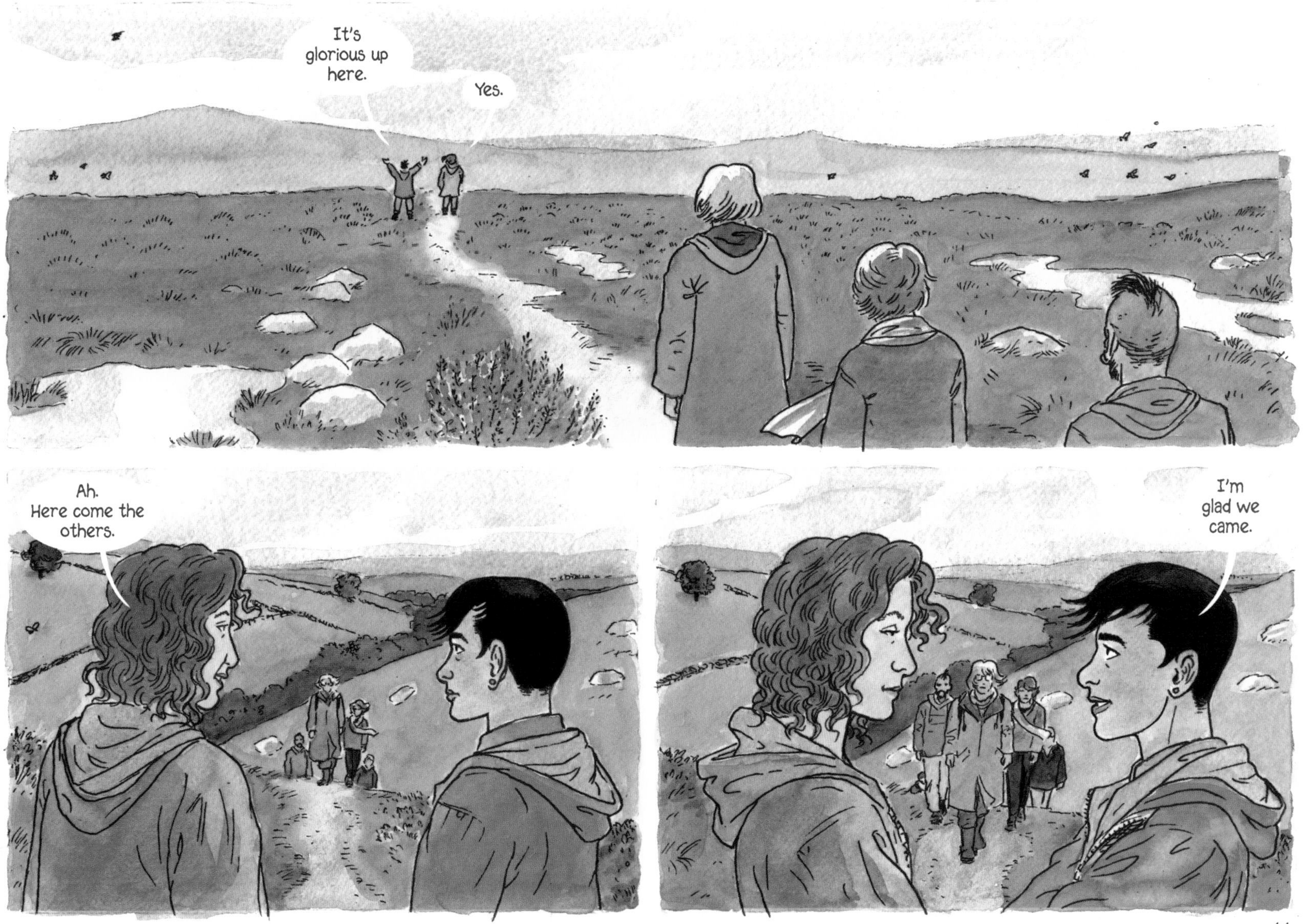
It's glorious up here.
Yes.
Ah. Here come the others.
I'm glad we came.

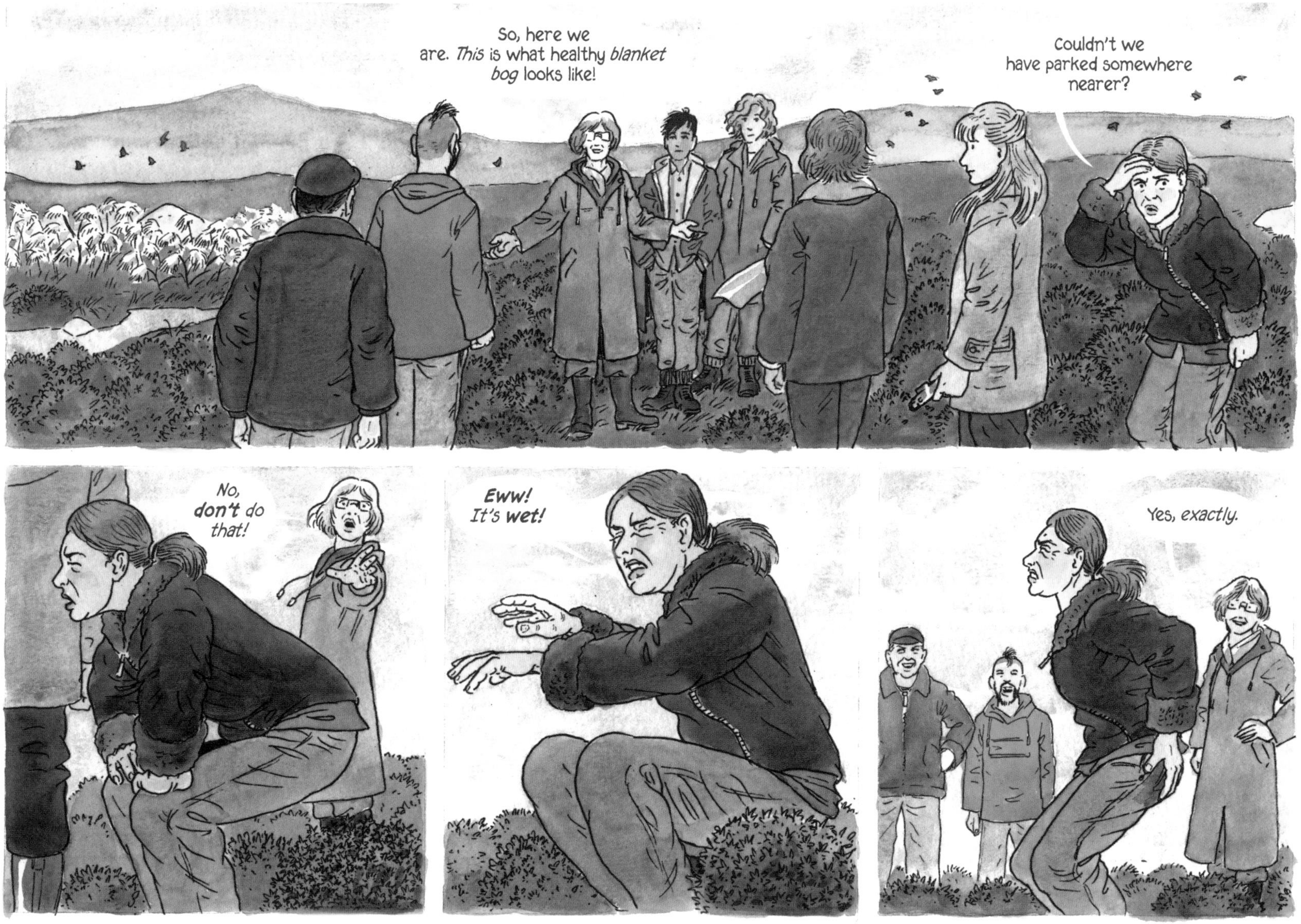
So, here we are. *This* is what healthy *blanket bog* looks like!
Couldn't we have parked somewhere nearer?
No, **don't** do that!
Eww! It's **wet!**
Yes, *exactly*.

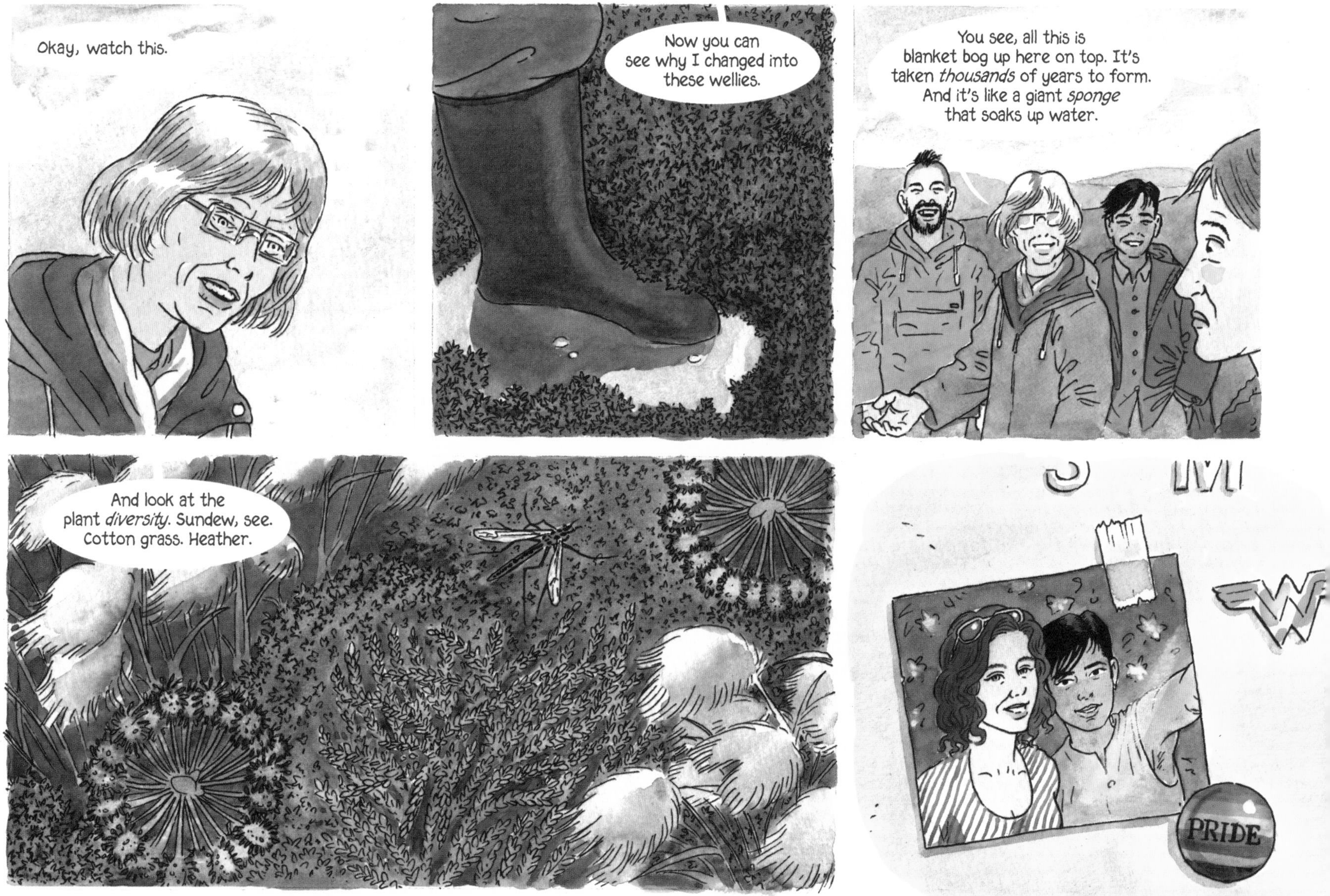

Okay, watch this.
Now you can see why I changed into these wellies.
You see, all this is blanket bog up here on top. It's taken *thousands* of years to form. And it's like a giant *sponge* that soaks up water.
And look at the plant *diversity*. Sundew, see. Cotton grass. Heather.
PRIDE

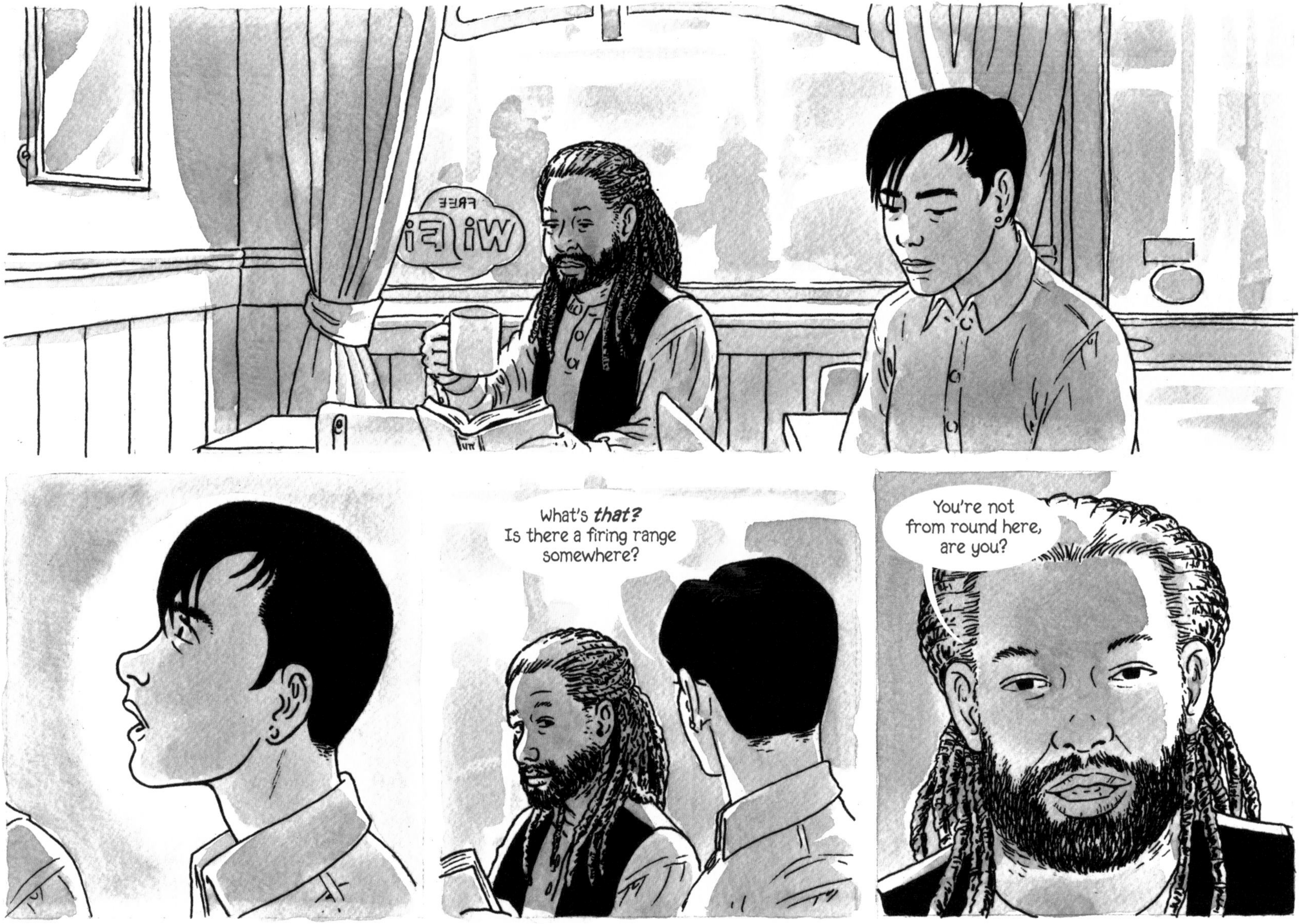
What's ***that?***
Is there a firing range
somewhere?
You're not
from round here,
are you?

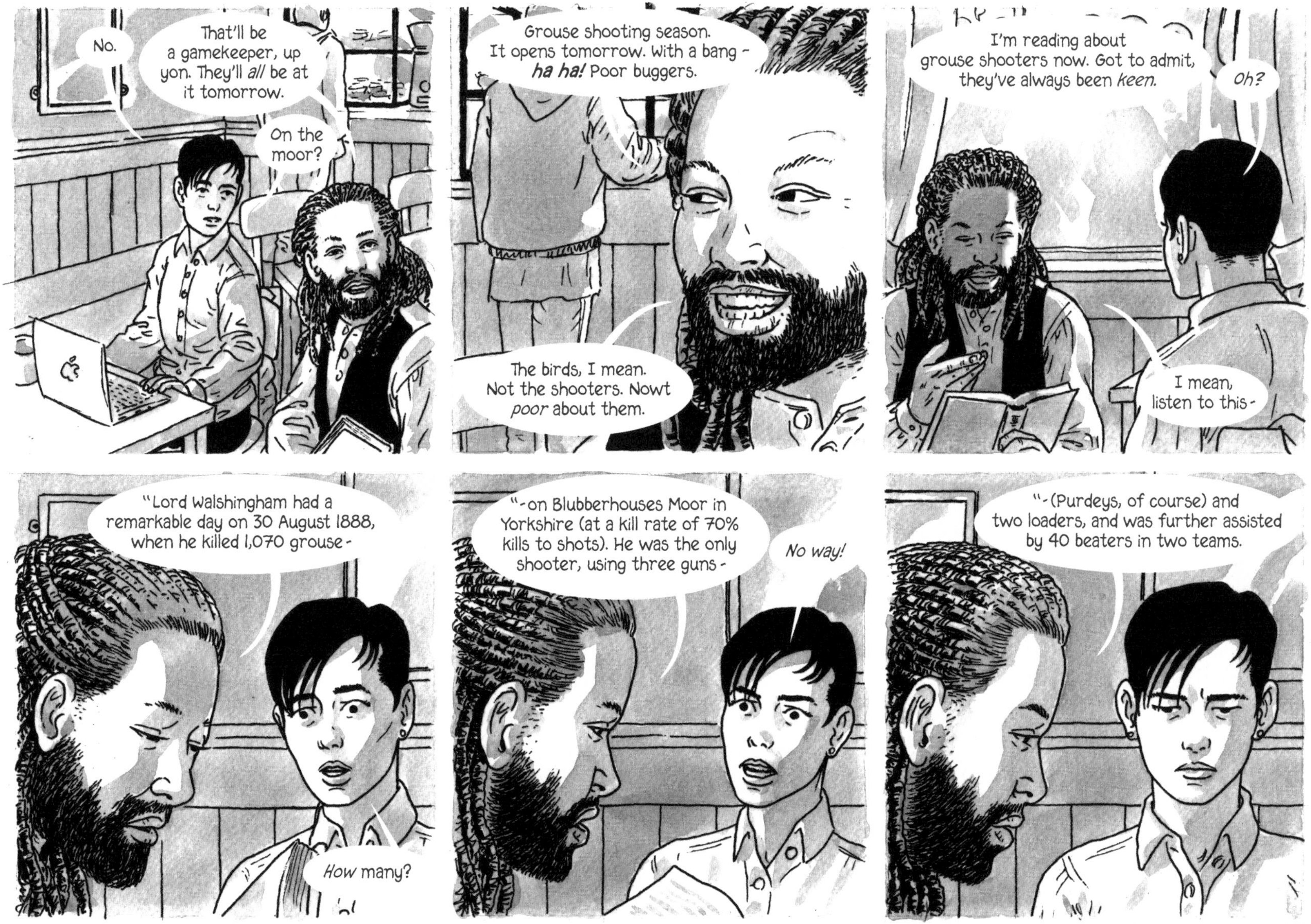
No.
That'll be a gamekeeper, up yon. They'll *all* be at it tomorrow.
On the moor?
Grouse shooting season. It opens tomorrow. With a bang - ***ha ha!*** Poor buggers.
The birds, I mean. Not the shooters. Nowt *poor* about them.
I'm reading about grouse shooters now. Got to admit, they've always been *keen.*
Oh?
I mean, listen to this -
"Lord Walshingham had a remarkable day on 30 August 1888, when he killed 1,070 grouse -
How many?
"- on Blubberhouses Moor in Yorkshire (at a kill rate of 70% kills to shots). He was the only shooter, using three guns -
No way!
"- (Purdeys, of course) and two loaders, and was further assisted by 40 beaters in two teams.

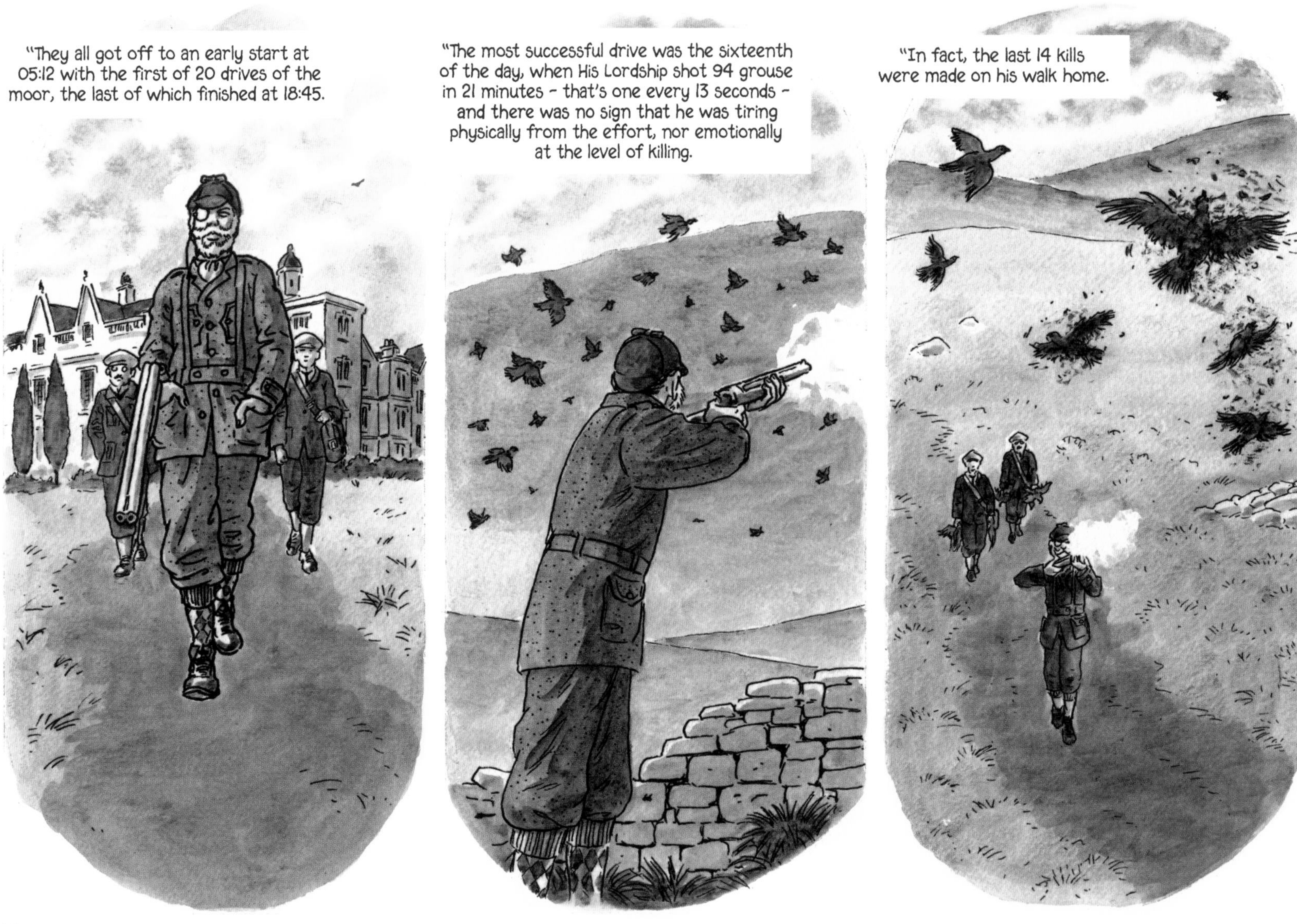
"They all got off to an early start at 05:12 with the first of 20 drives of the moor, the last of which finished at 18:45.
"The most successful drive was the sixteenth of the day, when His Lordship shot 94 grouse in 21 minutes - that's one every 13 seconds - and there was no sign that he was tiring physically from the effort, nor emotionally at the level of killing.
"In fact, the last 14 kills were made on his walk home.

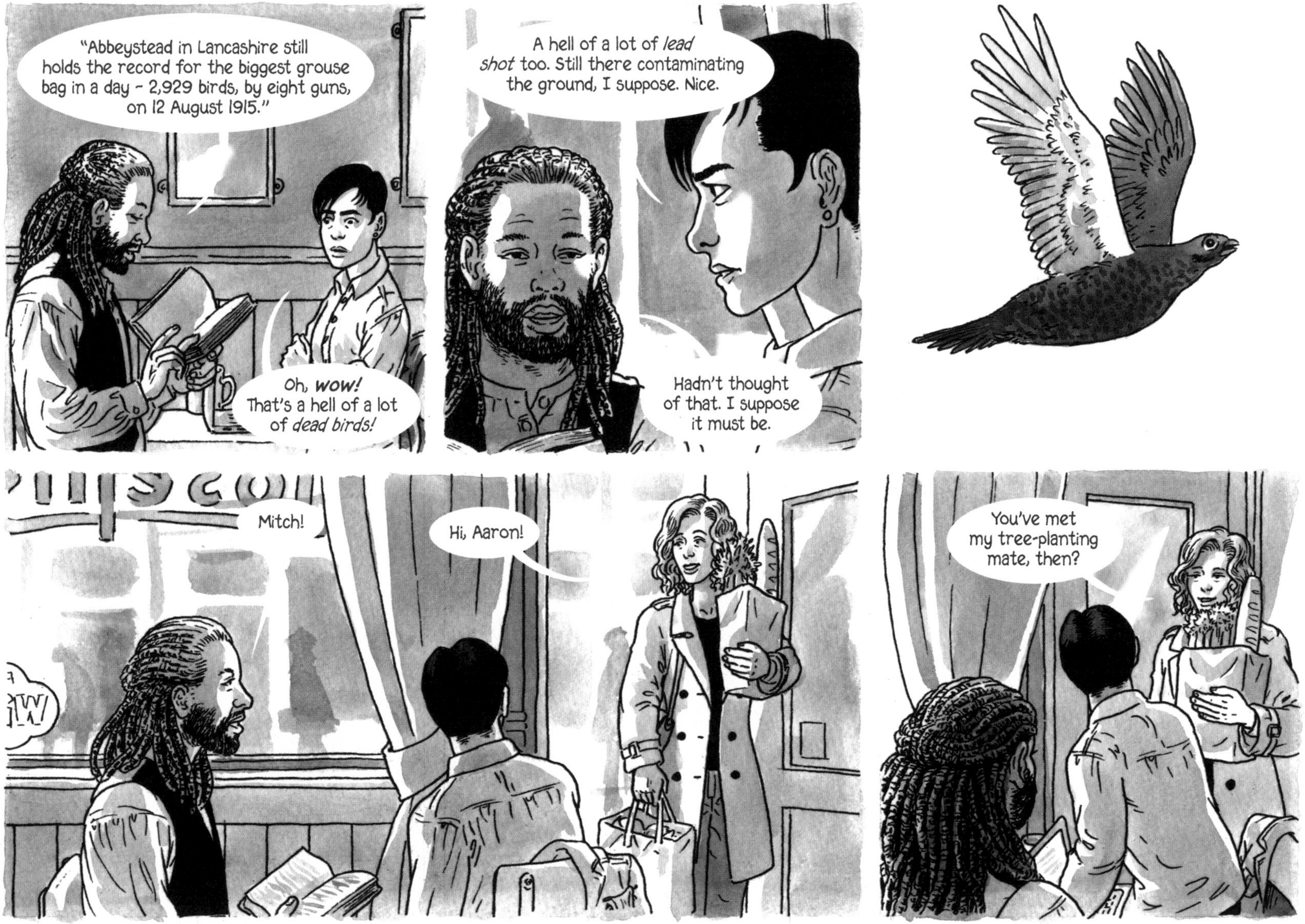
"Abbeystead in Lancashire still holds the record for the biggest grouse bag in a day - 2,929 birds, by eight guns, on 12 August 1915."
Oh, *WOW!* That's a hell of a lot of *dead birds!*
A hell of a lot of *lead shot* too. Still there contaminating the ground, I suppose. Nice.
Hadn't thought of that. I suppose it must be.
Mitch!
Hi, Aaron!
You've met my tree-planting mate, then?

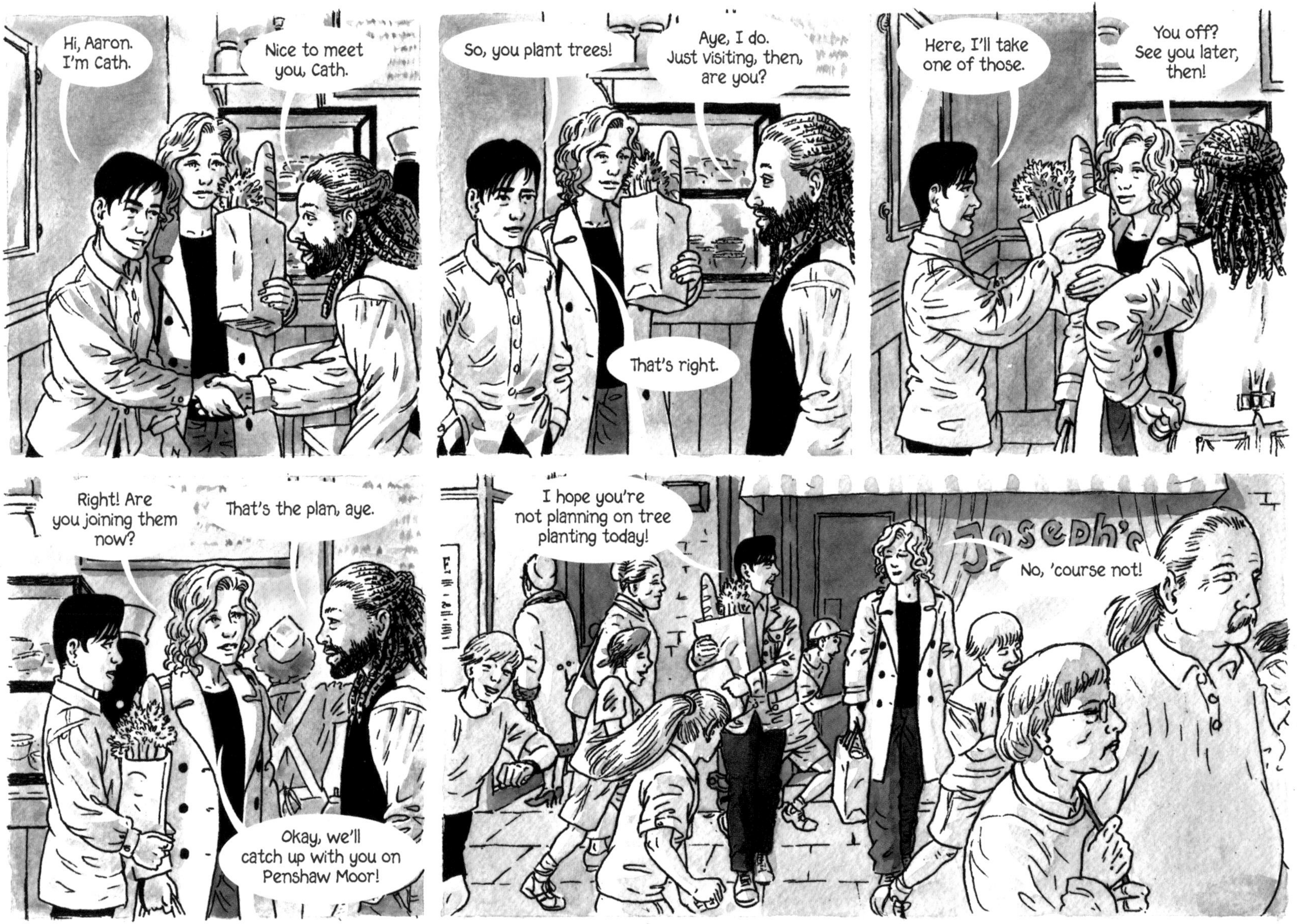

Hi, Aaron. I'm Cath.
Nice to meet you, Cath.
So, you plant trees!
Aye, I do. Just visiting, then, are you?
That's right.
Here, I'll take one of those.
You off? See you later, then!
Right! Are you joining them now?
That's the plan, aye.
Okay, we'll catch up with you on Penshaw Moor!
I hope you're not planning on tree planting today!
No, 'course not!

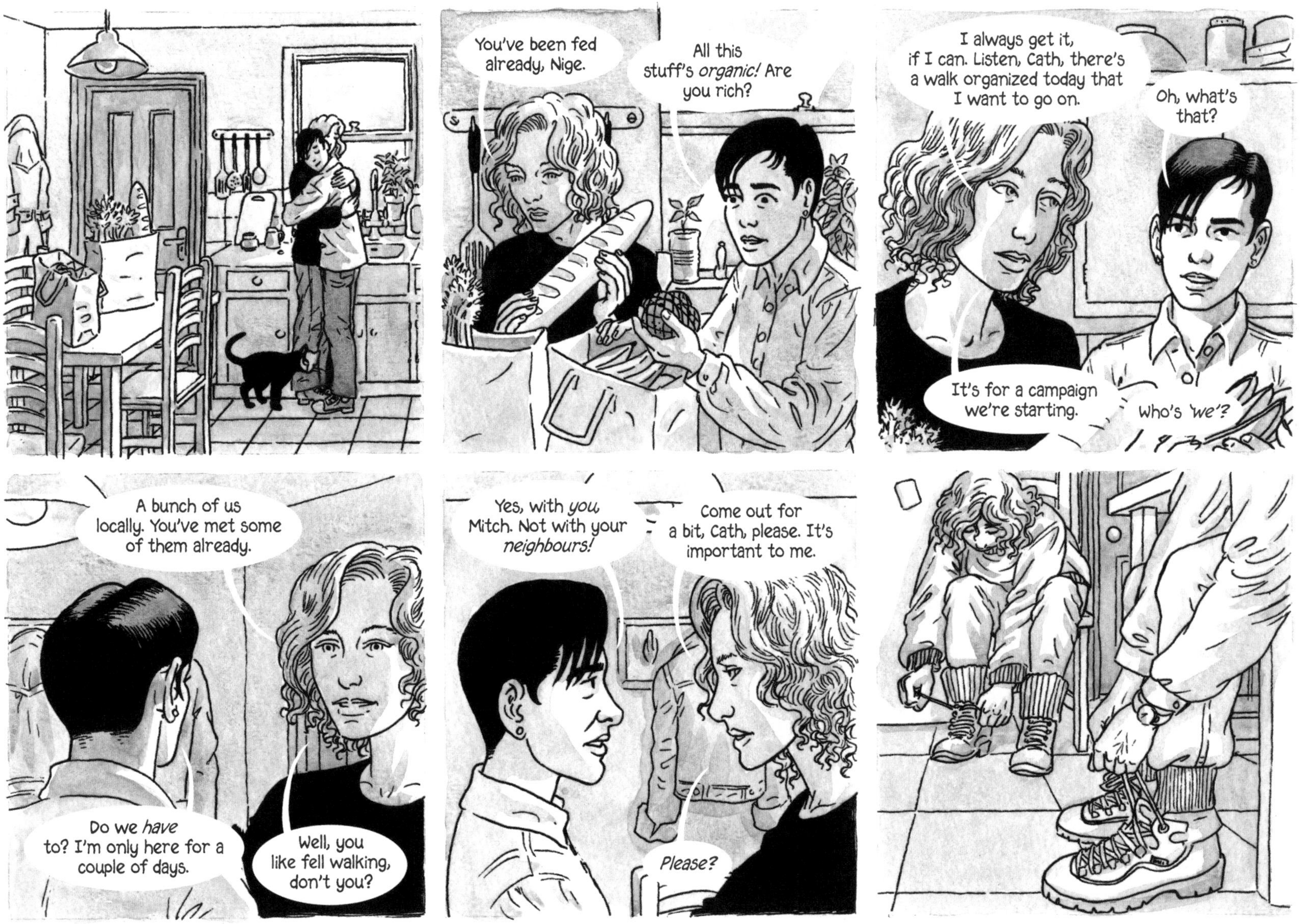
You've been fed already, Nige.
All this stuff's *organic!* Are you rich?
I always get it, if I can. Listen, Cath, there's a walk organized today that I want to go on.
Oh, what's that?
It's for a campaign we're starting.
Who's *'we'*?
A bunch of us locally. You've met some of them already.
Do we *have* to? I'm only here for a couple of days.
Well, you like fell walking, don't you?
Yes, with *you*, Mitch. Not with your *neighbours!*
Come out for a bit, Cath, please. It's important to me.
Please?

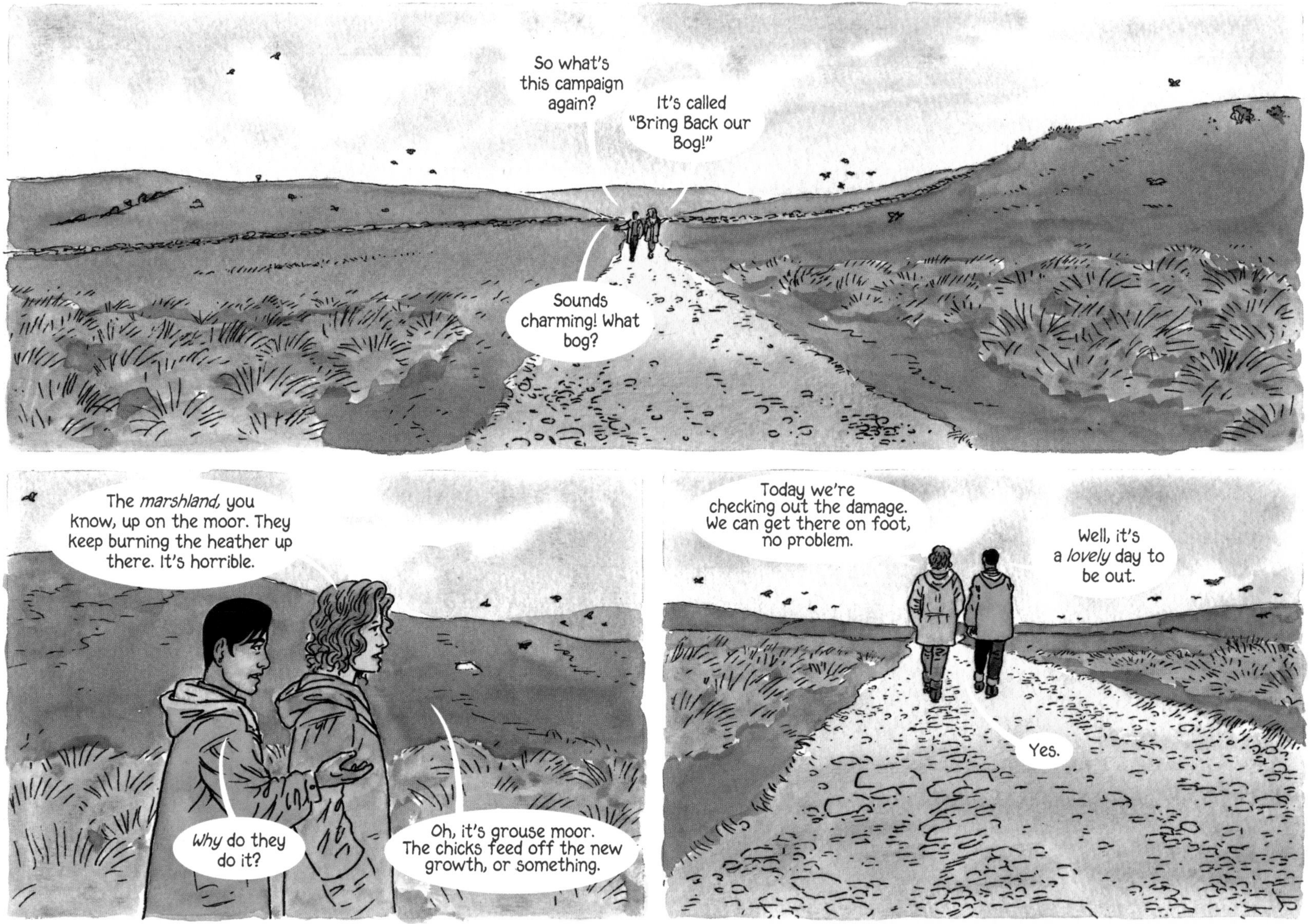
So what's this campaign again?
It's called "Bring Back our Bog!"
Sounds charming! What bog?
The *marshland,* you know, up on the moor. They keep burning the heather up there. It's horrible.
Why do they do it?
Oh, it's grouse moor. The chicks feed off the new growth, or something.
Today we're checking out the damage. We can get there on foot, no problem.
Well, it's a *lovely* day to be out.
Yes.

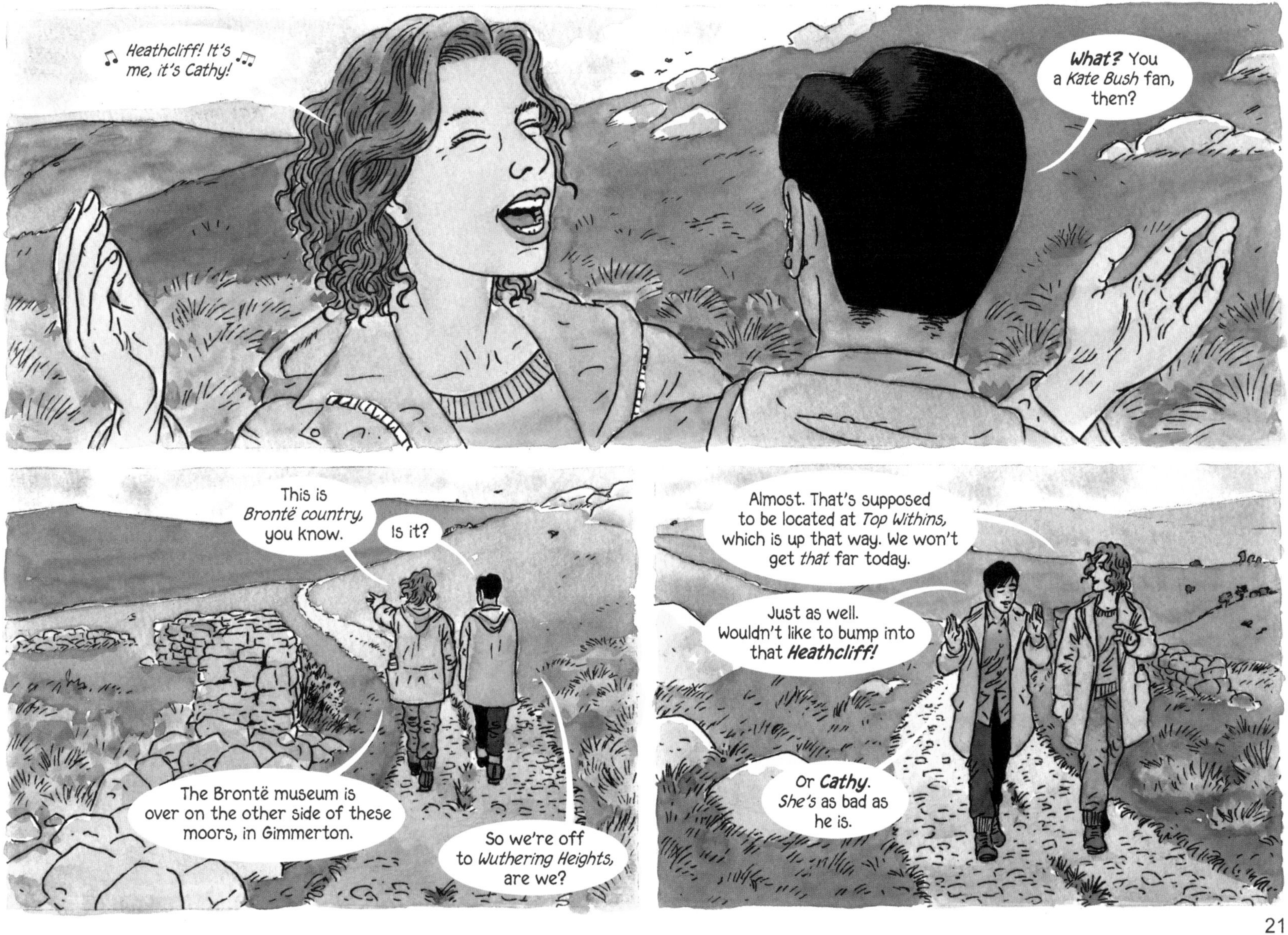
♫ Heathcliff! It's me, it's Cathy! ♫
What? You a *Kate Bush* fan, then?
This is *Brontë country,* you know.
Is it?
The Brontë museum is over on the other side of these moors, in Gimmerton.
So we're off to *Wuthering Heights,* are we?
Almost. That's supposed to be located at *Top Withins,* which is up that way. We won't get *that* far today.
Just as well. Wouldn't like to bump into that **Heathcliff!**
Or **Cathy**. *She's* as bad as he is.

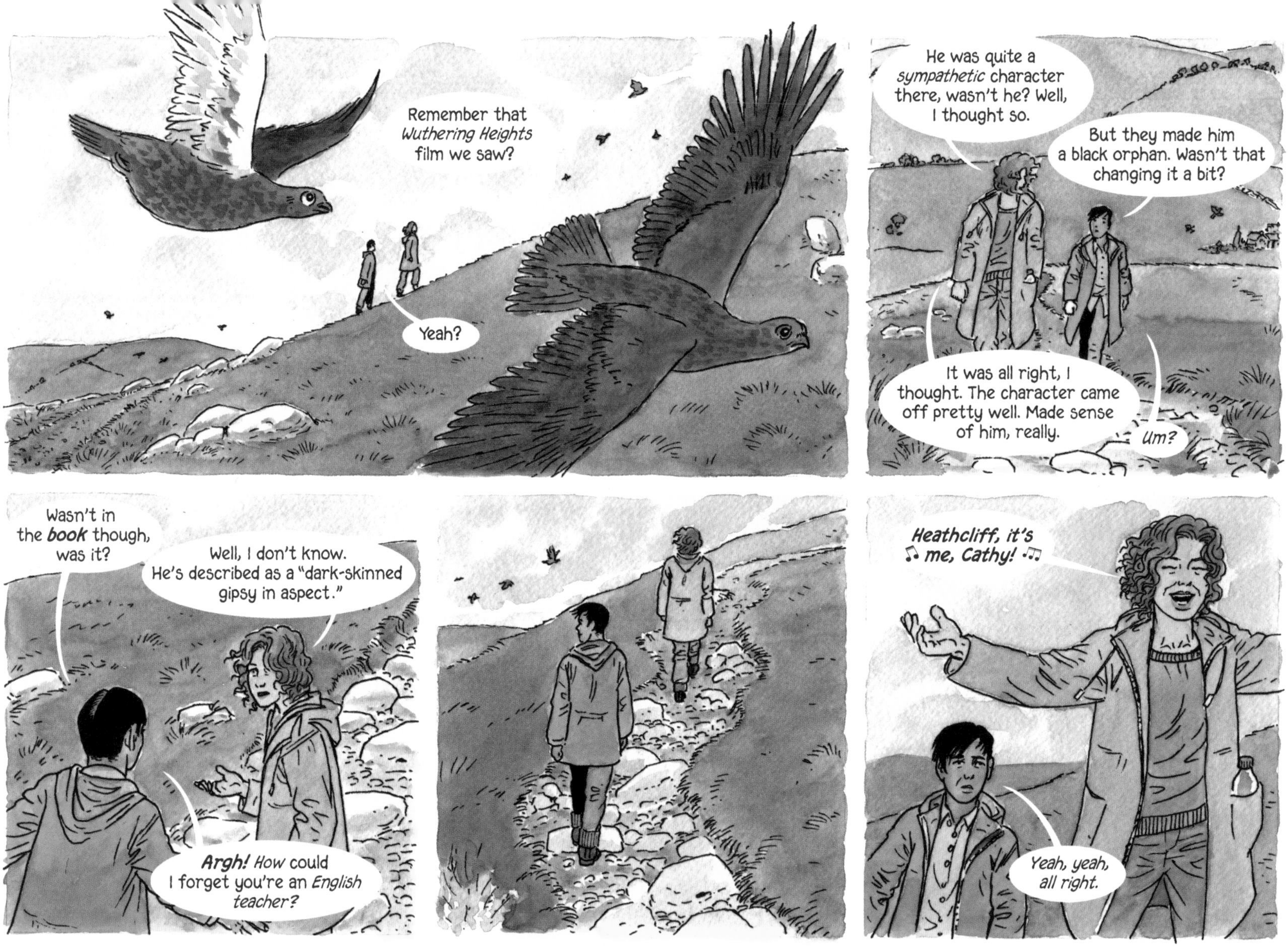
Remember that *Wuthering Heights* film we saw?
Yeah?
He was quite a *sympathetic* character there, wasn't he? Well, I thought so.
But they made him a black orphan. Wasn't that changing it a bit?
It was all right, I thought. The character came off pretty well. Made sense of him, really.
Um?
Wasn't in the **book** though, was it?
Well, I don't know. He's described as a "dark-skinned gipsy in aspect."
Argh! *How* could I forget you're an *English* teacher?
Heathcliff, it's ♫ me, Cathy! ♫
Yeah, yeah, all right.

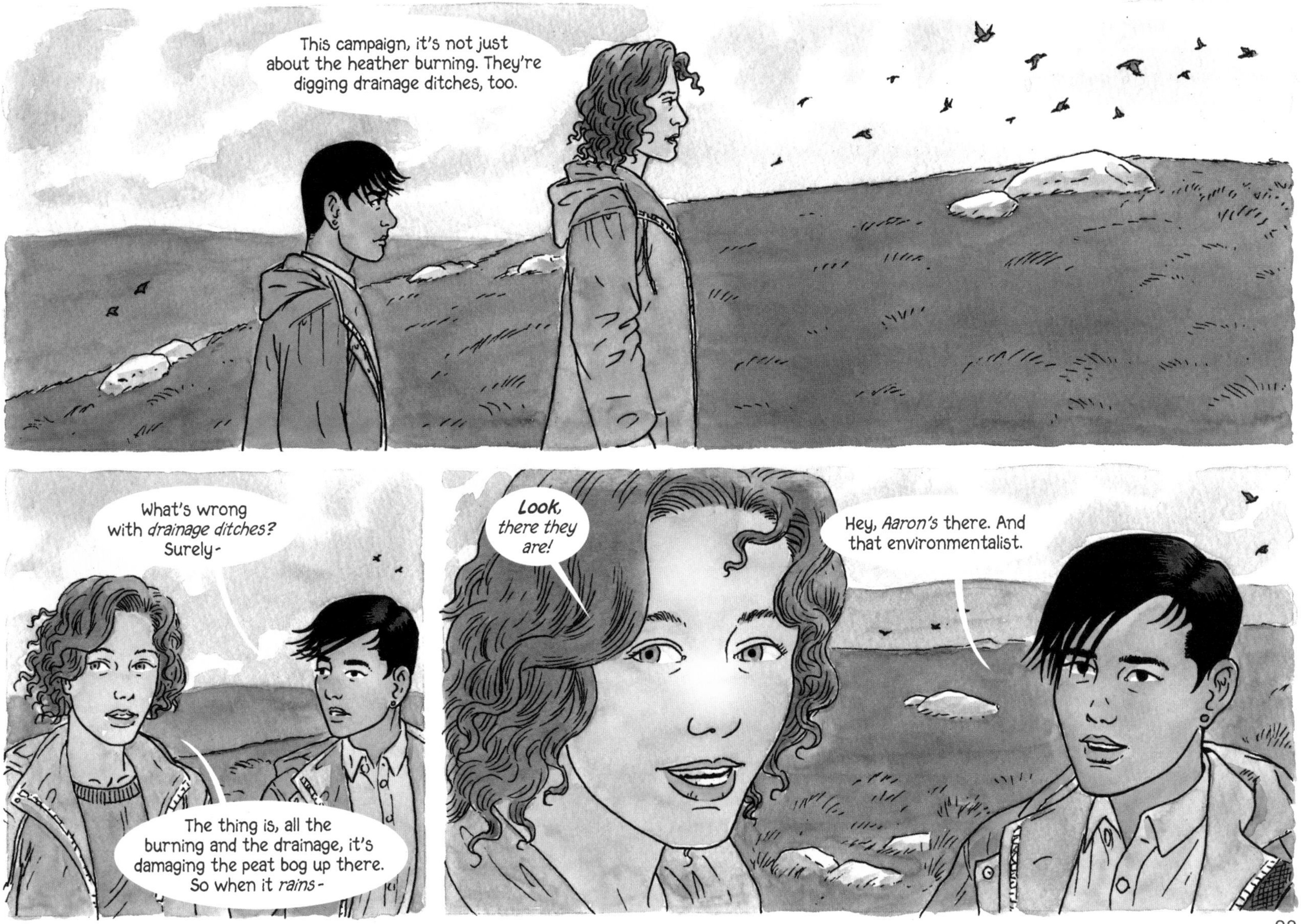
This campaign, it's not just about the heather burning. They're digging drainage ditches, too.
What's wrong with *drainage ditches?* Surely-
The thing is, all the burning and the drainage, it's damaging the peat bog up there. So when it *rains*-
Look, *there they are!*
Hey, *Aaron's* there. And that environmentalist.

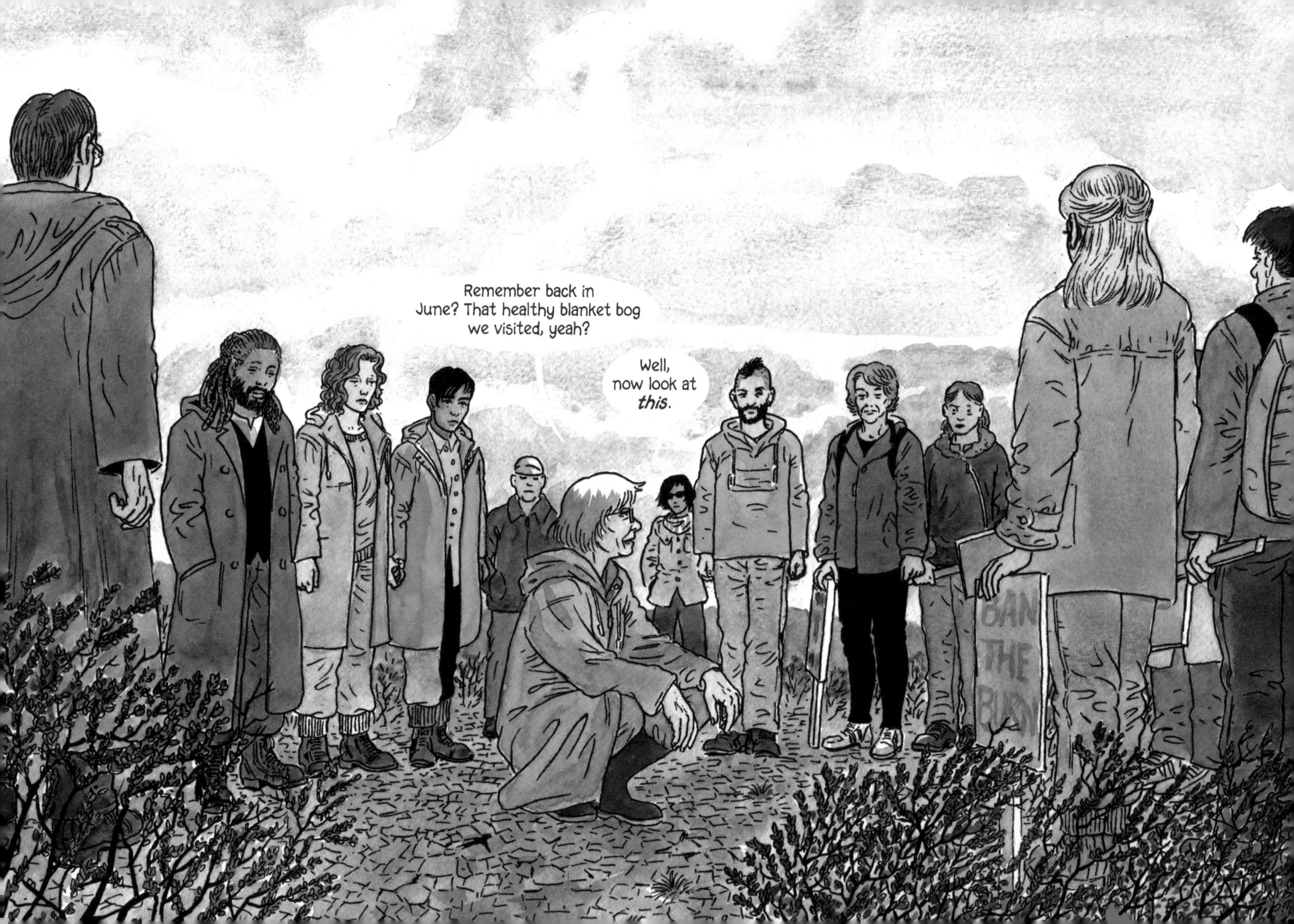
Remember back in June? That healthy blanket bog we visited, yeah?
Well, now look at *this*.
BAN THE BURN

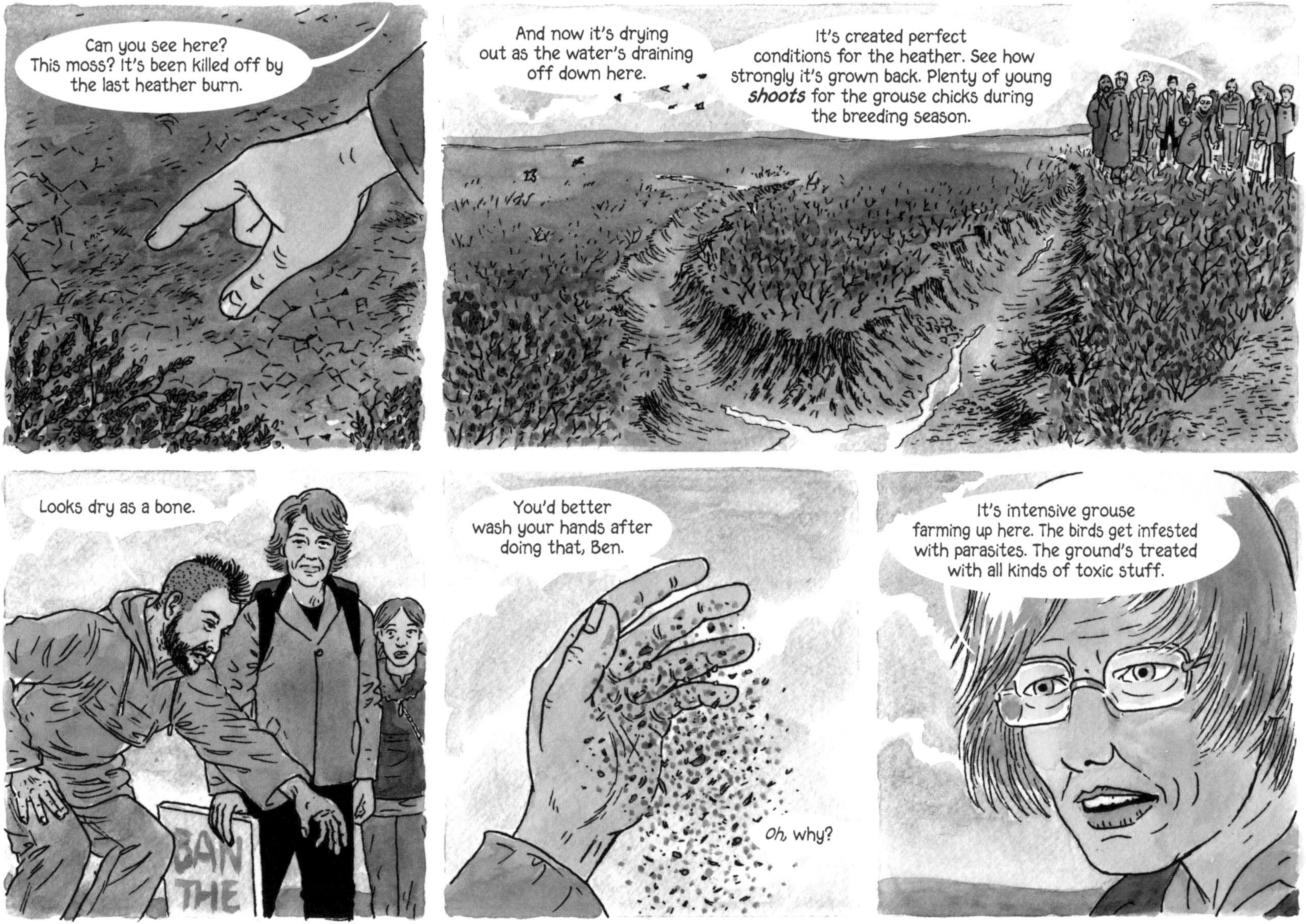
Can you see here? This moss? It's been killed off by the last heather burn.
And now it's drying out as the water's draining off down here.
It's created perfect conditions for the heather. See how strongly it's grown back. Plenty of young *shoots* for the grouse chicks during the breeding season.
Looks dry as a bone.
BAN THE
You'd better wash your hands after doing that, Ben.
Oh, why?
It's intensive grouse farming up here. The birds get infested with parasites. The ground's treated with all kinds of toxic stuff.

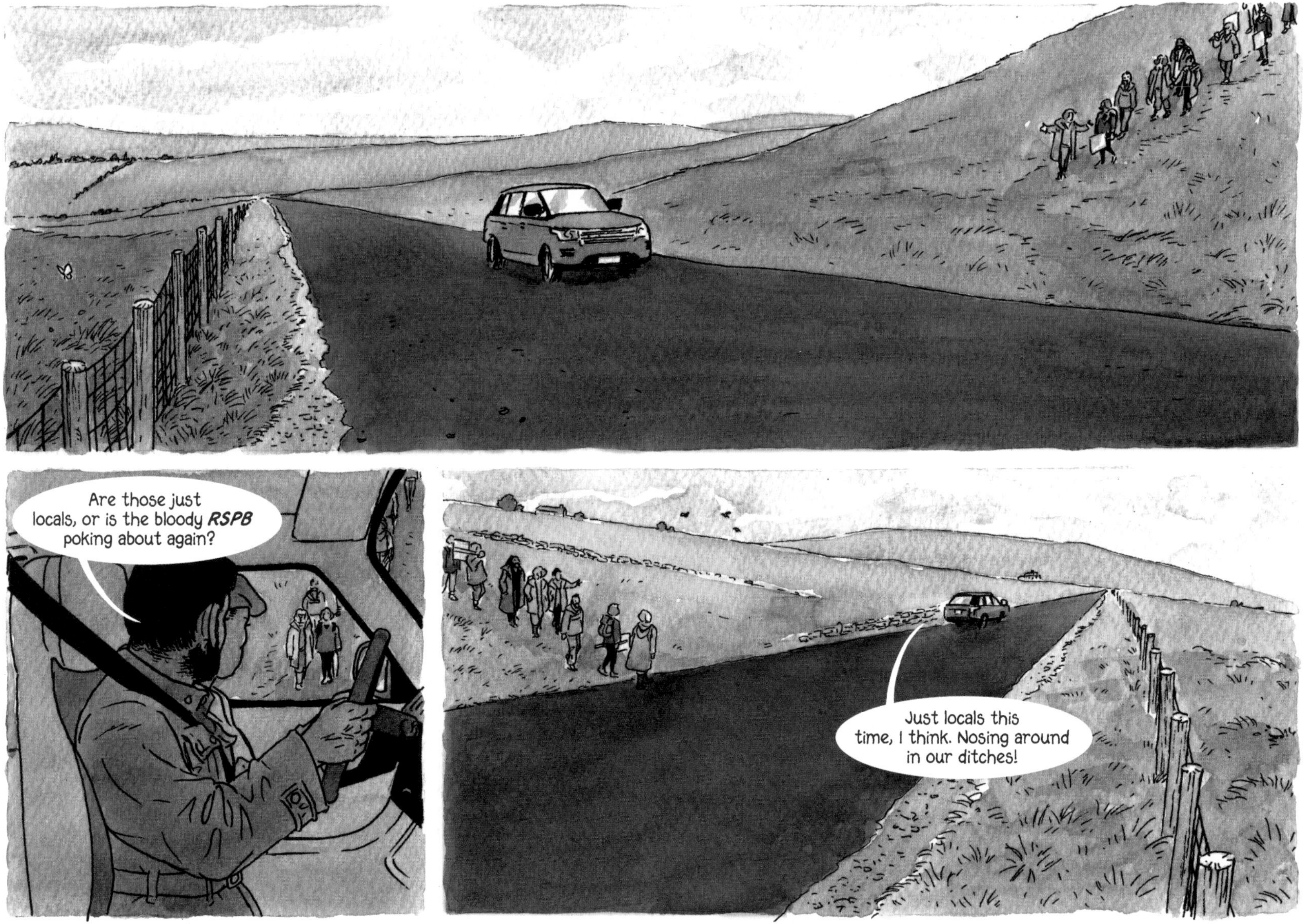
Are those just locals, or is the bloody **RSPB** poking about again?
Just locals this time, I think. Nosing around in our ditches!

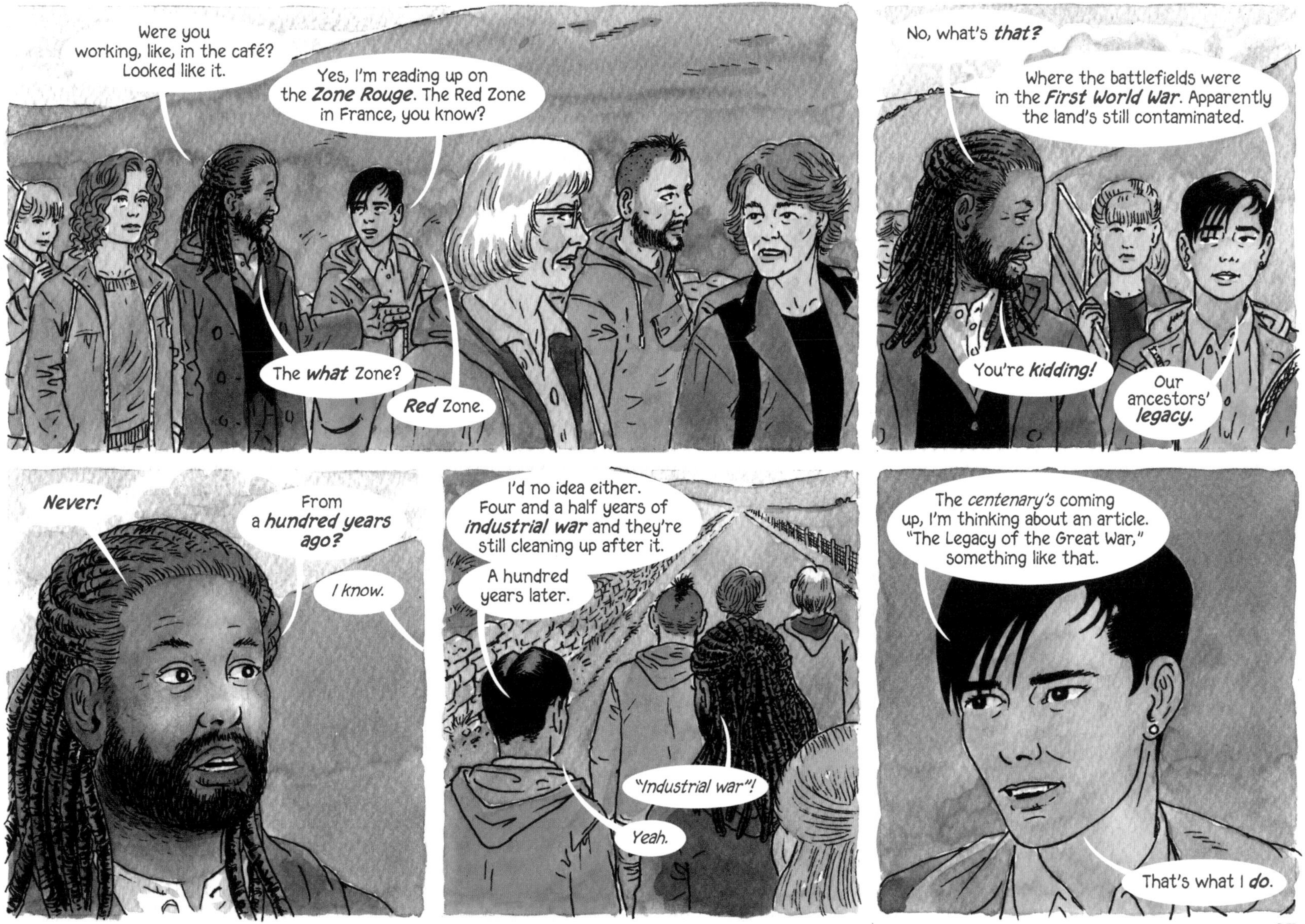
Were you working, like, in the café? Looked like it.
Yes, I'm reading up on the **Zone Rouge**. The Red Zone in France, you know?
The **what** Zone?
Red Zone.
No, what's **that?**
Where the battlefields were in the **First World War**. Apparently the land's still contaminated.
You're **kidding!**
Our ancestors' **legacy.**
Never!
From a **hundred years ago?**
I know.
I'd no idea either. Four and a half years of **industrial war** and they're still cleaning up after it.
A hundred years later.
"Industrial war"!
Yeah.
The *centenary's* coming up, I'm thinking about an article. "The Legacy of the Great War," something like that.
That's what I **do**.

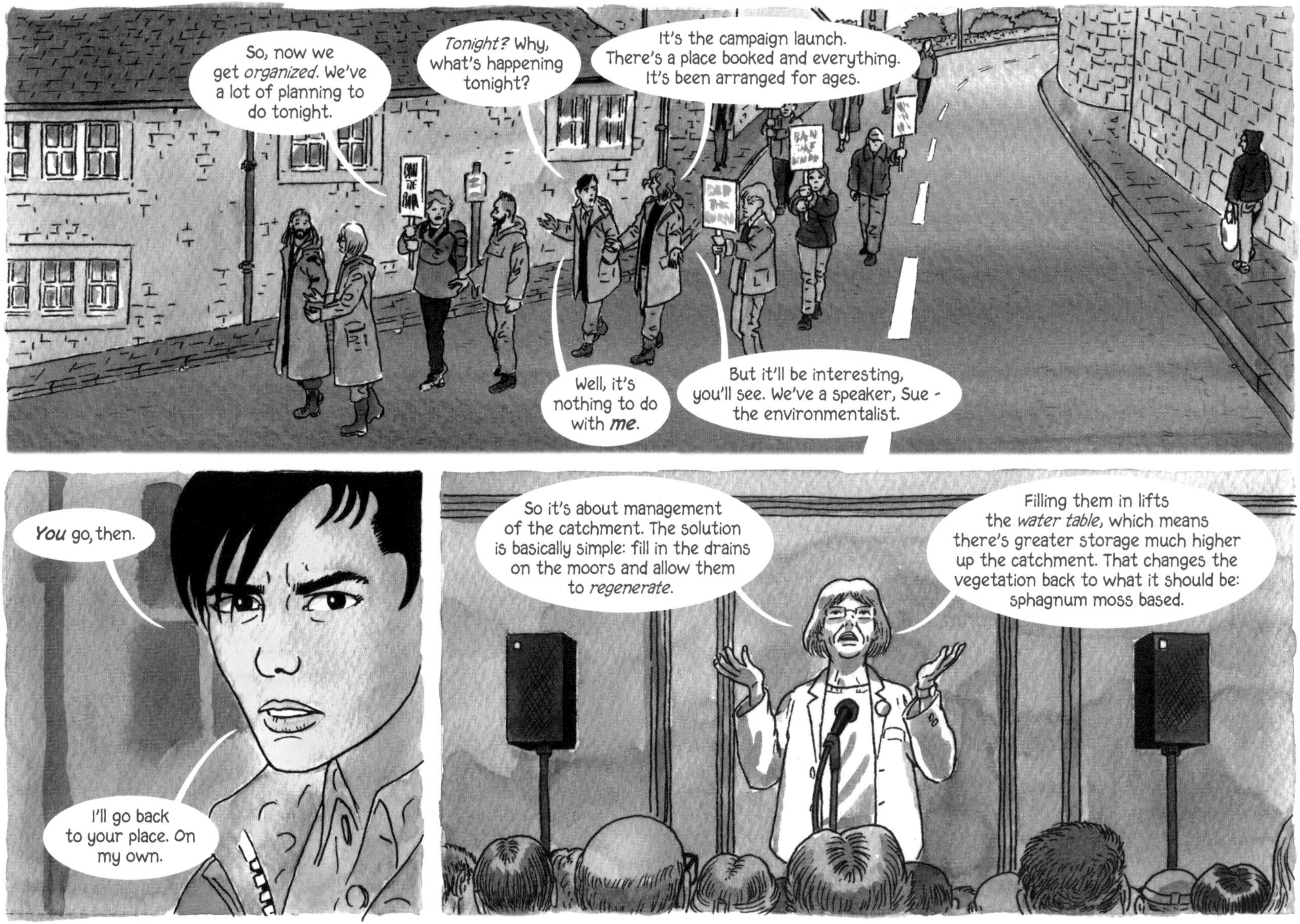
So, now we get *organized*. We've a lot of planning to do tonight.
Tonight? Why, what's happening tonight?
It's the campaign launch. There's a place booked and everything. It's been arranged for ages.
Well, it's nothing to do with ***me***.
But it'll be interesting, you'll see. We've a speaker, Sue - the environmentalist.
You go, then.
I'll go back to your place. On my own.
So it's about management of the catchment. The solution is basically simple: fill in the drains on the moors and allow them to *regenerate*.
Filling them in lifts the *water table*, which means there's greater storage much higher up the catchment. That changes the vegetation back to what it should be: sphagnum moss based.

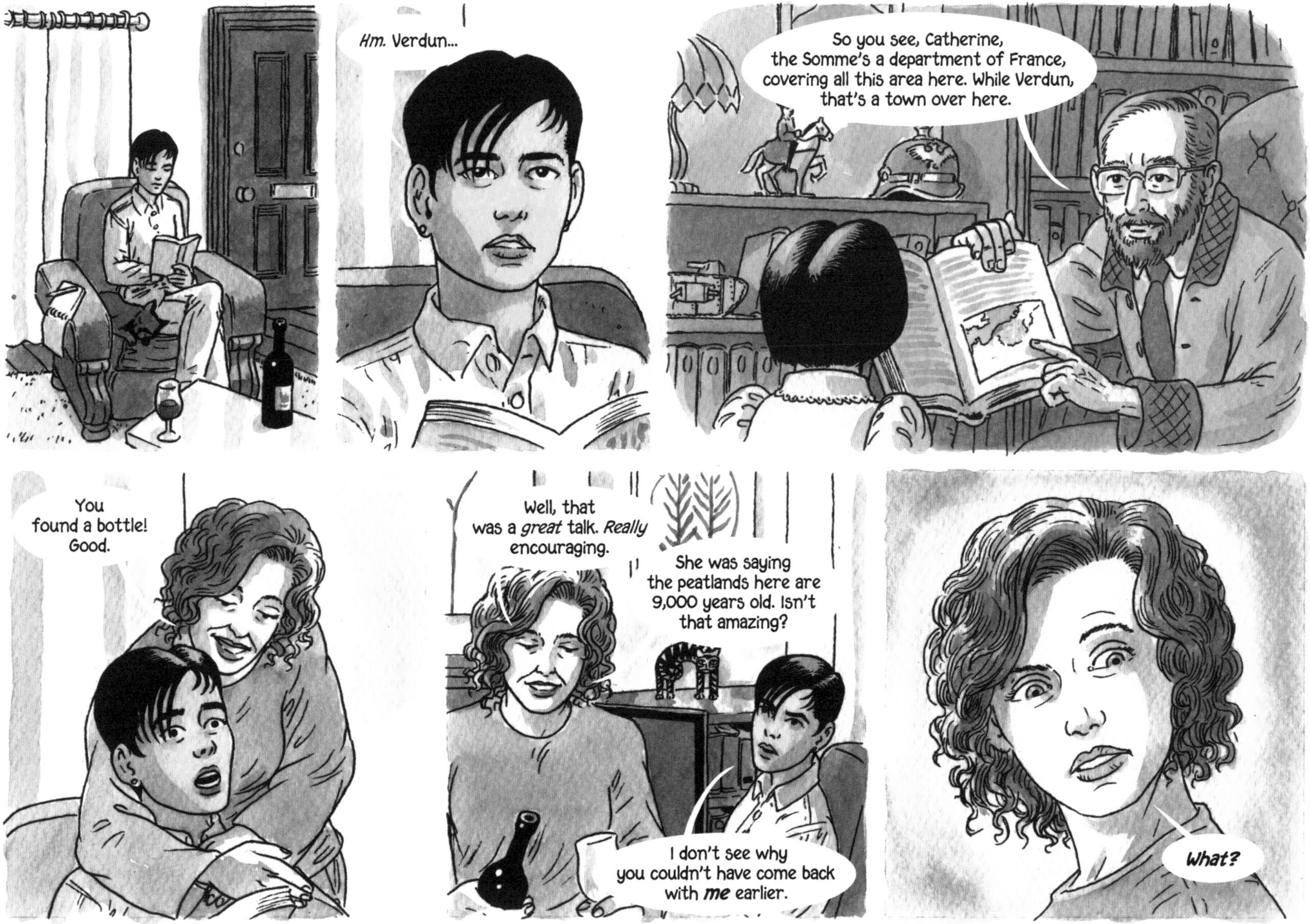
Hm. Verdun...
So you see, Catherine, the Somme's a department of France, covering all this area here. While Verdun, that's a town over here.
You found a bottle! Good.
Well, that was a *great* talk. *Really* encouraging.
She was saying the peatlands here are 9,000 years old. Isn't that amazing?
I don't see why you couldn't have come back with *me* earlier.
What?

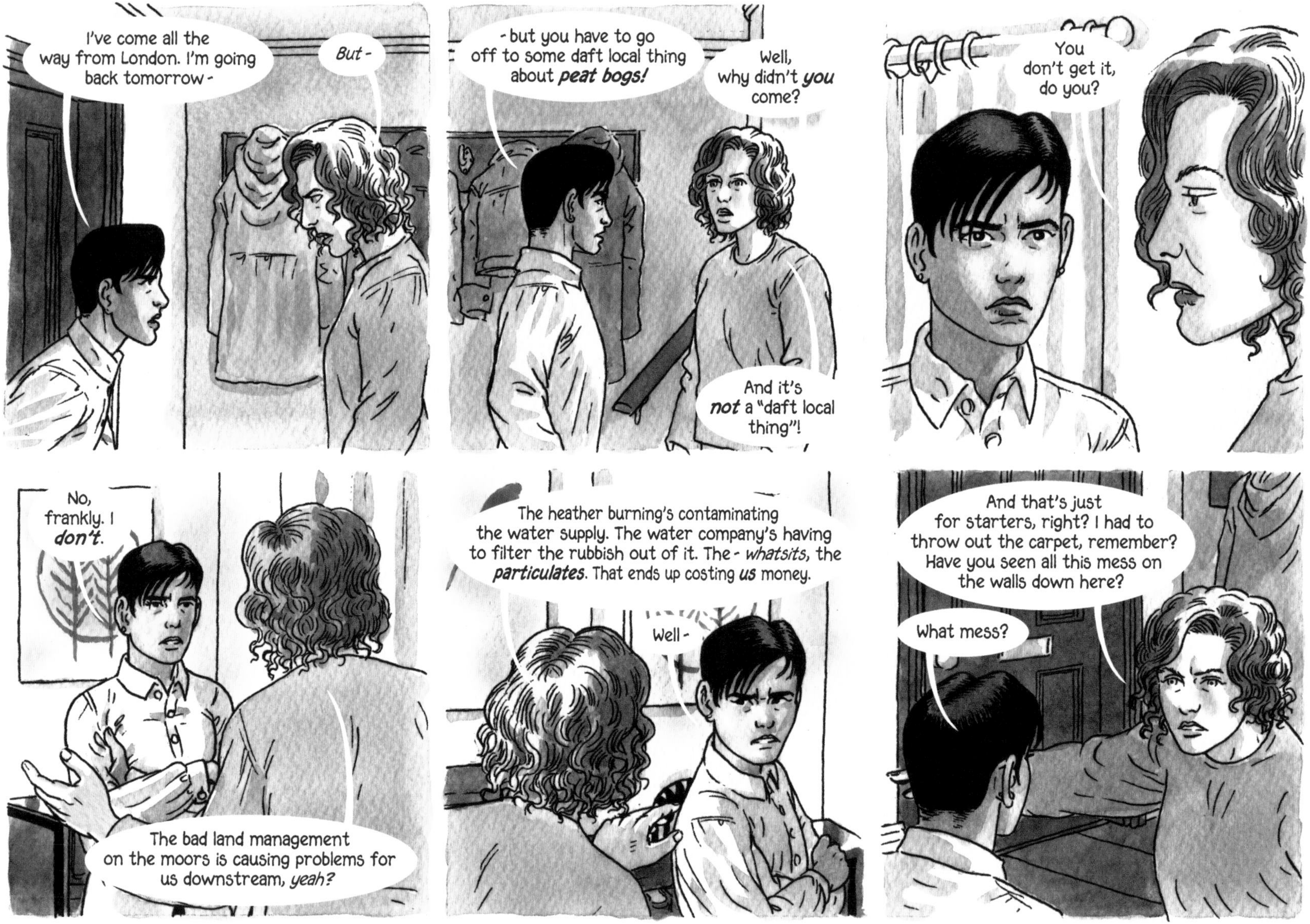
I've come all the way from London. I'm going back tomorrow -
But -
- but you have to go off to some daft local thing about ***peat bogs!***
Well, why didn't ***you*** come?
And it's ***not*** a "daft local thing"!
You don't get it, do you?
No, frankly. I ***don't***.
The bad land management on the moors is causing problems for us downstream, *yeah?*
The heather burning's contaminating the water supply. The water company's having to filter the rubbish out of it. The - *whatsits*, the ***particulates***. That ends up costing ***us*** money.
Well -
And that's just for starters, right? I had to throw out the carpet, remember? Have you seen all this mess on the walls down here?
What mess?

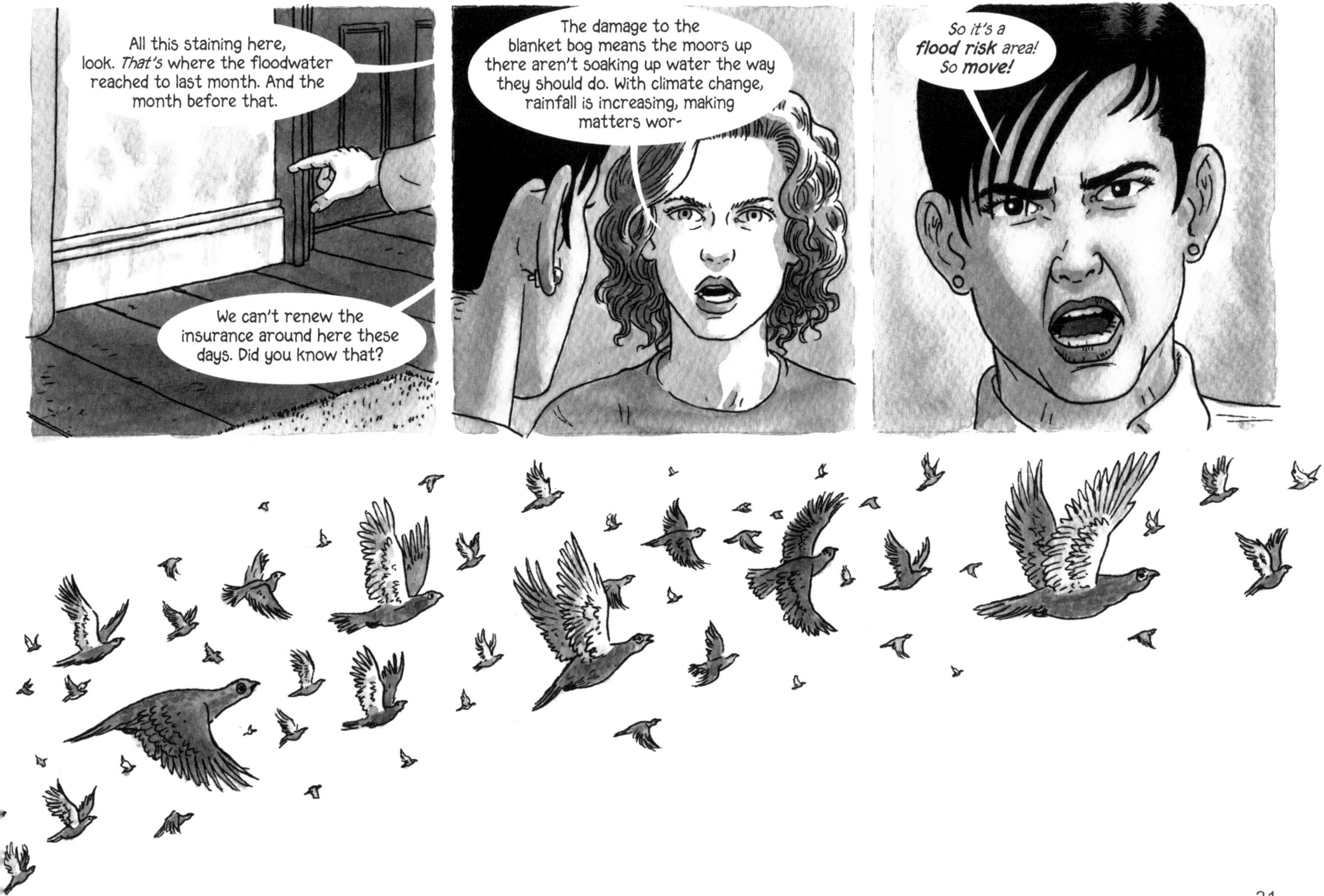
All this staining here, look. *That's* where the floodwater reached to last month. And the month before that.
We can't renew the insurance around here these days. Did you know that?
The damage to the blanket bog means the moors up there aren't soaking up water the way they should do. With climate change, rainfall is increasing, making matters wor-
*So it's a **flood risk** area! So **move!***

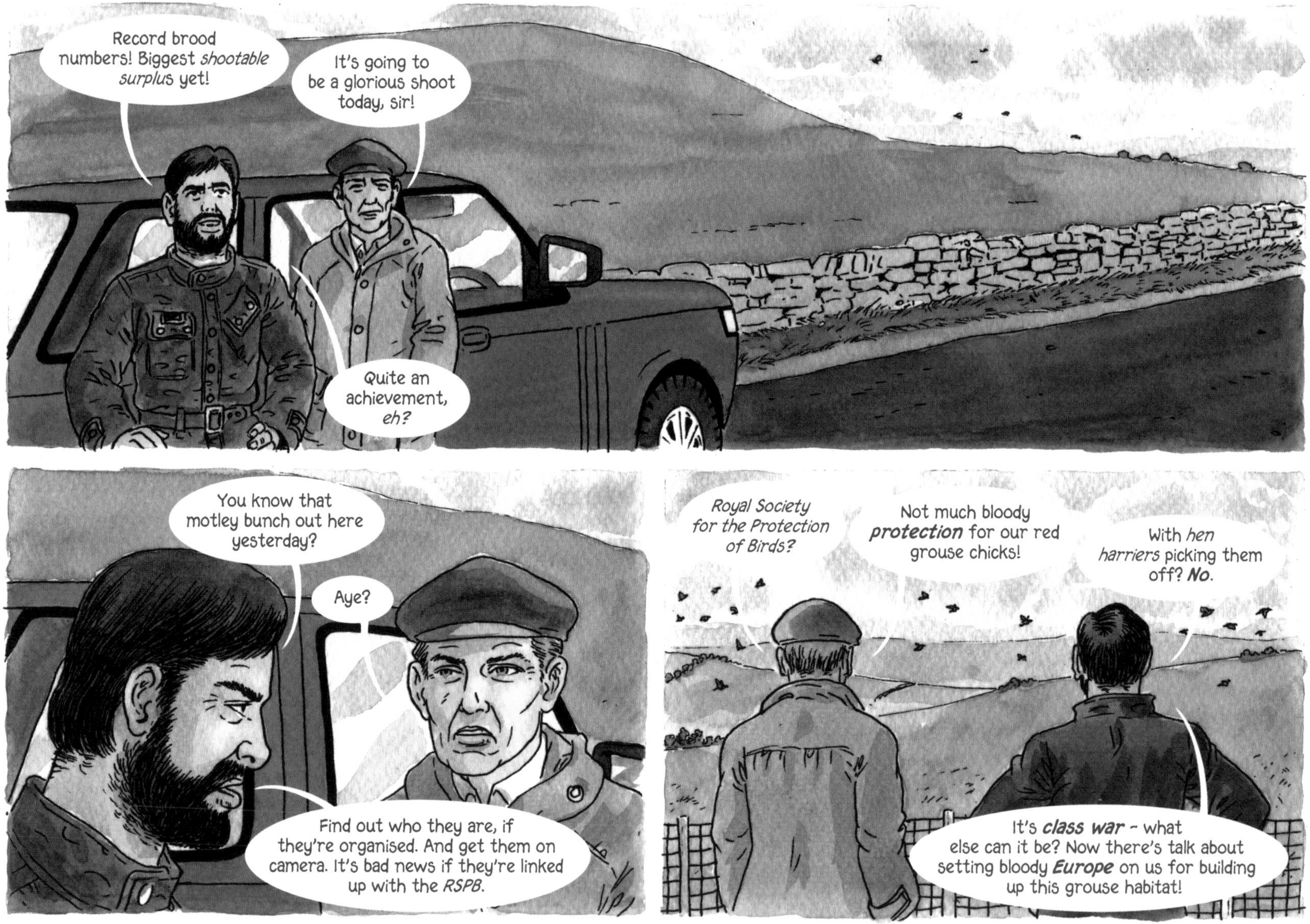
Record brood numbers! Biggest *shootable surplus* yet!
It's going to be a glorious shoot today, sir!
Quite an achievement, *eh?*
You know that motley bunch out here yesterday?
Aye?
Find out who they are, if they're organised. And get them on camera. It's bad news if they're linked up with the *RSPB*.
Royal Society for the Protection of Birds?
Not much bloody **protection** for our red grouse chicks!
With *hen harriers* picking them off? **No**.
It's **class war** – what else can it be? Now there's talk about setting bloody **Europe** on us for building up this grouse habitat!

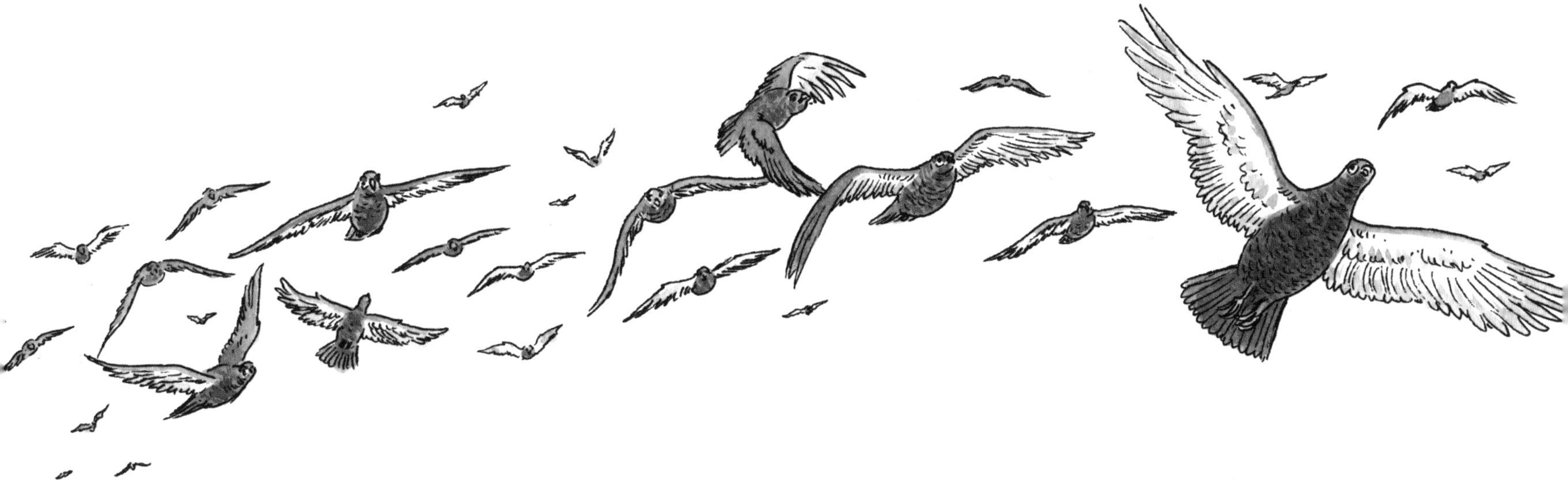

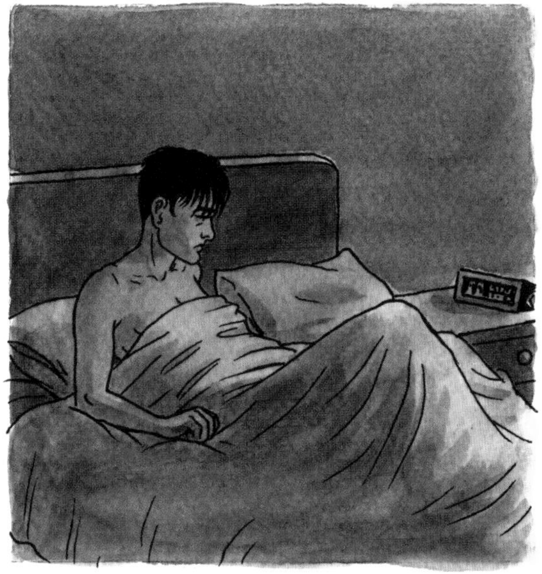

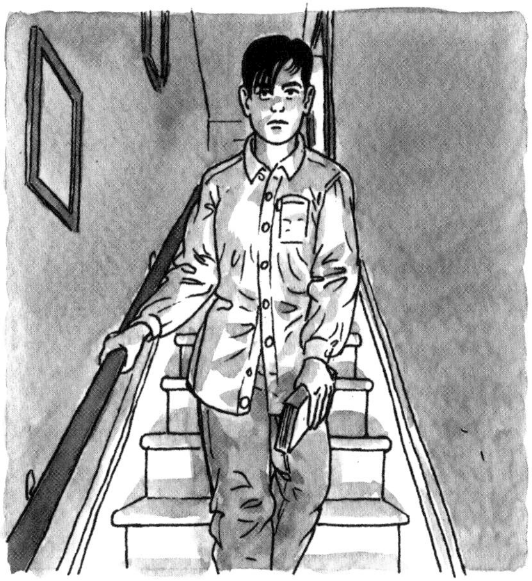

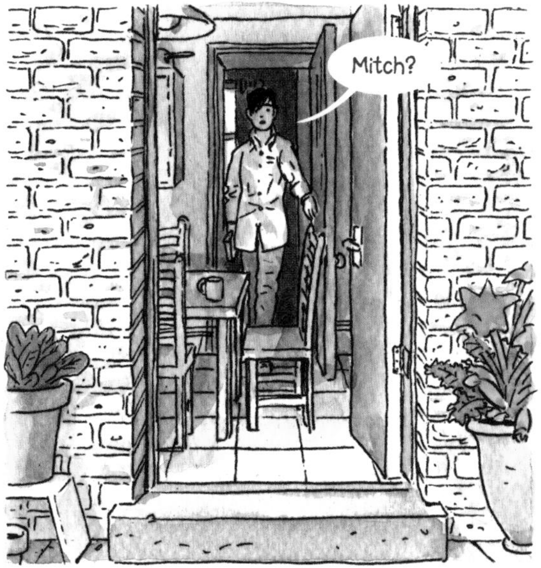
Mitch?

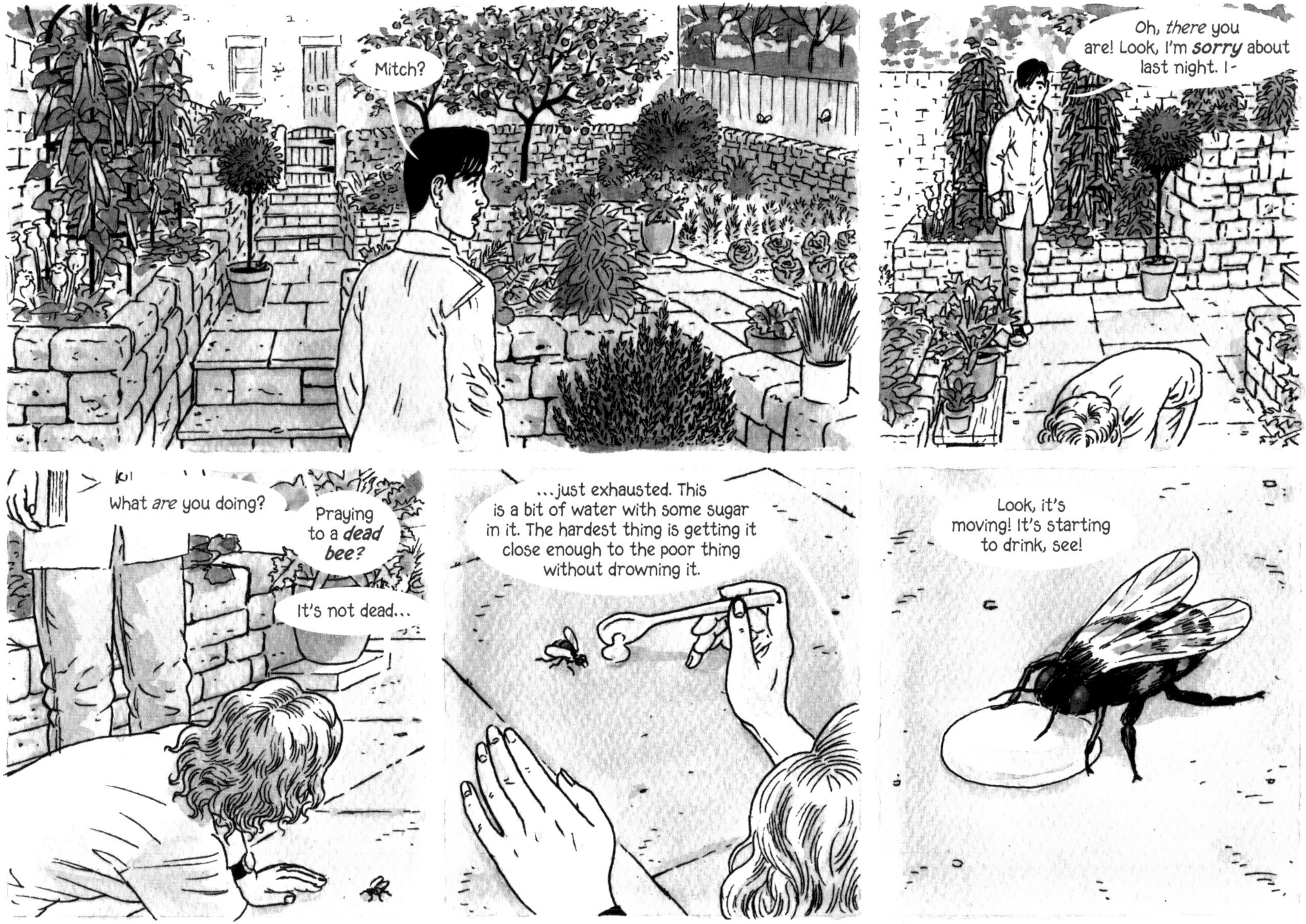
Mitch?
Oh, *there* you are! Look, I'm **sorry** about last night. I -
What *are* you doing?
Praying to a ***dead bee?***
It's not dead...
...just exhausted. This is a bit of water with some sugar in it. The hardest thing is getting it close enough to the poor thing without drowning it.
Look, it's moving! It's starting to drink, see!

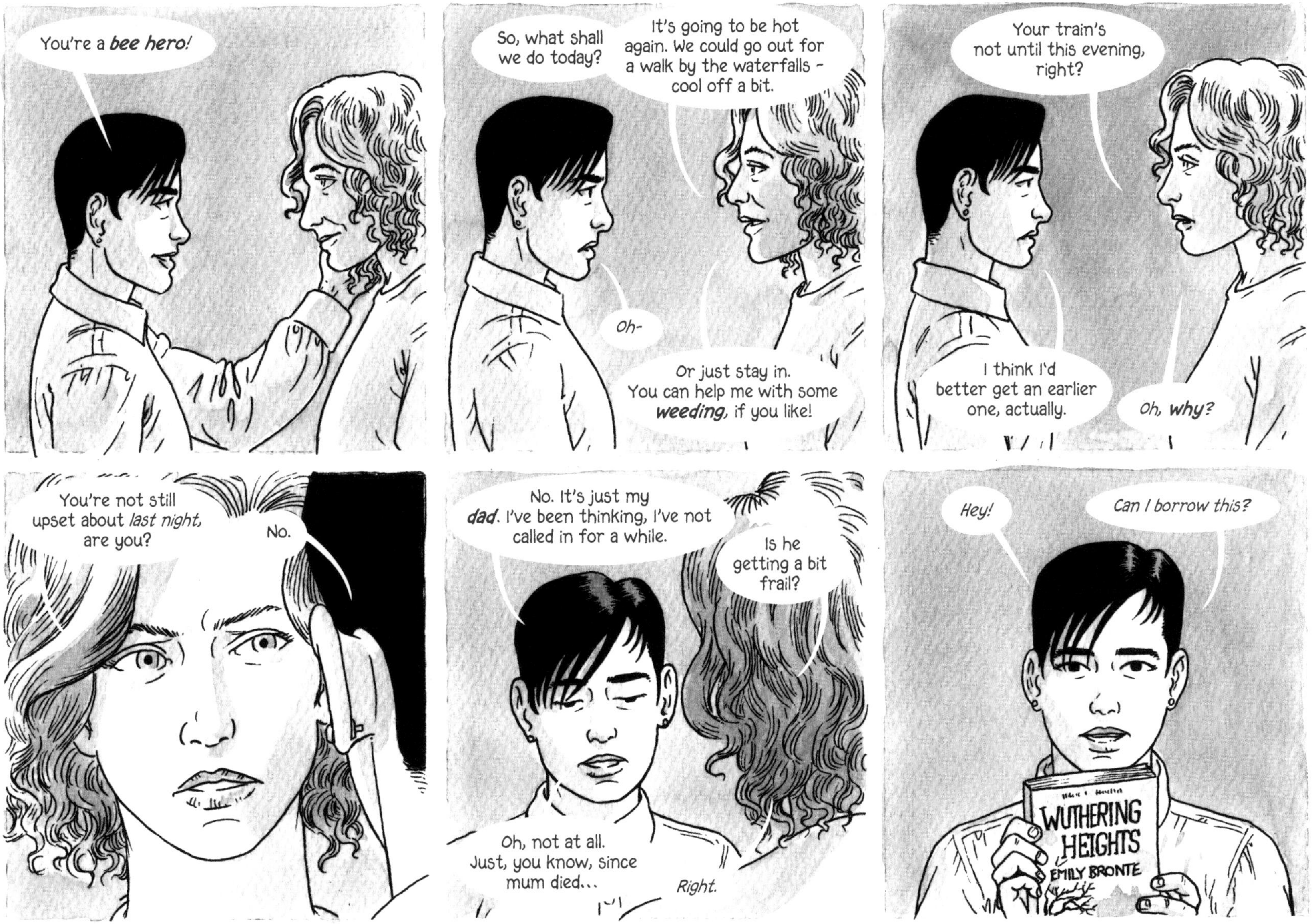
You're a *bee hero!*
So, what shall we do today?
It's going to be hot again. We could go out for a walk by the waterfalls - cool off a bit.
Oh-
Or just stay in. You can help me with some *weeding*, if you like!
Your train's not until this evening, right?
I think I'd better get an earlier one, actually.
Oh, *why?*
You're not still upset about *last night*, are you?
No.
No. It's just my *dad*. I've been thinking, I've not called in for a while.
Is he getting a bit frail?
Oh, not at all. Just, you know, since mum died...
Right.
Hey!
Can I borrow this?
WUTHERING HEIGHTS
EMILY BRONTE

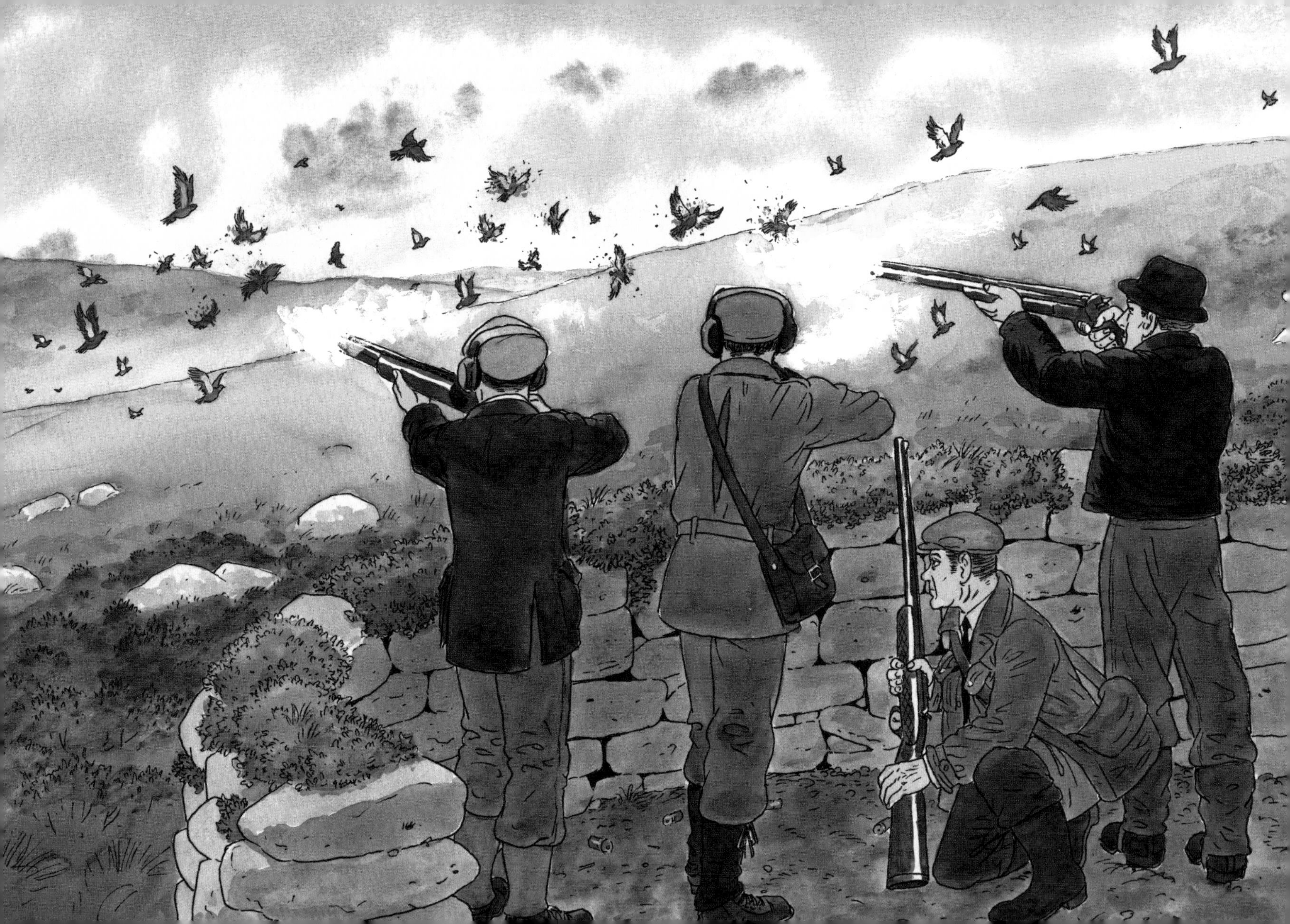

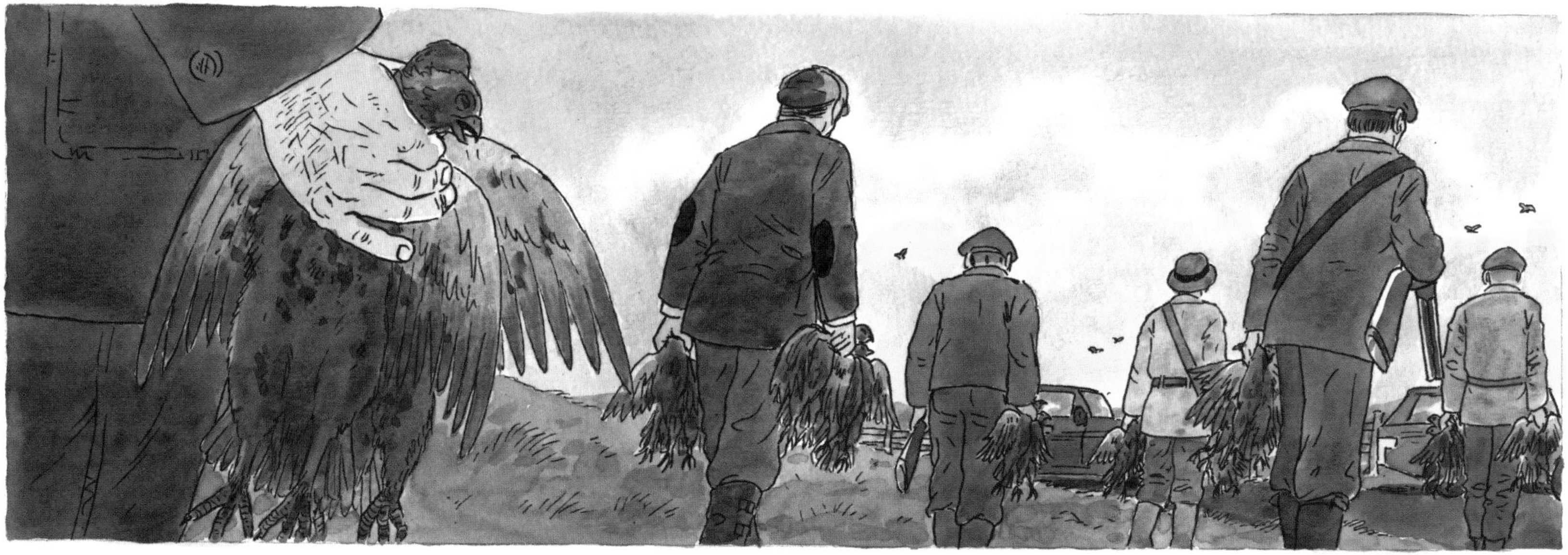

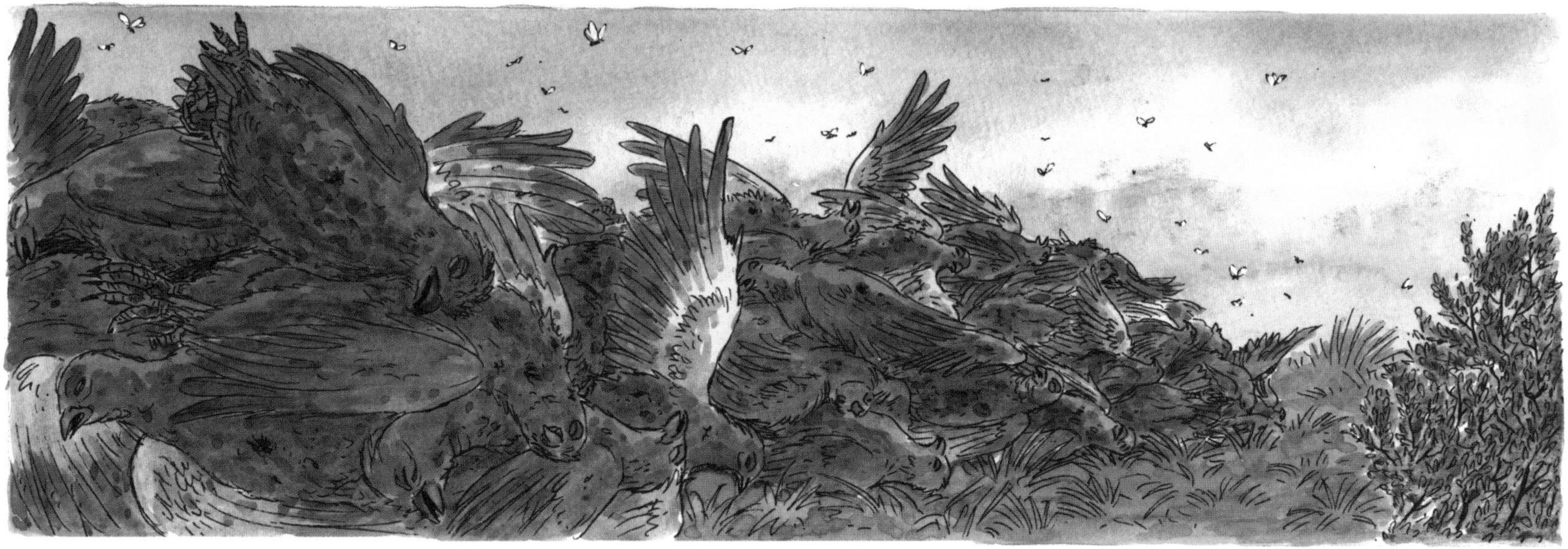

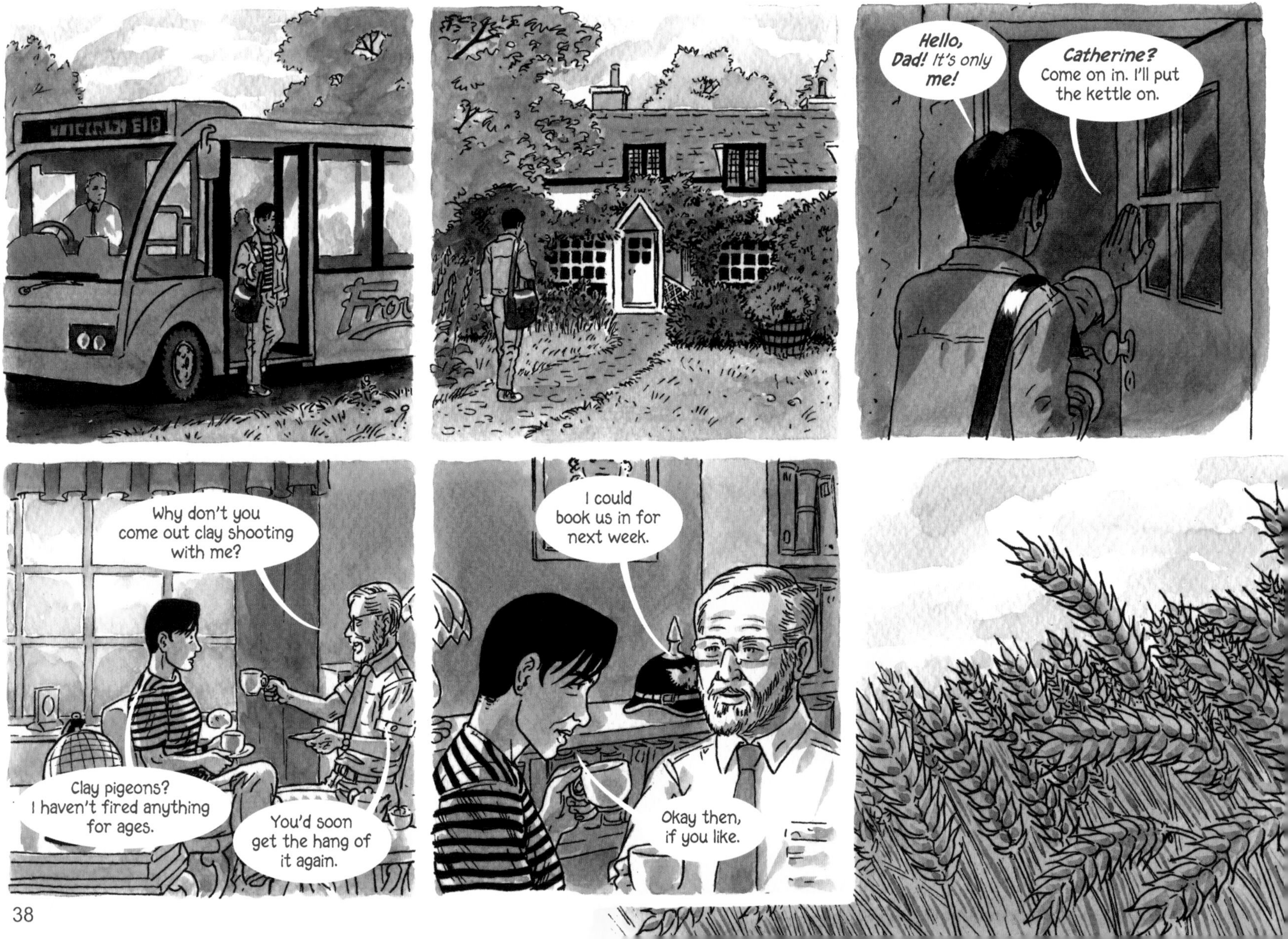
Hello, Dad! It's only me!
Catherine? Come on in. I'll put the kettle on.
Why don't you come out clay shooting with me?
Clay pigeons? I haven't fired anything for ages.
You'd soon get the hang of it again.
I could book us in for next week.
Okay then, if you like.

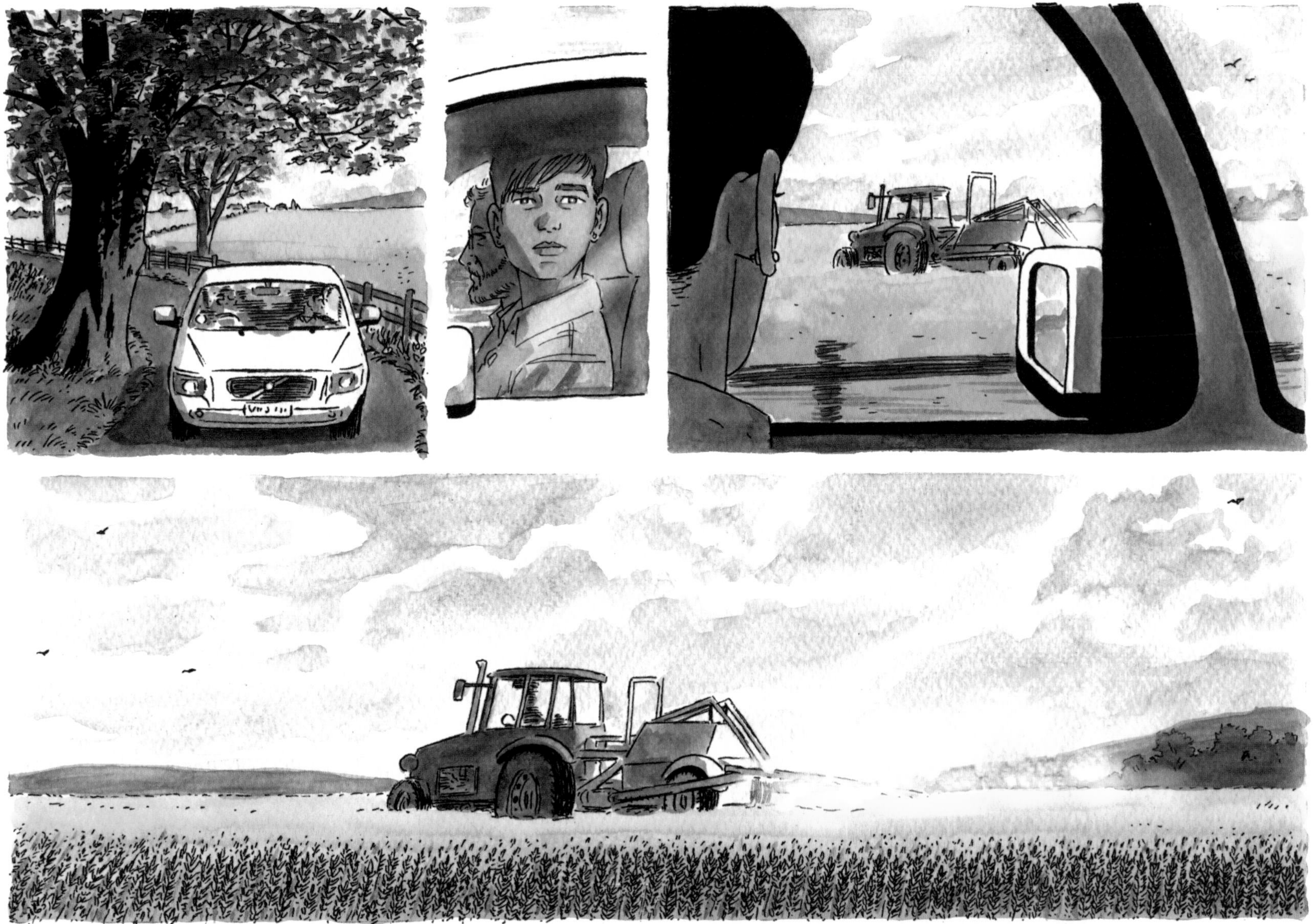

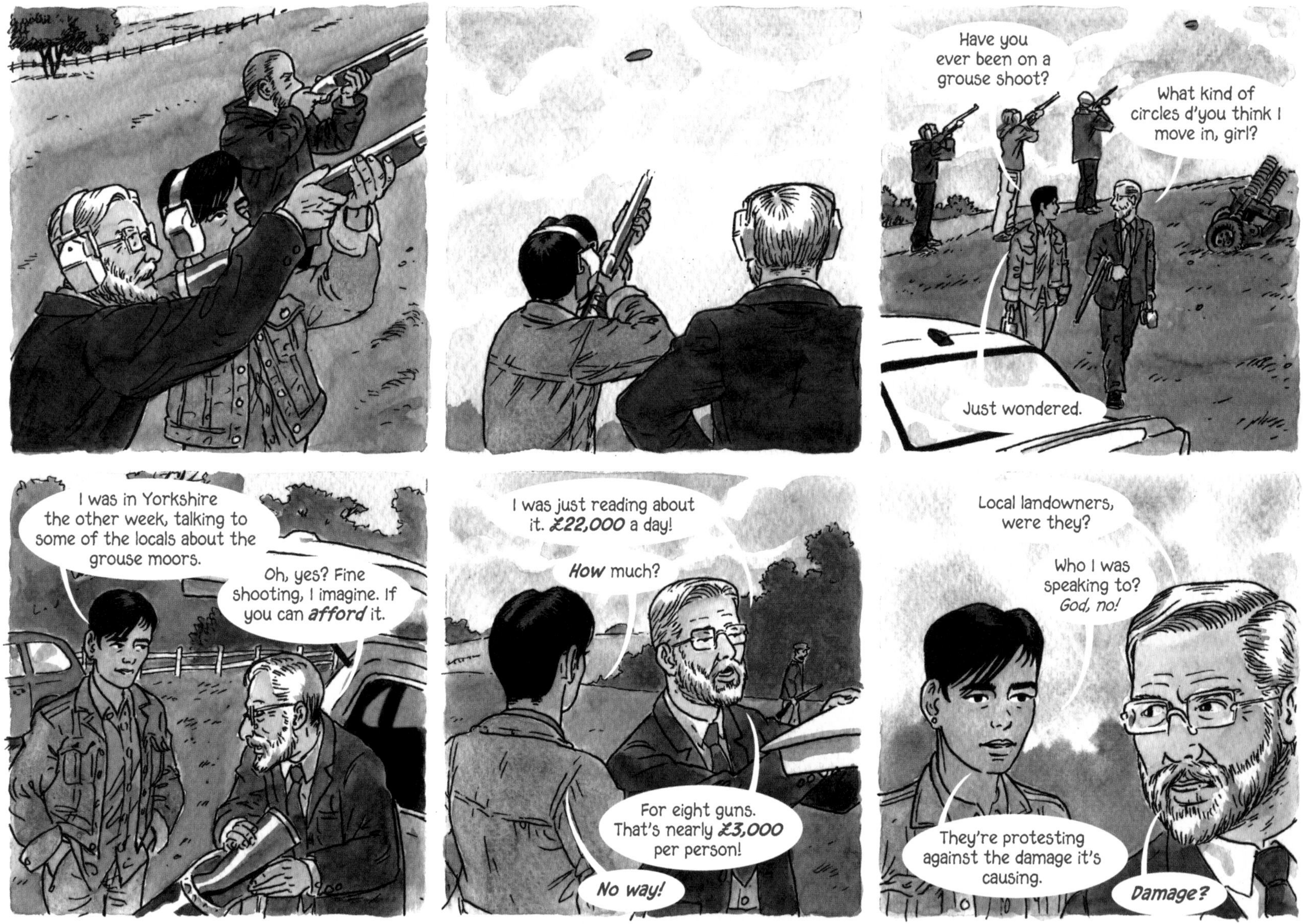

Have you ever been on a grouse shoot?
What kind of circles d'you think I move in, girl?
Just wondered.
I was in Yorkshire the other week, talking to some of the locals about the grouse moors.
Oh, yes? Fine shooting, I imagine. If you can *afford* it.
I was just reading about it. *£22,000* a day!
How much?
For eight guns. That's nearly *£3,000* per person!
No way!
Local landowners, were they?
Who I was speaking to? *God, no!*
They're protesting against the damage it's causing.
Damage?

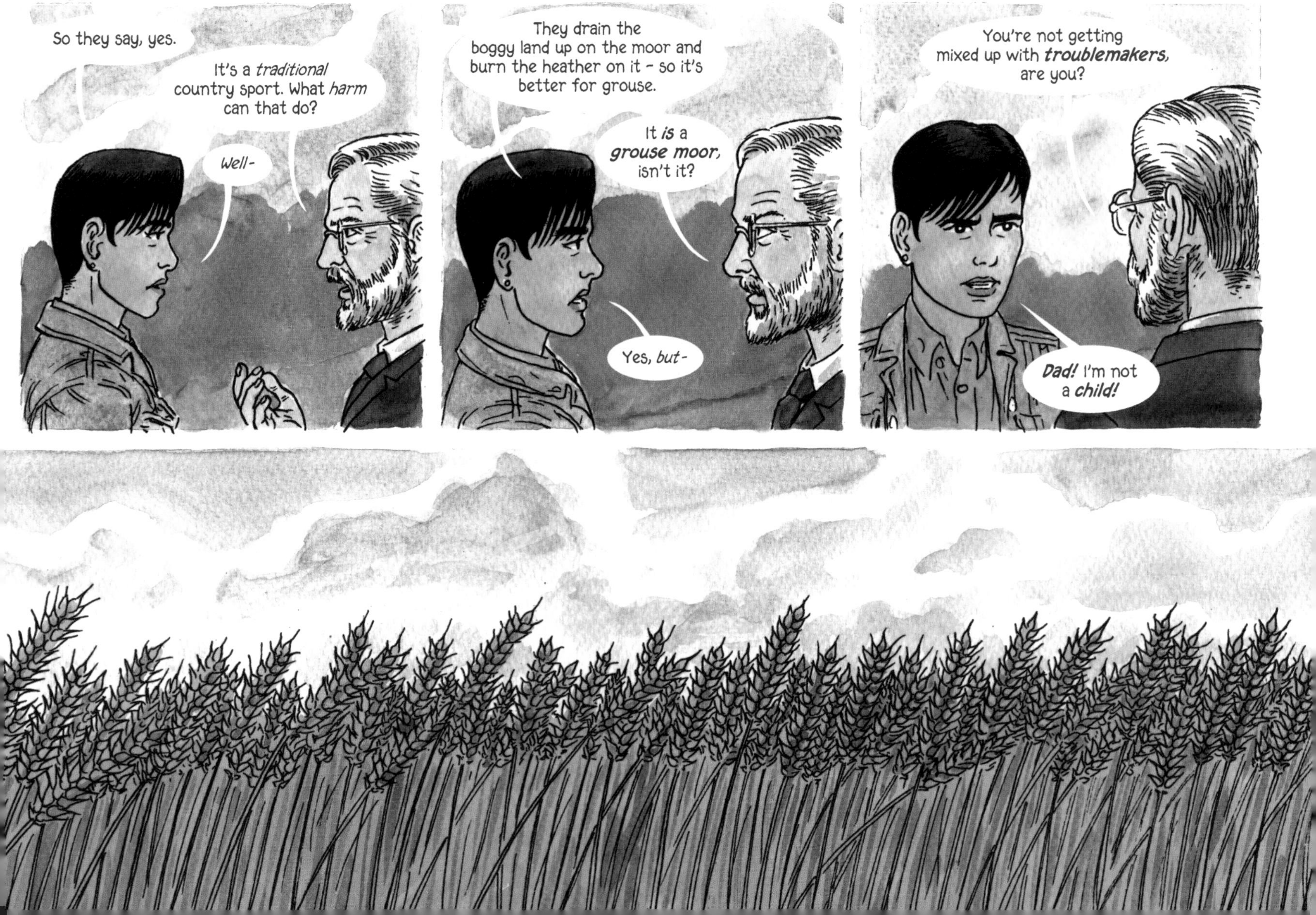
So they say, yes.
It's a *traditional* country sport. What *harm* can that do?
Well-
They drain the boggy land up on the moor and burn the heather on it - so it's better for grouse.
It ***is*** a ***grouse moor,*** isn't it?
Yes, *but-*
You're not getting mixed up with ***troublemakers,*** are you?
Dad! I'm not a ***child!***

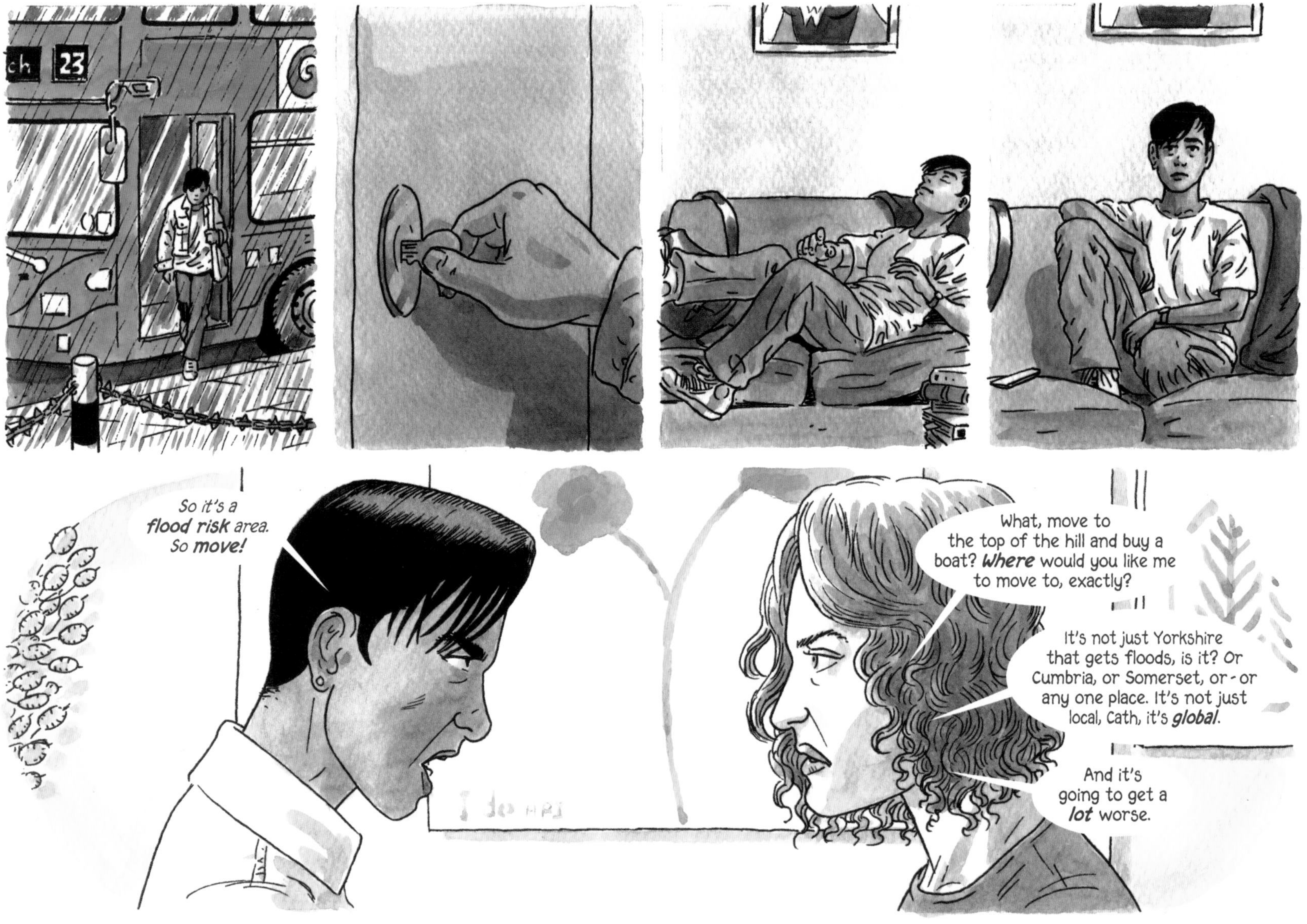
23
So it's a *flood risk* area. So *move!*
What, move to the top of the hill and buy a boat? *Where* would you like me to move to, exactly?
It's not just Yorkshire that gets floods, is it? Or Cumbria, or Somerset, or - or any one place. It's not just local, Cath, it's *global*.
And it's going to get a *lot* worse.

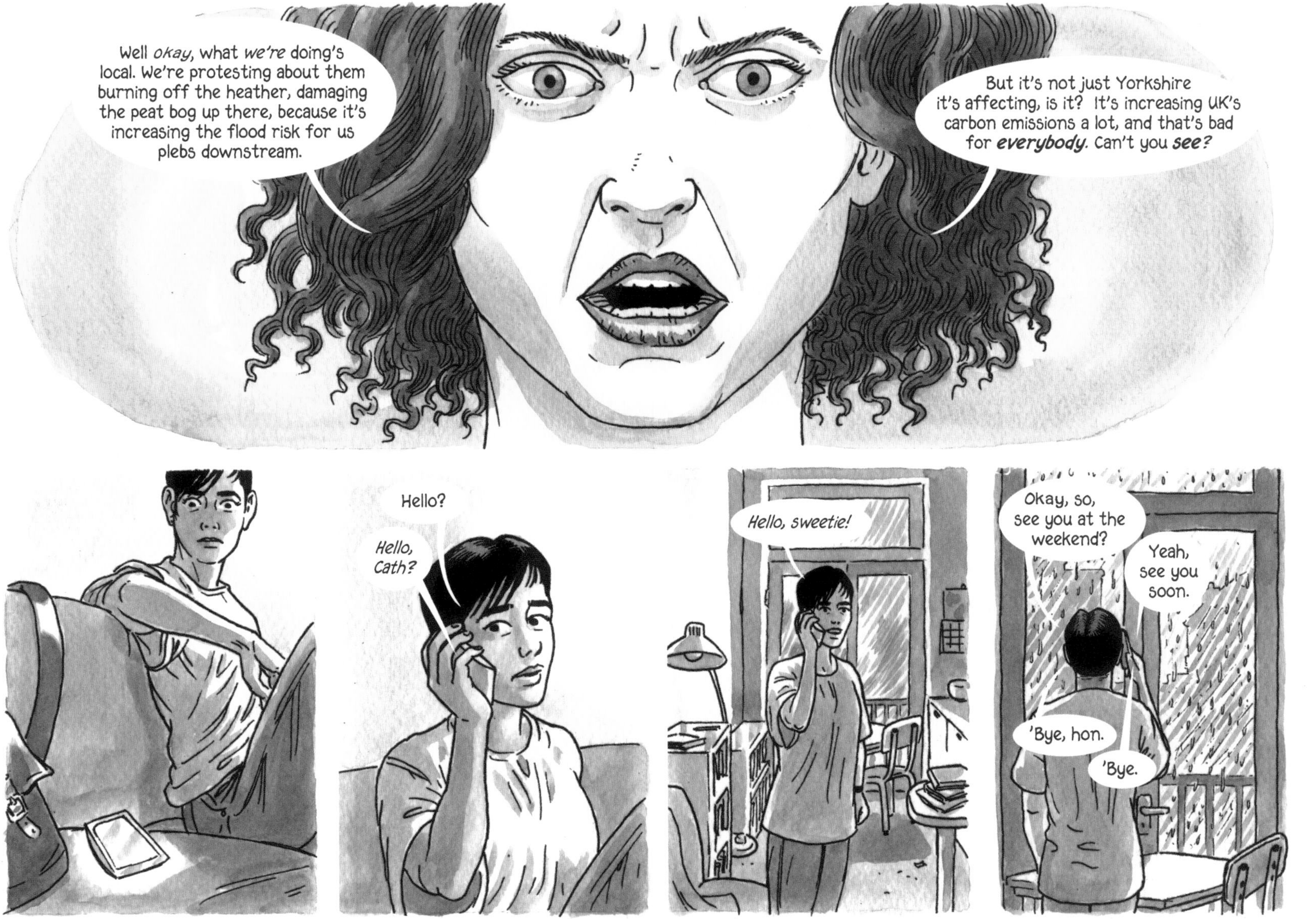
Well *okay*, what *we're* doing's local. We're protesting about them burning off the heather, damaging the peat bog up there, because it's increasing the flood risk for us plebs downstream.
But it's not just Yorkshire it's affecting, is it? It's increasing UK's carbon emissions a lot, and that's bad for ***everybody***. Can't you ***see?***
Hello?
Hello, Cath?
Hello, sweetie!
Okay, so, see you at the weekend?
Yeah, see you soon.
'Bye, hon.
'Bye.

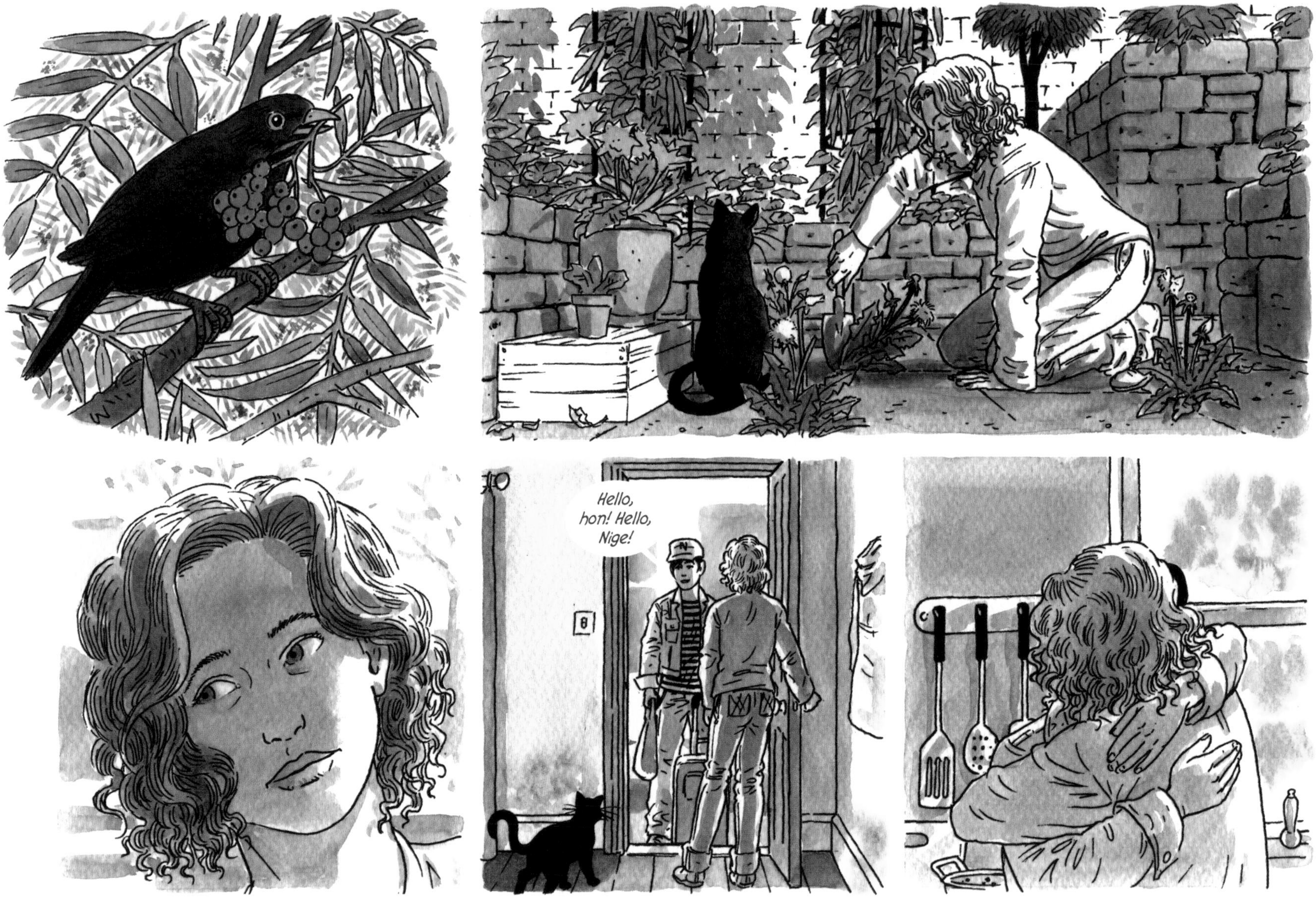
Hello, hon! Hello, Nige!

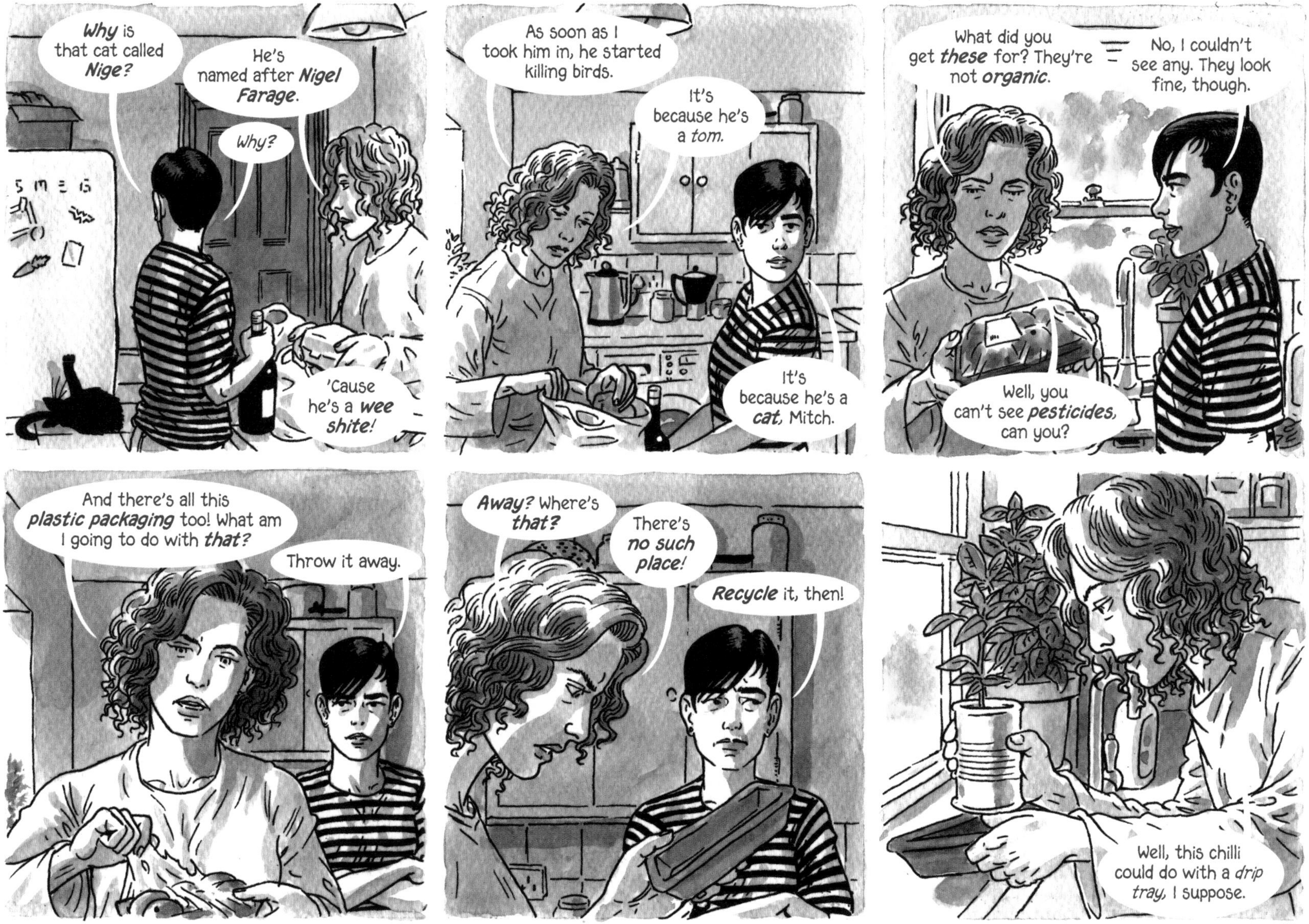
Why is that cat called ***Nige?***
He's named after ***Nigel Farage***.
Why?
'Cause he's a ***wee shite!***
As soon as I took him in, he started killing birds.
It's because he's a *tom.*
It's because he's a ***cat,*** Mitch.
What did you get ***these*** for? They're not ***organic***.
No, I couldn't see any. They look fine, though.
Well, you can't see ***pesticides,*** can you?
And there's all this ***plastic packaging*** too! What am I going to do with ***that?***
Throw it away.
Away? Where's ***that?***
There's ***no such place!***
Recycle it, then!
Well, this chilli could do with a *drip tray,* I suppose.

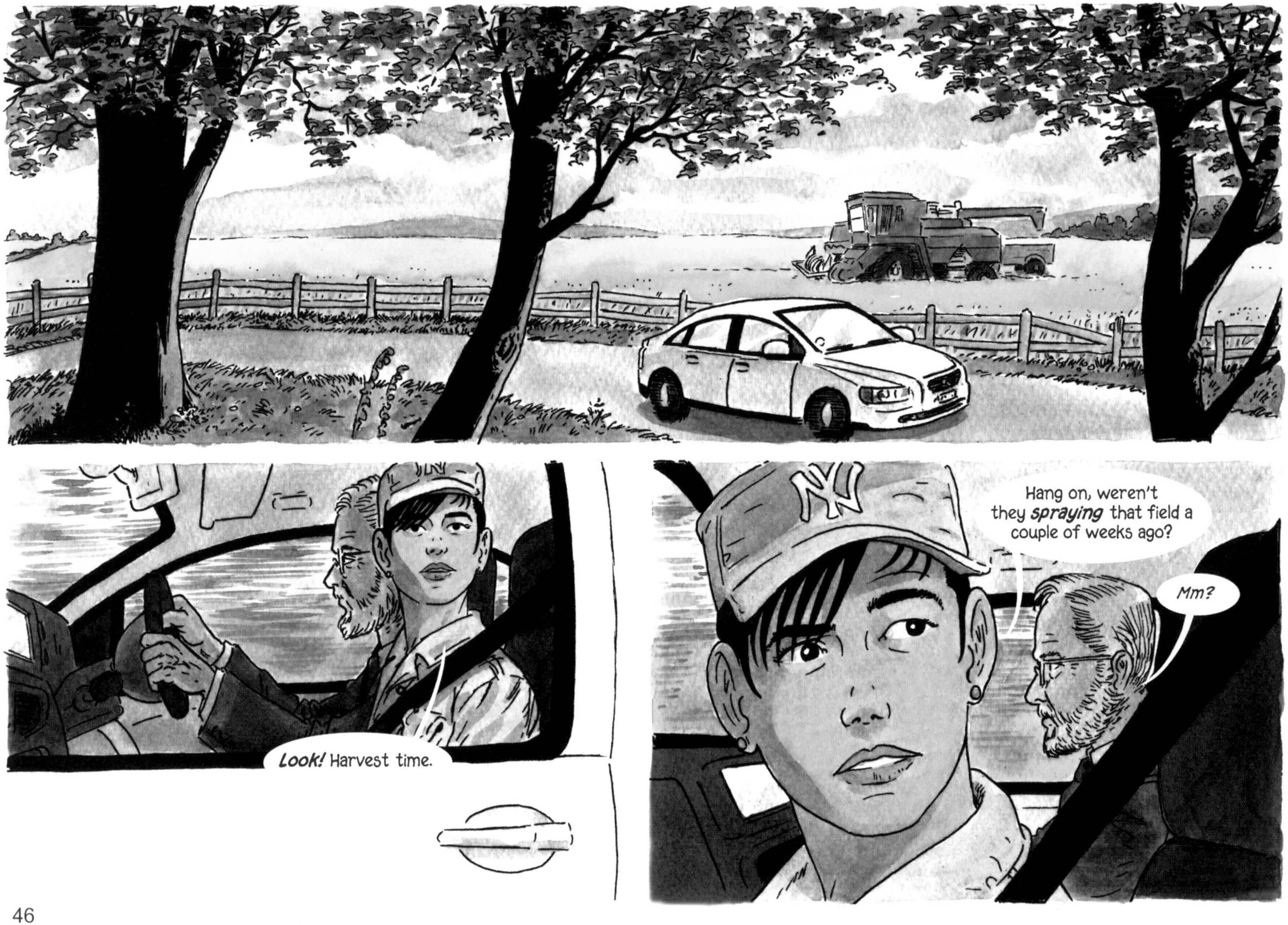
Look! Harvest time.
Hang on, weren't they spraying that field a couple of weeks ago?
Mm?

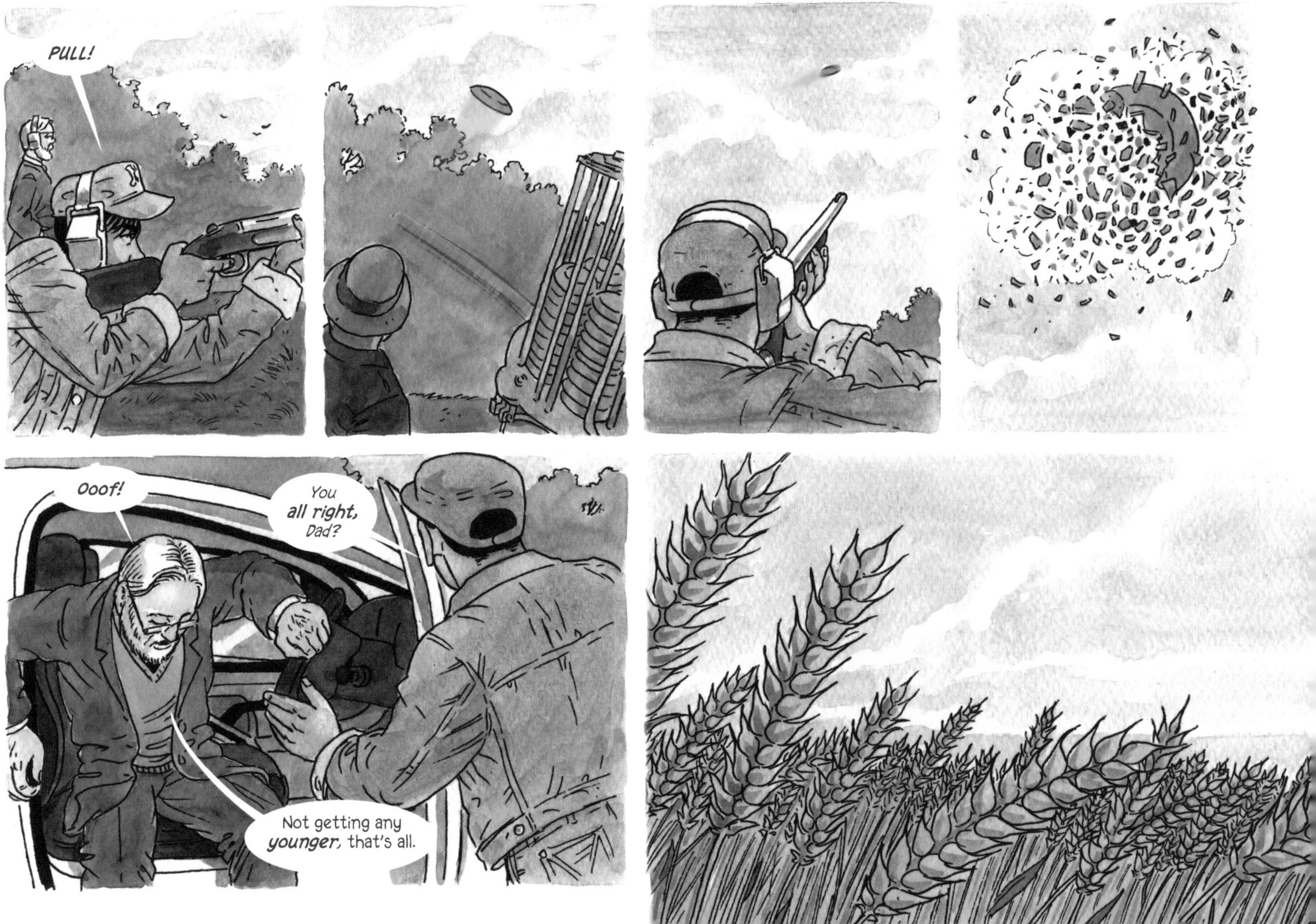
PULL!
Ooof!
You all right, Dad?
Not getting any younger, that's all.

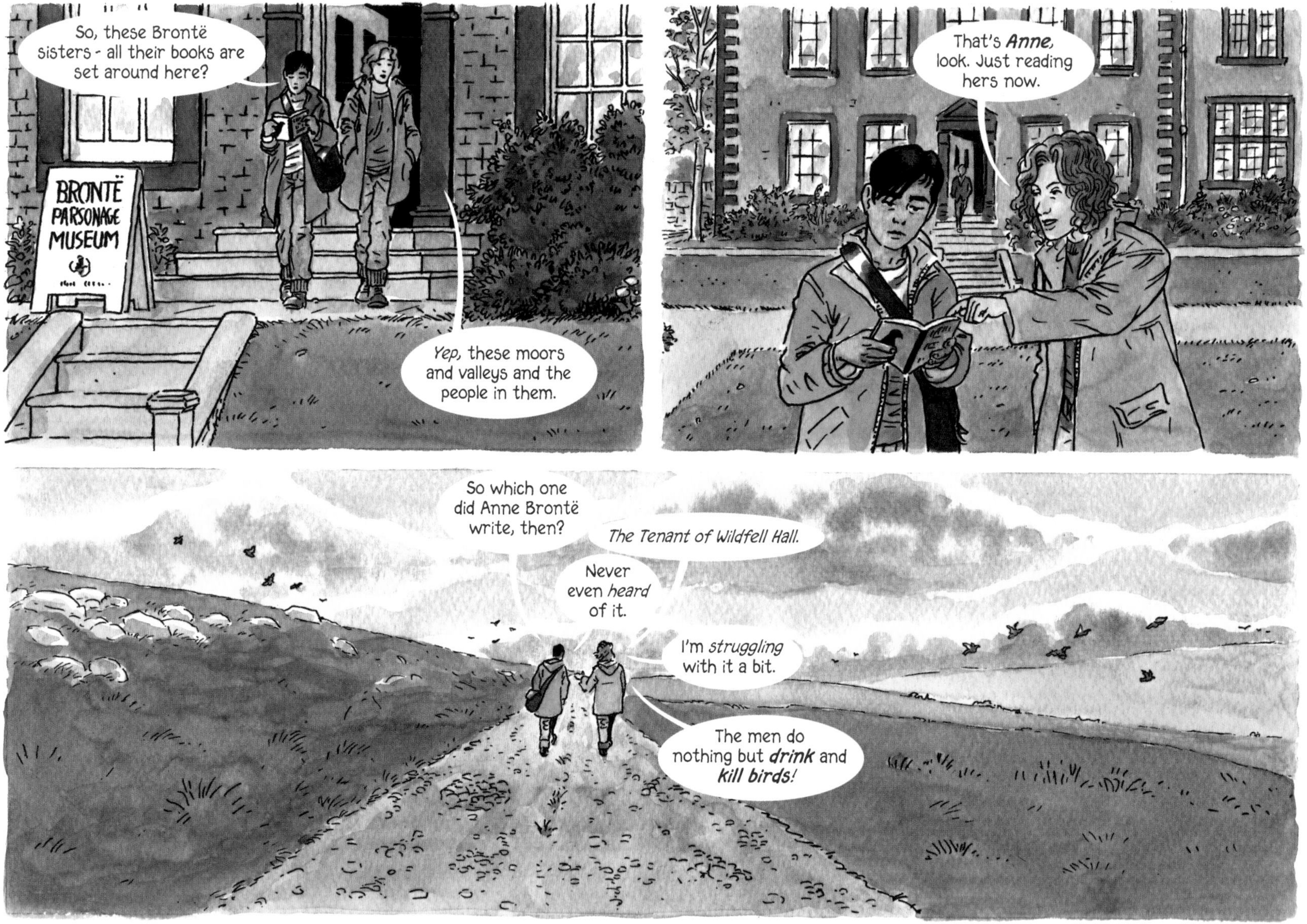
So, these Brontë sisters - all their books are set around here?
BRONTË PARSONAGE MUSEUM
Yep, these moors and valleys and the people in them.
That's ***Anne,*** look. Just reading hers now.
So which one did Anne Brontë write, then?
The Tenant of Wildfell Hall.
Never even *heard* of it.
I'm *struggling* with it a bit.
The men do nothing but ***drink*** and ***kill birds***!

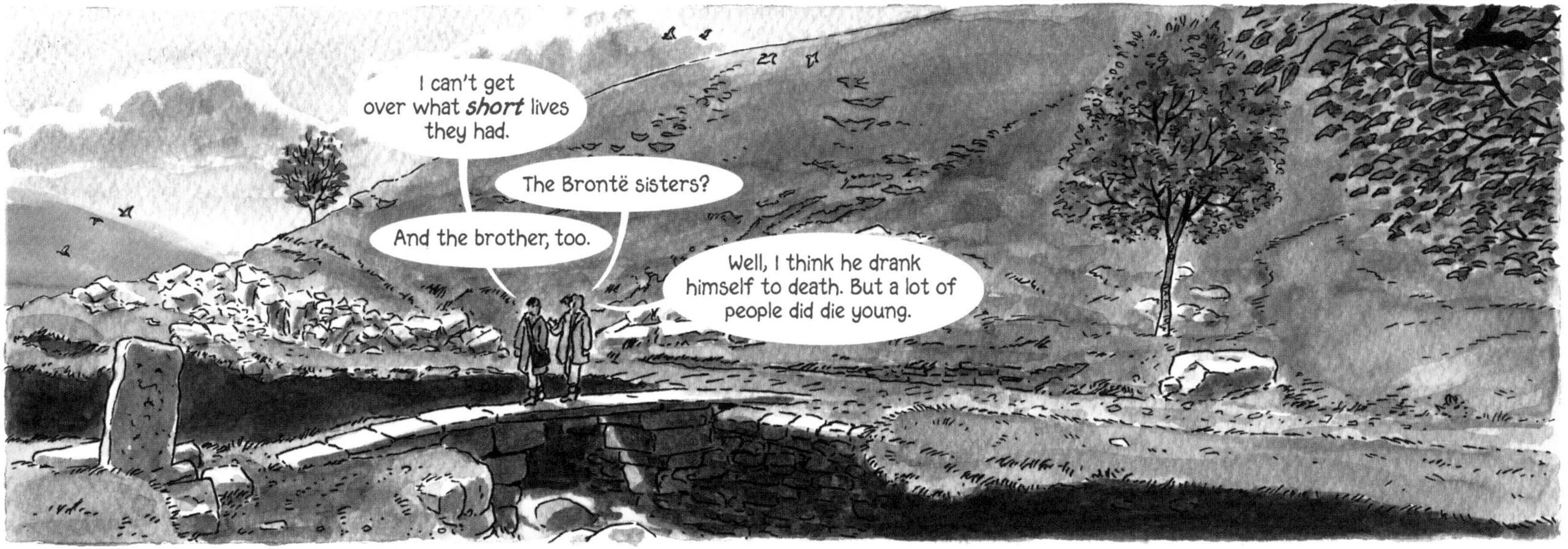
I can't get over what **short** lives they had.
The Brontë sisters?
And the brother, too.
Well, I think he drank himself to death. But a lot of people did die young.

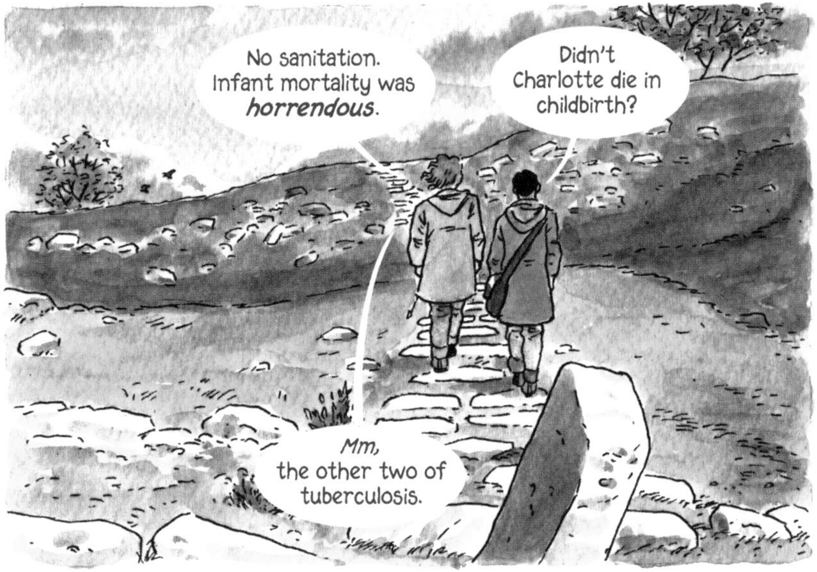
No sanitation. Infant mortality was **horrendous**.
Didn't Charlotte die in childbirth?
Mm, the other two of tuberculosis.

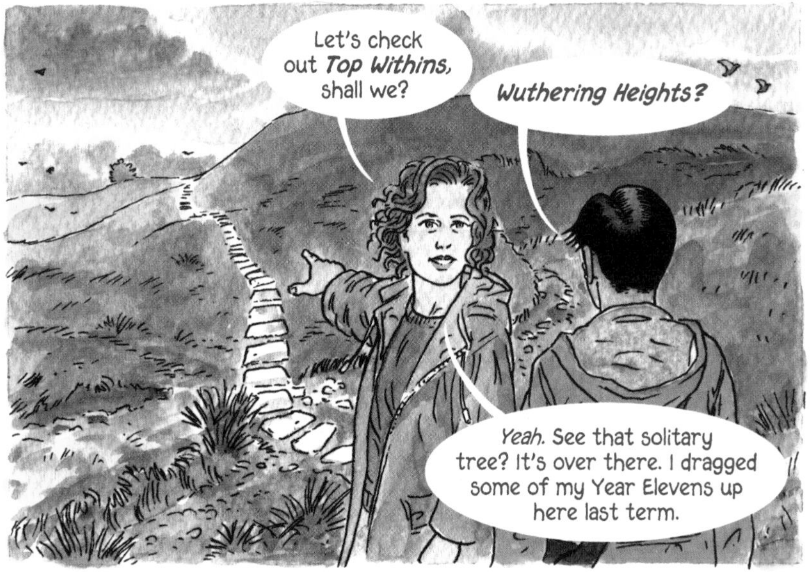
Let's check out ***Top Withins,*** shall we?
Wuthering Heights?
Yeah. See that solitary tree? It's over there. I dragged some of my Year Elevens up here last term.

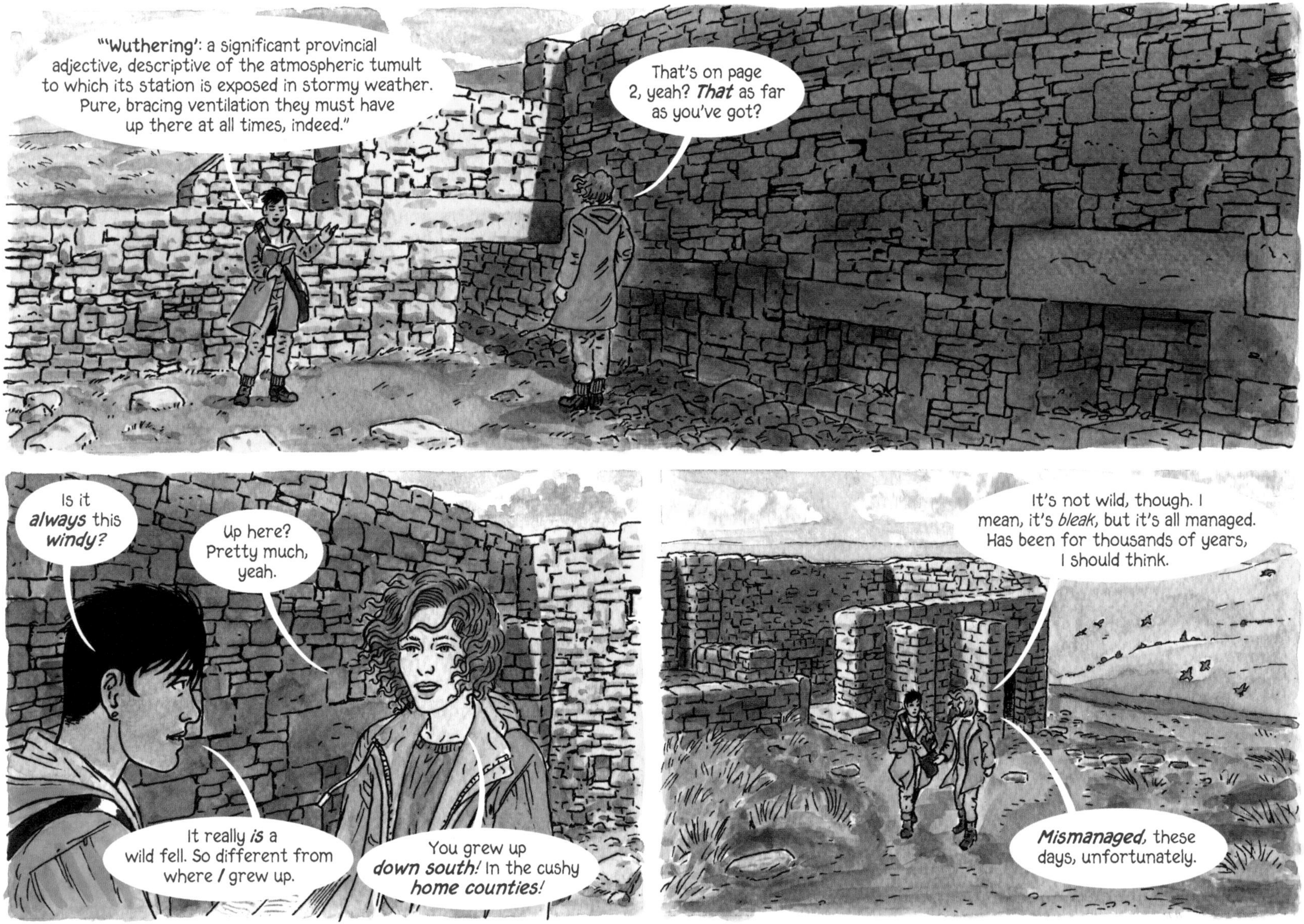

"'**Wuthering**': a significant provincial adjective, descriptive of the atmospheric tumult to which its station is exposed in stormy weather. Pure, bracing ventilation they must have up there at all times, indeed."
That's on page 2, yeah? ***That*** as far as you've got?
Is it ***always*** this ***windy?***
Up here? Pretty much, yeah.
It really ***is*** a wild fell. So different from where ***I*** grew up.
You grew up ***down south!*** In the cushy ***home counties!***
It's not wild, though. I mean, it's *bleak*, but it's all managed. Has been for thousands of years, I should think.
Mismanaged, these days, unfortunately.

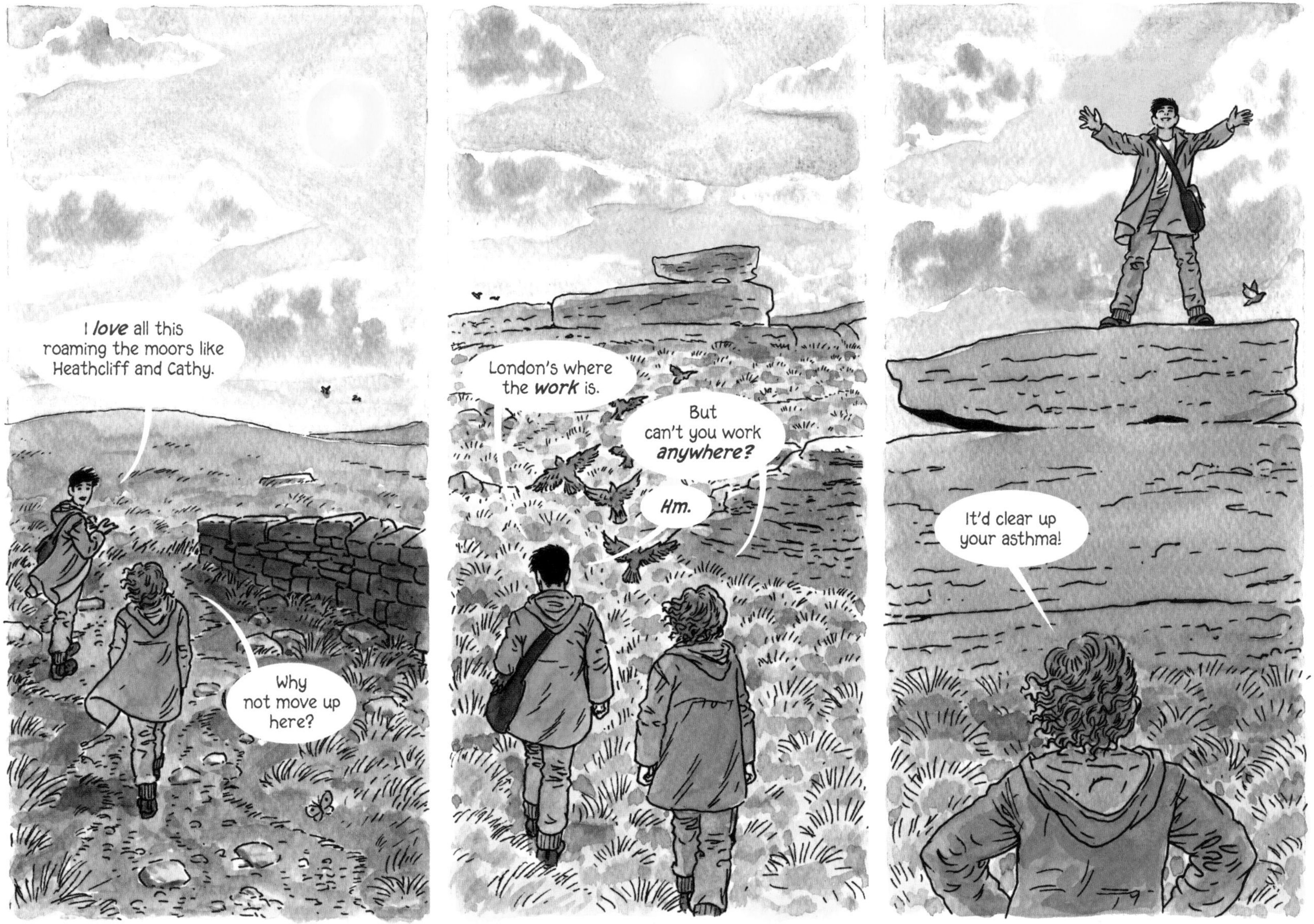
I *love* all this roaming the moors like Heathcliff and Cathy.
Why not move up here?
London's where the *work* is.
But can't you work *anywhere?*
Hm.
It'd clear up your asthma!

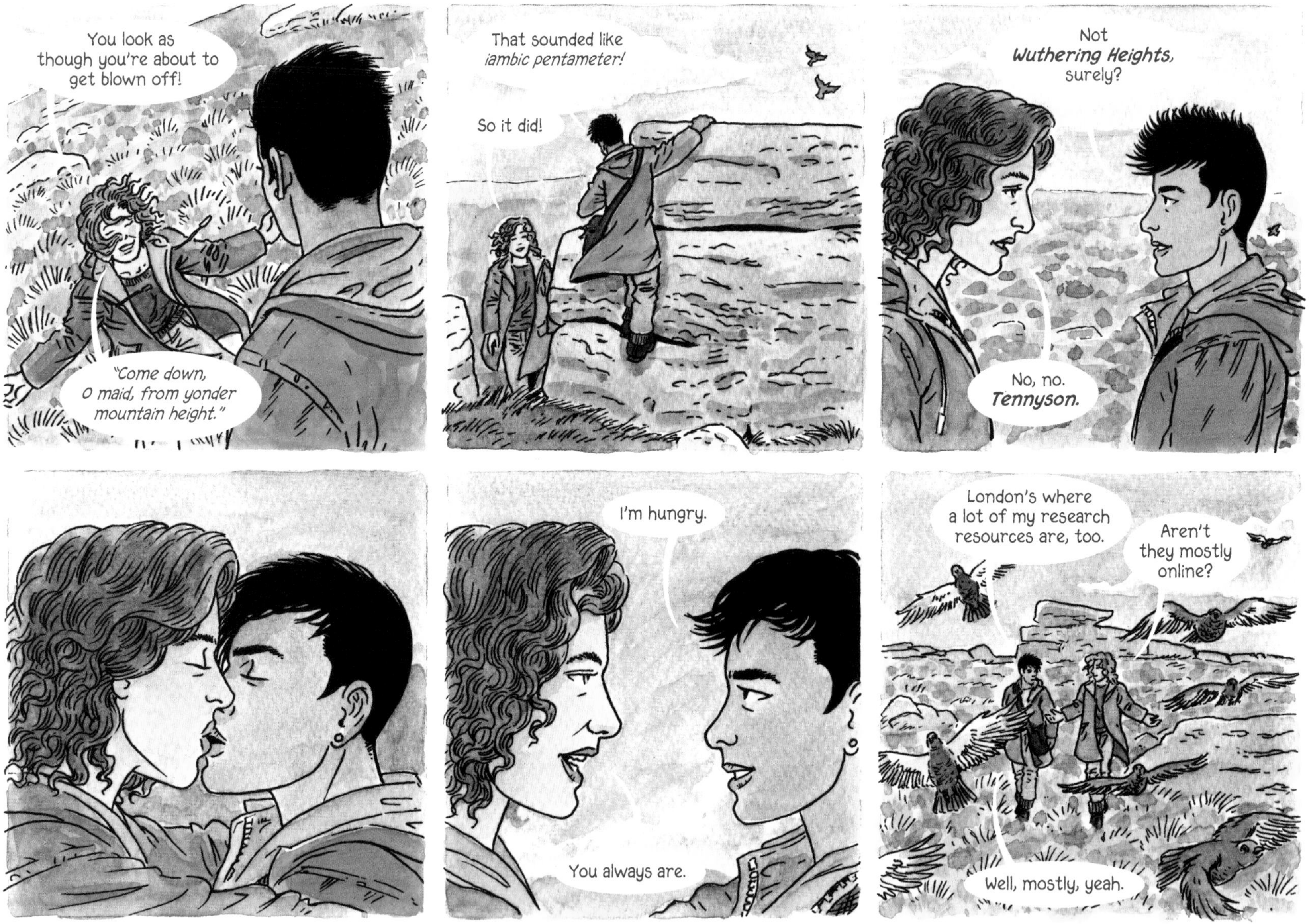
You look as though you're about to get blown off!
"Come down, O maid, from yonder mountain height."
That sounded like iambic pentameter!
So it did!
Not Wuthering Heights, surely?
No, no. Tennyson.
I'm hungry.
You always are.
London's where a lot of my research resources are, too.
Aren't they mostly online?
Well, mostly, yeah.

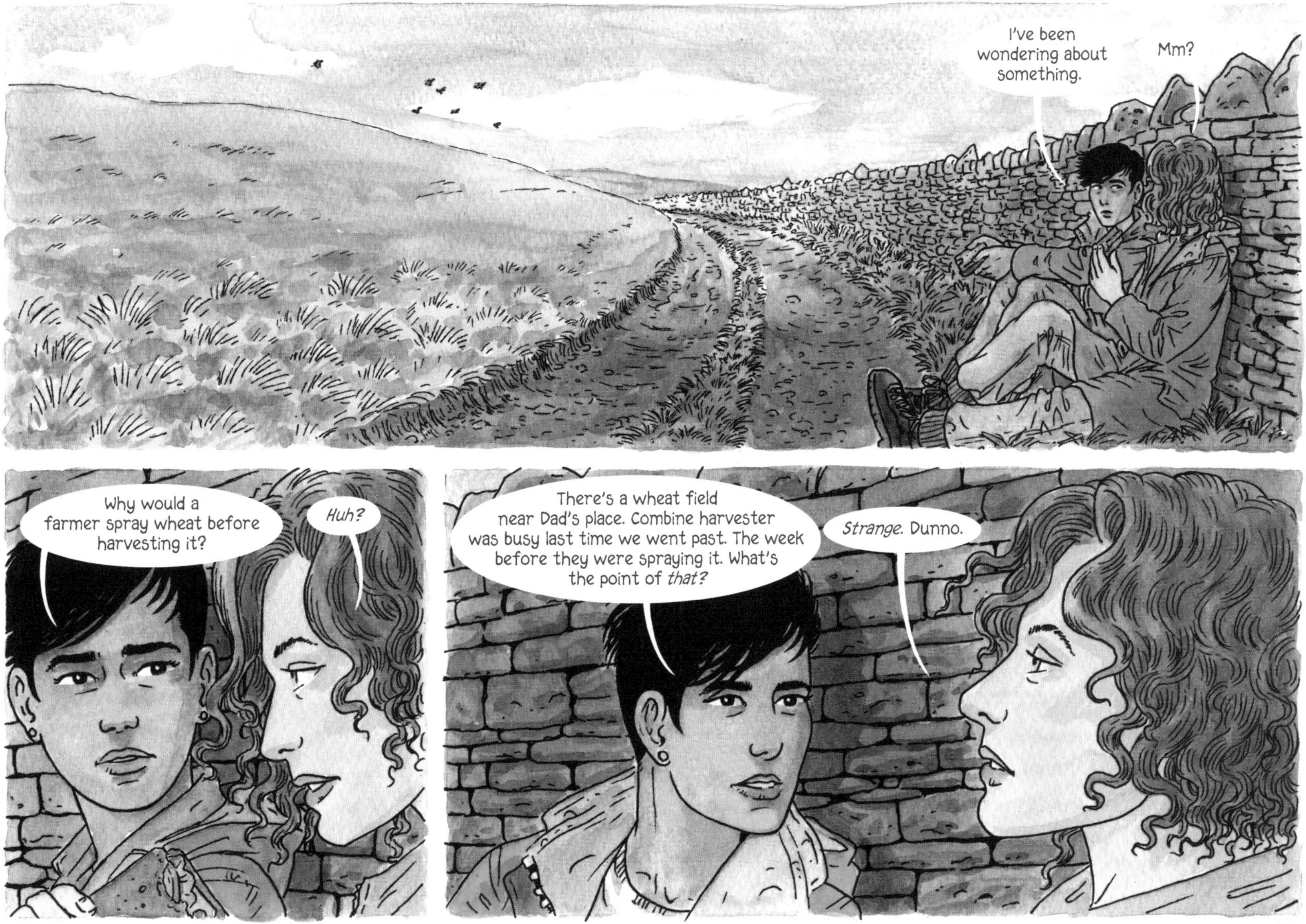
I've been wondering about something.
Mm?
Why would a farmer spray wheat before harvesting it?
Huh?
There's a wheat field near Dad's place. Combine harvester was busy last time we went past. The week before they were spraying it. What's the point of *that?*
Strange. Dunno.

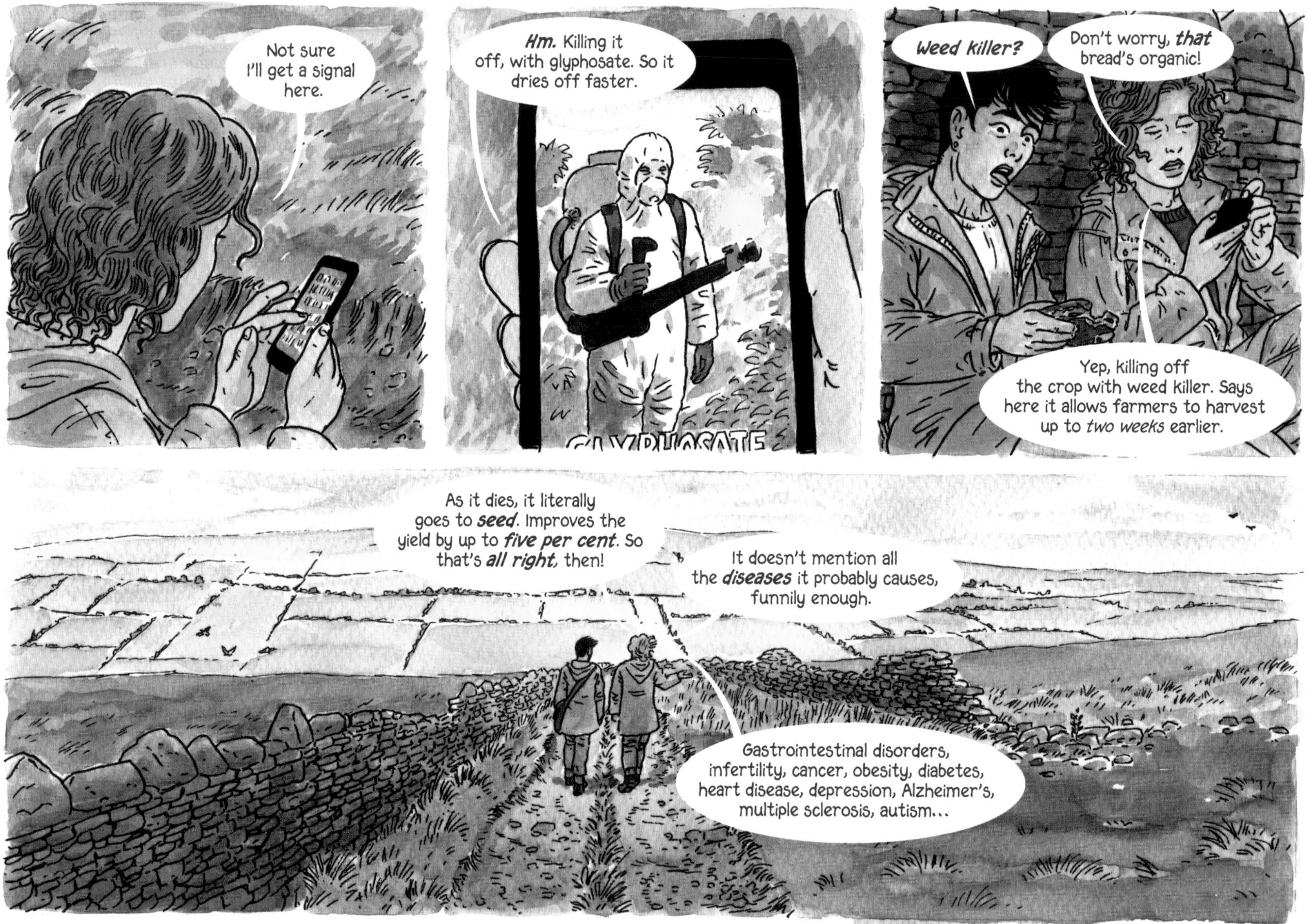
Not sure I'll get a signal here.
Hm. Killing it off, with glyphosate. So it dries off faster.
Weed killer?
Don't worry, *that* bread's organic!
Yep, killing off the crop with weed killer. Says here it allows farmers to harvest up to *two weeks* earlier.
As it dies, it literally goes to *seed*. Improves the yield by up to *five per cent*. So that's *all right,* then!
It doesn't mention all the *diseases* it probably causes, funnily enough.
Gastrointestinal disorders, infertility, cancer, obesity, diabetes, heart disease, depression, Alzheimer's, multiple sclerosis, autism...

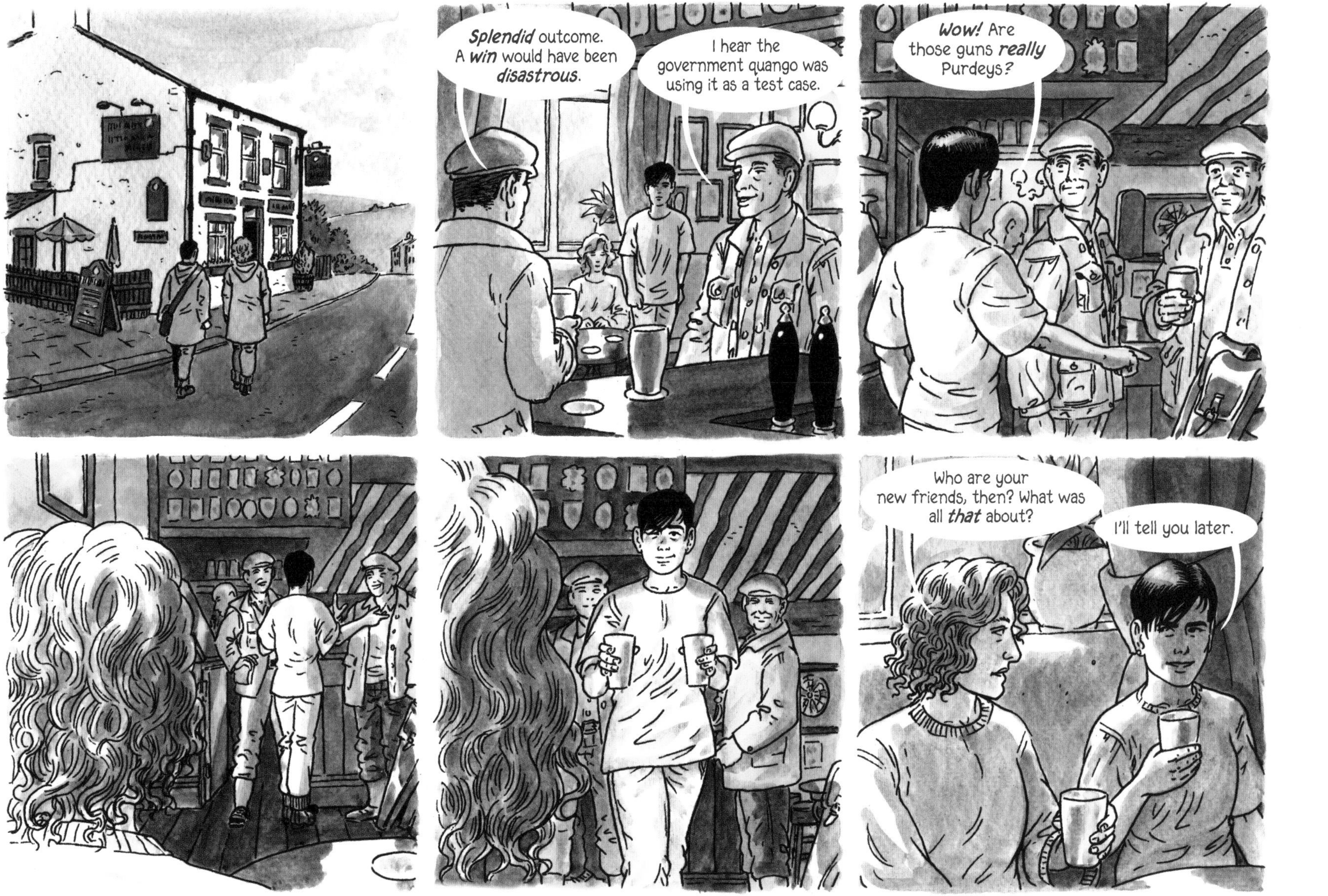
Splendid outcome. A win would have been disastrous.
I hear the government quango was using it as a test case.
Wow! Are those guns really Purdeys?
Who are your new friends, then? What was all that about?
I'll tell you later.

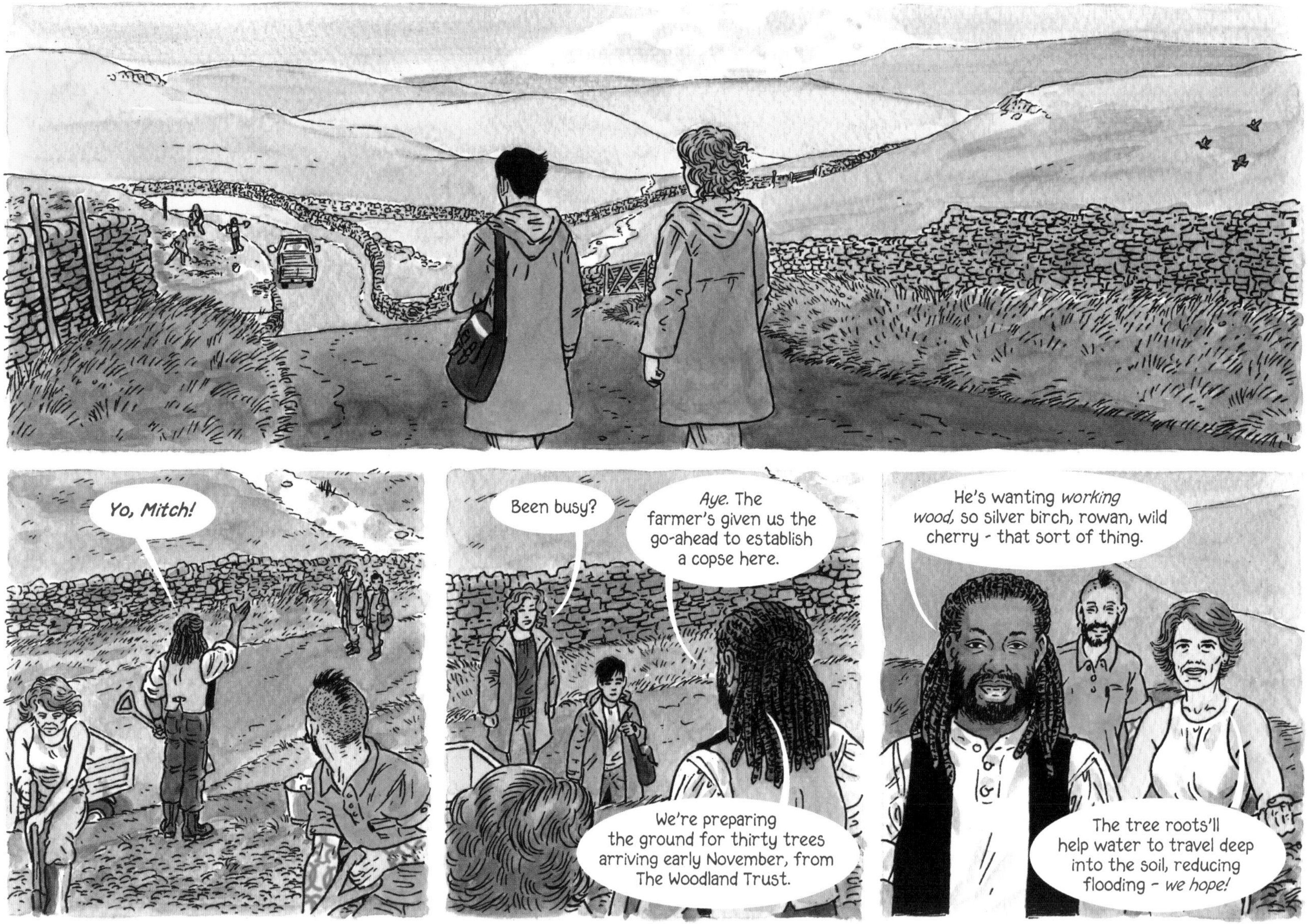
Yo, Mitch!
Been busy?
Aye. The farmer's given us the go-ahead to establish a copse here.
We're preparing the ground for thirty trees arriving early November, from The Woodland Trust.
He's wanting *working wood,* so silver birch, rowan, wild cherry - that sort of thing.
The tree roots'll help water to travel deep into the soil, reducing flooding - *we hope!*

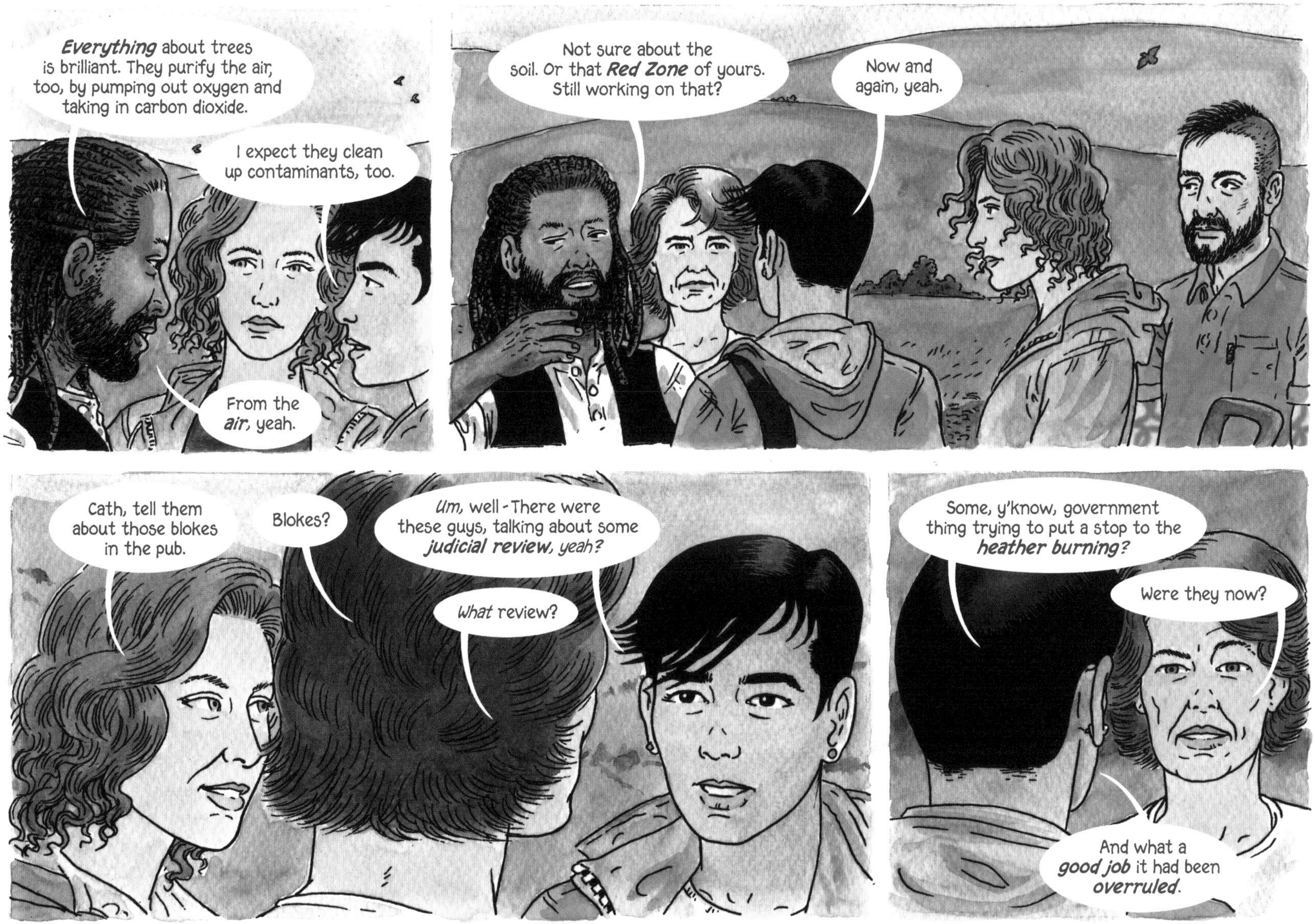
Everything about trees is brilliant. They purify the air, too, by pumping out oxygen and taking in carbon dioxide.
I expect they clean up contaminants, too.
From the *air*, yeah.
Not sure about the soil. Or that *Red Zone* of yours. Still working on that?
Now and again, yeah.
Cath, tell them about those blokes in the pub.
Blokes?
Um, well - There were these guys, talking about some *judicial review, yeah?*
What review?
Some, y'know, government thing trying to put a stop to the *heather burning?*
Were they now?
And what a *good job* it had been *overruled*.

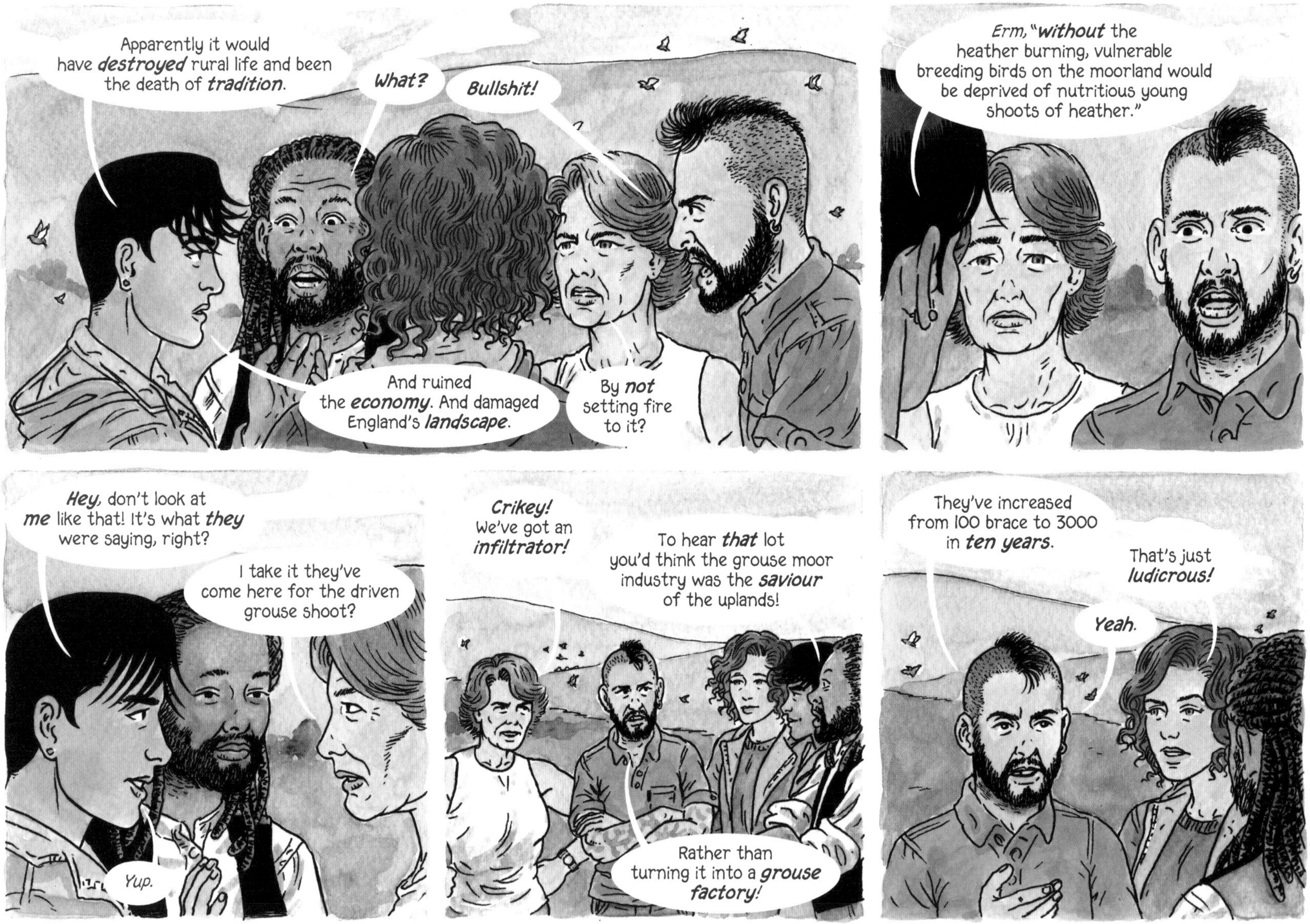
Apparently it would have destroyed rural life and been the death of tradition.
What?
Bullshit!
And ruined the economy. And damaged England's landscape.
By not setting fire to it?
Erm, "without the heather burning, vulnerable breeding birds on the moorland would be deprived of nutritious young shoots of heather."
Hey, don't look at me like that! It's what they were saying, right?
I take it they've come here for the driven grouse shoot?
Yup.
Crikey! We've got an infiltrator!
To hear that lot you'd think the grouse moor industry was the saviour of the uplands!
Rather than turning it into a grouse factory!
They've increased from 100 brace to 3000 in ten years.
That's just ludicrous!
Yeah.

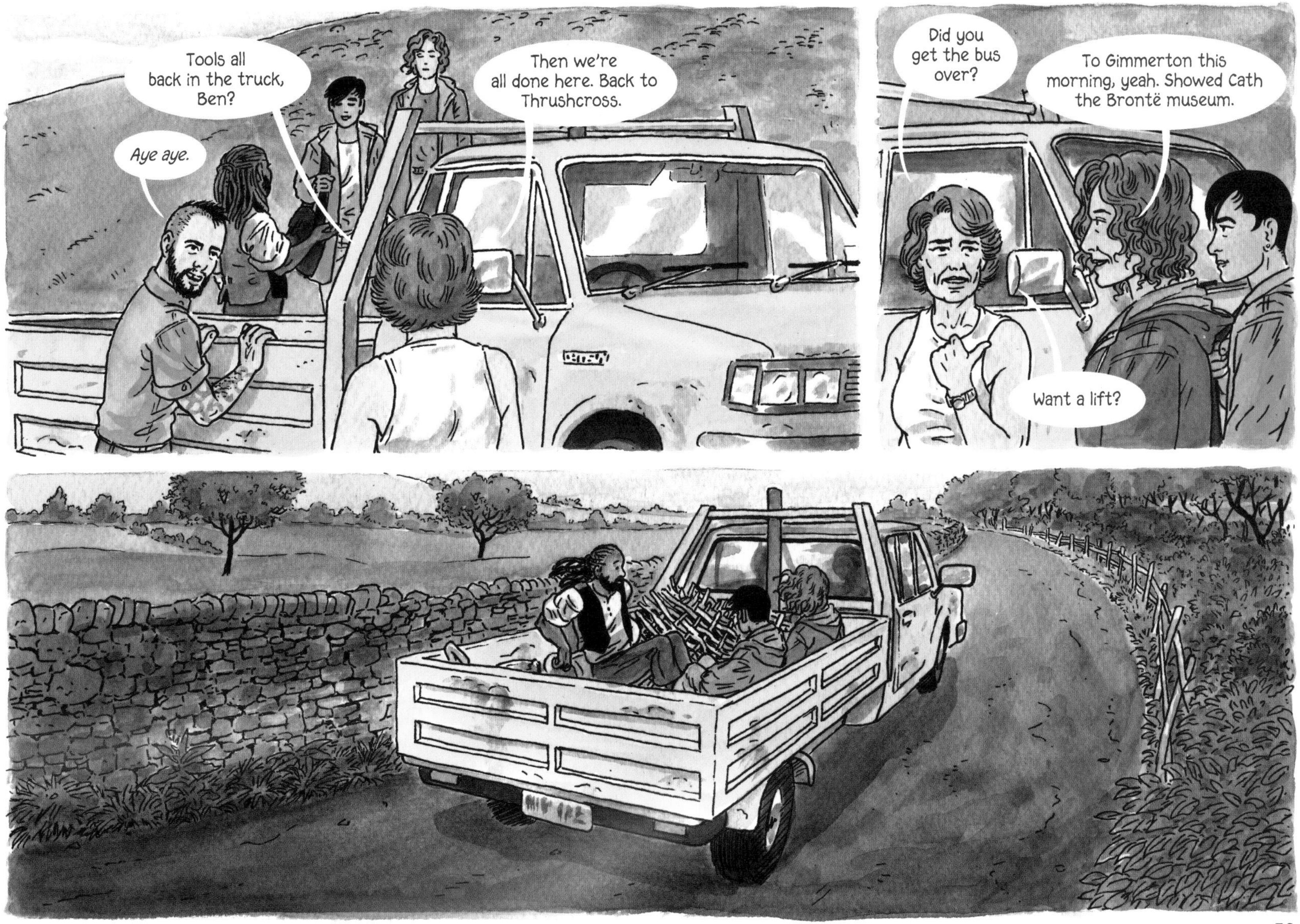
Tools all back in the truck, Ben?
Aye aye.
Then we're all done here. Back to Thrushcross.
Did you get the bus over?
To Gimmerton this morning, yeah. Showed Cath the Brontë museum.
Want a lift?

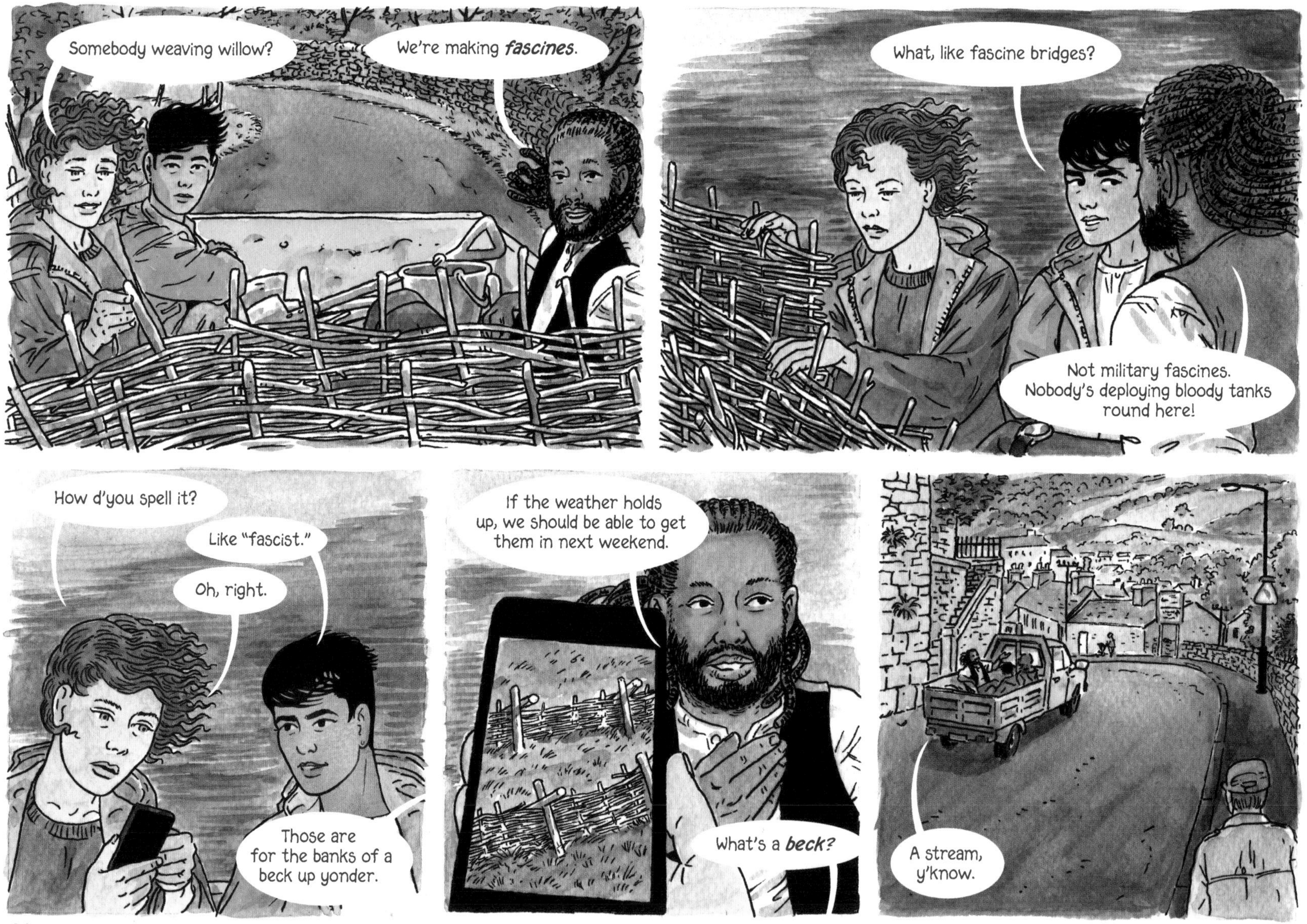
Somebody weaving willow?
We're making *fascines*.
What, like fascine bridges?
Not military fascines. Nobody's deploying bloody tanks round here!
How d'you spell it?
Like "fascist."
Oh, right.
Those are for the banks of a beck up yonder.
If the weather holds up, we should be able to get them in next weekend.
What's a *beck?*
A stream, y'know.

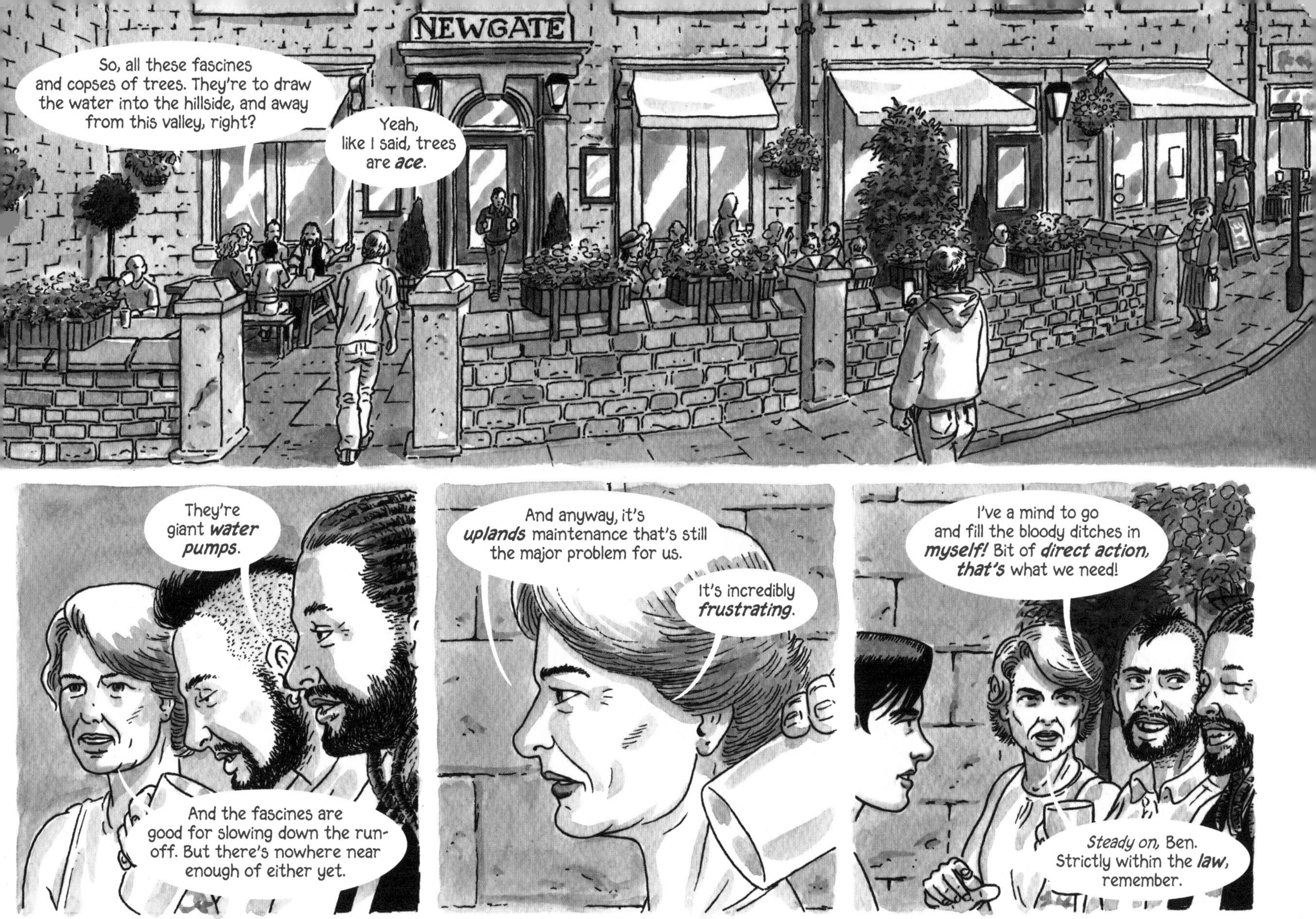
NEWGATE
So, all these fascines and copses of trees. They're to draw the water into the hillside, and away from this valley, right?
Yeah, like I said, trees are *ace*.
They're giant *water pumps*.
And the fascines are good for slowing down the run-off. But there's nowhere near enough of either yet.
And anyway, it's *uplands* maintenance that's still the major problem for us.
It's incredibly *frustrating*.
I've a mind to go and fill the bloody ditches in *myself!* Bit of *direct action, that's* what we need!
Steady on, Ben. Strictly within the *law,* remember.

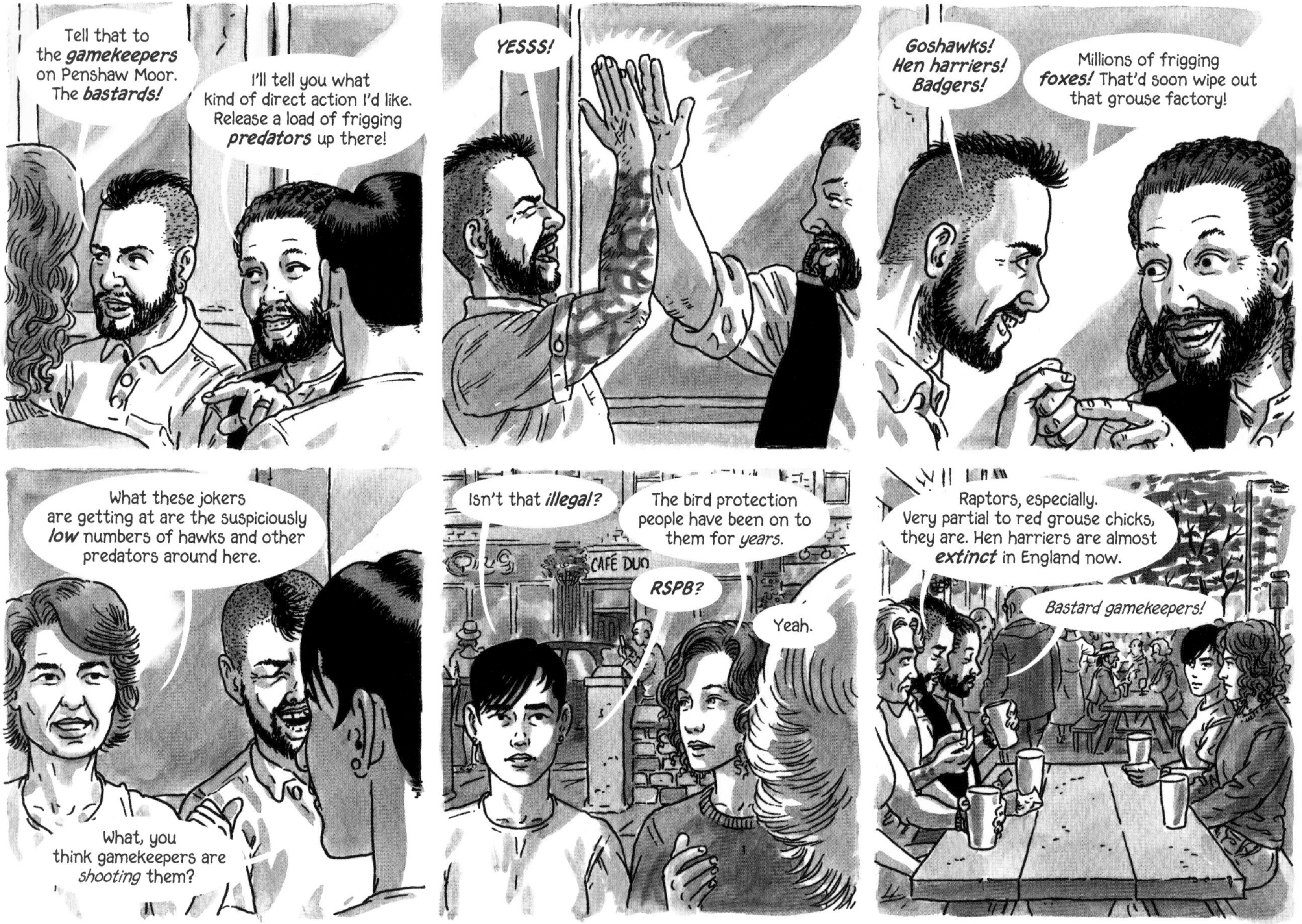
Tell that to the *gamekeepers* on Penshaw Moor. The ***bastards!***
I'll tell you what kind of direct action I'd like. Release a load of frigging ***predators*** up there!
YESSS!
Goshawks! Hen harriers! Badgers!
Millions of frigging ***foxes!*** That'd soon wipe out that grouse factory!
What these jokers are getting at are the suspiciously ***low*** numbers of hawks and other predators around here.
What, you think gamekeepers are *shooting* them?
Isn't that ***illegal?***
The bird protection people have been on to them for *years.*
CAFÉ DUO
RSPB?
Yeah.
Raptors, especially. Very partial to red grouse chicks, they are. Hen harriers are almost ***extinct*** in England now.
Bastard gamekeepers!

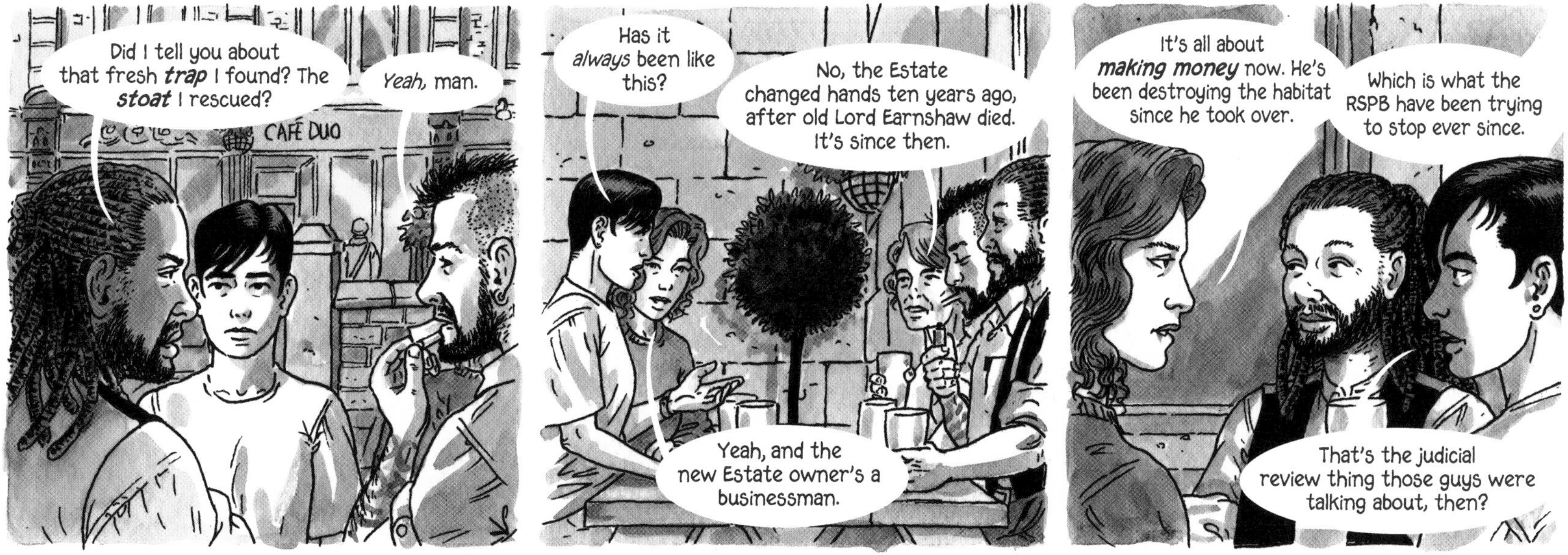
Did I tell you about that fresh *trap* I found? The *stoat* I rescued?
Yeah, man.
CAFÉ DUO
Has it *always* been like this?
No, the Estate changed hands ten years ago, after old Lord Earnshaw died. It's since then.
Yeah, and the new Estate owner's a businessman.
It's all about ***making money*** now. He's been destroying the habitat since he took over.
Which is what the RSPB have been trying to stop ever since.
That's the judicial review thing those guys were talking about, then?

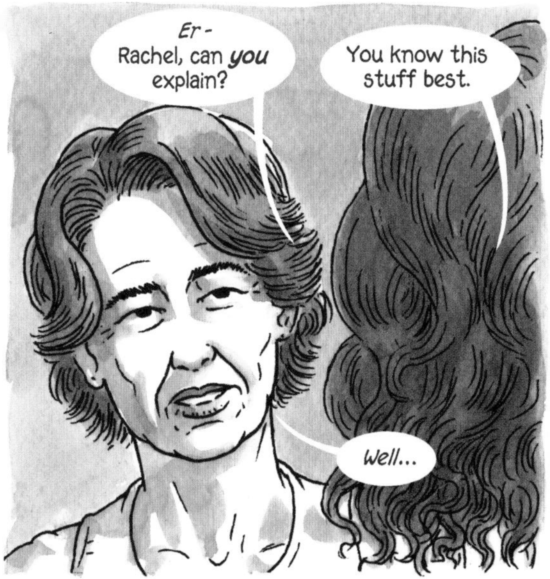
Er - Rachel, can ***you*** explain?
You know this stuff best.
Well...

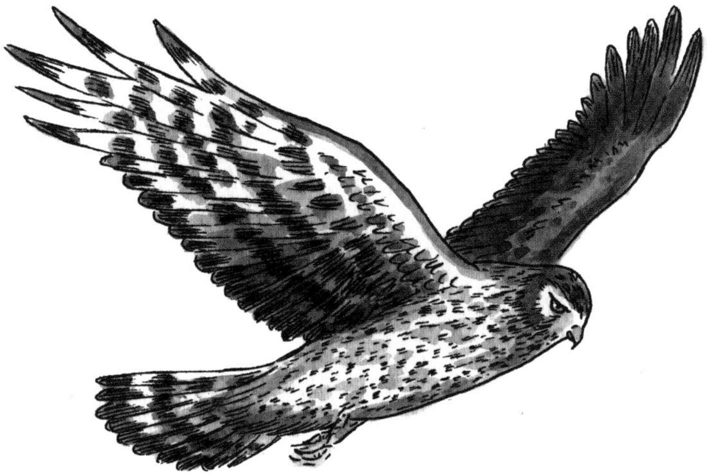

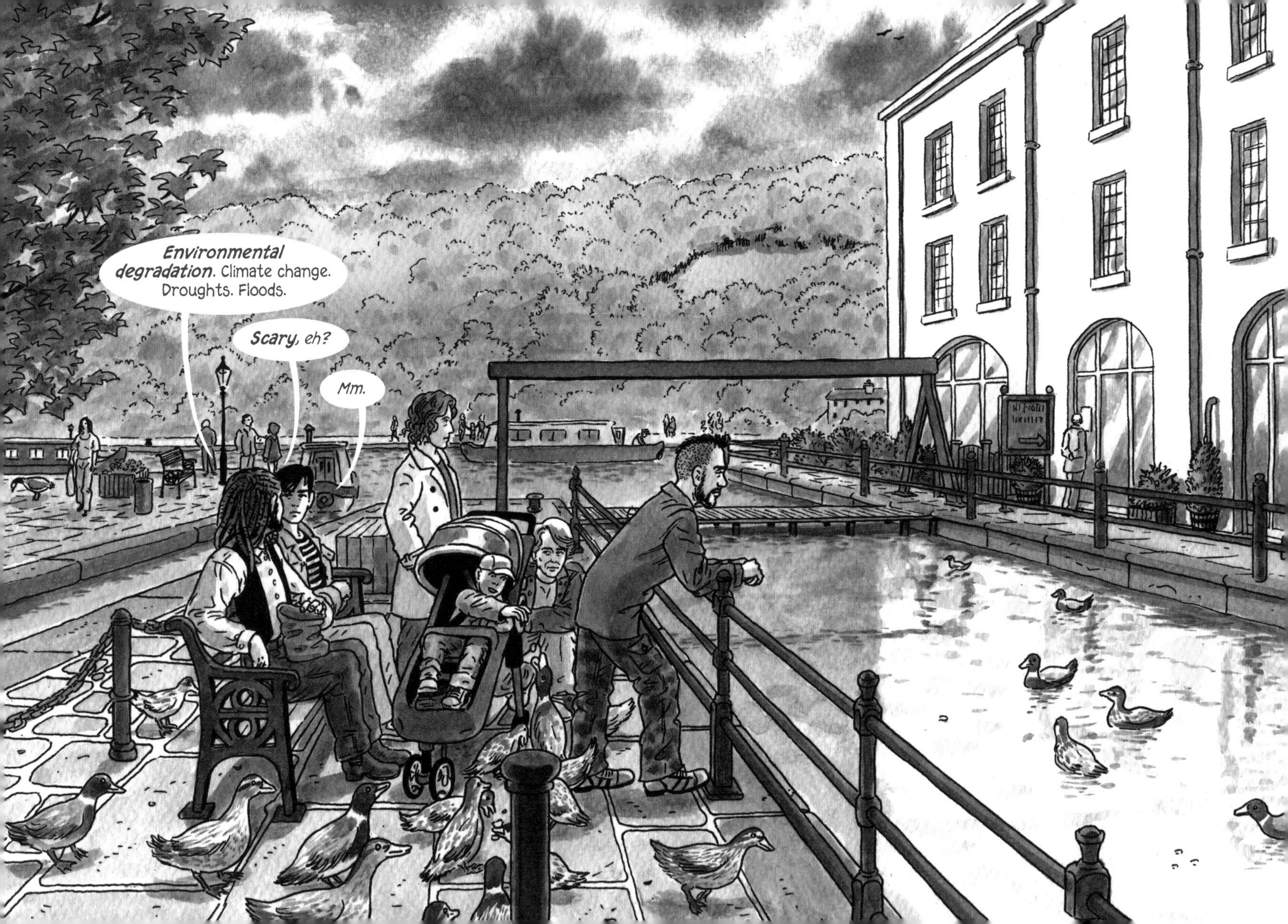
Environmental degradation. Climate change. Droughts. Floods.
Scary, eh?
Mm.

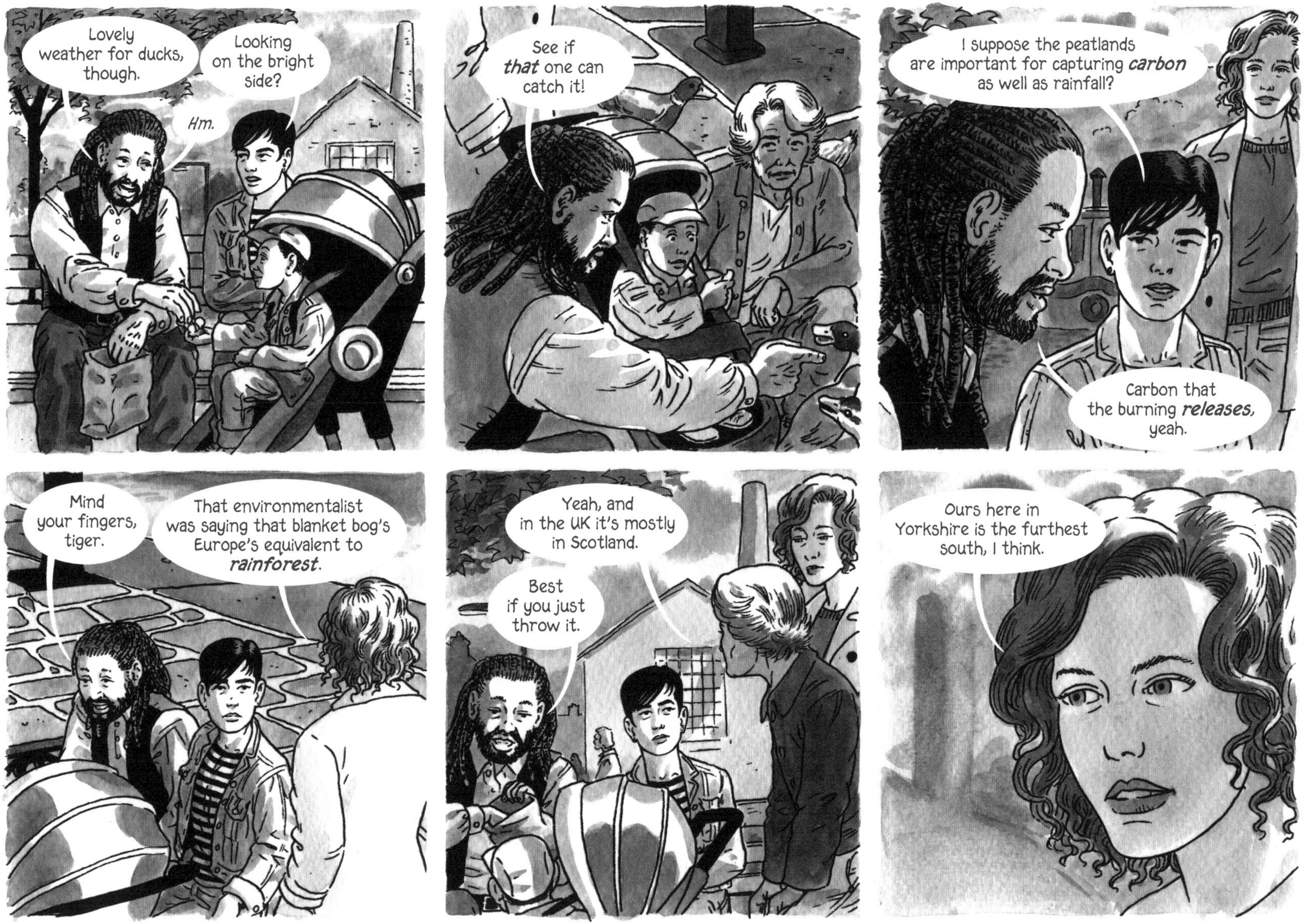
Lovely weather for ducks, though.
Hm.
Looking on the bright side?
See if *that* one can catch it!
I suppose the peatlands are important for capturing *carbon* as well as rainfall?
Carbon that the burning *releases*, yeah.
Mind your fingers, tiger.
That environmentalist was saying that blanket bog's Europe's equivalent to *rainforest*.
Yeah, and in the UK it's mostly in Scotland.
Best if you just throw it.
Ours here in Yorkshire is the furthest south, I think.

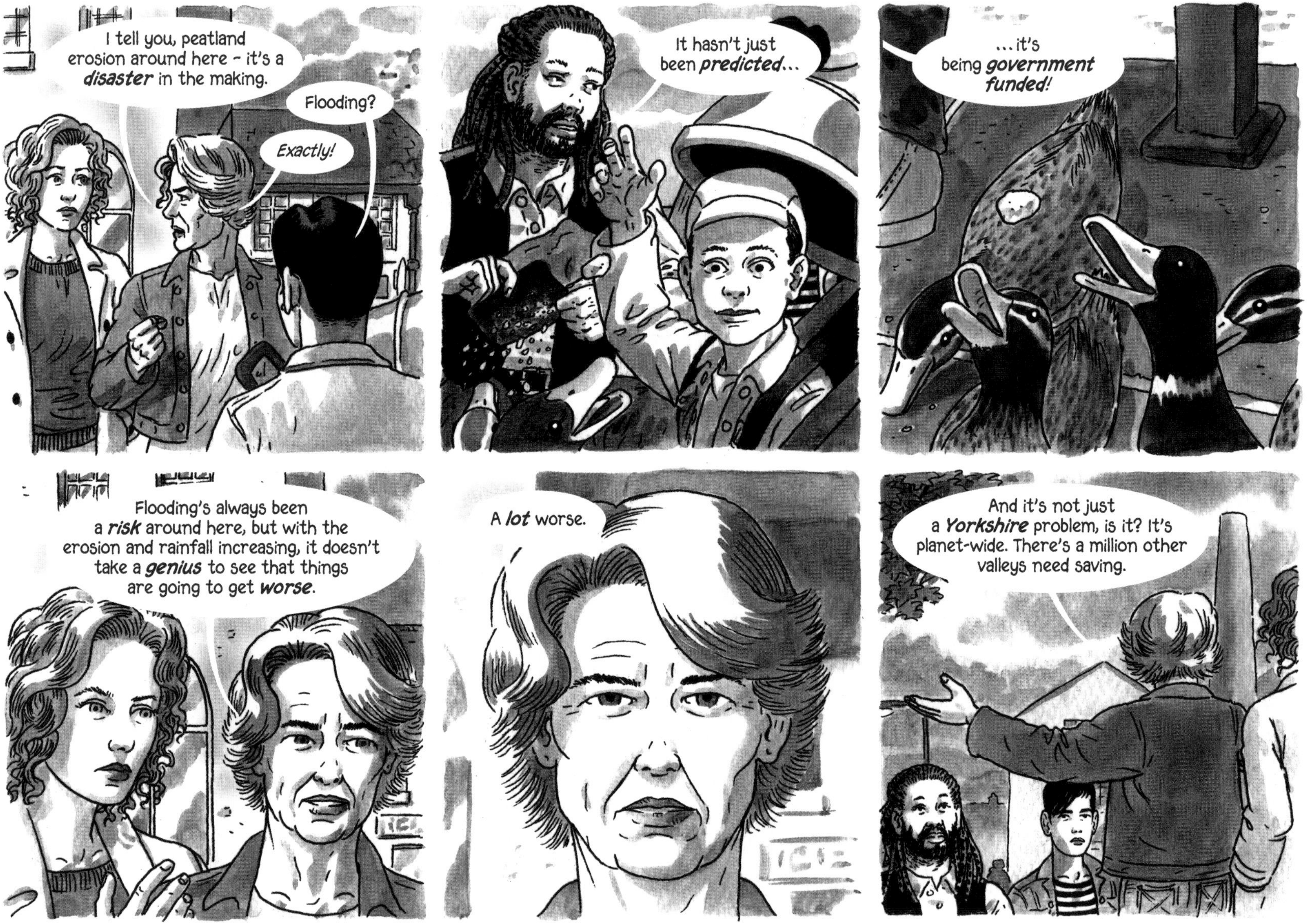
I tell you, peatland erosion around here - it's a *disaster* in the making.
Flooding?
Exactly!
It hasn't just been *predicted*...
...it's being *government funded*!
Flooding's always been a *risk* around here, but with the erosion and rainfall increasing, it doesn't take a *genius* to see that things are going to get *worse*.
A *lot* worse.
And it's not just a *Yorkshire* problem, is it? It's planet-wide. There's a million other valleys need saving.

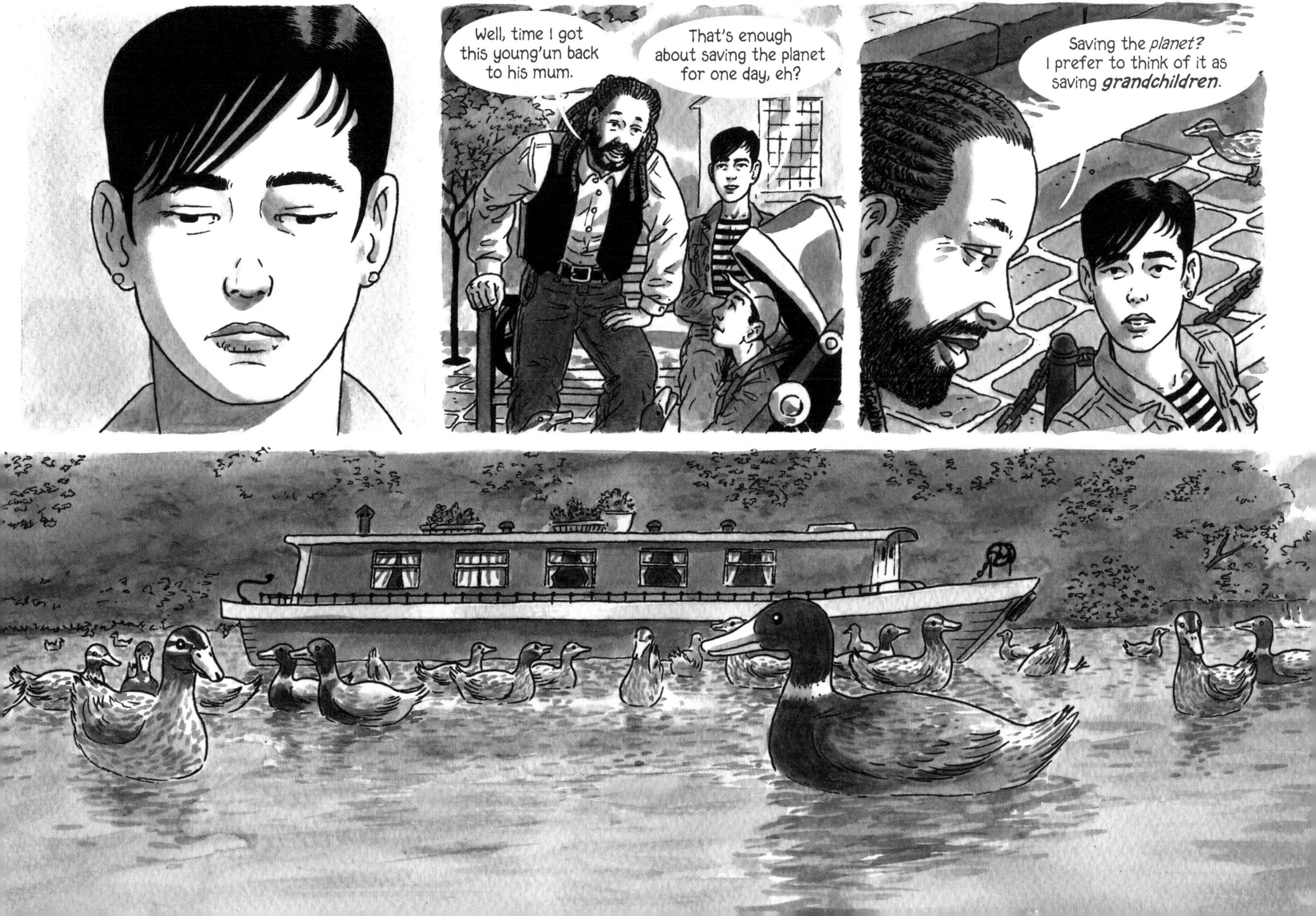
Well, time I got this young'un back to his mum.
That's enough about saving the planet for one day, eh?
Saving the planet? I prefer to think of it as saving grandchildren.

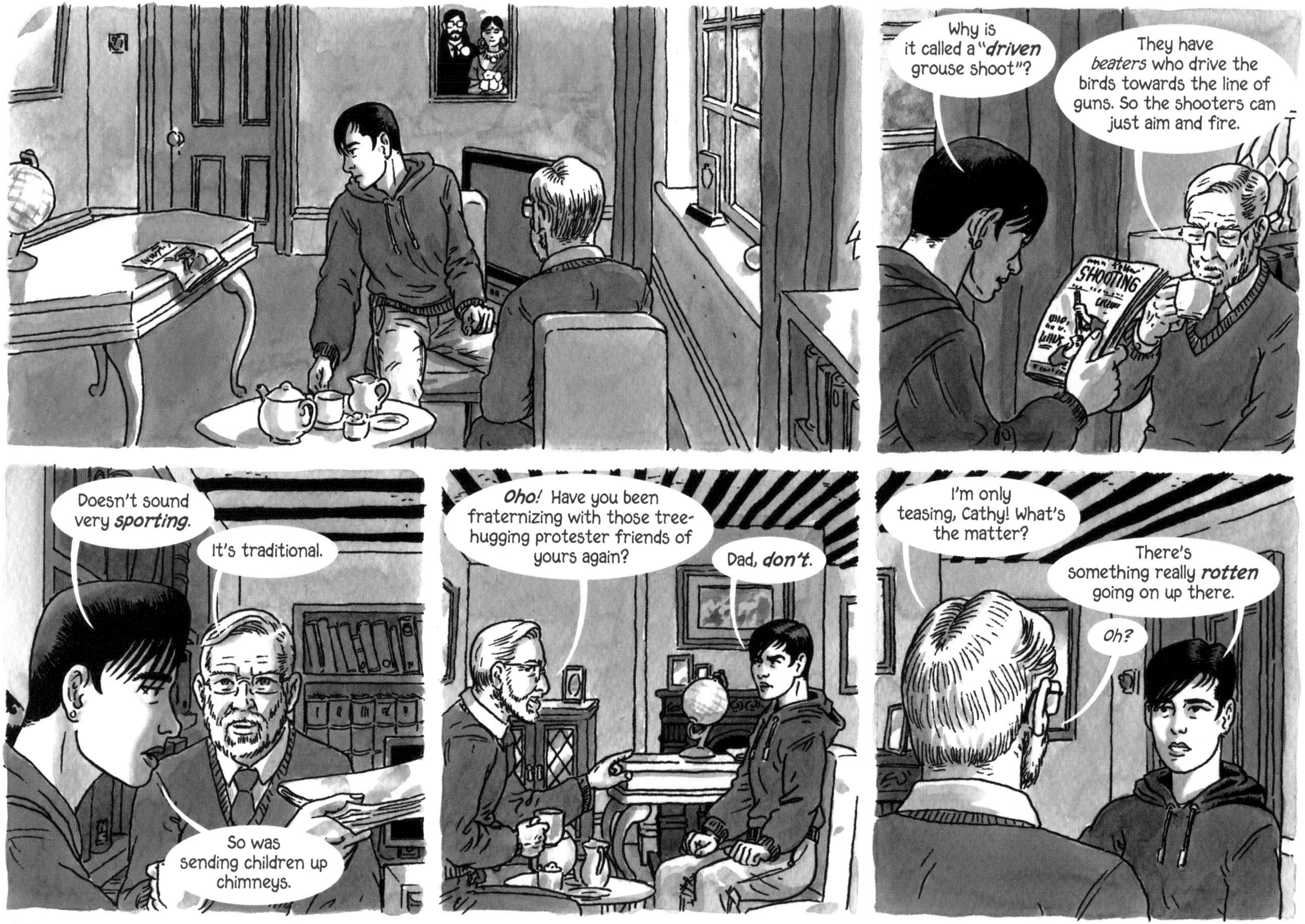
Why is it called a "*driven* grouse shoot"?
They have *beaters* who drive the birds towards the line of guns. So the shooters can just aim and fire.
SHOOTING
Doesn't sound very *sporting*.
It's traditional.
So was sending children up chimneys.
Oho! Have you been fraternizing with those tree-hugging protester friends of yours again?
Dad, *don't*.
I'm only teasing, Cathy! What's the matter?
There's something really *rotten* going on up there.
Oh?

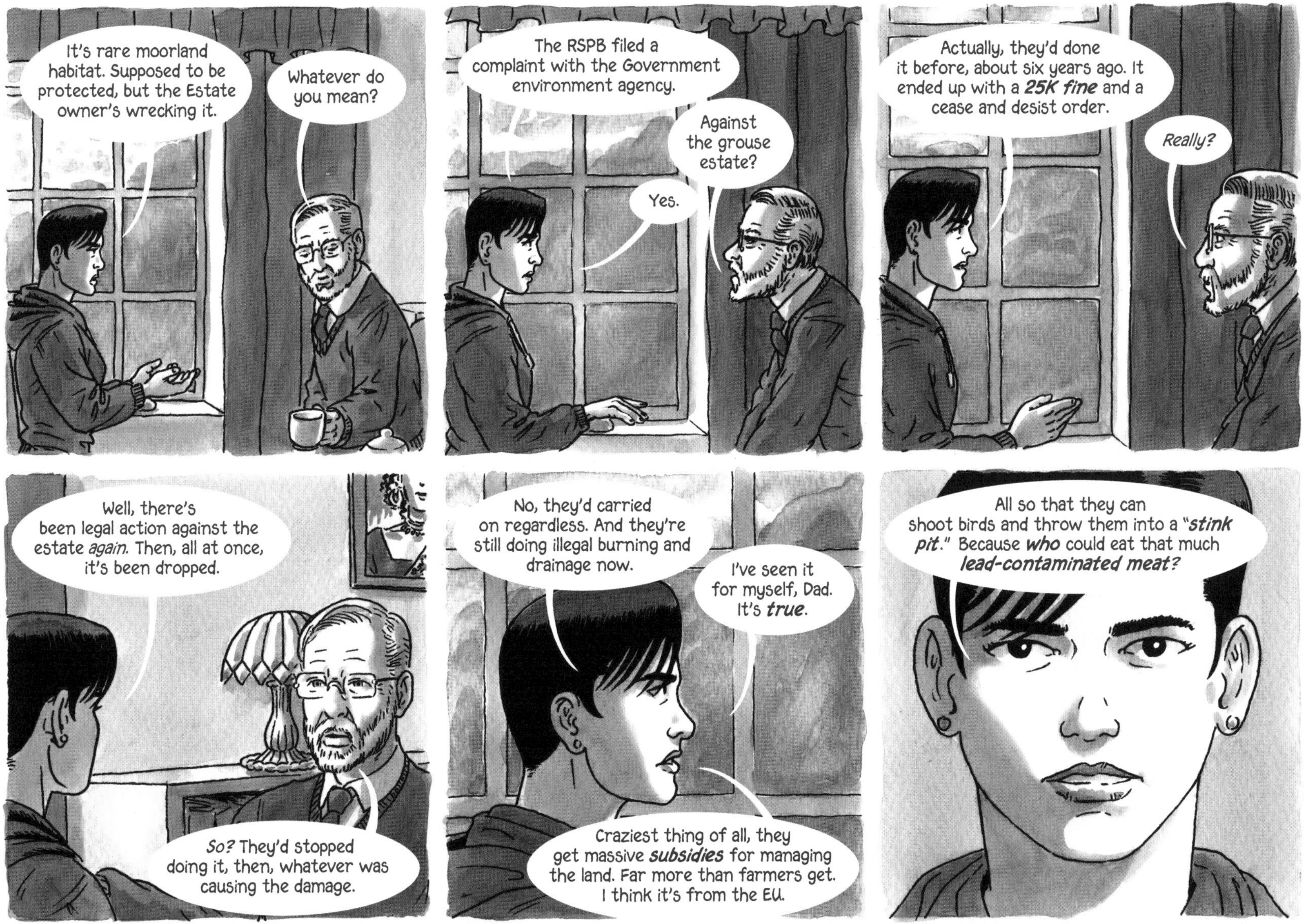
It's rare moorland habitat. Supposed to be protected, but the Estate owner's wrecking it.
Whatever do you mean?
The RSPB filed a complaint with the Government environment agency.
Against the grouse estate?
Yes.
Actually, they'd done it before, about six years ago. It ended up with a 25K fine and a cease and desist order.
Really?
Well, there's been legal action against the estate again. Then, all at once, it's been dropped.
So? They'd stopped doing it, then, whatever was causing the damage.
No, they'd carried on regardless. And they're still doing illegal burning and drainage now.
I've seen it for myself, Dad. It's true.
Craziest thing of all, they get massive subsidies for managing the land. Far more than farmers get. I think it's from the EU.
All so that they can shoot birds and throw them into a "stink pit." Because who could eat that much lead-contaminated meat?

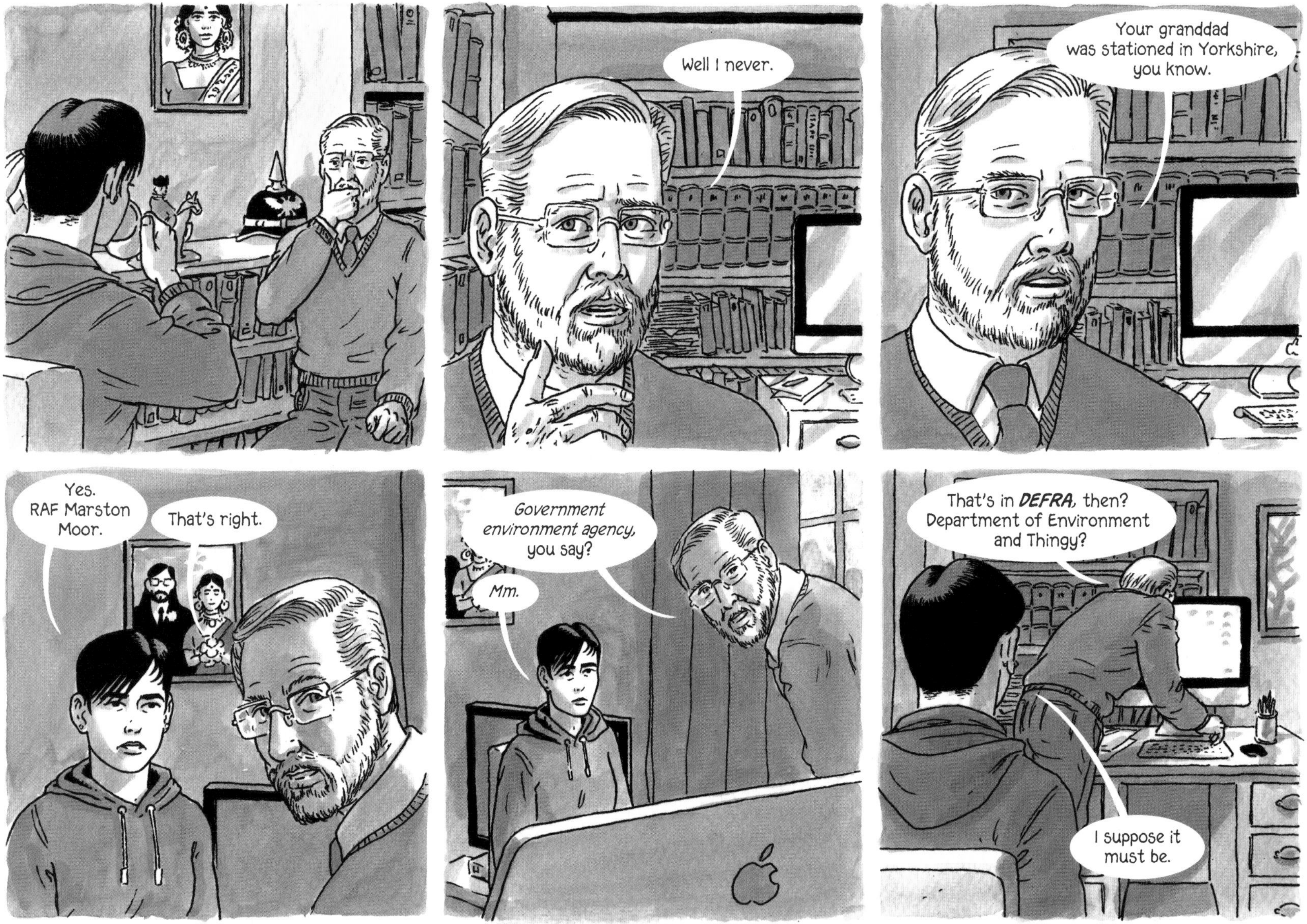
Well I never.
Your granddad was stationed in Yorkshire, you know.
Yes. RAF Marston Moor.
That's right.
Government environment agency, you say?
Mm.
That's in DEFRA, then? Department of Environment and Thingy?
I suppose it must be.

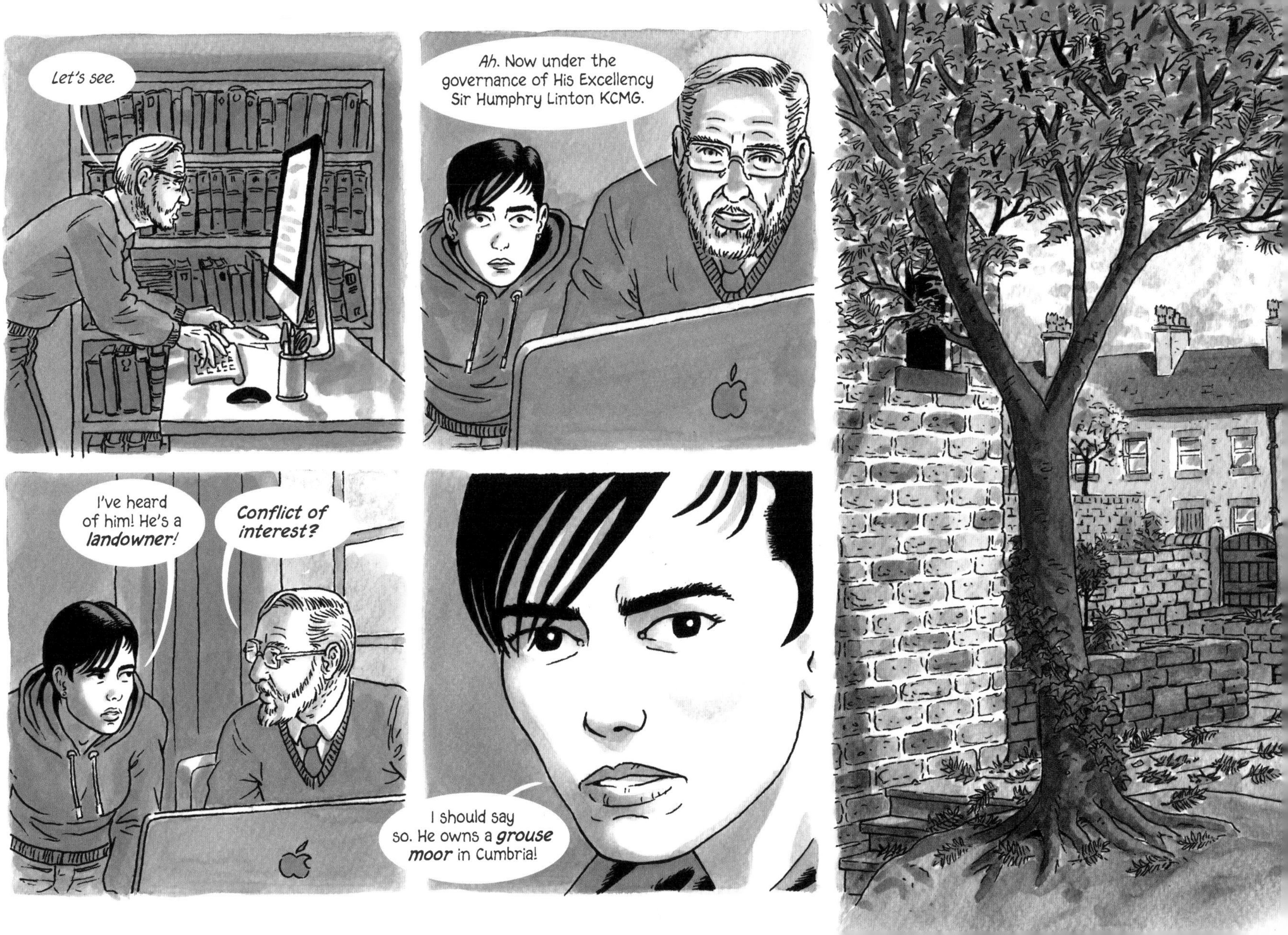
Let's see.
Ah. Now under the governance of His Excellency Sir Humphry Linton KCMG.
I've heard of him! He's a landowner!
Conflict of interest?
I should say so. He owns a grouse moor in Cumbria!

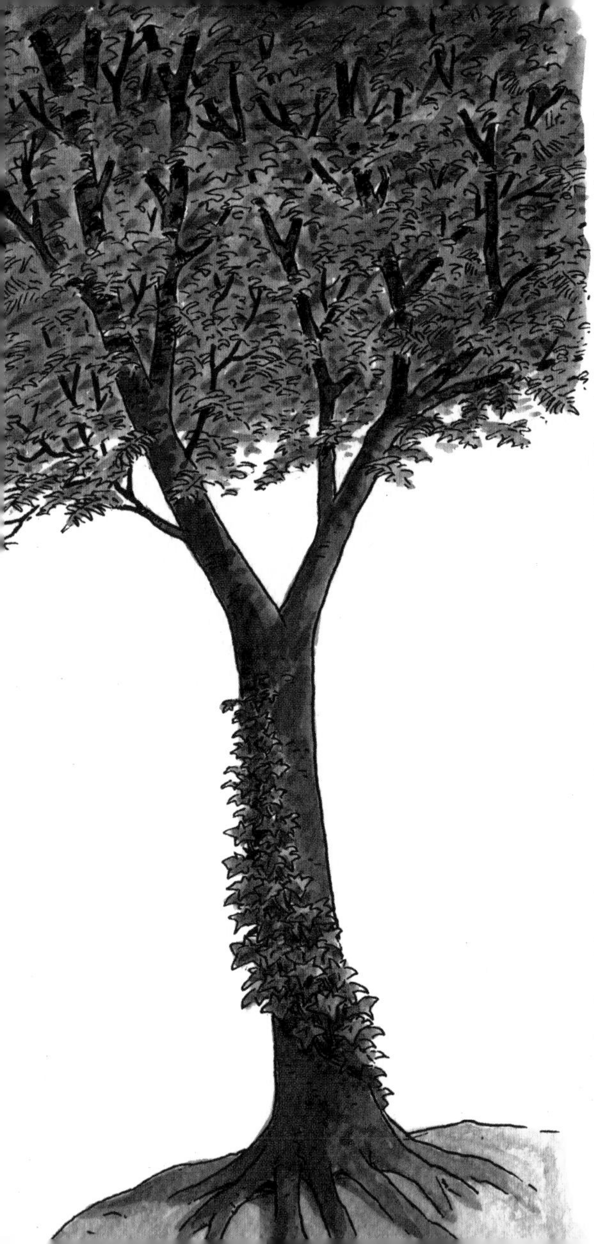

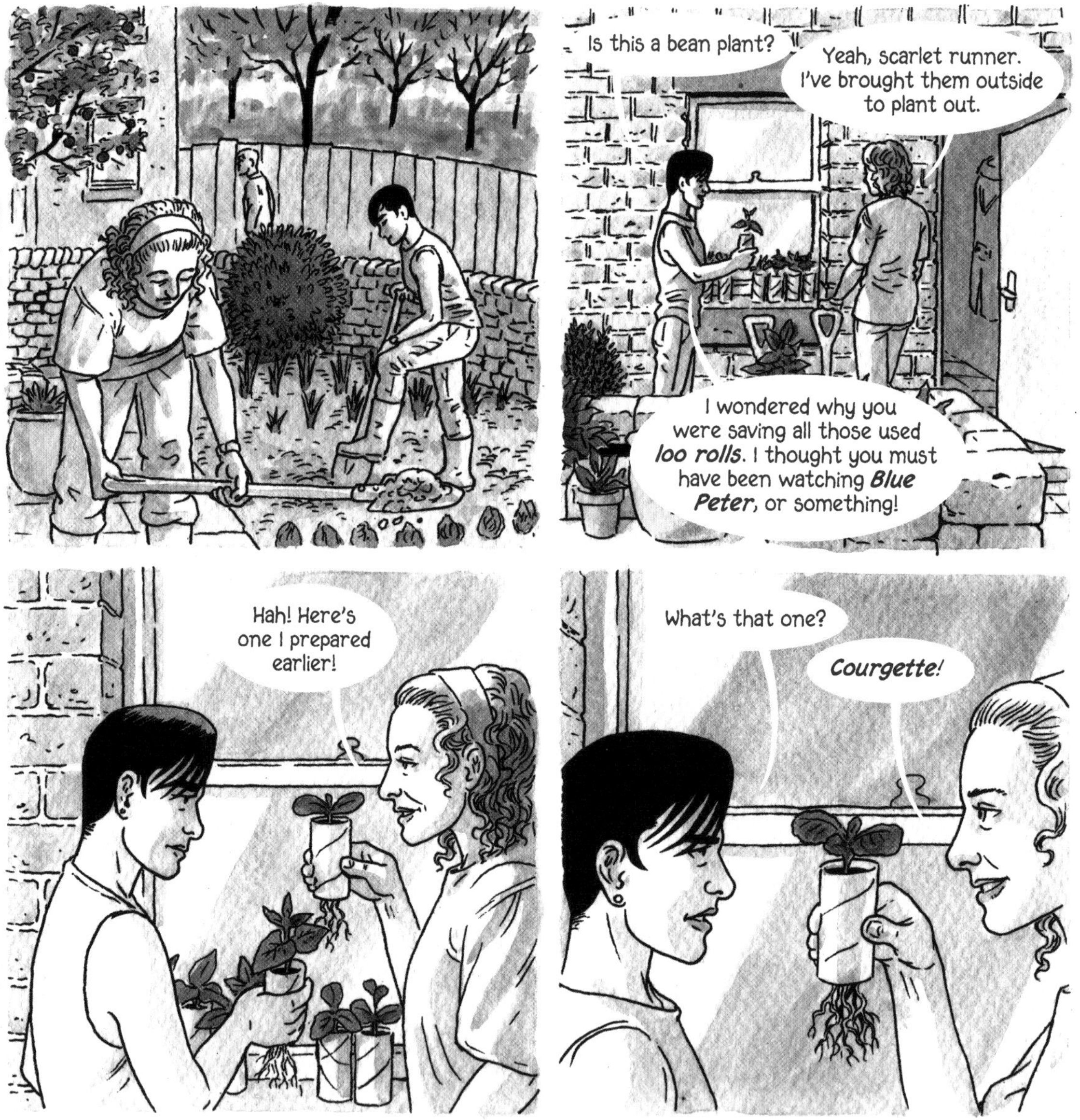

Is this a bean plant?
Yeah, scarlet runner. I've brought them outside to plant out.
I wondered why you were saving all those used loo rolls. I thought you must have been watching Blue Peter, or something!
Hah! Here's one I prepared earlier!
What's that one?
Courgette!

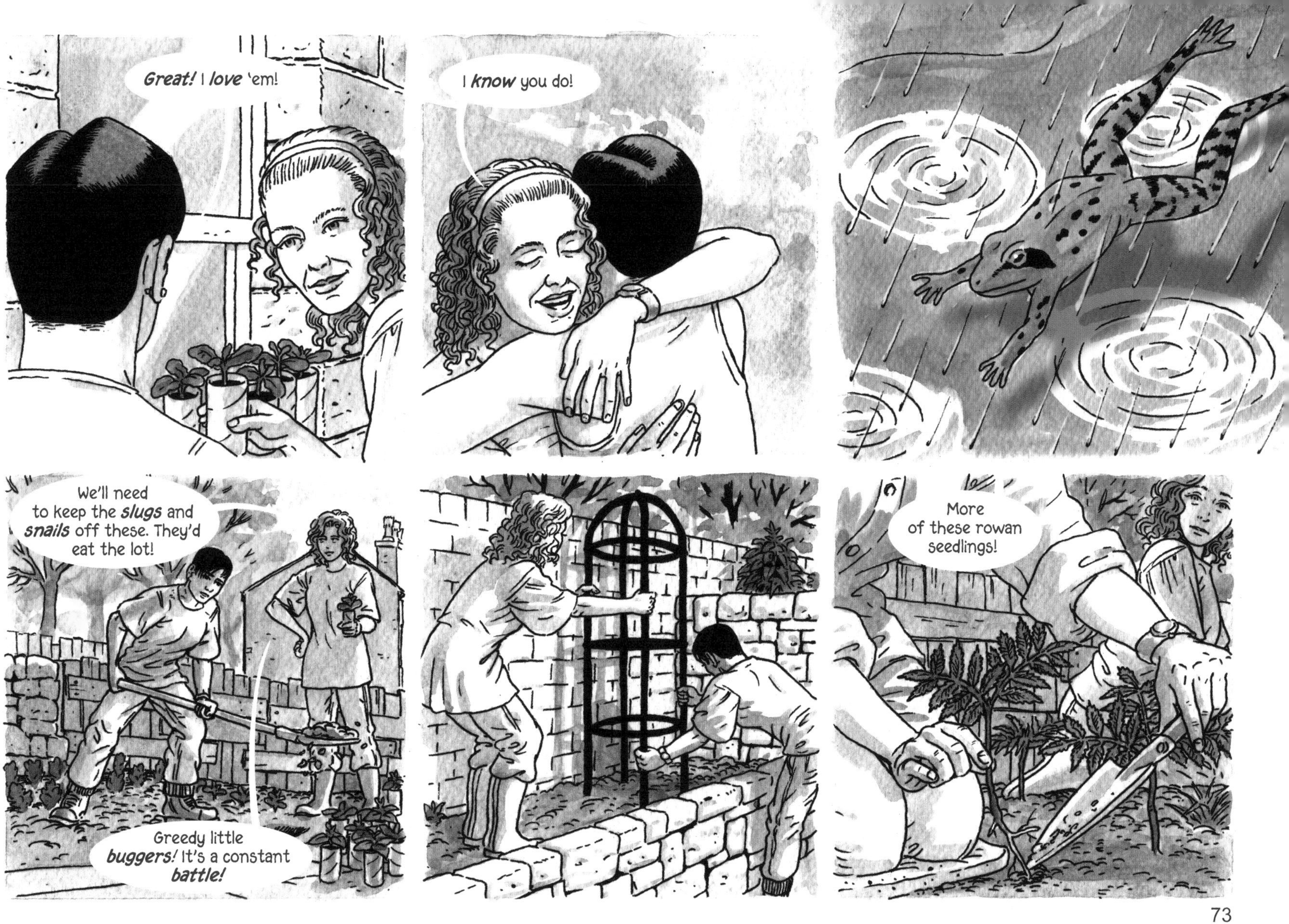
Great! I love 'em!
I know you do!
We'll need to keep the slugs and snails off these. They'd eat the lot!
Greedy little buggers! It's a constant battle!
More of these rowan seedlings!

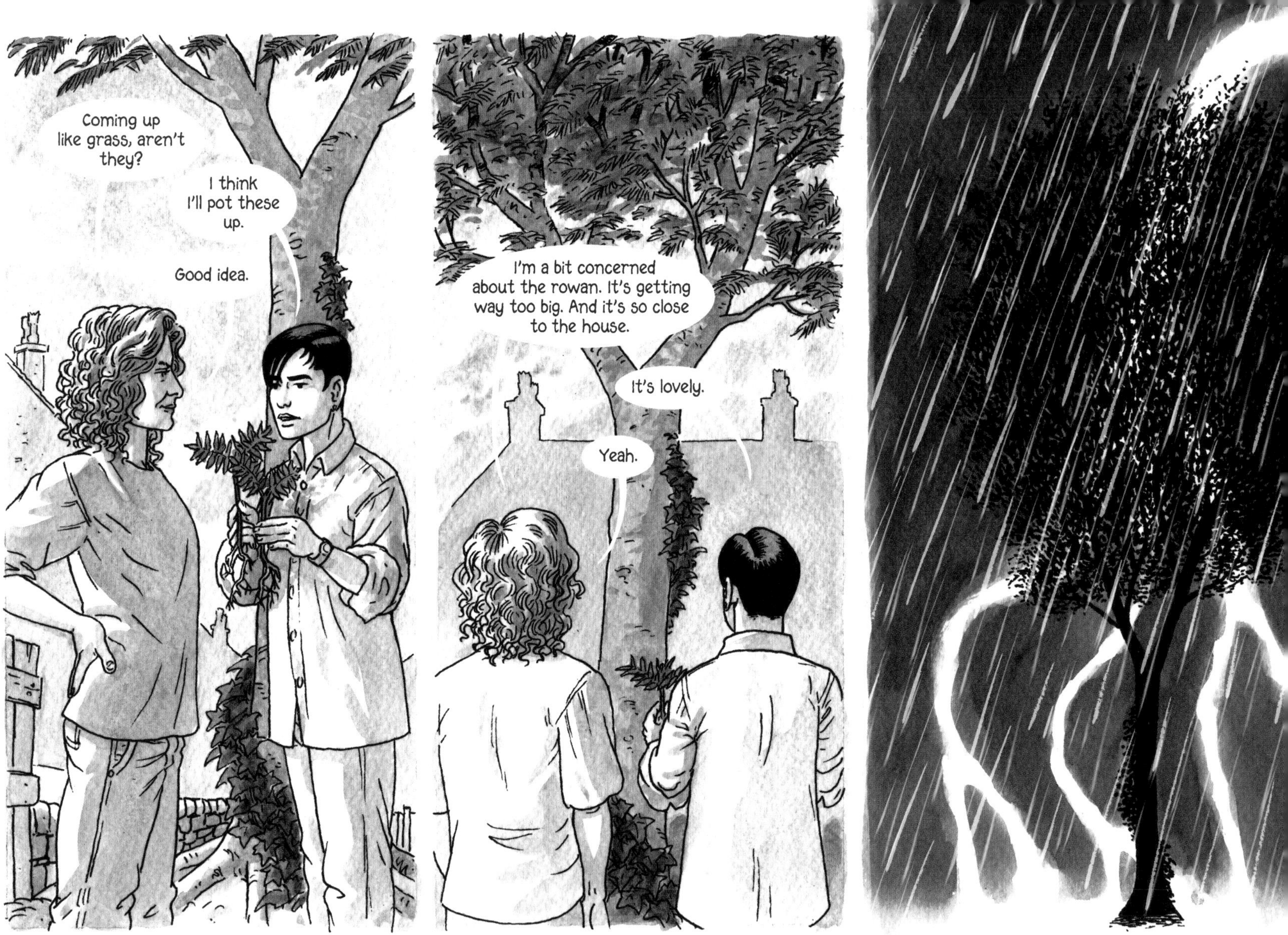
Coming up like grass, aren't they?
I think I'll pot these up.
Good idea.
I'm a bit concerned about the rowan. It's getting way too big. And it's so close to the house.
It's lovely.
Yeah.

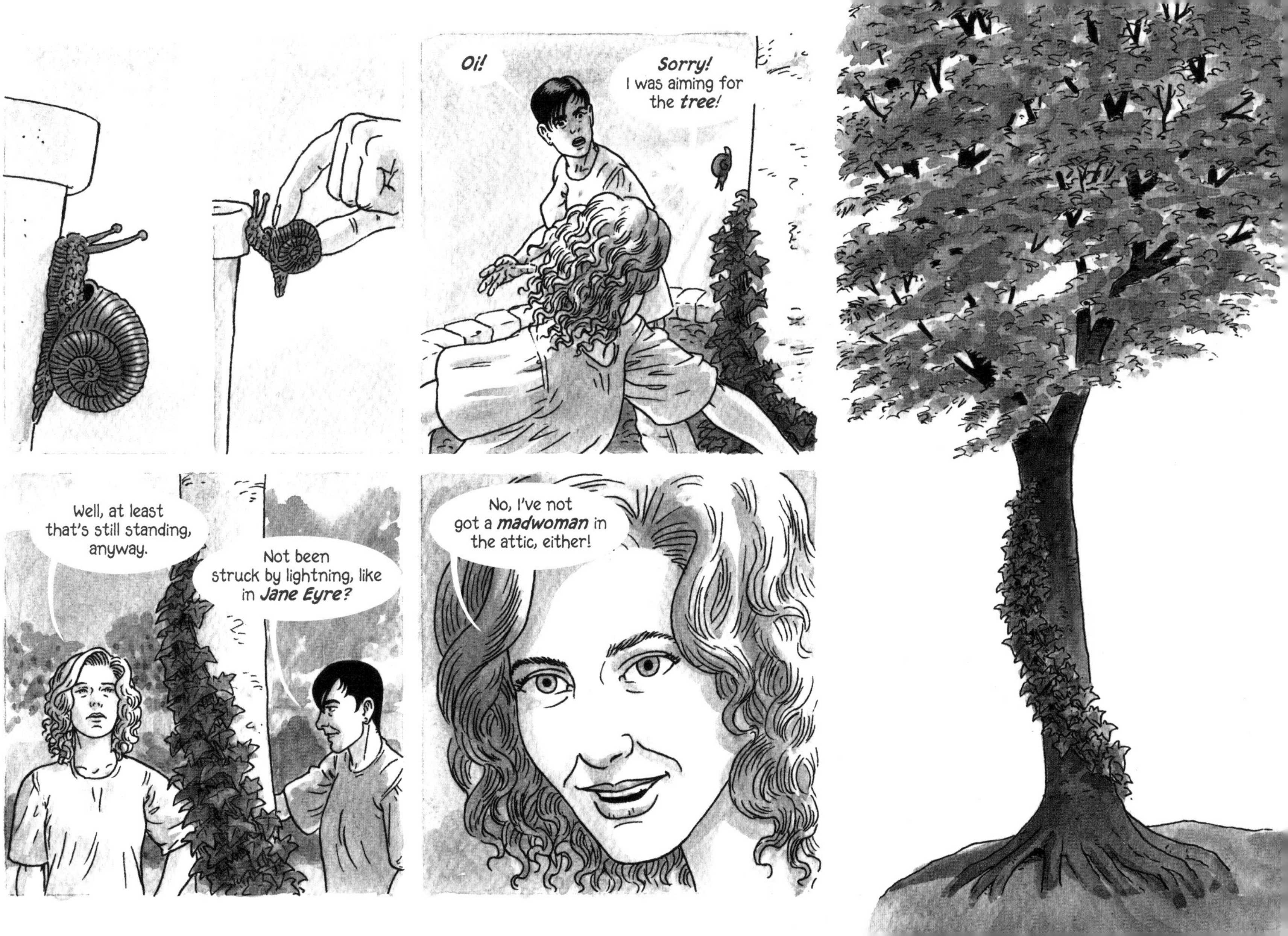
Oi!
Sorry! I was aiming for the *tree!*
Well, at least that's still standing, anyway.
Not been struck by lightning, like in *Jane Eyre?*
No, I've not got a *madwoman* in the attic, either!

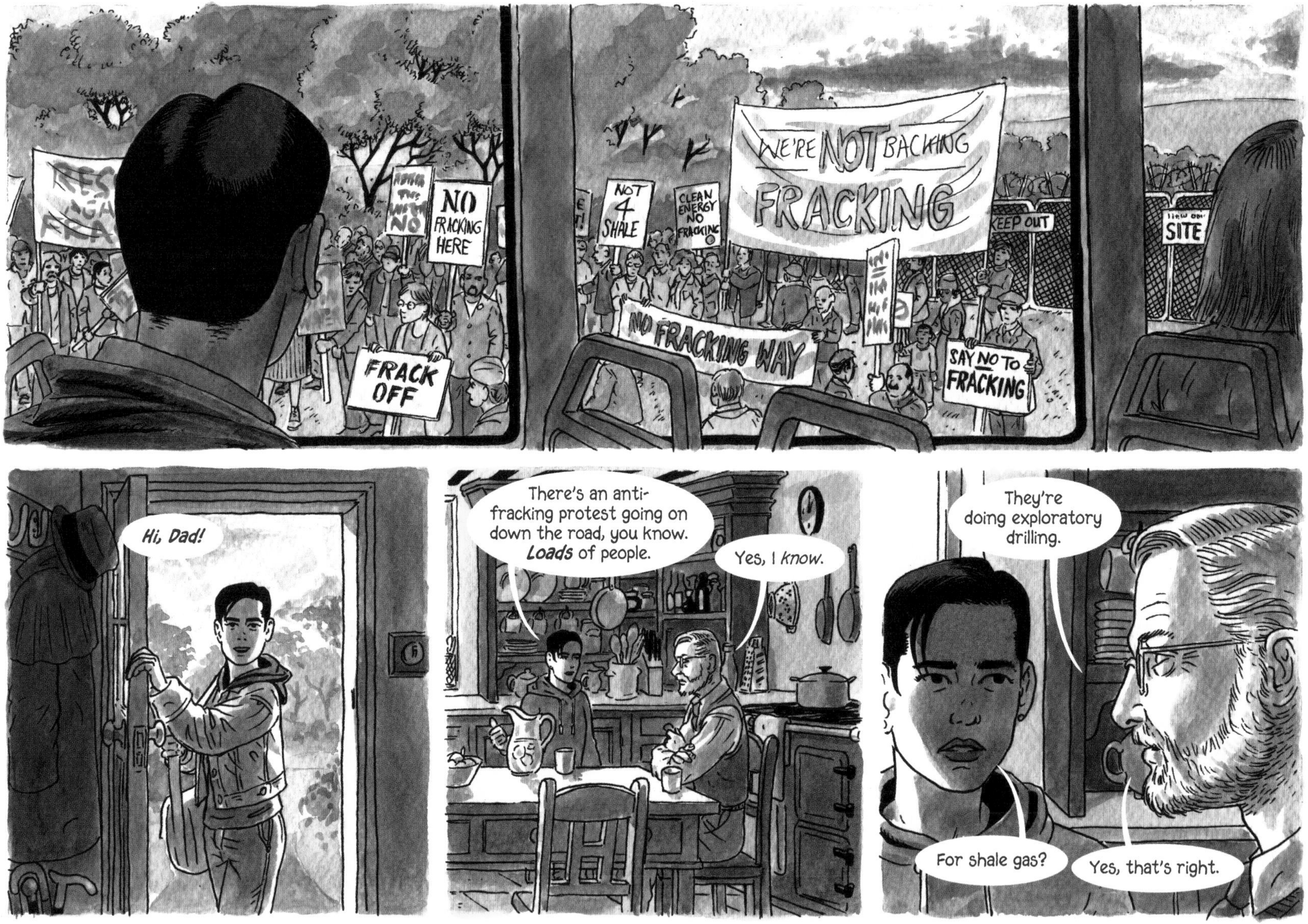
NO FRACKING HERE
FRACK OFF
NOT 4 SHALE
CLEAN ENERGY NO FRACKING
WE'RE NOT BACKING FRACKING
KEEP OUT
SITE
NO FRACKING WAY
SAY NO TO FRACKING
Hi, Dad!
There's an anti-fracking protest going on down the road, you know. *Loads* of people.
Yes, I *know*.
They're doing exploratory drilling.
For shale gas?
Yes, that's right.

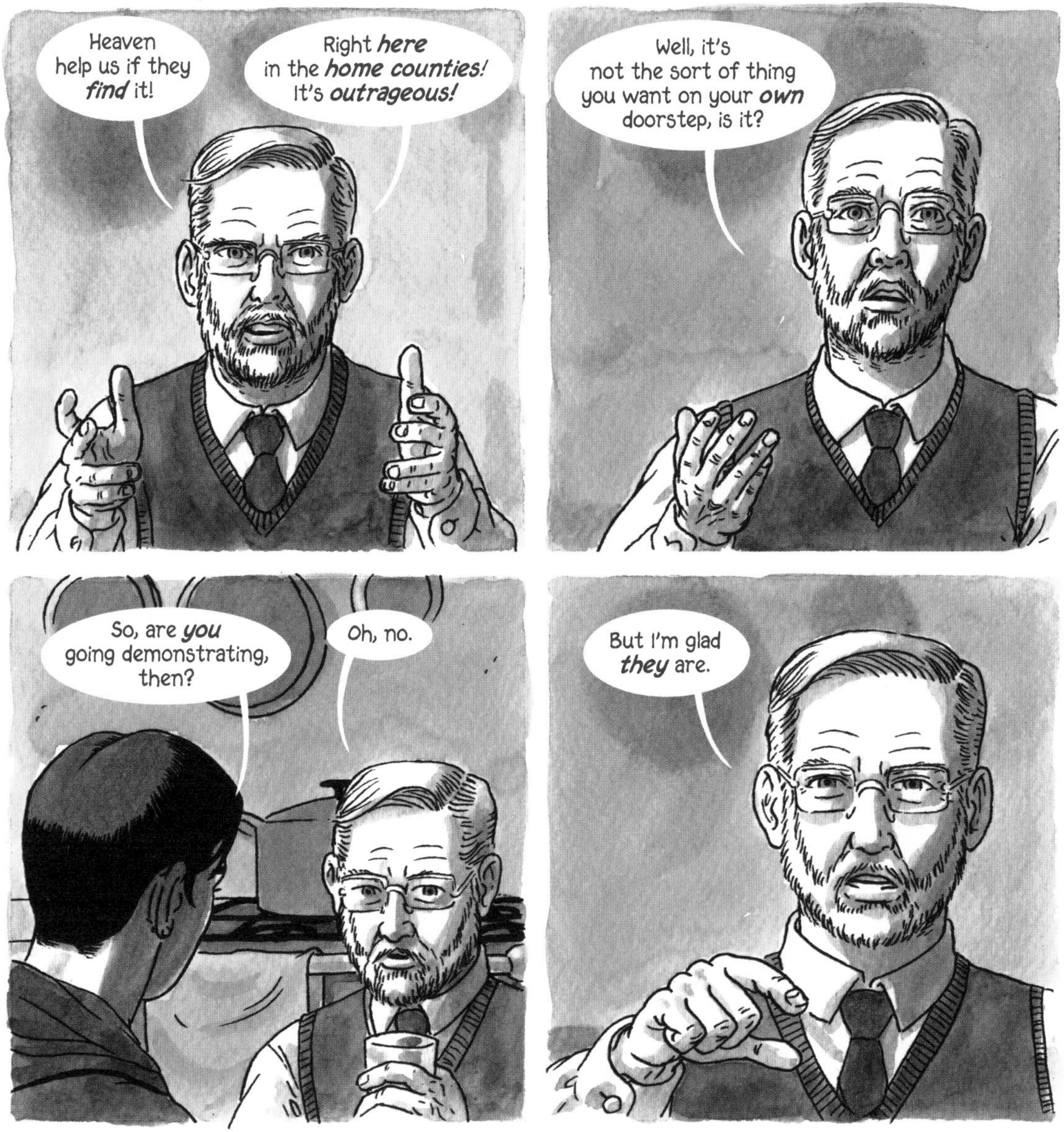

Heaven help us if they *find* it!
Right *here* in the *home counties!* It's *outrageous!*
Well, it's not the sort of thing you want on your *own* doorstep, is it?
So, are *you* going demonstrating, then?
Oh, no.
But I'm glad *they* are.

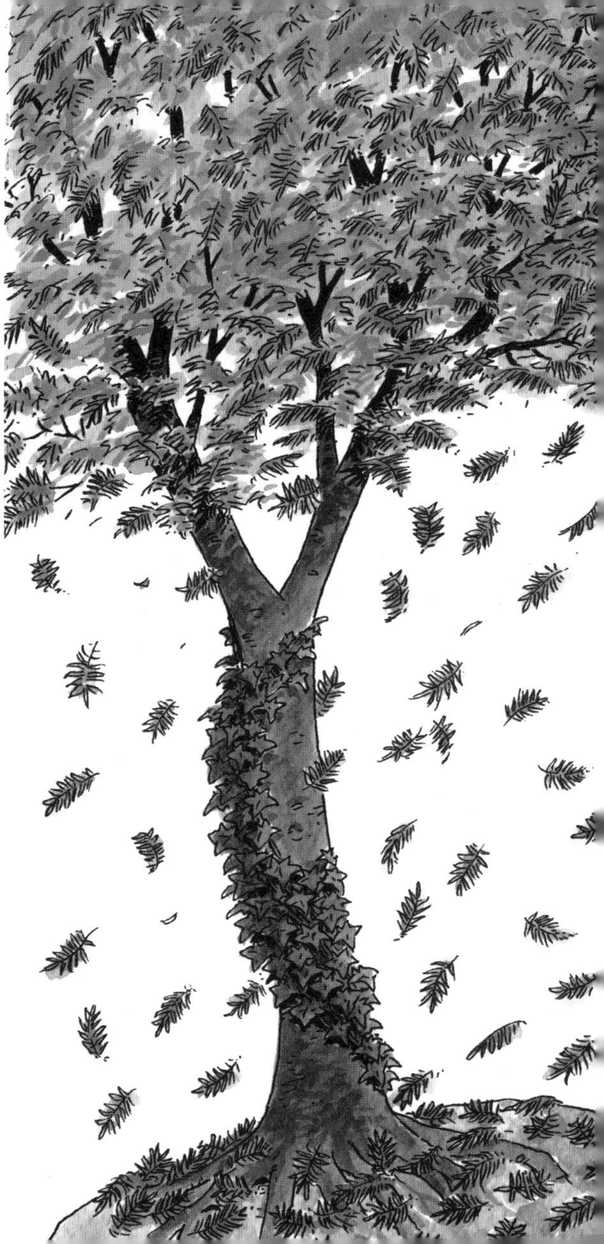

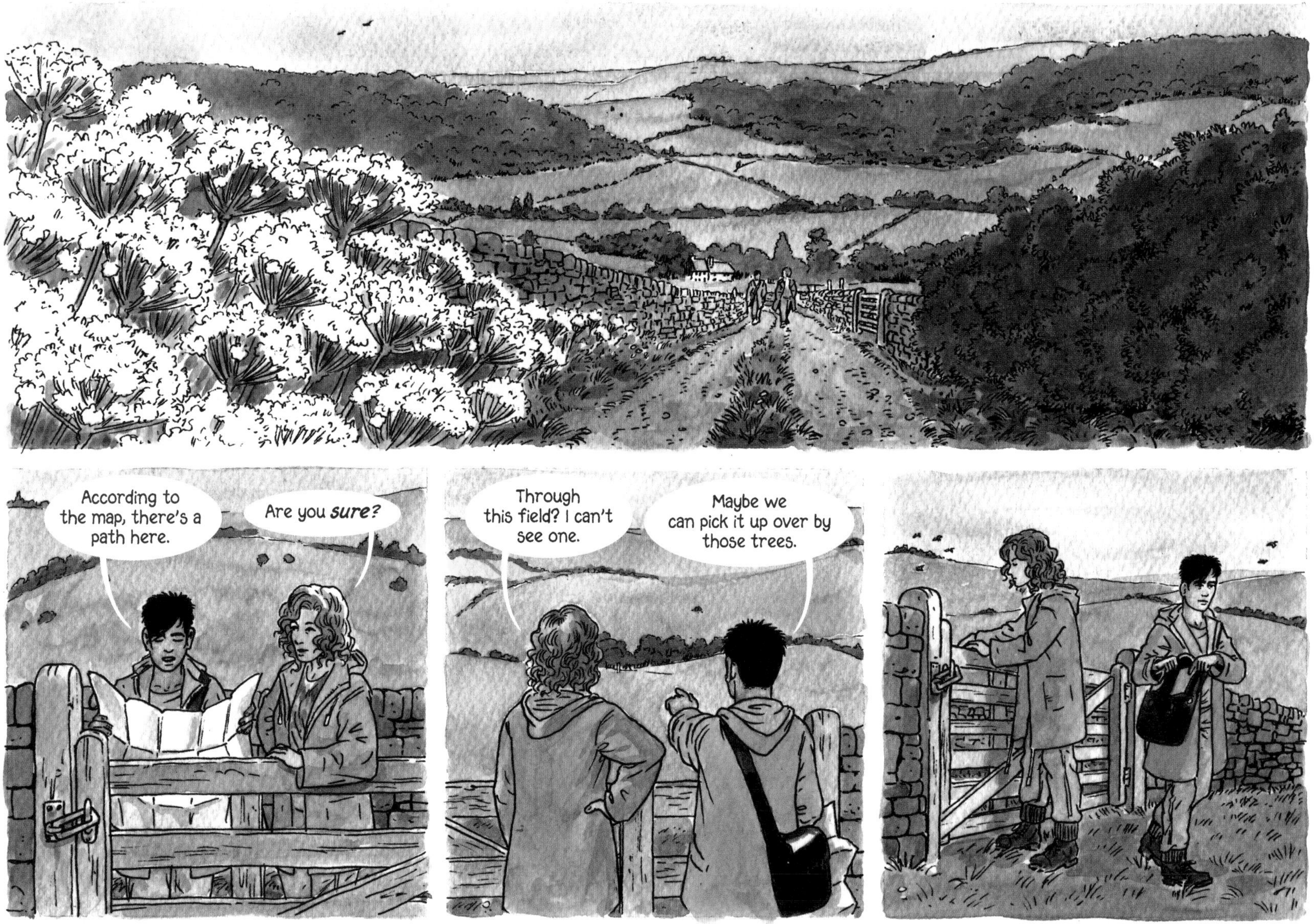
According to the map, there's a path here.
Are you *sure?*
Through this field? I can't see one.
Maybe we can pick it up over by those trees.

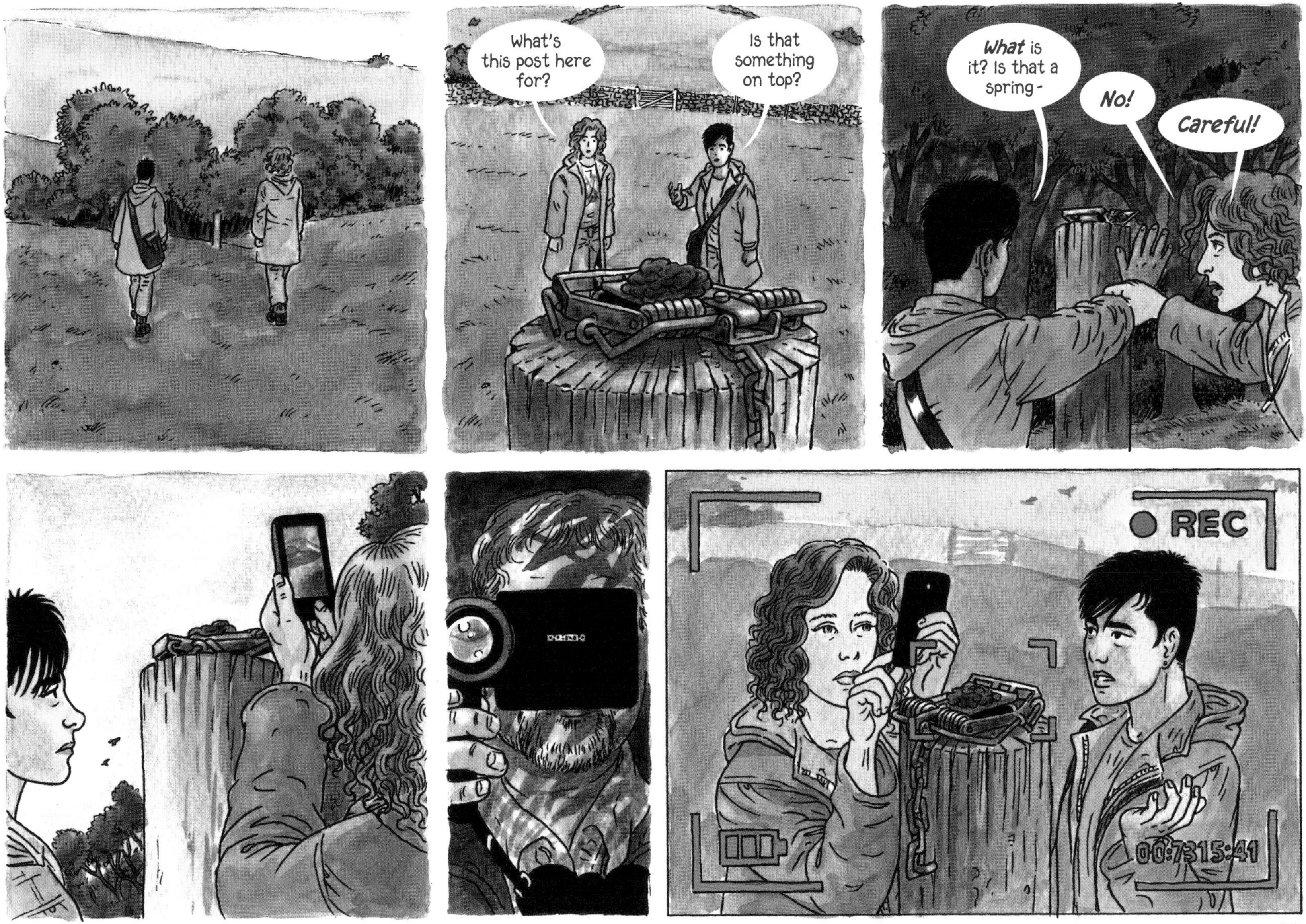
What's this post here for?
Is that something on top?
What is it? Is that a spring -
No!
Careful!
REC
00:73 15:41

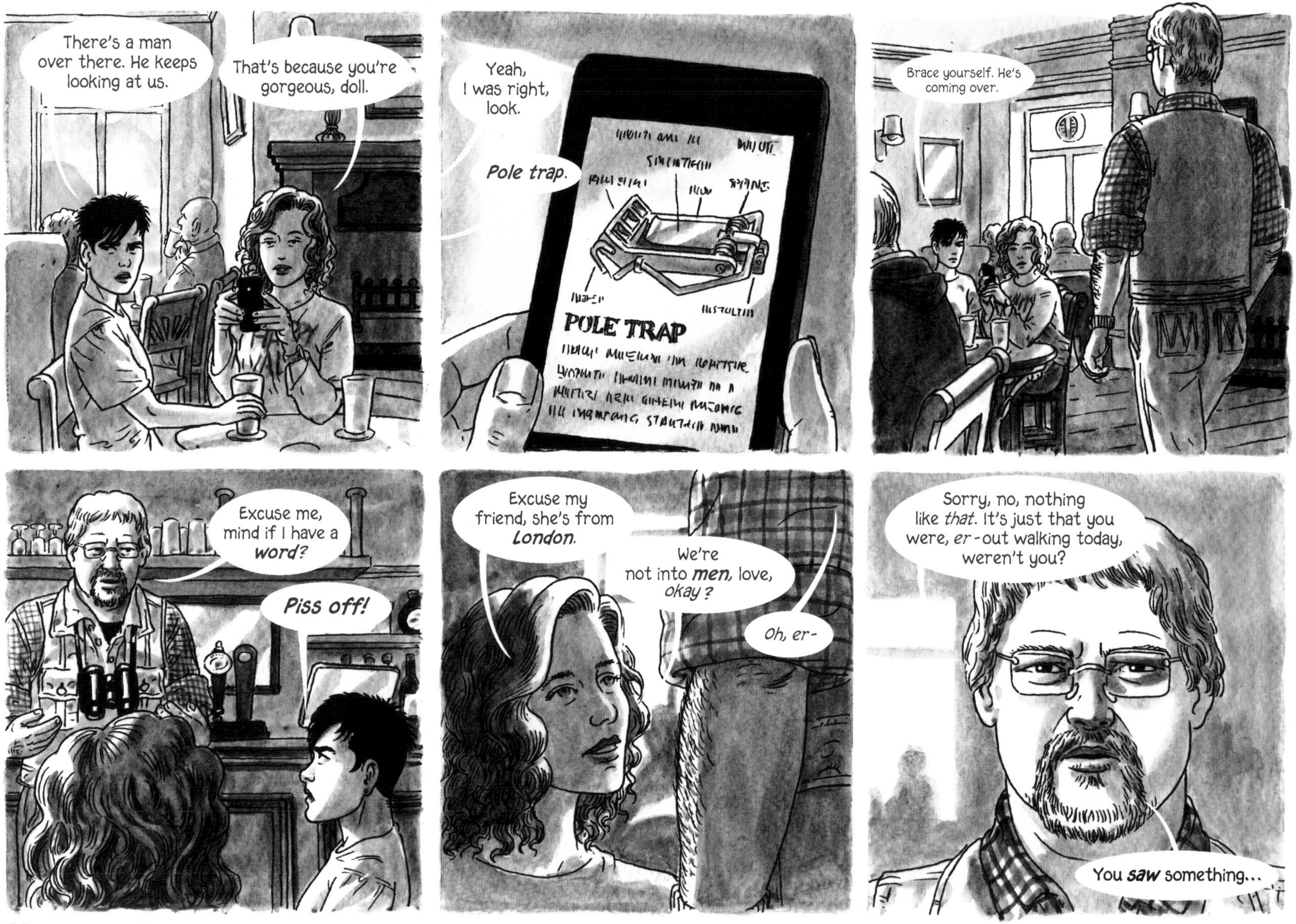
There's a man over there. He keeps looking at us.
That's because you're gorgeous, doll.
Yeah, I was right, look.
Pole trap.
POLE TRAP
Brace yourself. He's coming over.
Excuse me, mind if I have a ***word?***
Piss off!
Excuse my friend, she's from ***London***.
We're not into ***men***, love, *okay?*
Oh, er-
Sorry, no, nothing like *that*. It's just that you were, *er*-out walking today, weren't you?
You ***saw*** something...

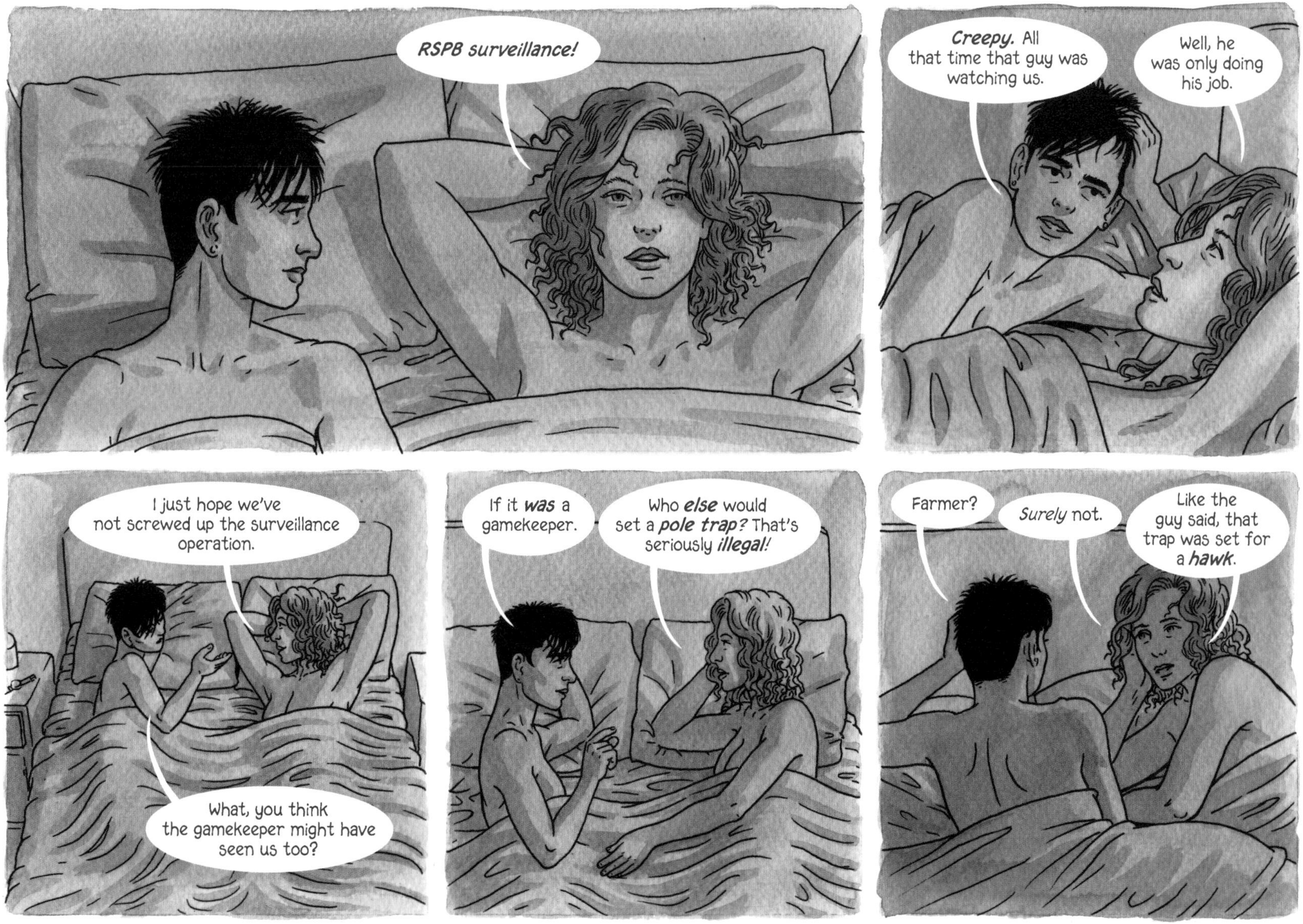
RSPB surveillance!
Creepy. All that time that guy was watching us.
Well, he was only doing his job.
I just hope we've not screwed up the surveillance operation.
What, you think the gamekeeper might have seen us too?
If it was a gamekeeper.
Who else would set a pole trap? That's seriously illegal!
Farmer?
Surely not.
Like the guy said, that trap was set for a hawk.

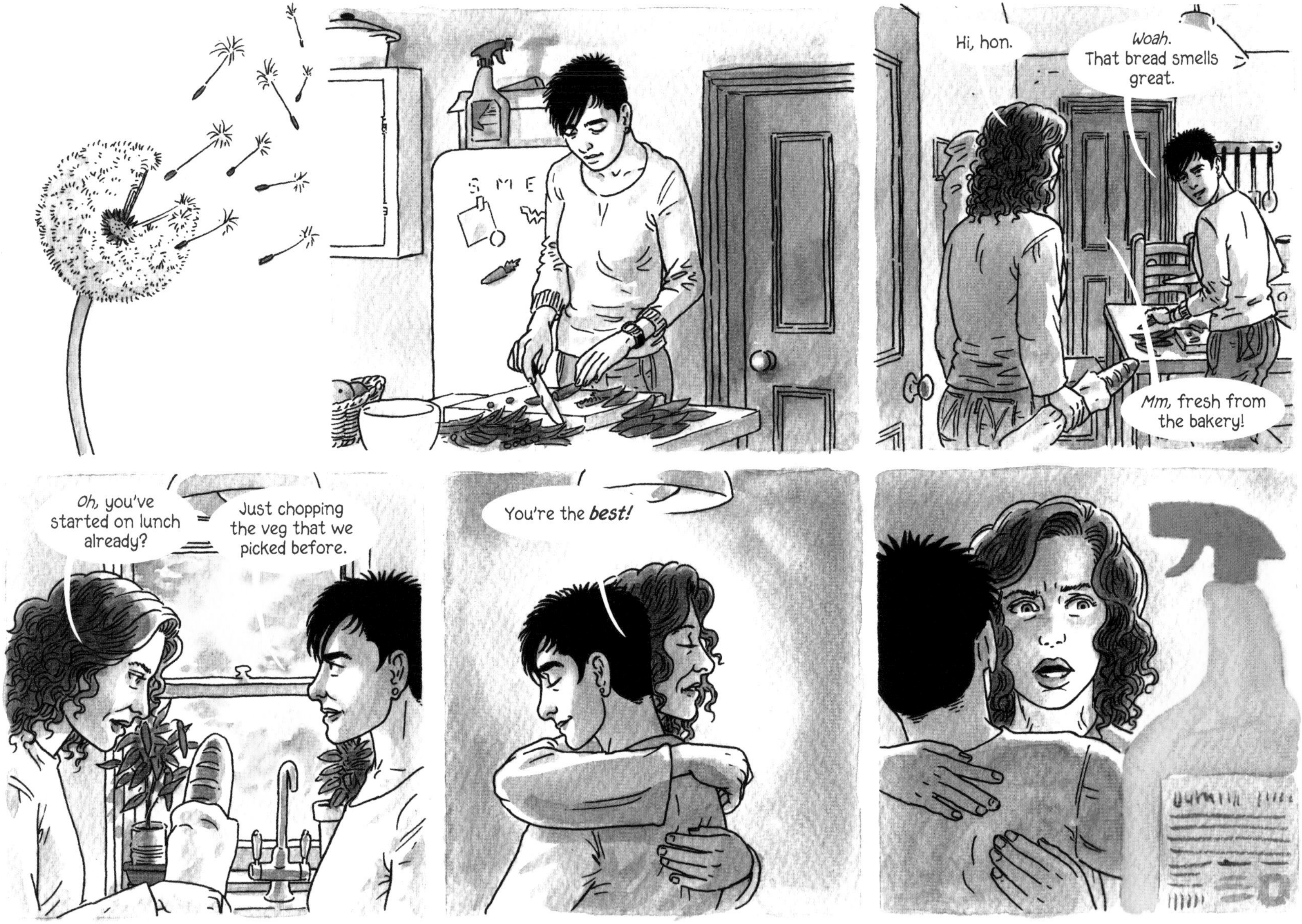
Hi, hon.
Woah. That bread smells great.
Mm, fresh from the bakery!
Oh, you've started on lunch already?
Just chopping the veg that we picked before.
You're the ***best!***

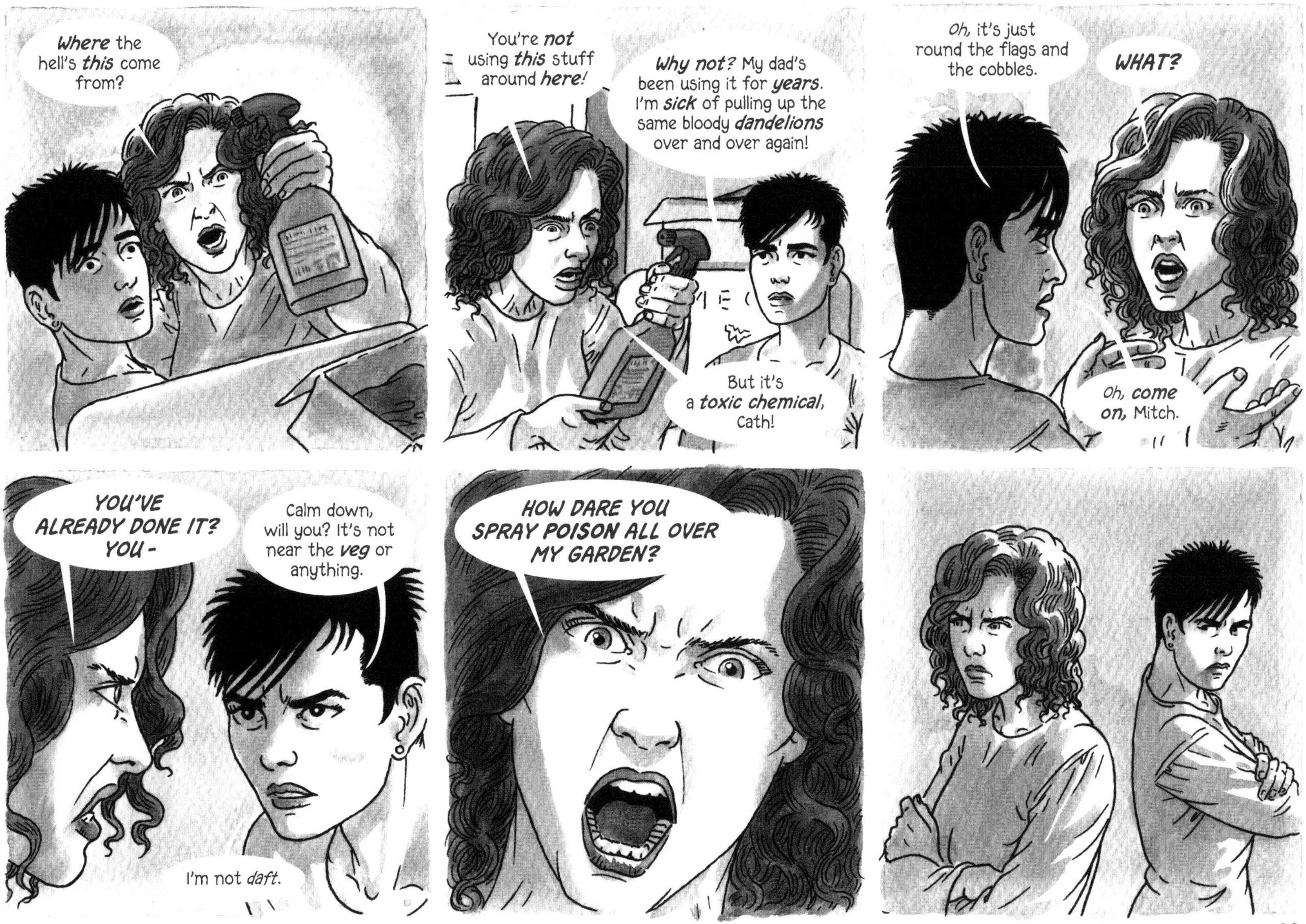

Where the hell's this come from?
You're not using this stuff around here!
Why not? My dad's been using it for years. I'm sick of pulling up the same bloody dandelions over and over again!
But it's a toxic chemical, Cath!
Oh, it's just round the flags and the cobbles.
WHAT?
Oh, come on, Mitch.
YOU'VE ALREADY DONE IT? YOU -
Calm down, will you? It's not near the veg or anything.
I'm not daft.
HOW DARE YOU SPRAY POISON ALL OVER MY GARDEN?

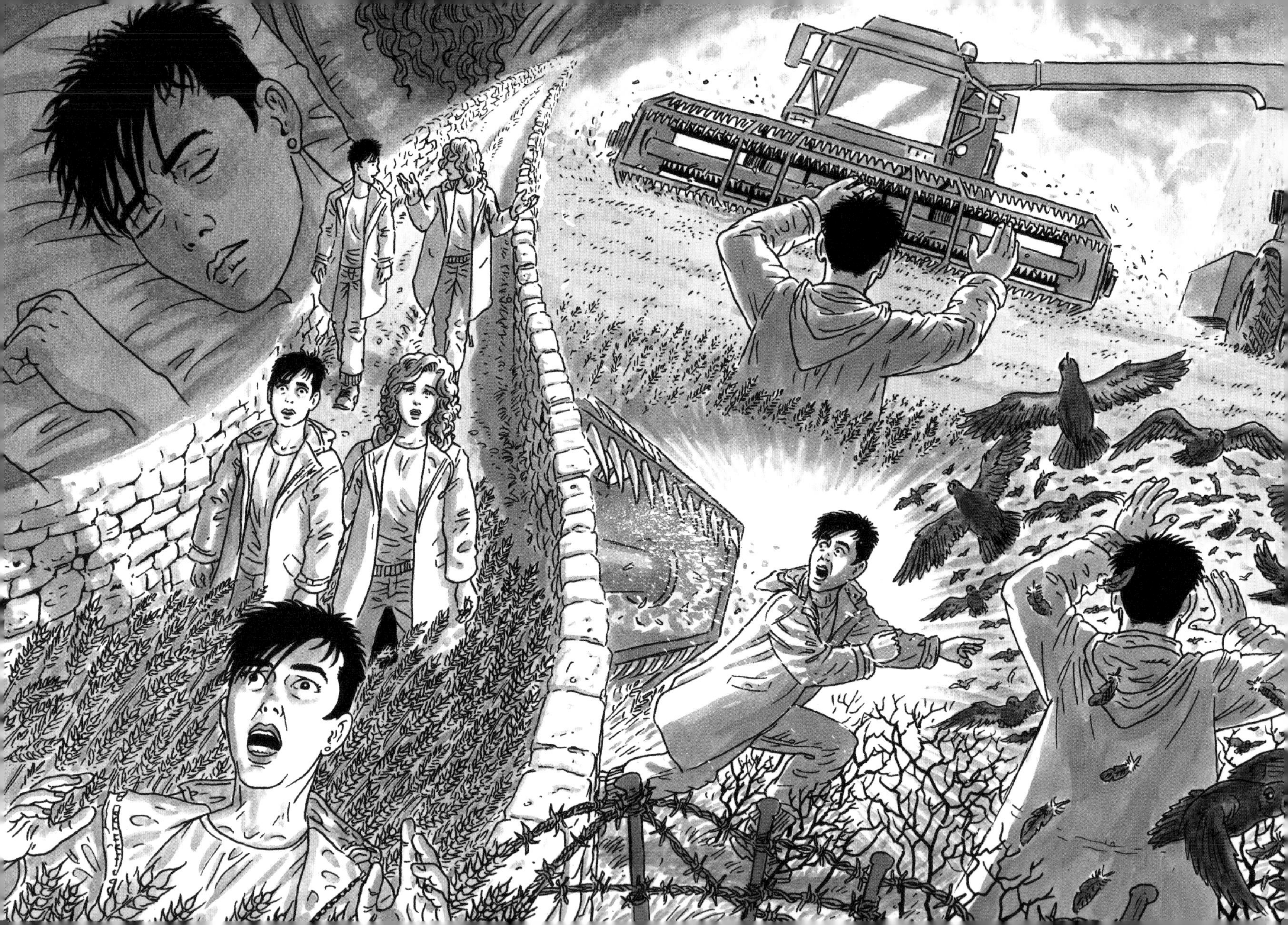

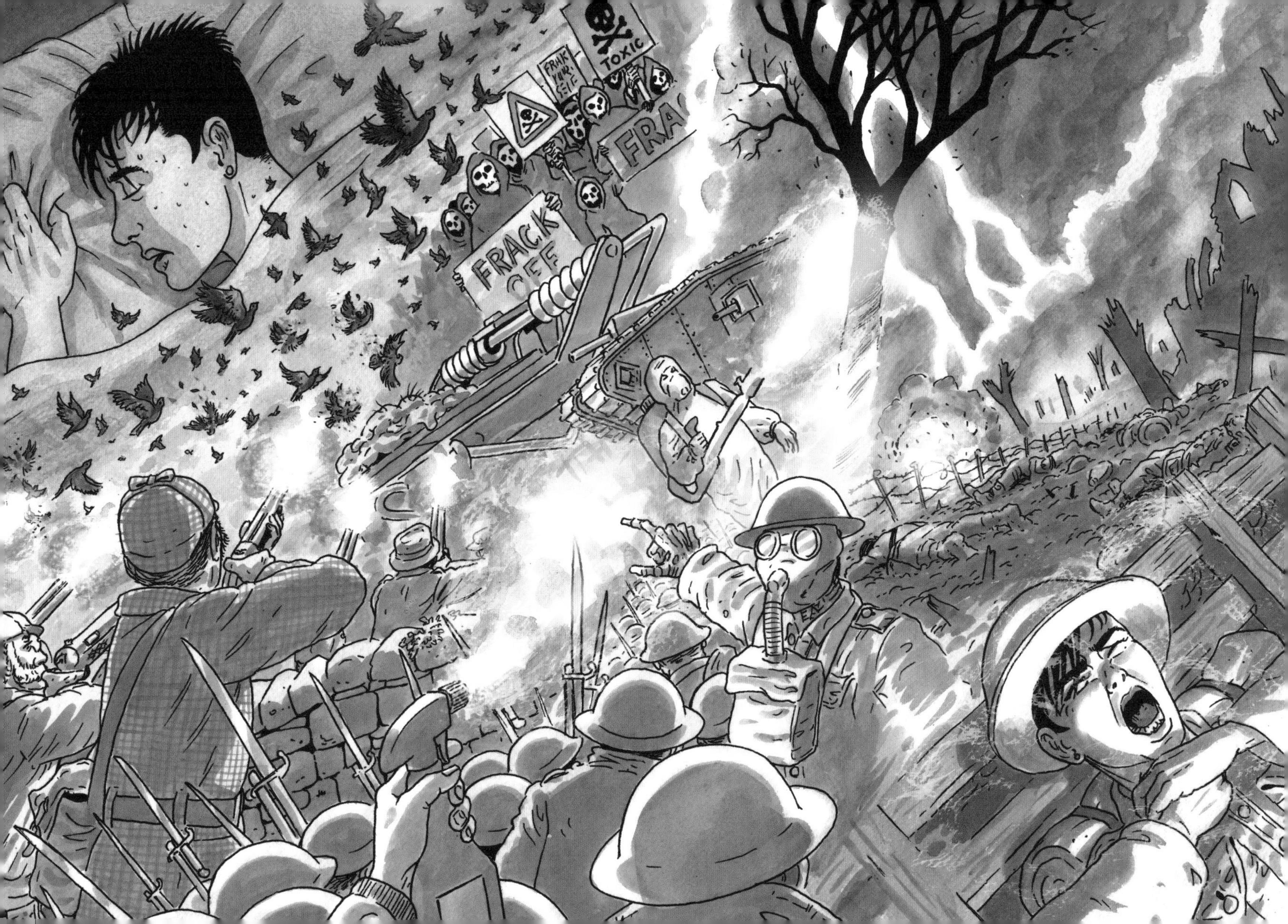
TOXIC
FRAK YUR SELF
FRA
FRACK OFF

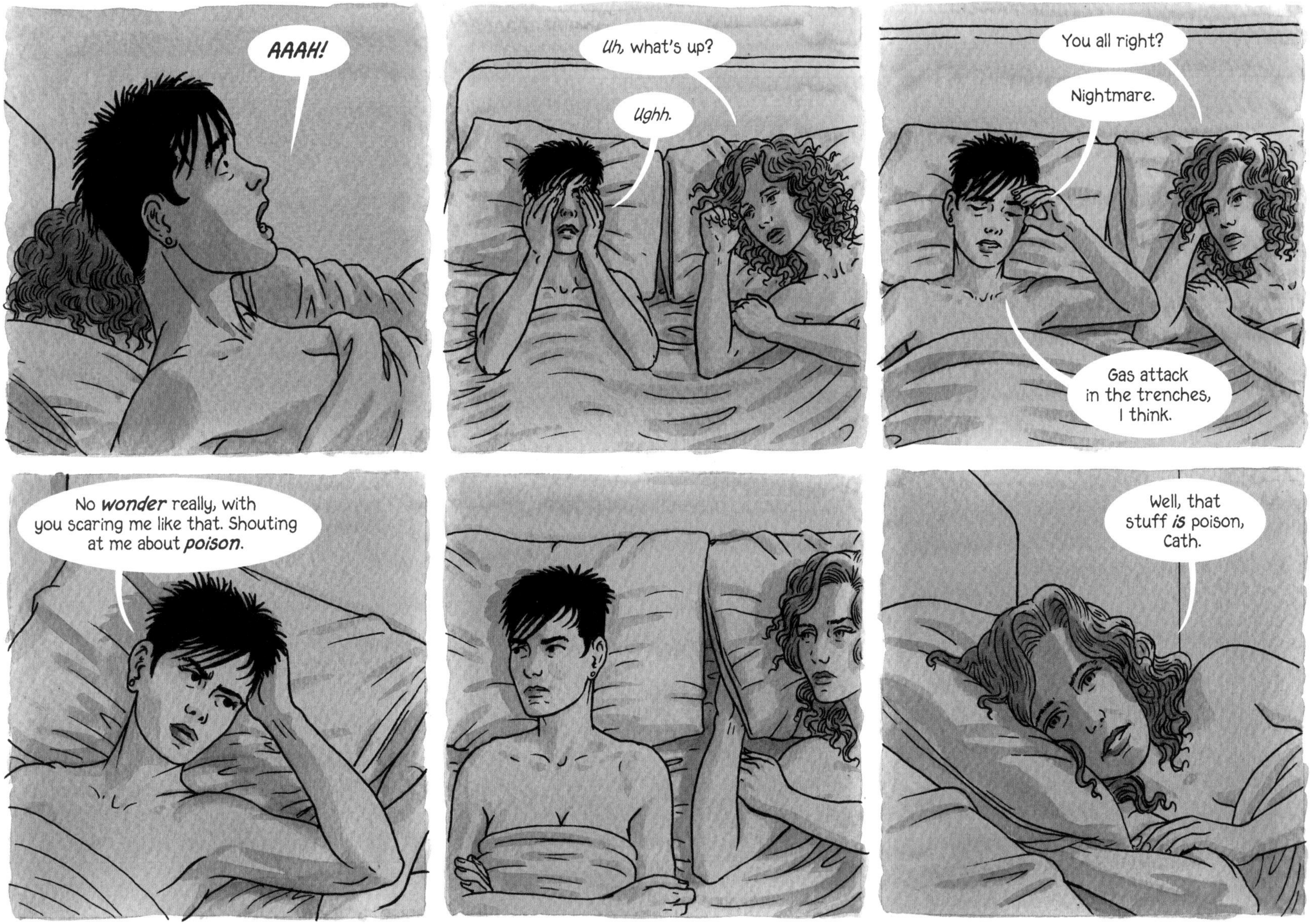
AAAH!
Uh, what's up?
Ughh.
You all right?
Nightmare.
Gas attack in the trenches, I think.
No wonder really, with you scaring me like that. Shouting at me about poison.
Well, that stuff is poison, Cath.

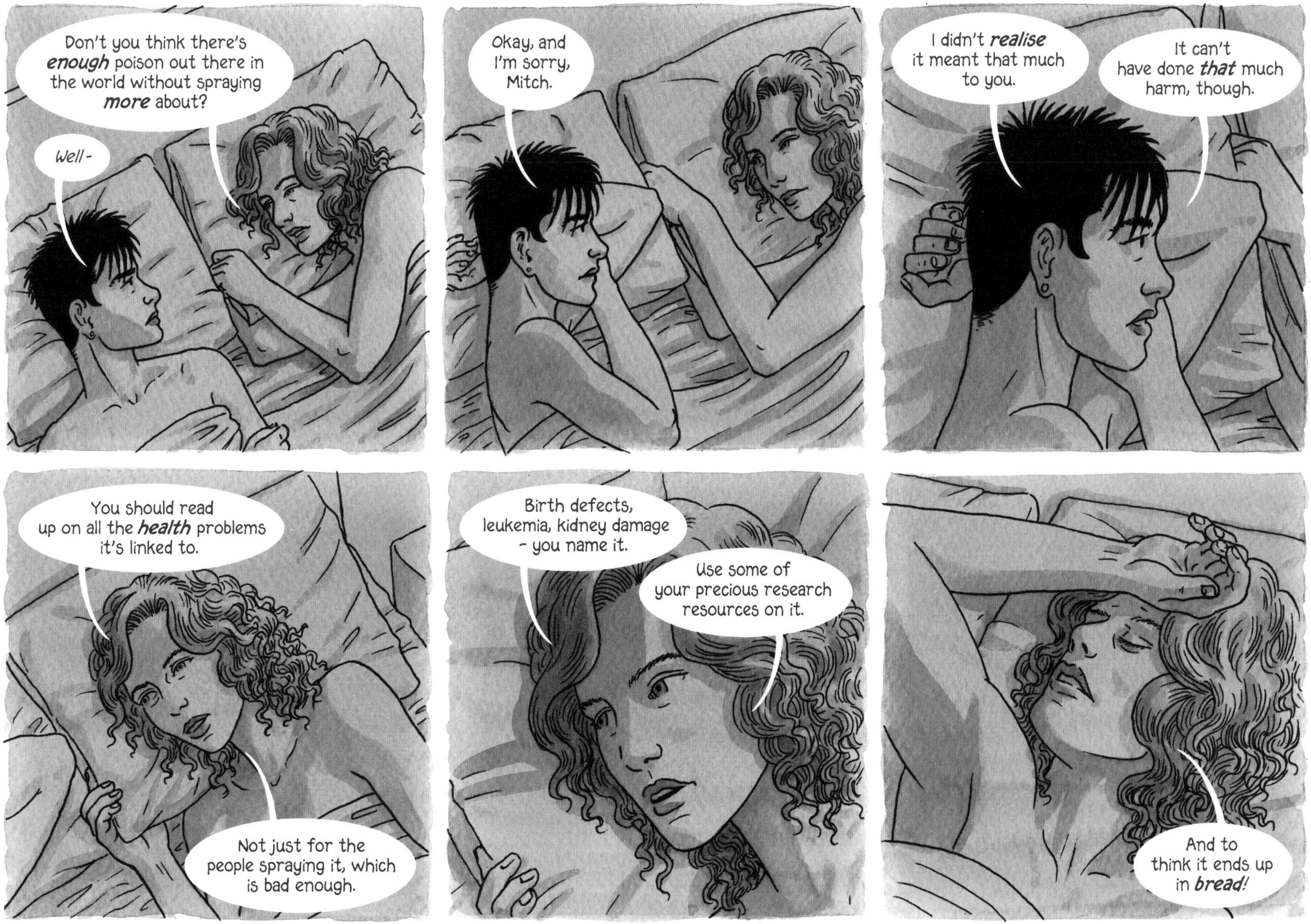
Don't you think there's **enough** poison out there in the world without spraying **more** about?
Well-
Okay, and I'm sorry, Mitch.
I didn't **realise** it meant that much to you.
It can't have done **that** much harm, though.
You should read up on all the **health** problems it's linked to.
Not just for the people spraying it, which is bad enough.
Birth defects, leukemia, kidney damage - you name it.
Use some of your precious research resources on it.
And to think it ends up in **bread**!

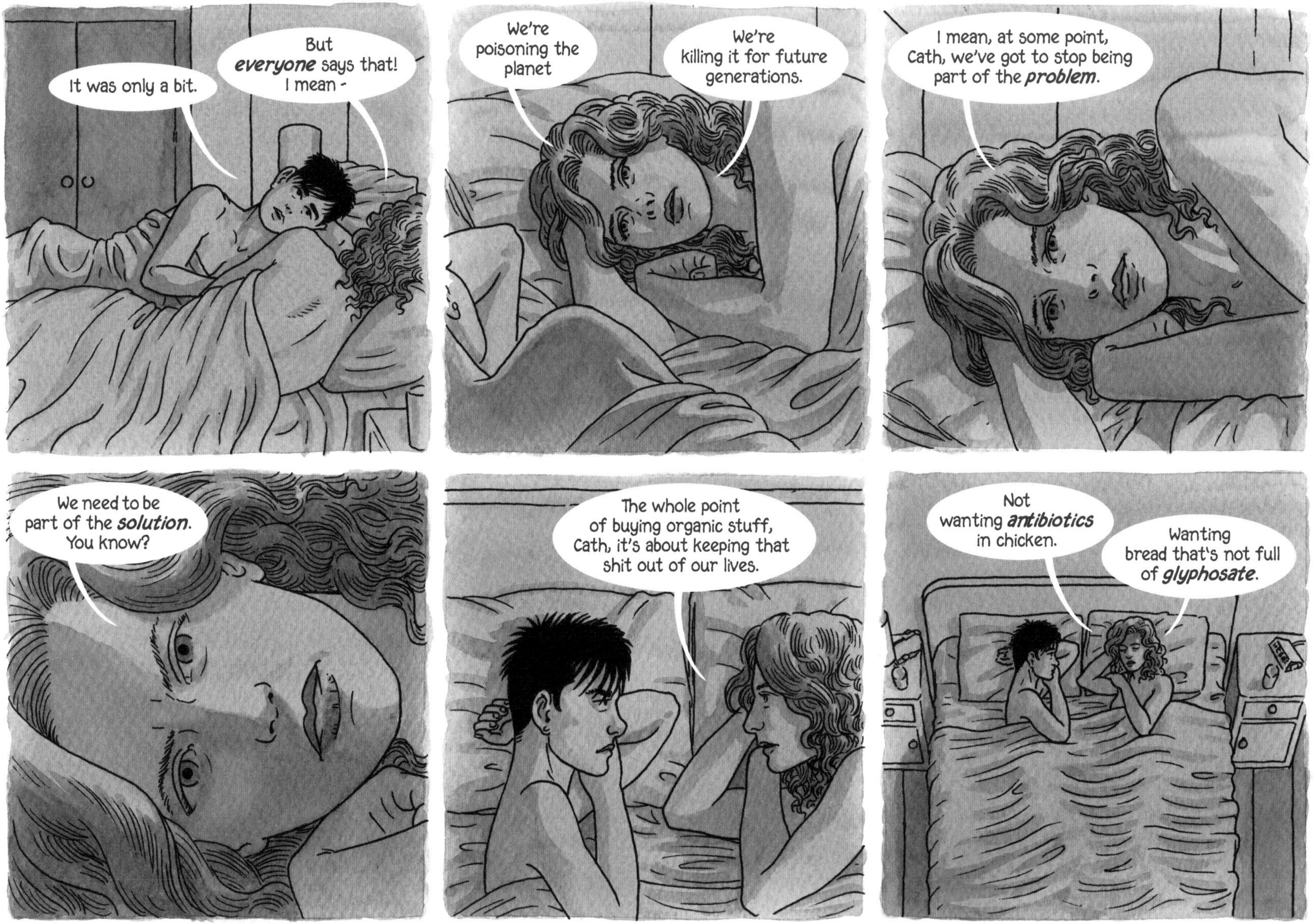
It was only a bit.
But *everyone* says that! I mean -
We're poisoning the planet
We're killing it for future generations.
I mean, at some point, Cath, we've got to stop being part of the *problem*.
We need to be part of the *solution*. You know?
The whole point of buying organic stuff, Cath, it's about keeping that shit out of our lives.
Not wanting *antibiotics* in chicken.
Wanting bread that's not full of *glyphosate*.

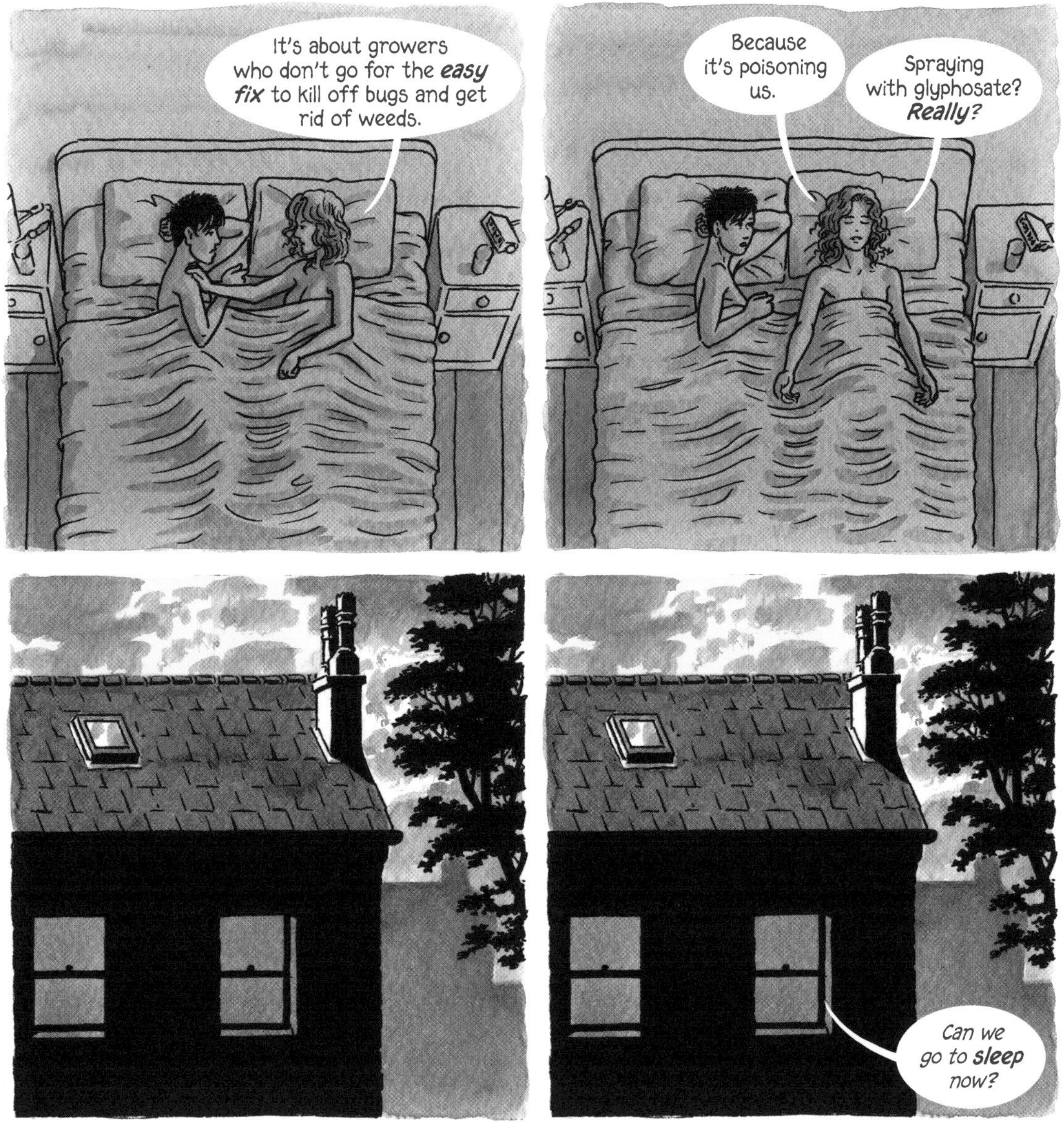
It's about growers who don't go for the ***easy fix*** to kill off bugs and get rid of weeds.
Because it's poisoning us.
Spraying with glyphosate? ***Really?***
*Can we go to **sleep** now?*

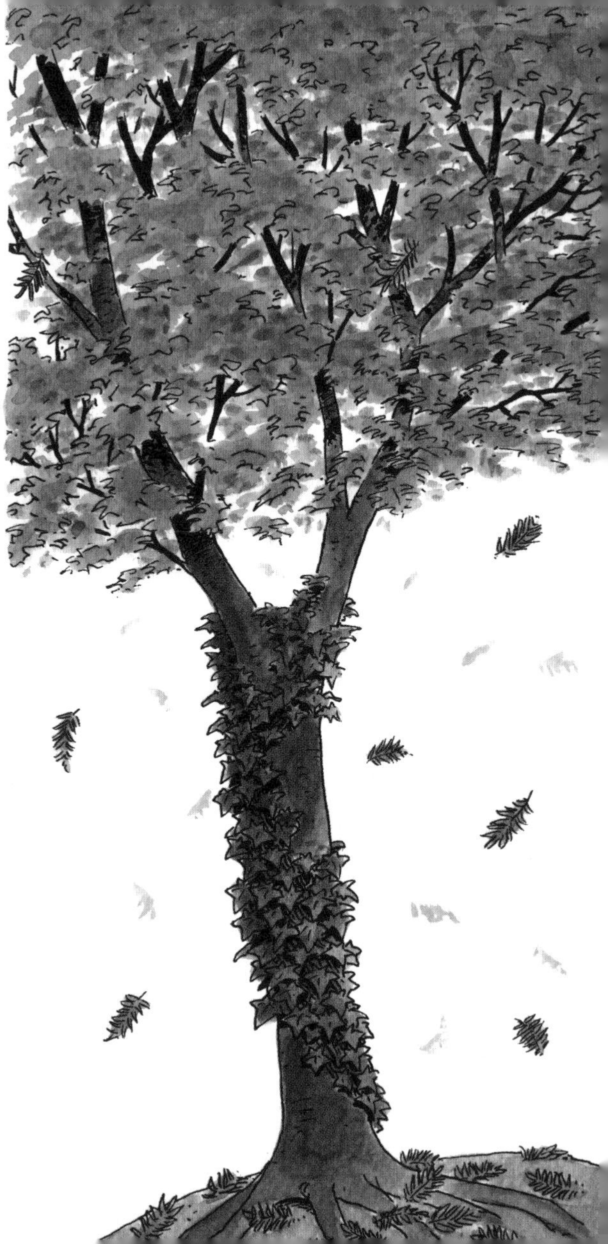

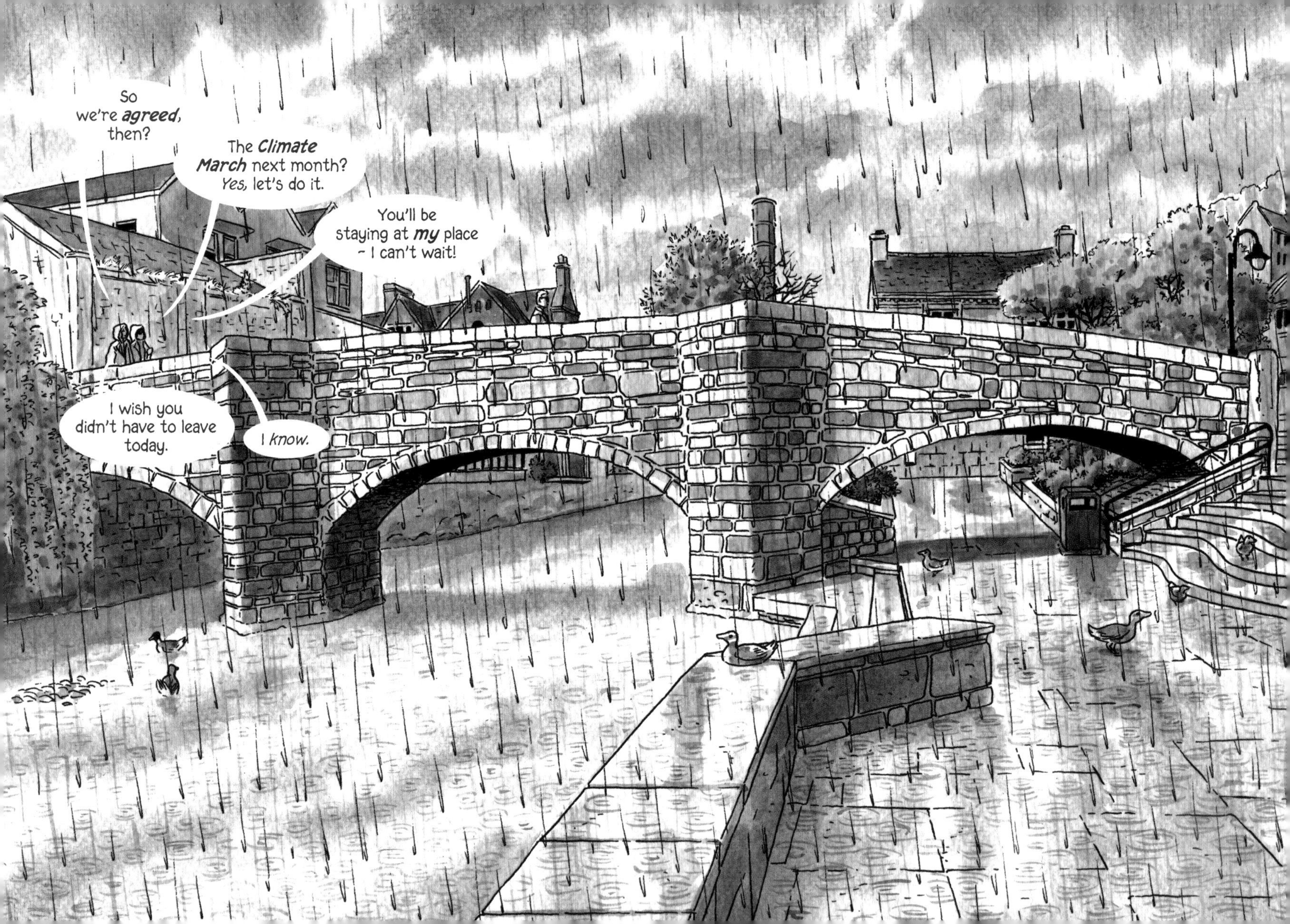
So we're **agreed**, then?
The **Climate March** next month? *Yes,* let's do it.
You'll be staying at **my** place - I can't wait!
I wish you didn't have to leave today.
I *know.*

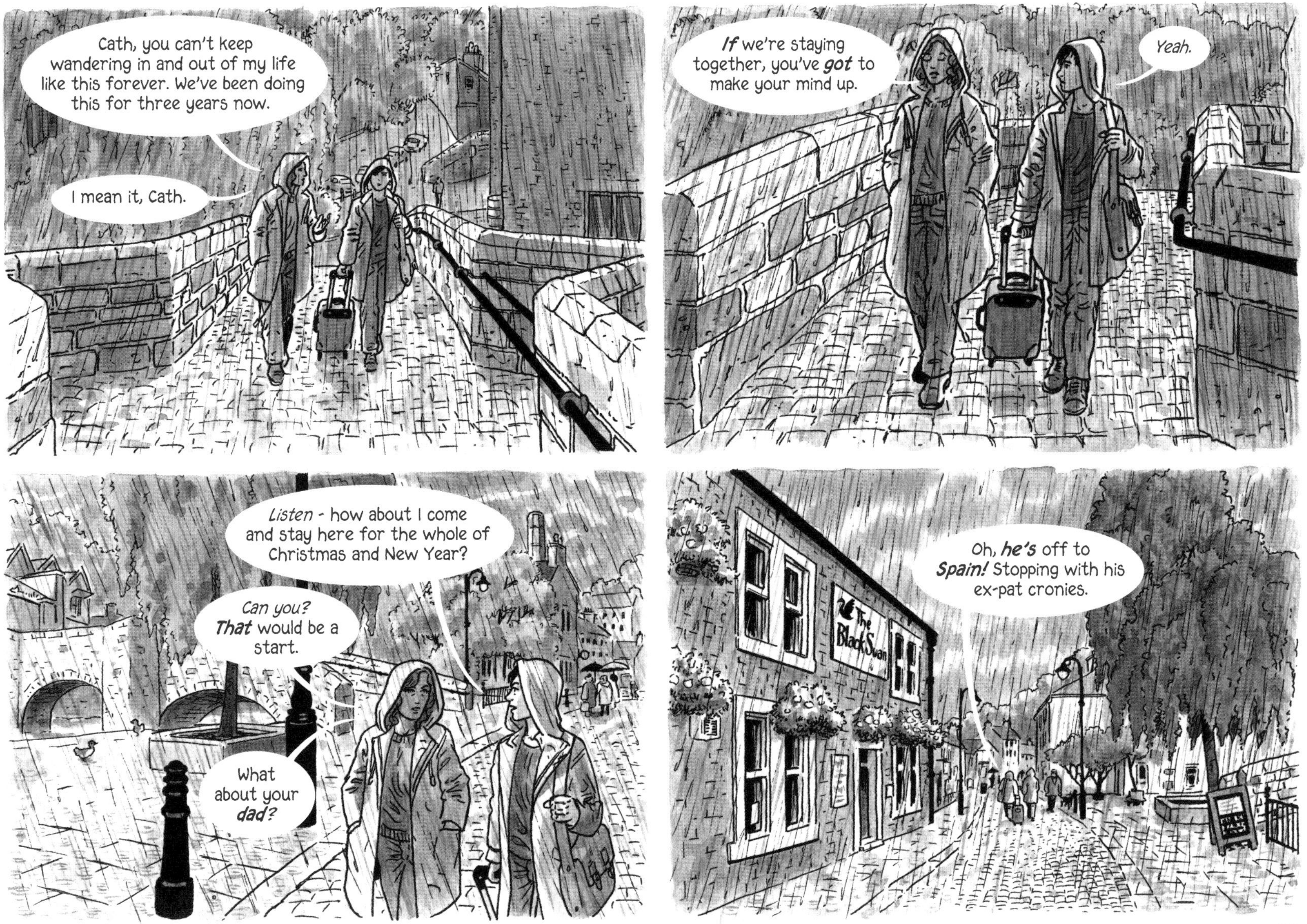
Cath, you can't keep wandering in and out of my life like this forever. We've been doing this for three years now.
I mean it, Cath.
If we're staying together, you've ***got*** to make your mind up.
Yeah.
Listen - how about I come and stay here for the whole of Christmas and New Year?
Can you? ***That*** would be a start.
What about your ***dad?***
The Black Swan
Oh, ***he's*** off to ***Spain!*** Stopping with his ex-pat cronies.

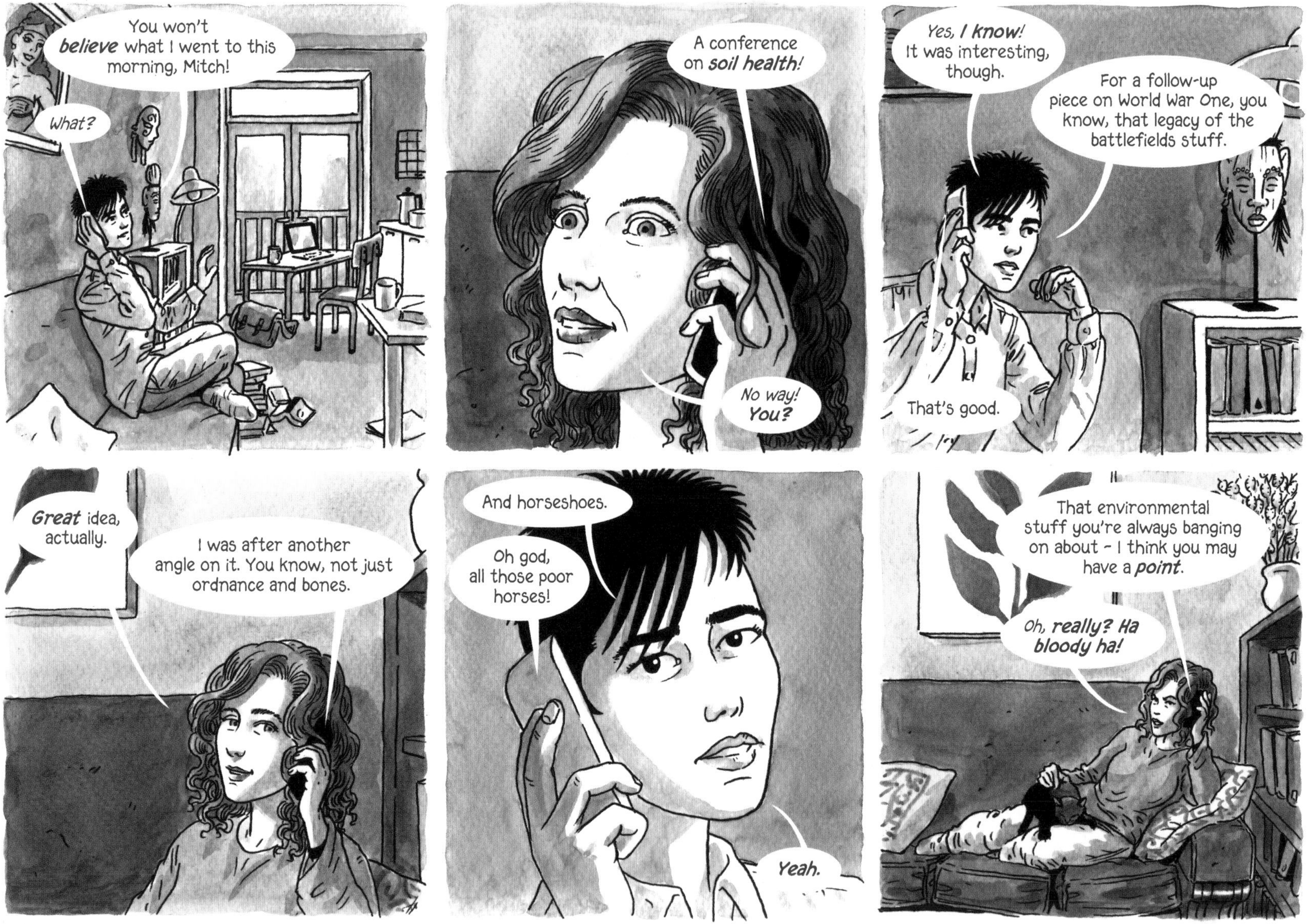

You won't **believe** what I went to this morning, Mitch!
What?
A conference on ***soil health!***
No way! ***You?***
Yes, ***I know!*** It was interesting, though.
For a follow-up piece on World War One, you know, that legacy of the battlefields stuff.
That's good.
Great idea, actually.
I was after another angle on it. You know, not just ordnance and bones.
And horseshoes.
Oh god, all those poor horses!
Yeah.
That environmental stuff you're always banging on about - I think you may have a ***point***.
Oh, ***really? Ha bloody ha!***

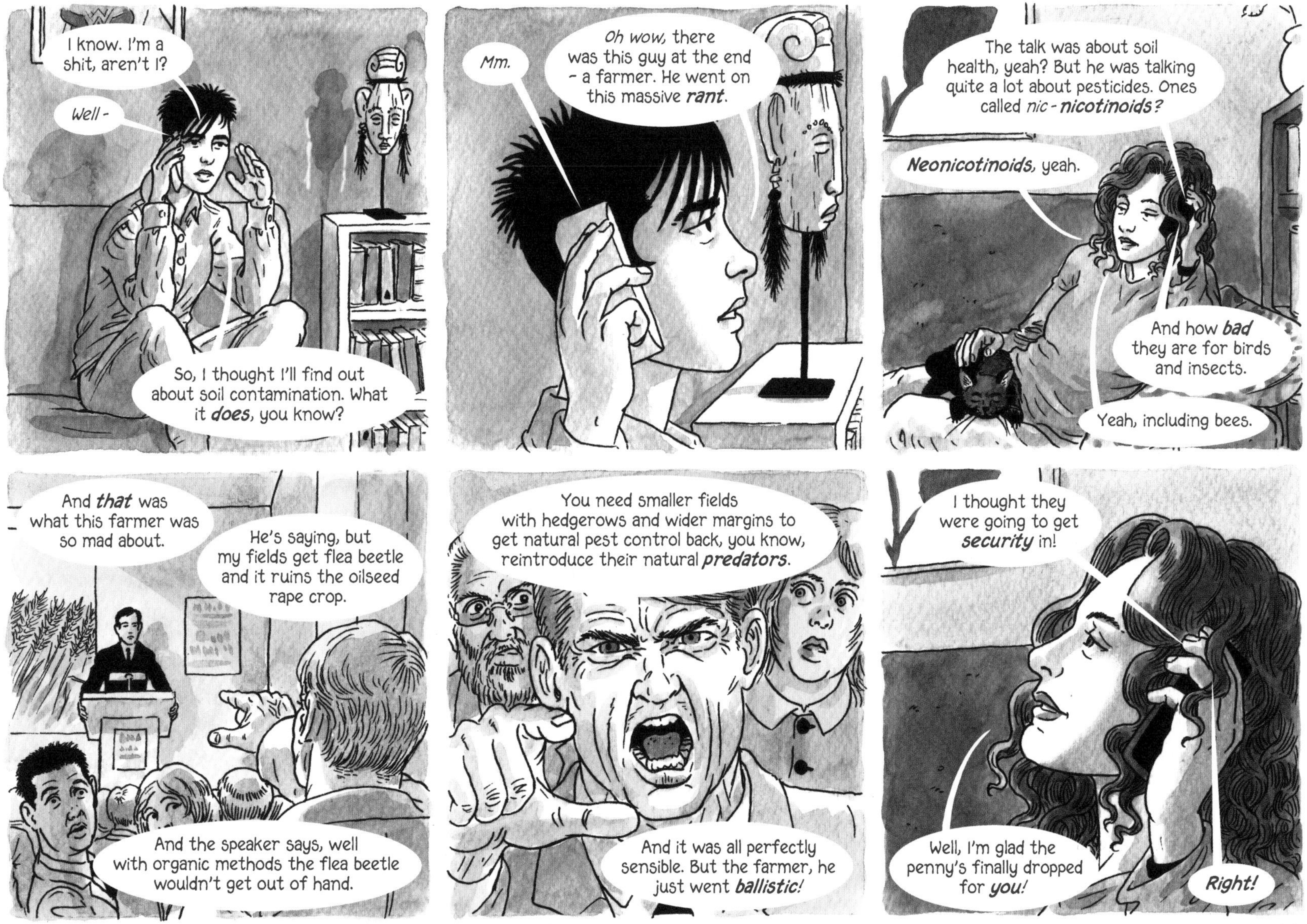
I know. I'm a shit, aren't I?
Well -
So, I thought I'll find out about soil contamination. What it *does*, you know?
Mm.
Oh wow, there was this guy at the end - a farmer. He went on this massive ***rant***.
The talk was about soil health, yeah? But he was talking quite a lot about pesticides. Ones called *nic* - ***nicotinoids?***
Neonicotinoids, yeah.
And how ***bad*** they are for birds and insects.
Yeah, including bees.
And ***that*** was what this farmer was so mad about.
He's saying, but my fields get flea beetle and it ruins the oilseed rape crop.
And the speaker says, well with organic methods the flea beetle wouldn't get out of hand.
You need smaller fields with hedgerows and wider margins to get natural pest control back, you know, reintroduce their natural ***predators***.
And it was all perfectly sensible. But the farmer, he just went ***ballistic!***
I thought they were going to get ***security*** in!
Well, I'm glad the penny's finally dropped for ***you!***
Right!

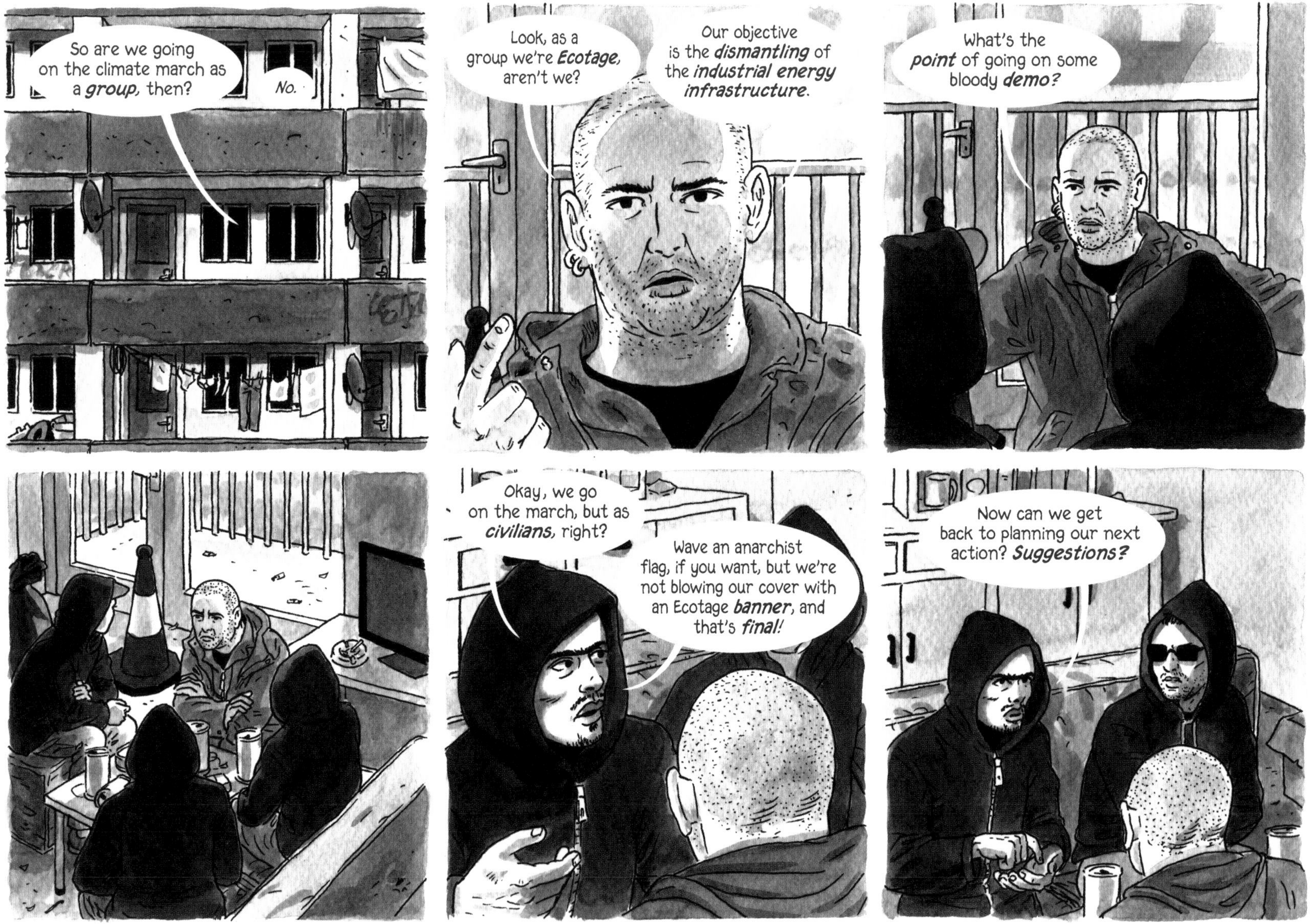
So are we going on the climate march as a *group*, then?
No.
Look, as a group we're *Ecotage*, aren't we?
Our objective is the *dismantling* of the *industrial energy infrastructure*.
What's the *point* of going on some bloody *demo?*
Okay, we go on the march, but as *civilians*, right?
Wave an anarchist flag, if you want, but we're not blowing our cover with an Ecotage *banner*, and that's *final!*
Now can we get back to planning our next action? *Suggestions?*

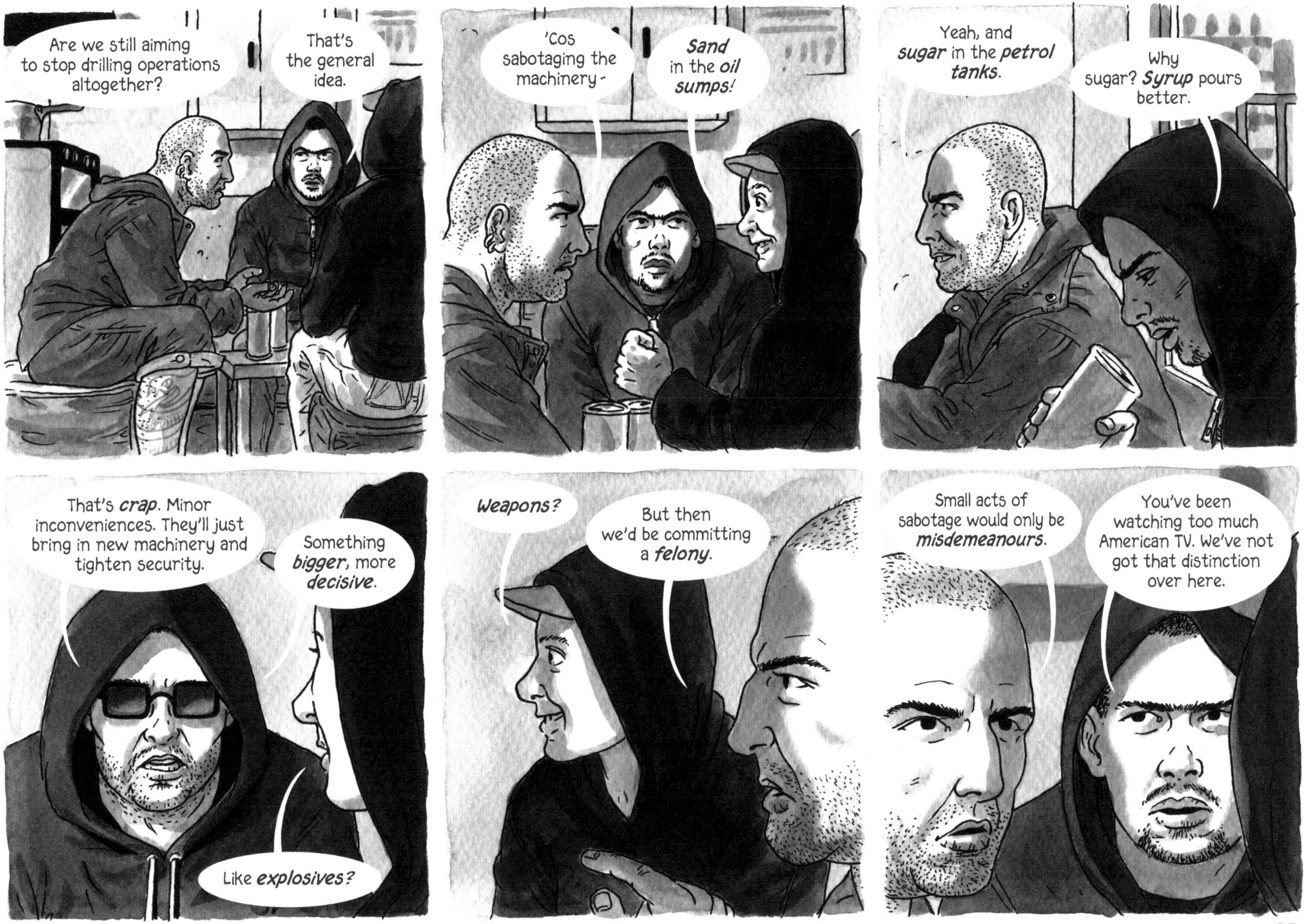

Are we still aiming to stop drilling operations altogether?
That's the general idea.
'Cos sabotaging the machinery -
Sand in the oil sumps!
Yeah, and sugar in the petrol tanks.
Why sugar? Syrup pours better.
That's crap. Minor inconveniences. They'll just bring in new machinery and tighten security.
Something bigger, more decisive.
Like explosives?
Weapons?
But then we'd be committing a felony.
Small acts of sabotage would only be misdemeanours.
You've been watching too much American TV. We've not got that distinction over here.

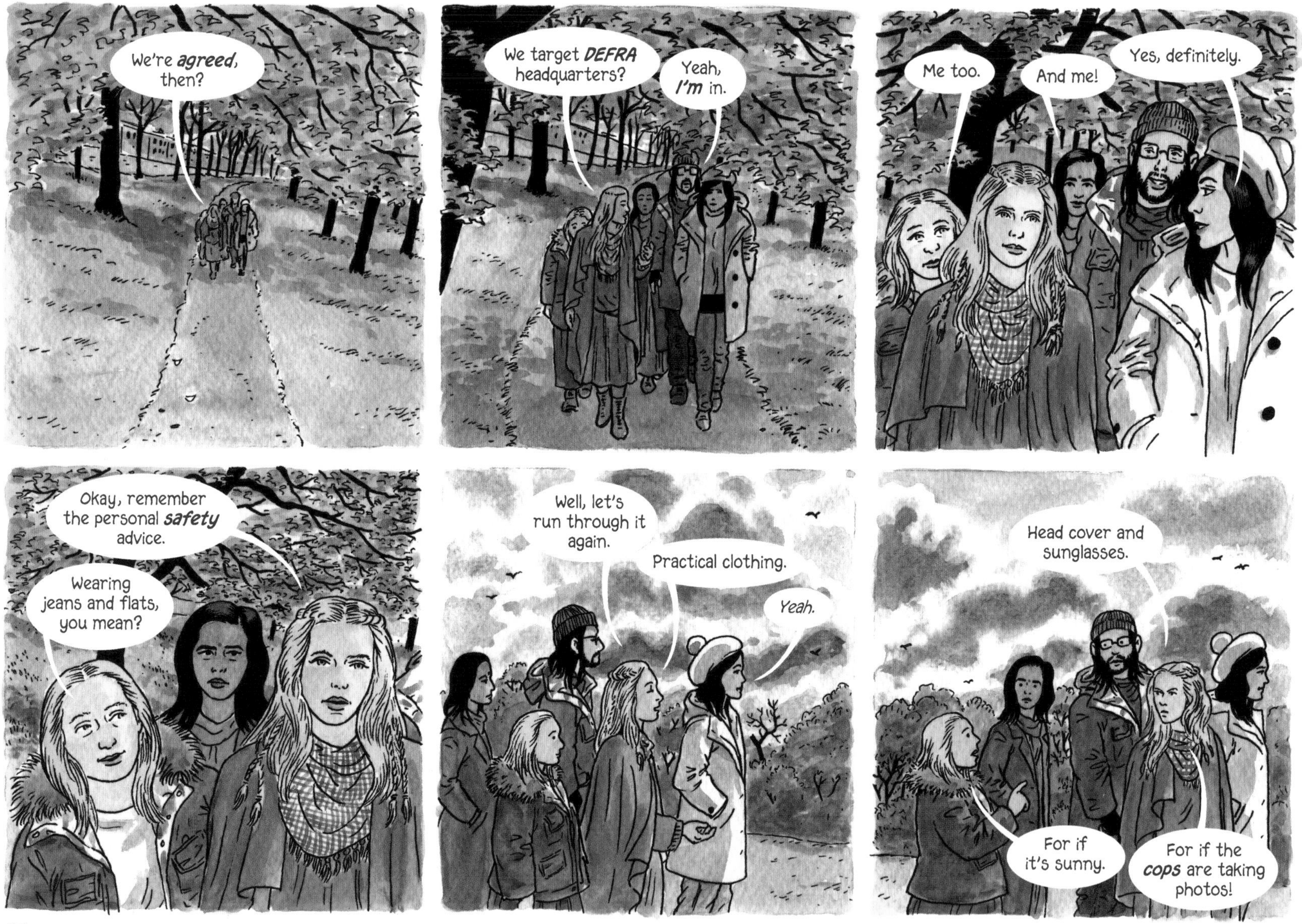
We're agreed, then?
We target DEFRA headquarters?
Yeah, I'm in.
Me too.
And me!
Yes, definitely.
Okay, remember the personal safety advice.
Wearing jeans and flats, you mean?
Well, let's run through it again.
Practical clothing.
Yeah.
Head cover and sunglasses.
For if it's sunny.
For if the cops are taking photos!

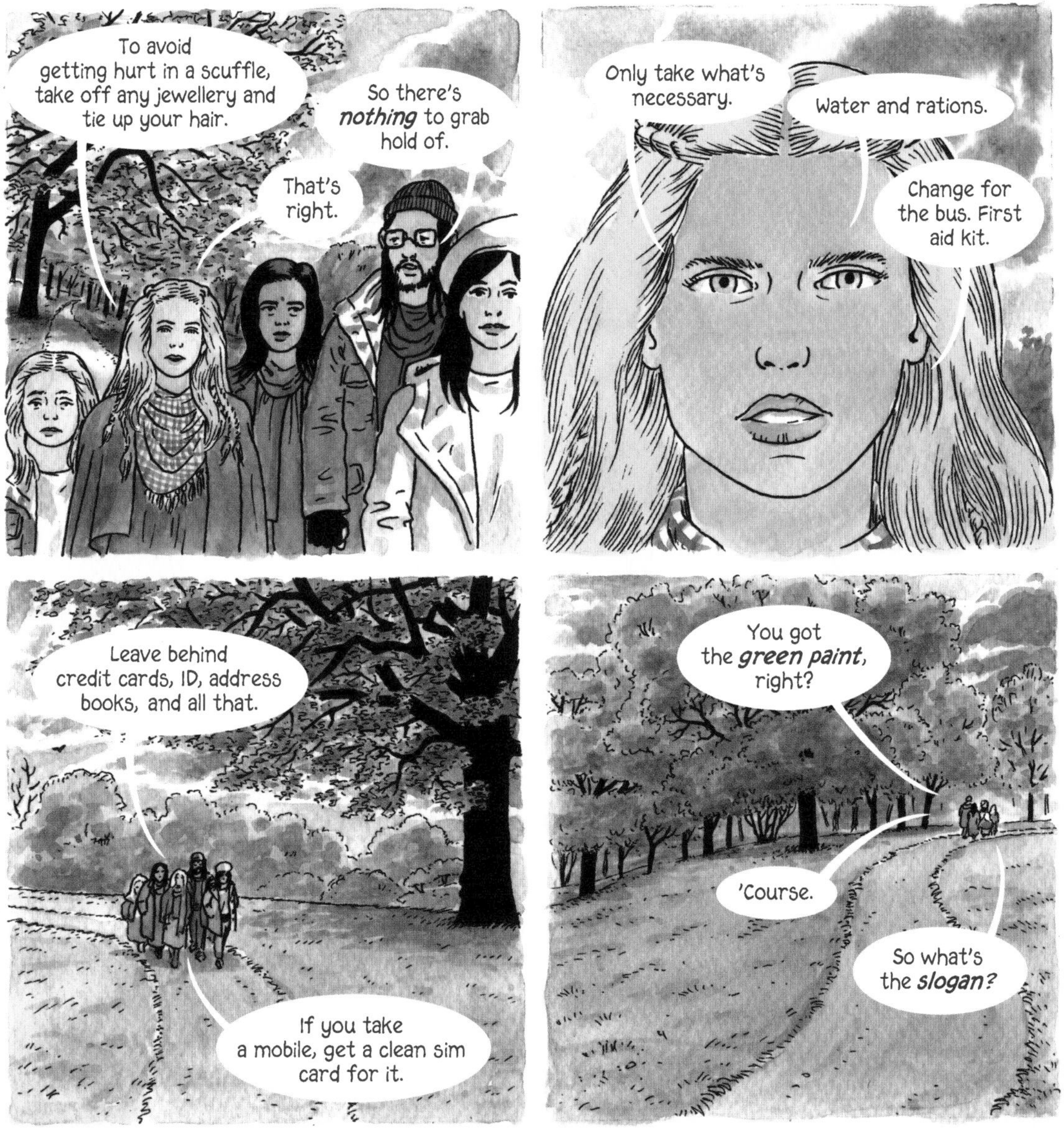
To avoid getting hurt in a scuffle, take off any jewellery and tie up your hair.
So there's ***nothing*** to grab hold of.
That's right.
Only take what's necessary.
Water and rations.
Change for the bus. First aid kit.
Leave behind credit cards, ID, address books, and all that.
If you take a mobile, get a clean sim card for it.
You got the ***green paint***, right?
'Course.
So what's the ***slogan?***

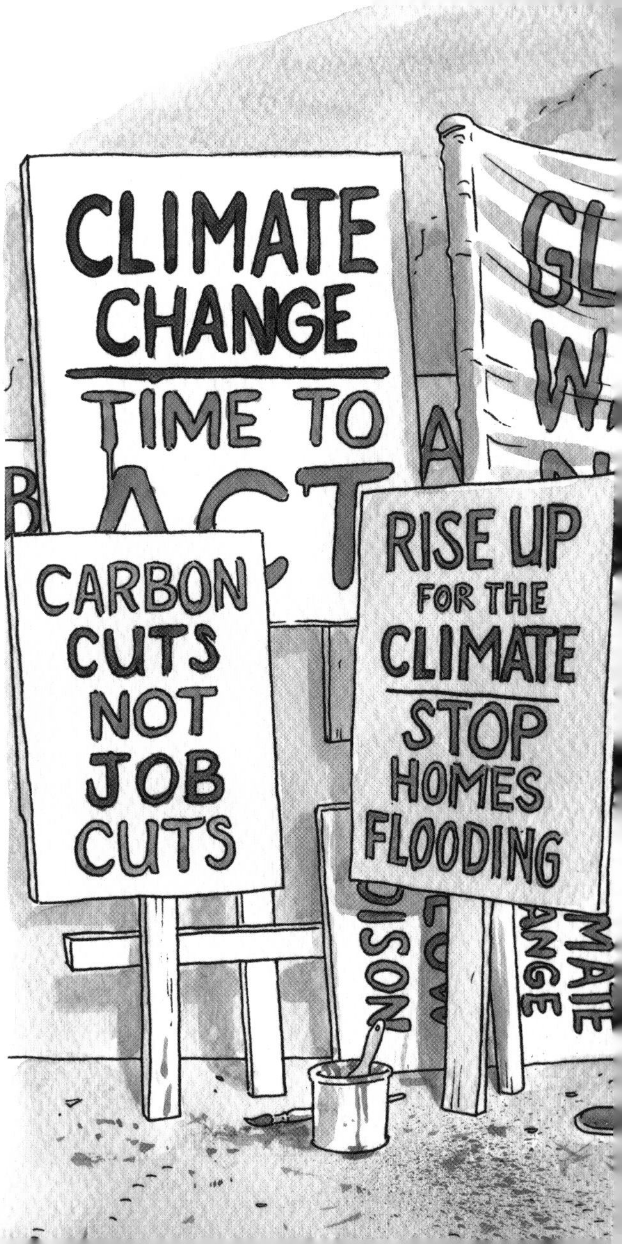
CLIMATE CHANGE
TIME TO
CARBON CUTS NOT JOB CUTS
RISE UP FOR THE CLIMATE
STOP HOMES FLOODING

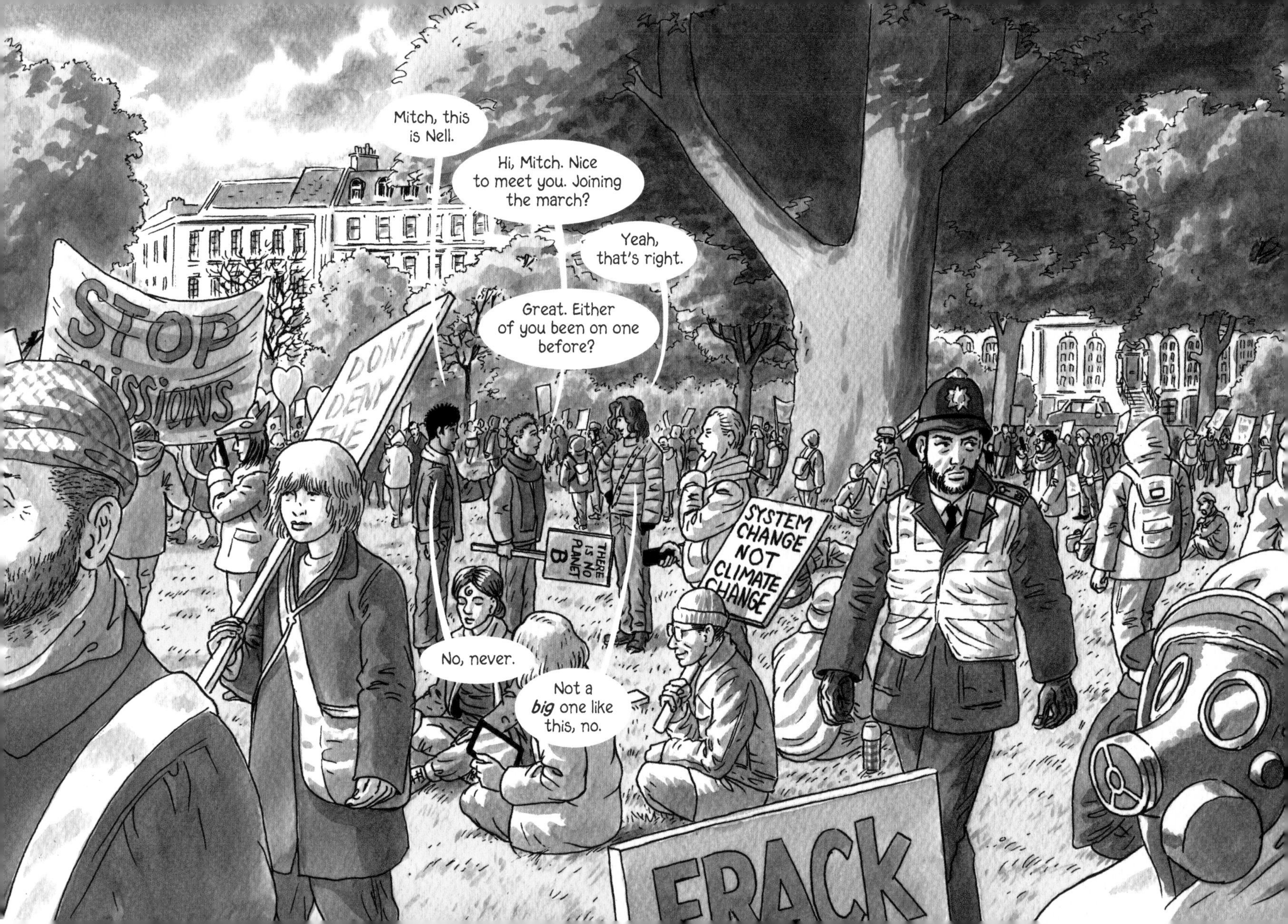
STOP
DON'T DENY THE
Mitch, this is Nell.
Hi, Mitch. Nice to meet you. Joining the march?
Yeah, that's right.
Great. Either of you been on one before?
THERE IS NO PLANET B
SYSTEM CHANGE NOT CLIMATE CHANGE
No, never.
Not a *big* one like this, no.
FRACK

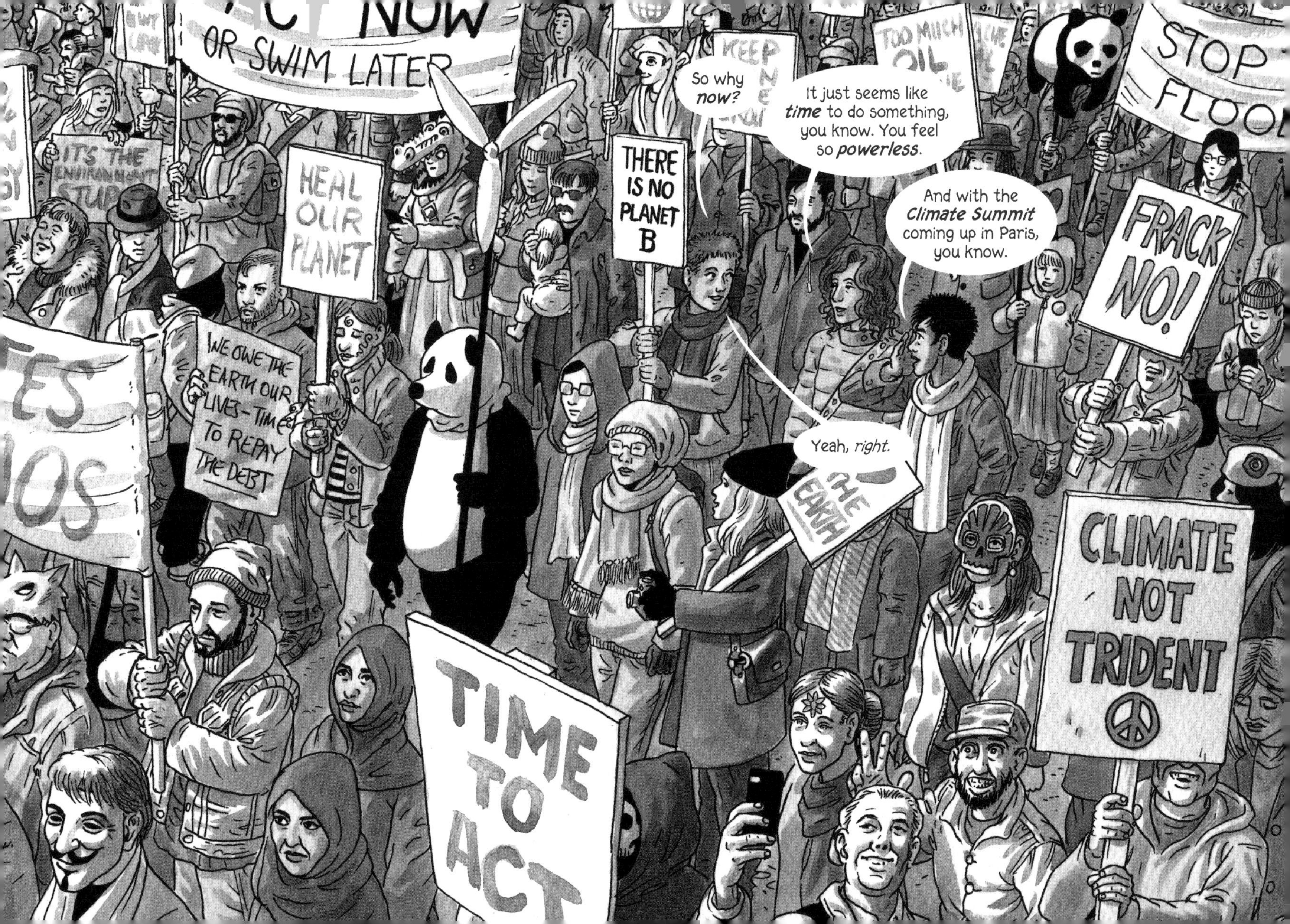

NOW
OR SWIM LATER
HEAL OUR PLANET
THERE IS NO PLANET B
So why *now?*
It just seems like *time* to do something, you know. You feel so *powerless.*
And with the *Climate Summit* coming up in Paris, you know.
FRACK NO!
WE OWE THE EARTH OUR LIVES-TIME TO REPAY THE DEBT
Yeah, *right.*
CLIMATE NOT TRIDENT
TIME TO ACT

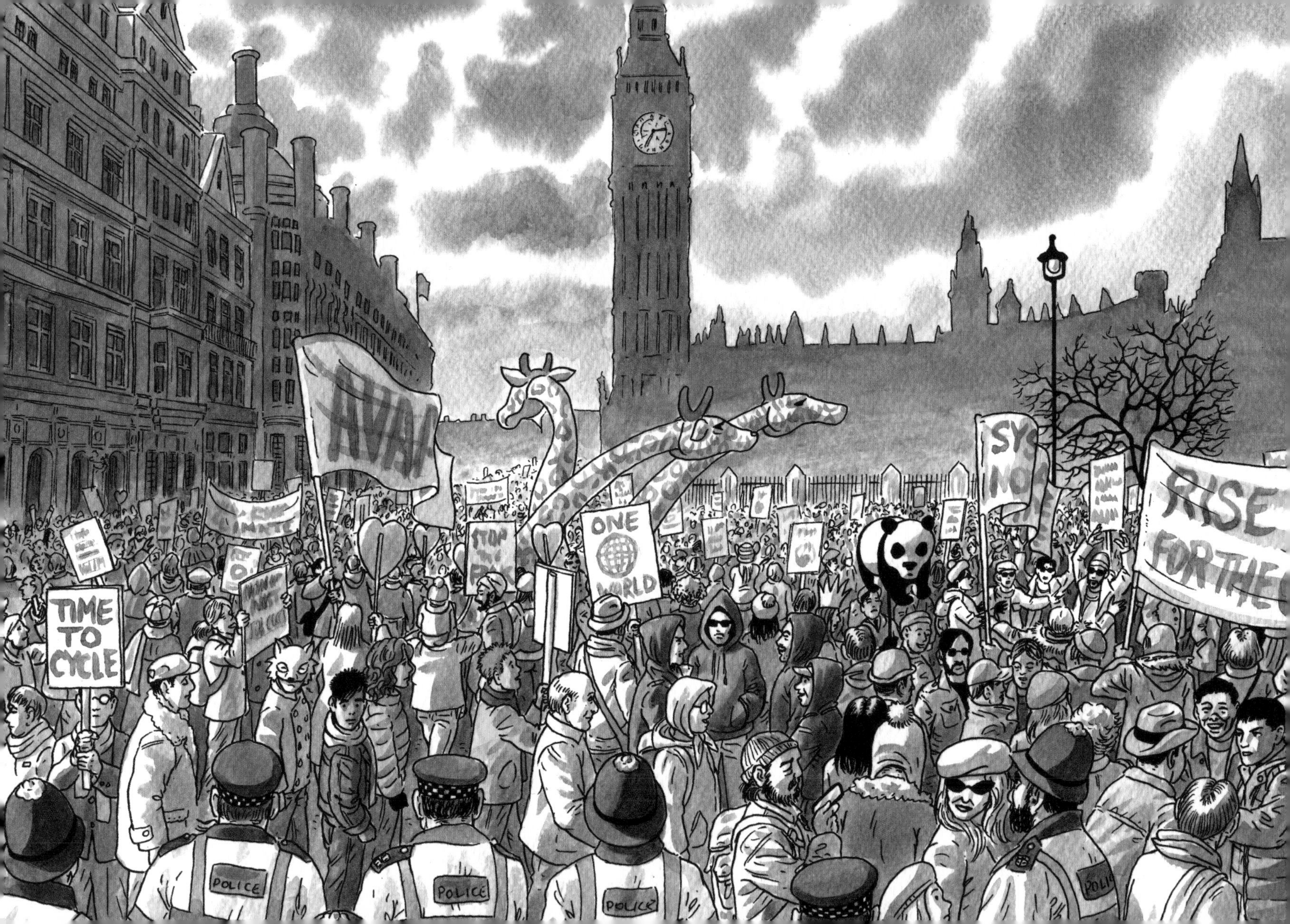
TIME TO CYCLE
ONE WORLD
RISE FOR THE
POLICE
POLICE
POLICE
POLICE

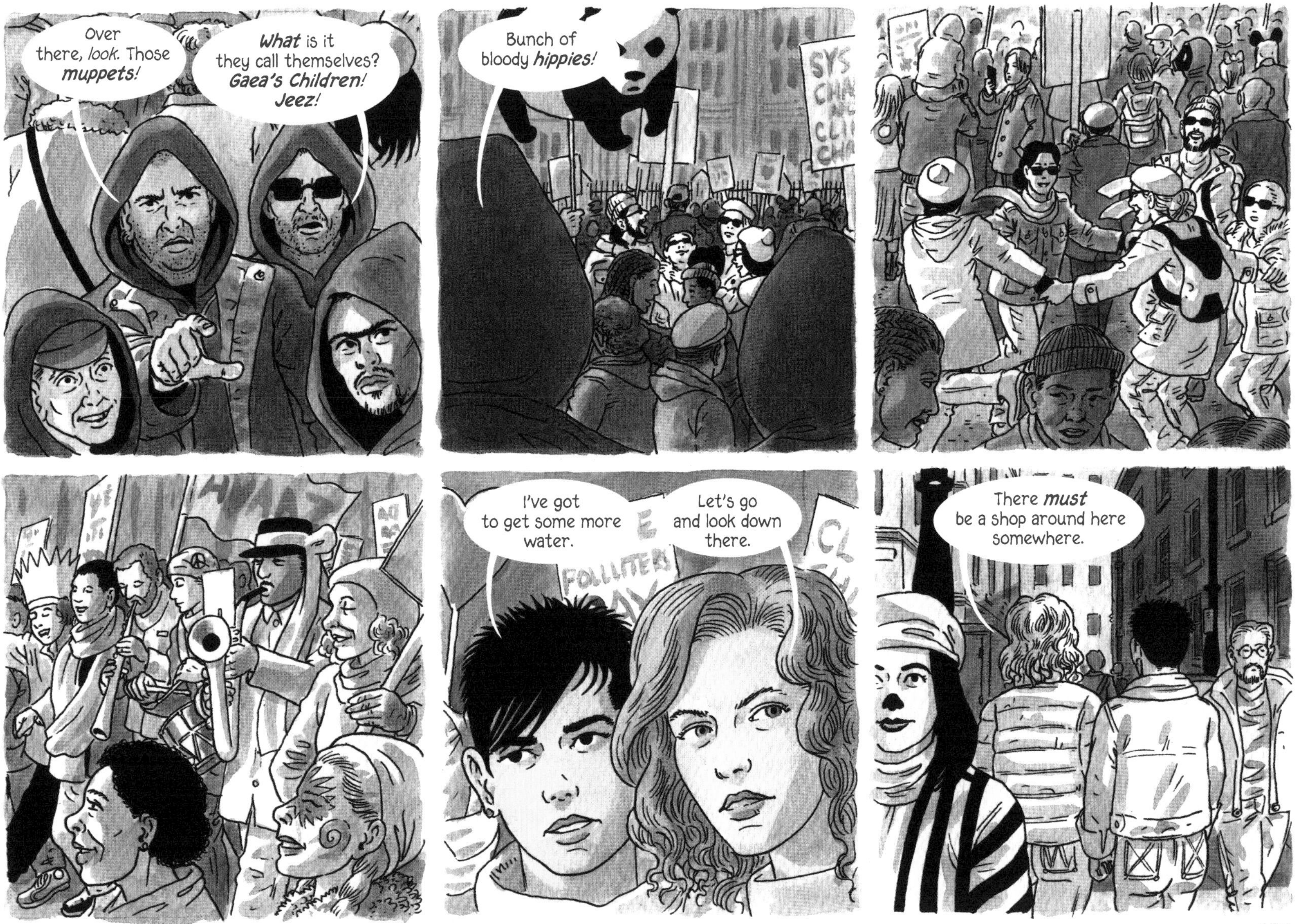
Over there, *look*. Those **muppets**!
What is it they call themselves? **Gaea's Children**! **Jeez**!
Bunch of bloody **hippies**!
SYS CHA
I've got to get some more water.
Let's go and look down there.
There **must** be a shop around here somewhere.

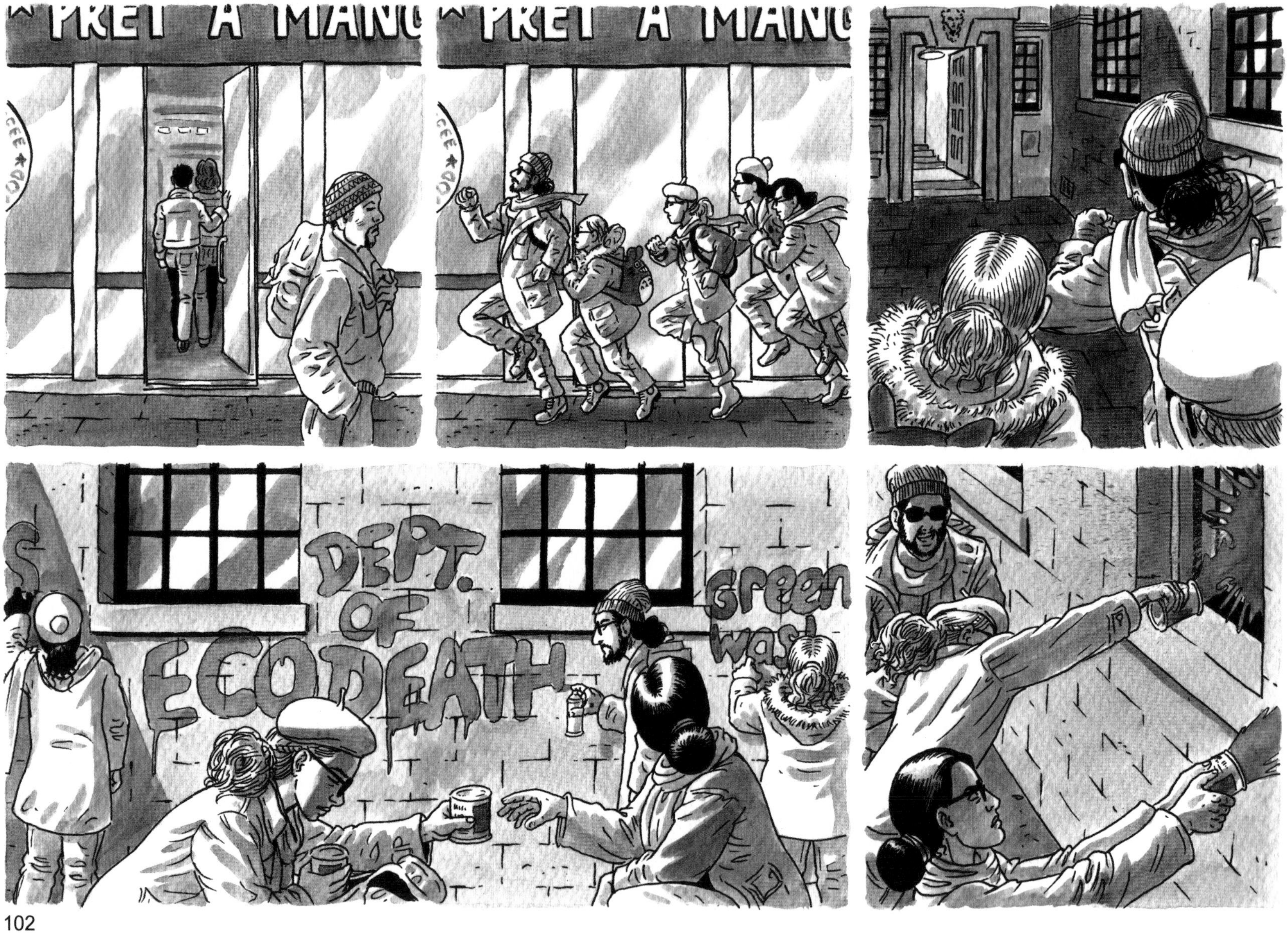
PRET A MANG
PRET A MANG
DEPT. OF ECODEATH
green was

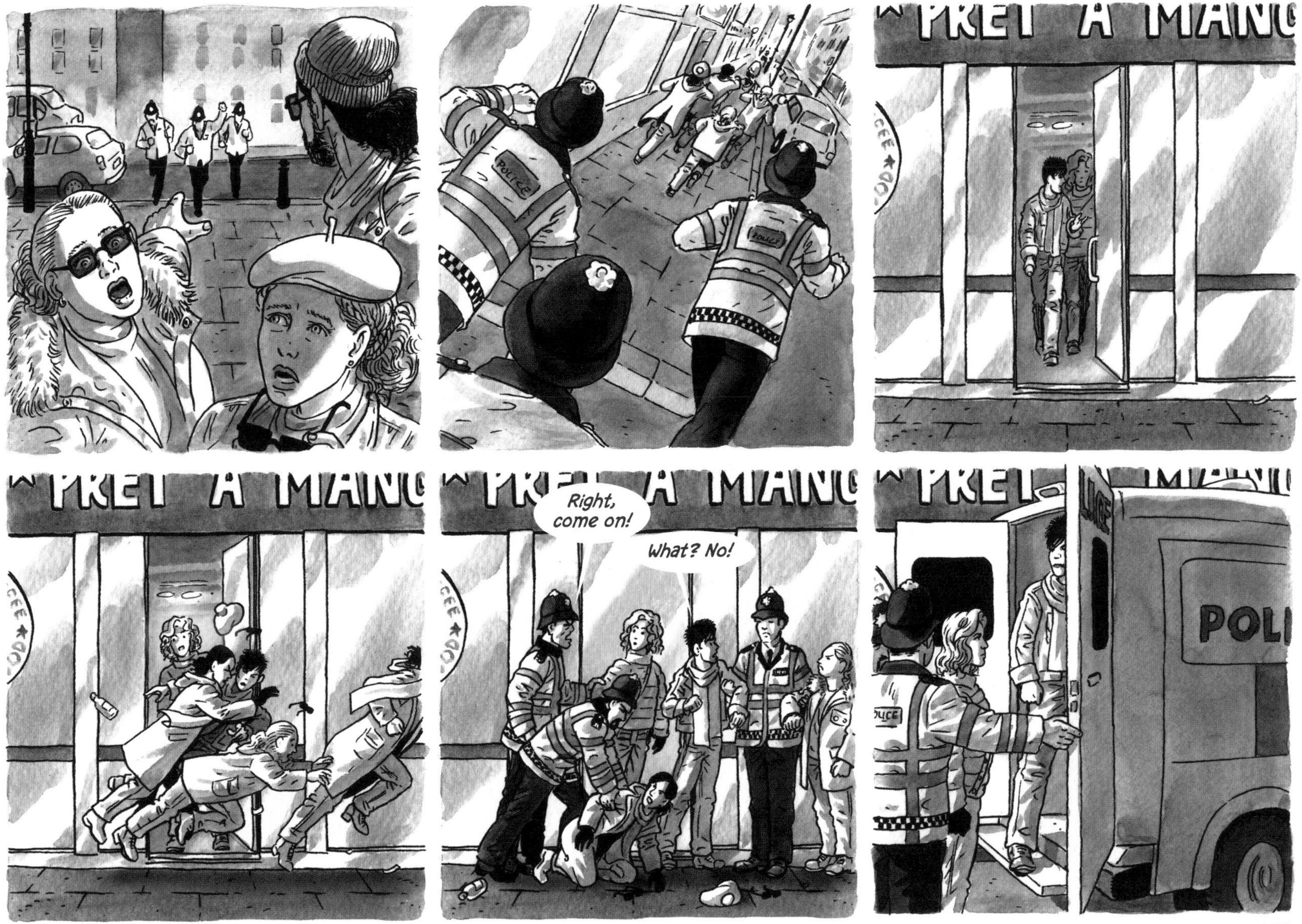
PRET A MANG
PRET A MANG
PRET A MANG
Right, come on!
What? No!
POLI

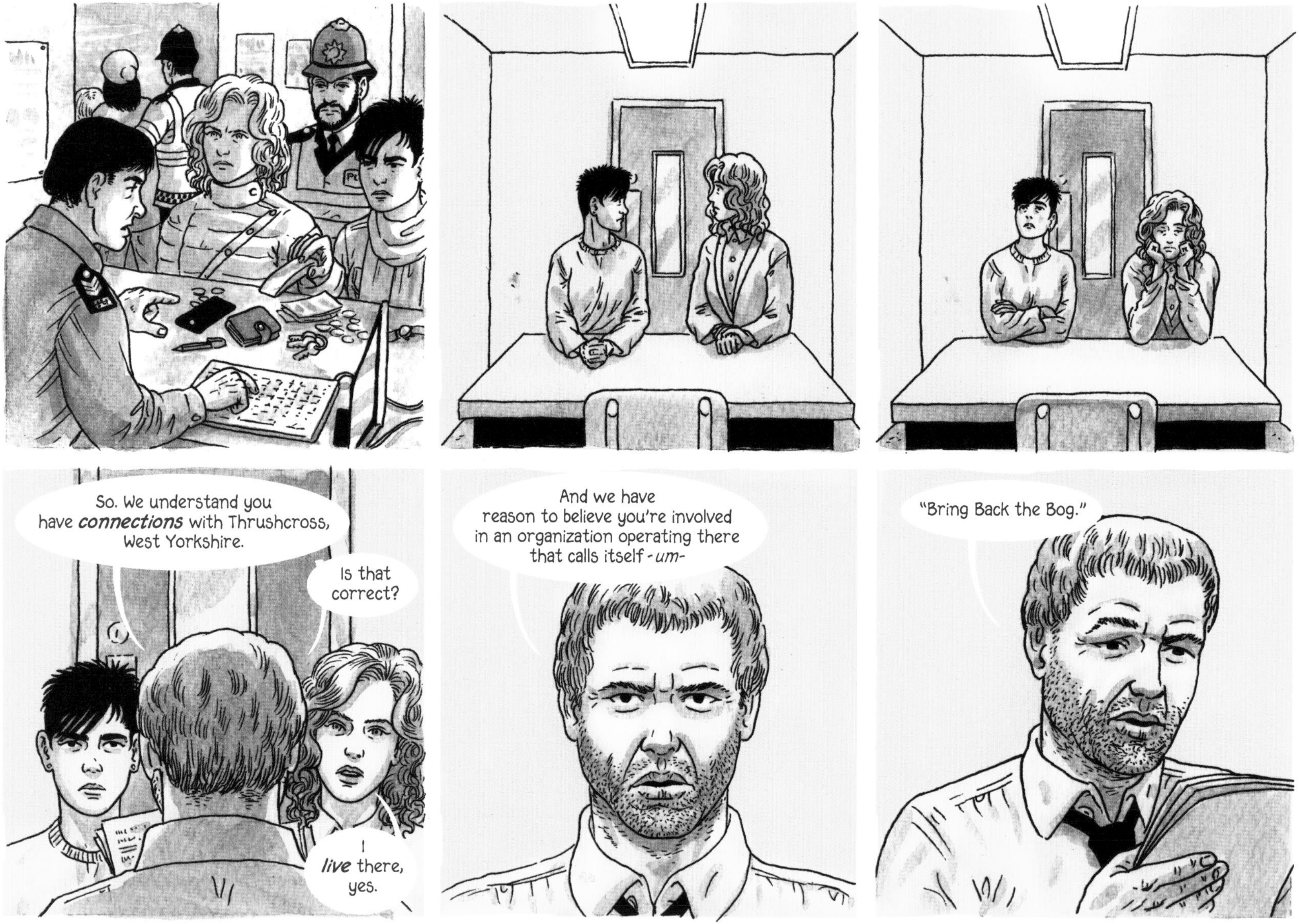
So. We understand you have *connections* with Thrushcross, West Yorkshire.
Is that correct?
I *live* there, yes.
And we have reason to believe you're involved in an organization operating there that calls itself *-um-*
"Bring Back the Bog."

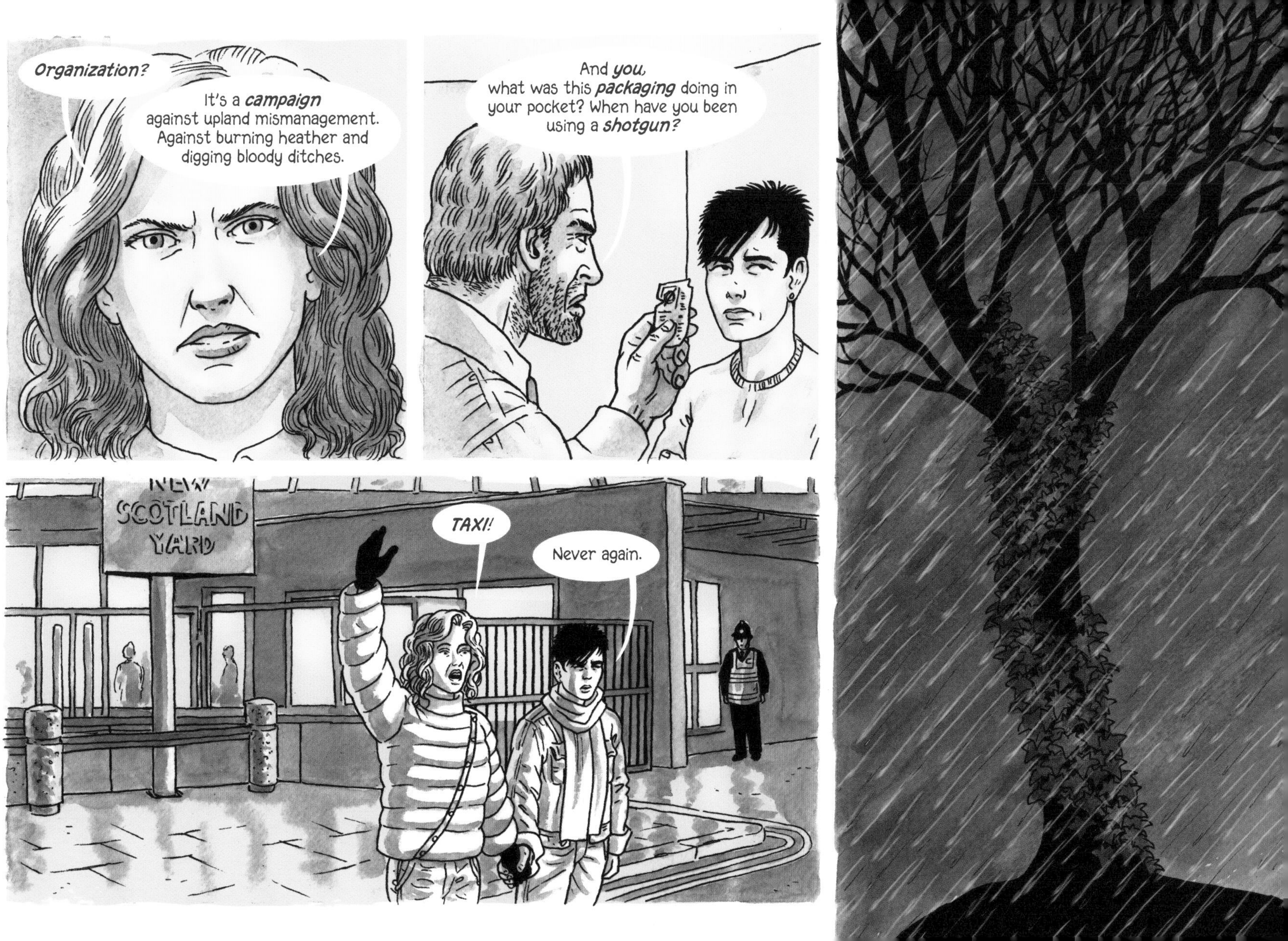
Organization?
It's a *campaign* against upland mismanagement. Against burning heather and digging bloody ditches.
And *you*, what was this *packaging* doing in your pocket? When have you been using a *shotgun?*
SCOTLAND YARD
TAXI!
Never again.

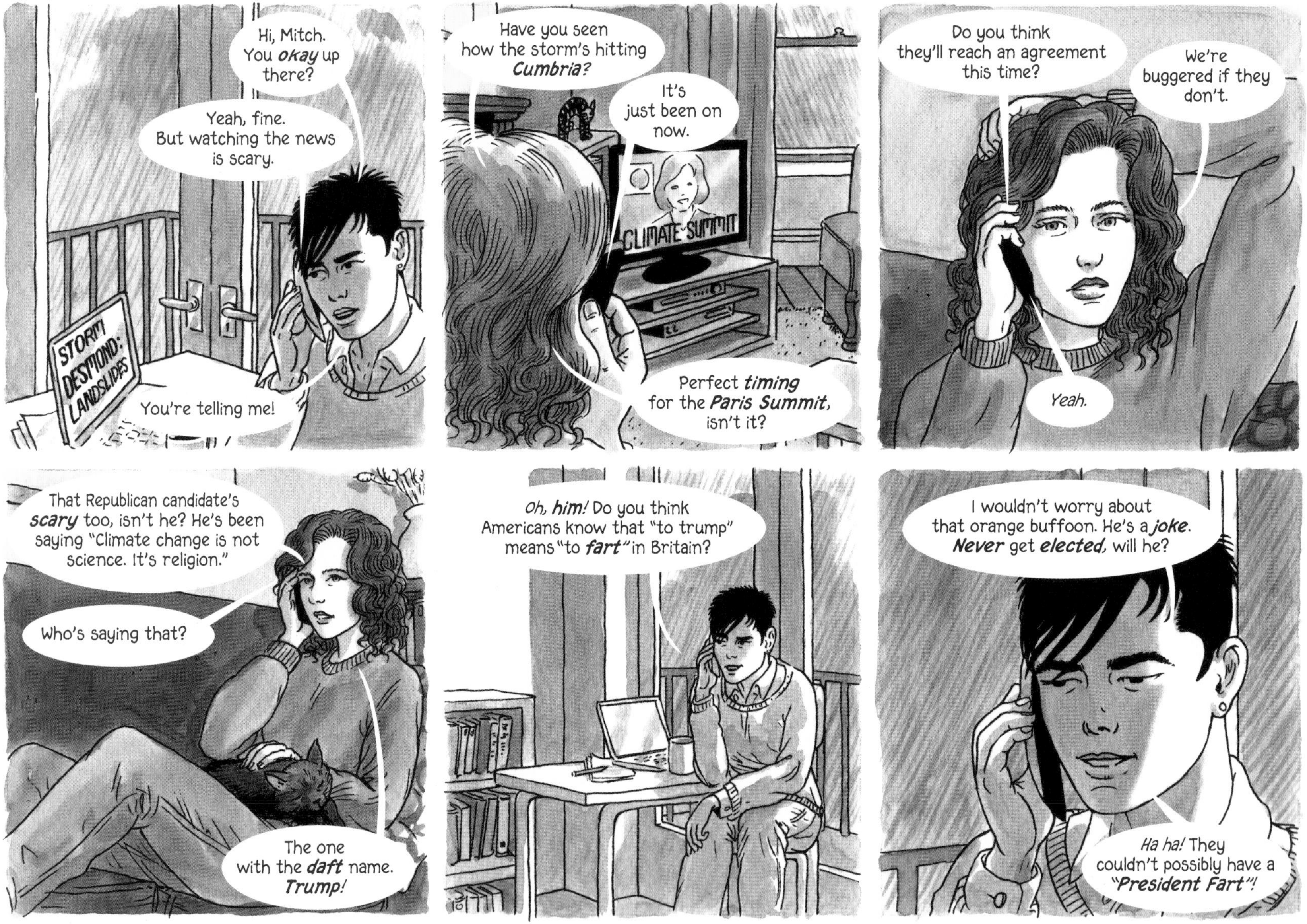
Hi, Mitch. You *okay* up there?
Yeah, fine. But watching the news is scary.
STORM DESMOND: LANDSLIDES
You're telling me!
Have you seen how the storm's hitting *Cumbria?*
It's just been on now.
CLIMATE SUMMIT
Perfect *timing* for the *Paris Summit*, isn't it?
Do you think they'll reach an agreement this time?
We're buggered if they don't.
Yeah.
That Republican candidate's *scary* too, isn't he? He's been saying "Climate change is not science. It's religion."
Who's saying that?
The one with the *daft* name. *Trump!*
Oh, him! Do you think Americans know that "to trump" means "to *fart*" in Britain?
I wouldn't worry about that orange buffoon. He's a *joke*. *Never* get *elected*, will he?
Ha ha! They couldn't possibly have a *"President Fart"!*

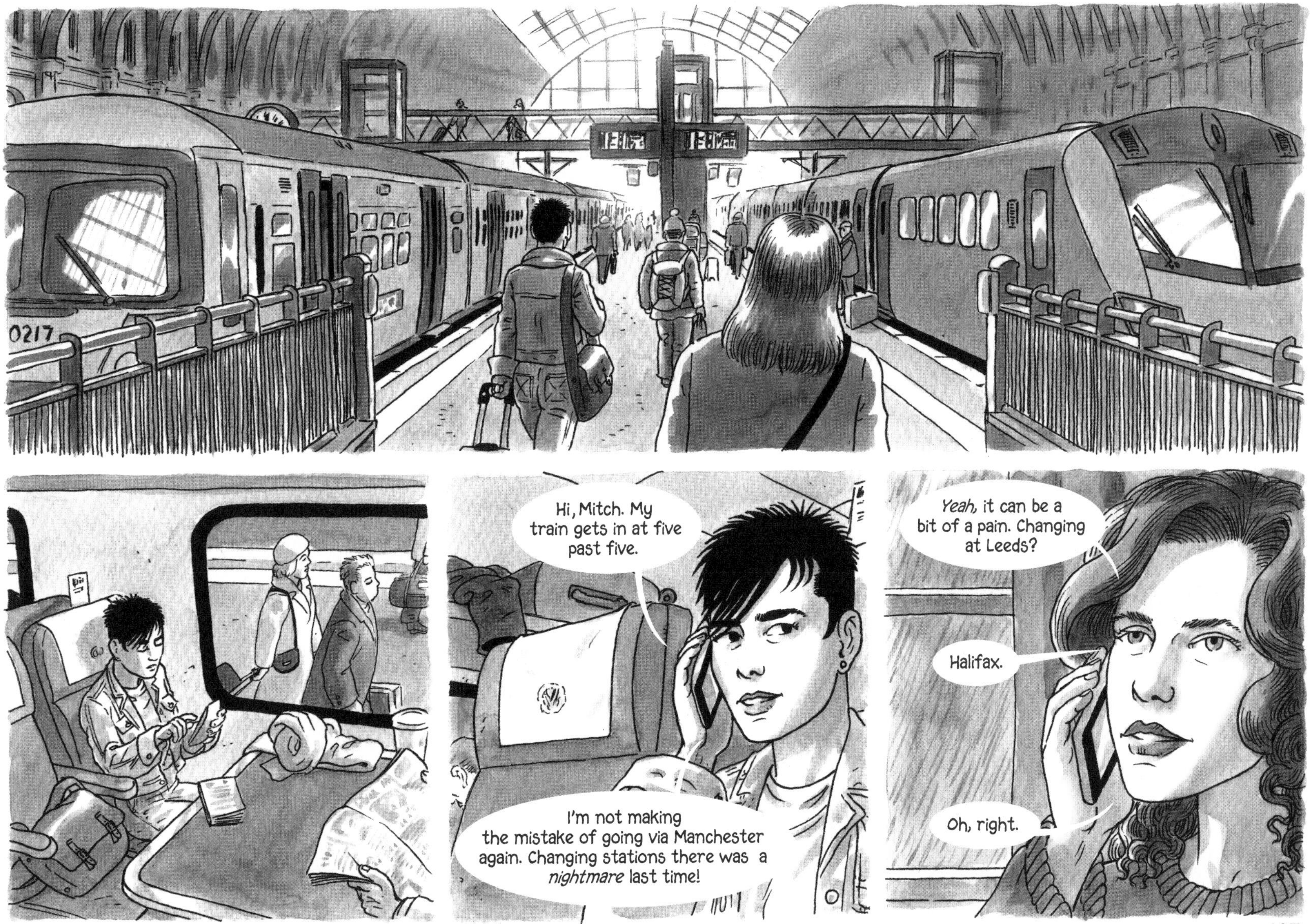
Hi, Mitch. My train gets in at five past five.
I'm not making the mistake of going via Manchester again. Changing stations there was a *nightmare* last time!
Yeah, it can be a bit of a pain. Changing at Leeds?
Halifax.
Oh, right.

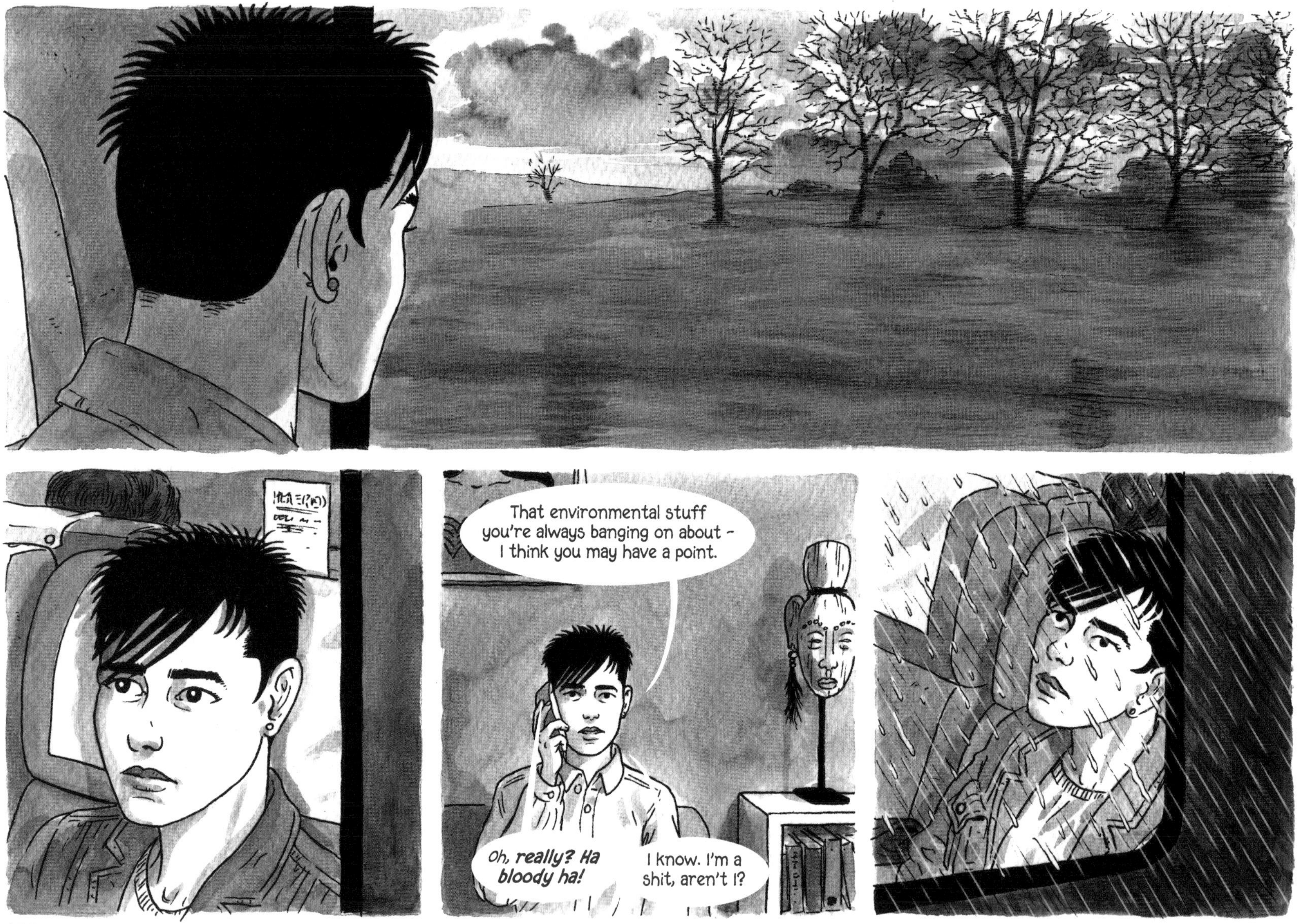
That environmental stuff you're always banging on about – I think you may have a point.
Oh, really? Ha bloody ha!
I know. I'm a shit, aren't I?

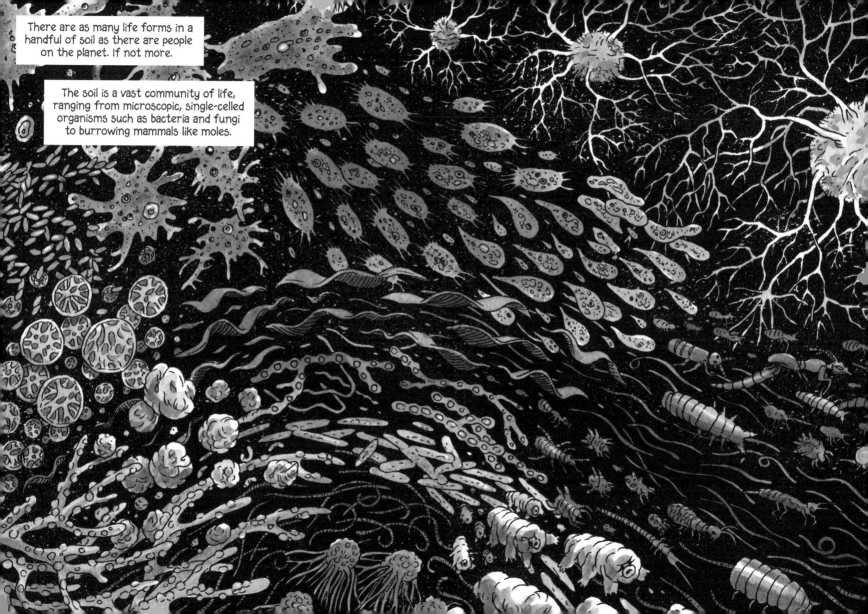

There are as many life forms in a handful of soil as there are people on the planet. If not more.

The soil is a vast community of life, ranging from microscopic, single-celled organisms such as bacteria and fungi to burrowing mammals like moles.

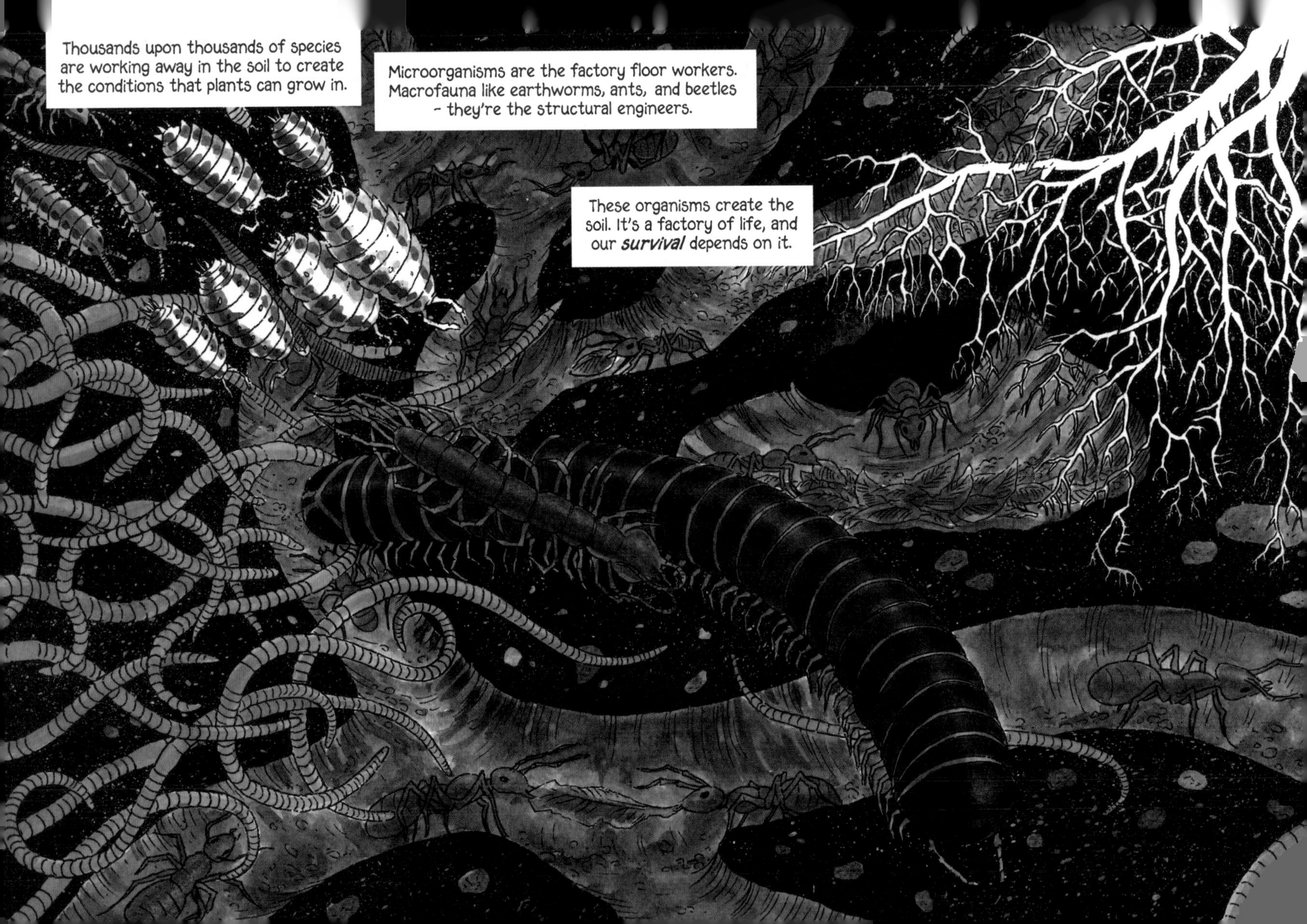
Thousands upon thousands of species are working away in the soil to create the conditions that plants can grow in.
Microorganisms are the factory floor workers. Macrofauna like earthworms, ants, and beetles – they're the structural engineers.
These organisms create the soil. It's a factory of life, and our *survival* depends on it.

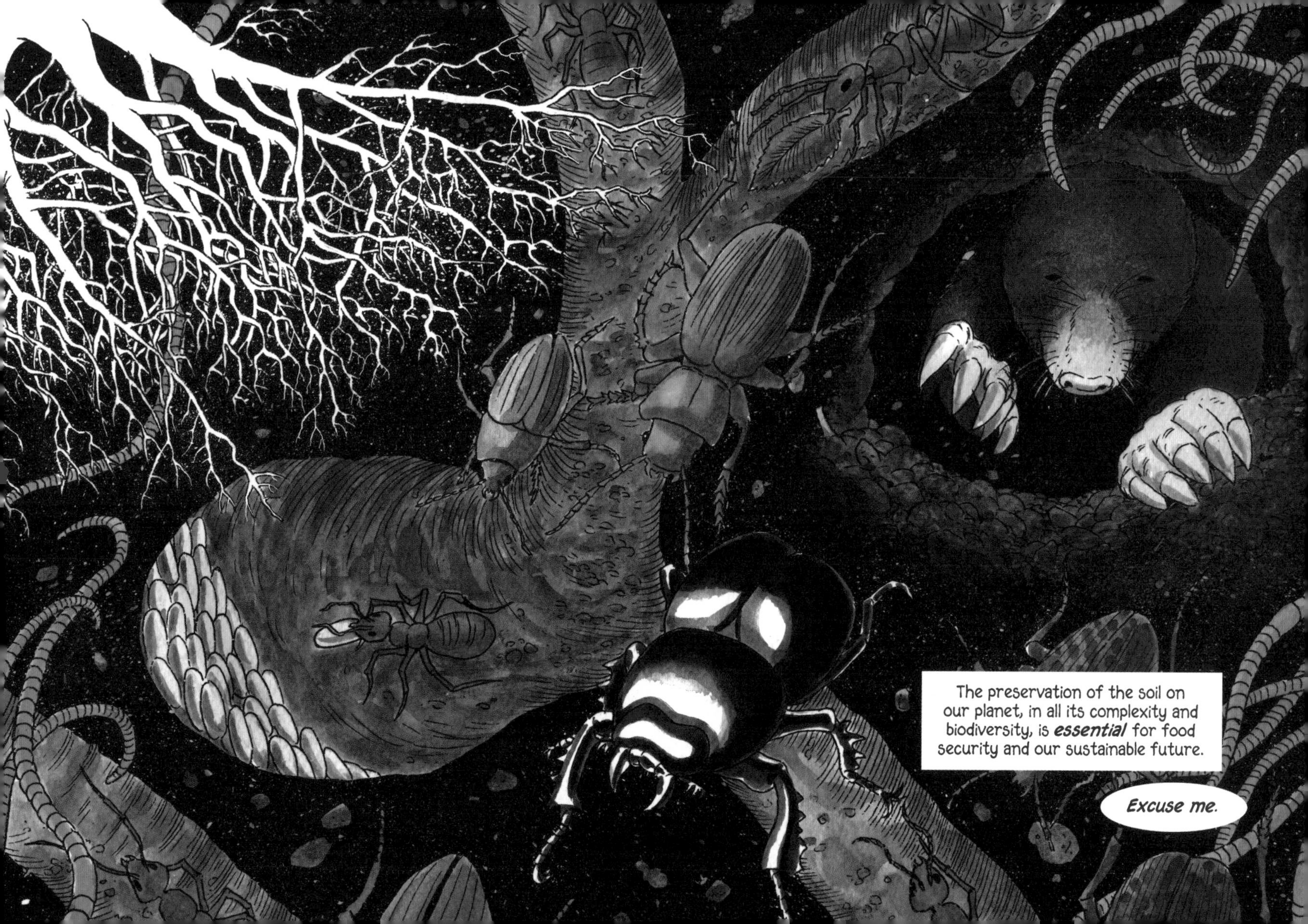
The preservation of the soil on our planet, in all its complexity and biodiversity, is *essential* for food security and our sustainable future.
Excuse me.

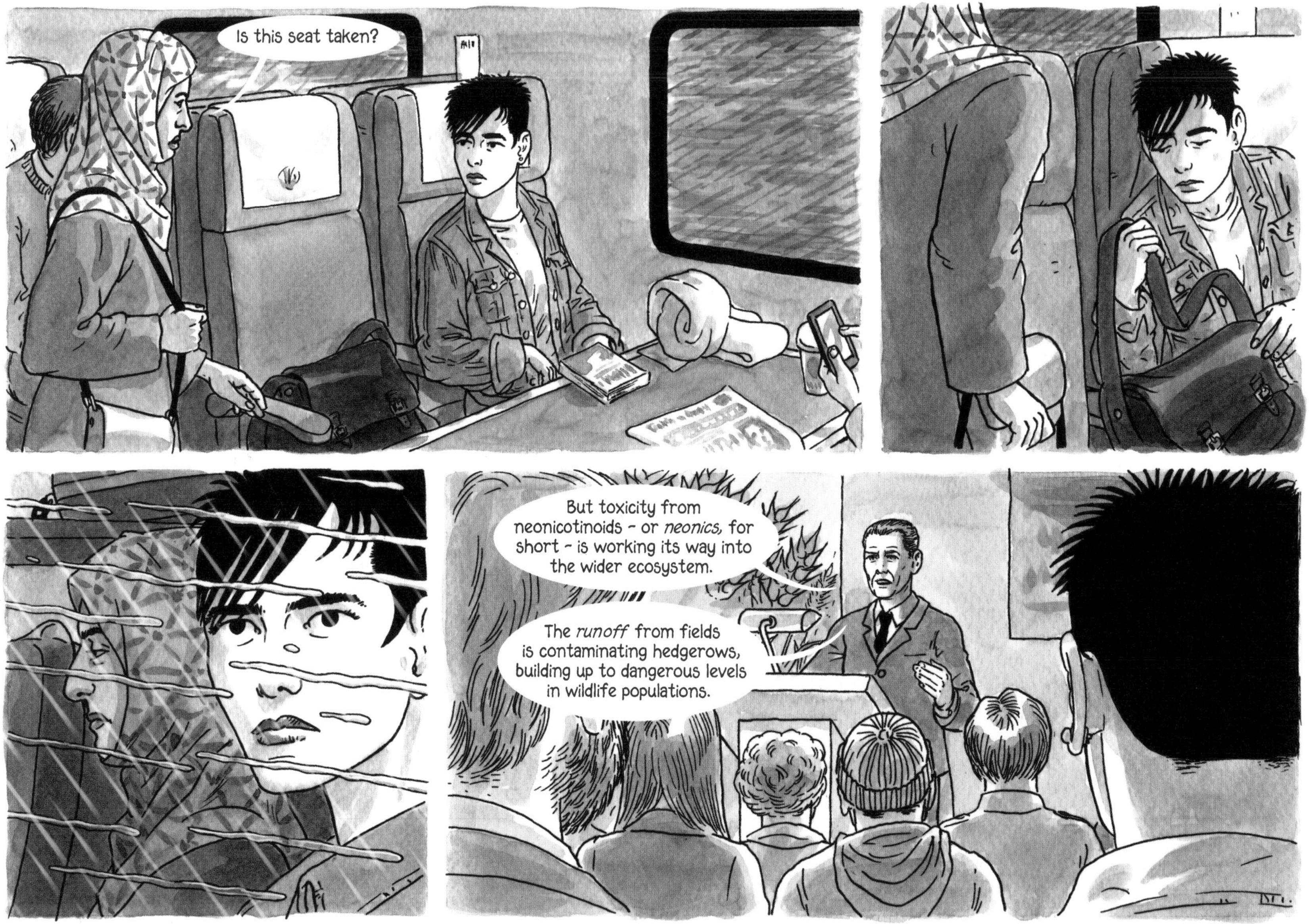

Is this seat taken?
But toxicity from neonicotinoids - or *neonics,* for short - is working its way into the wider ecosystem.
The *runoff* from fields is contaminating hedgerows, building up to dangerous levels in wildlife populations.

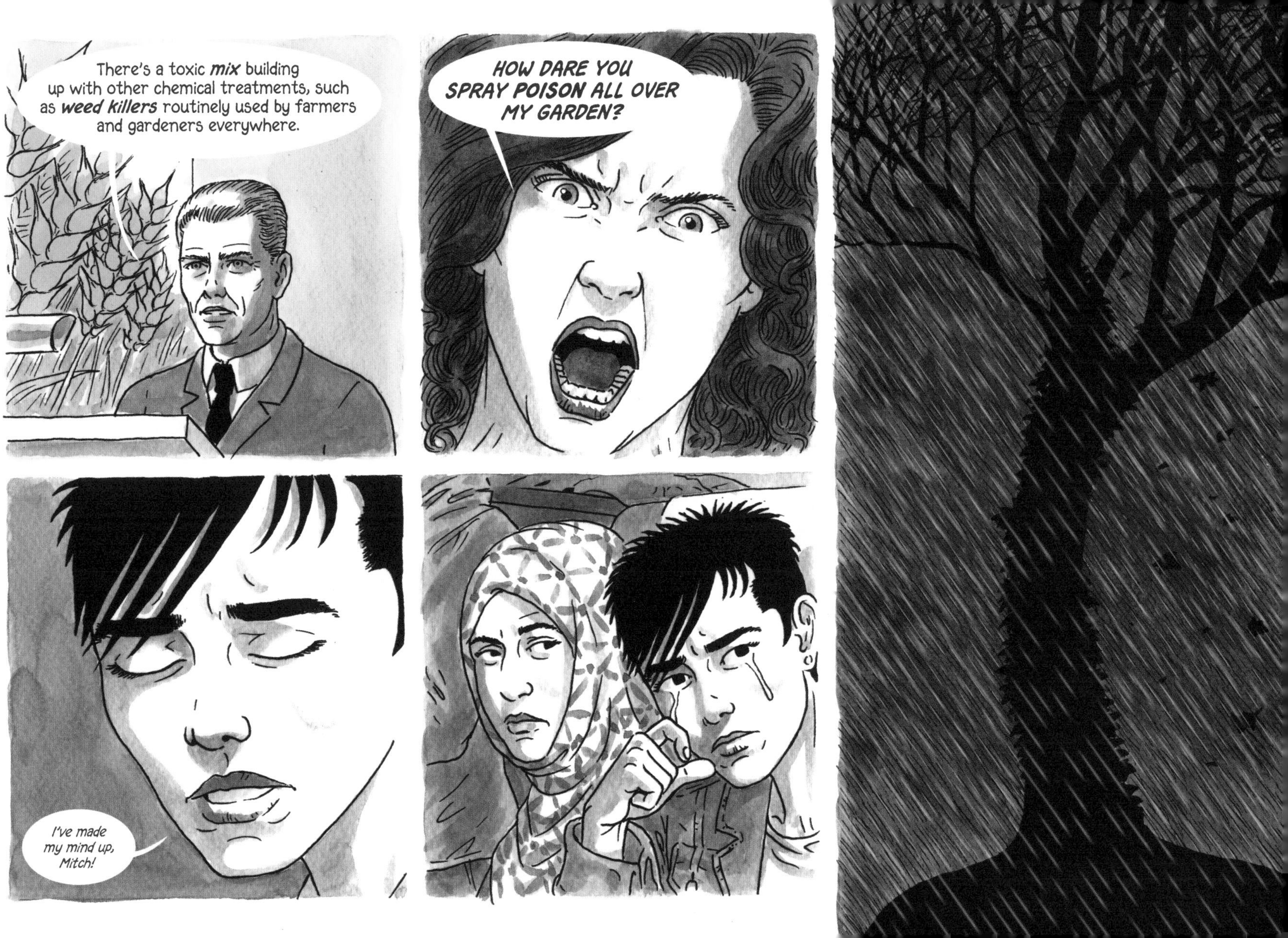
There's a toxic mix building up with other chemical treatments, such as weed killers routinely used by farmers and gardeners everywhere.
HOW DARE YOU SPRAY POISON ALL OVER MY GARDEN?
I've made my mind up, Mitch!

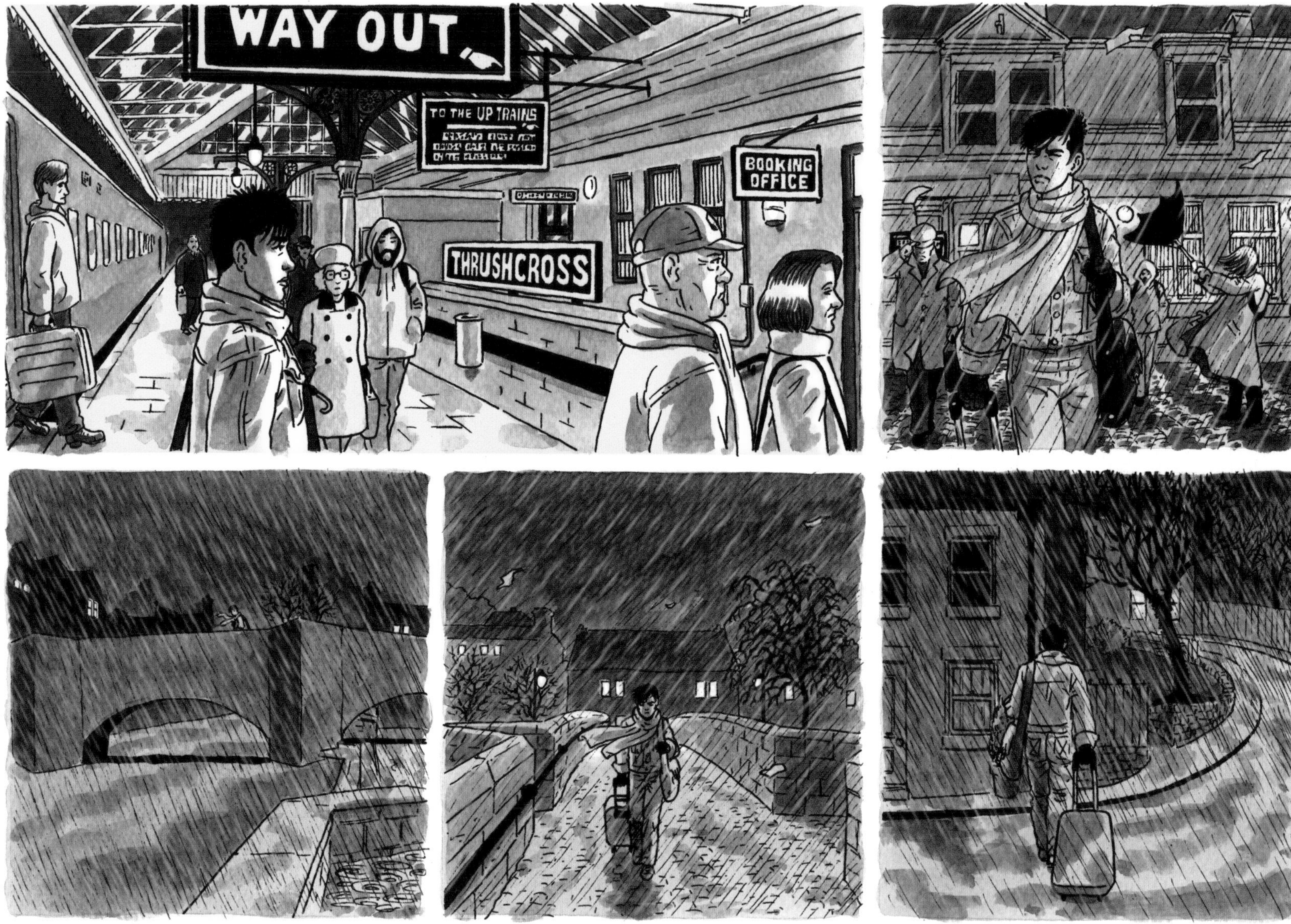
WAY OUT
TO THE UP TRAINS
BOOKING OFFICE
THRUSHCROSS

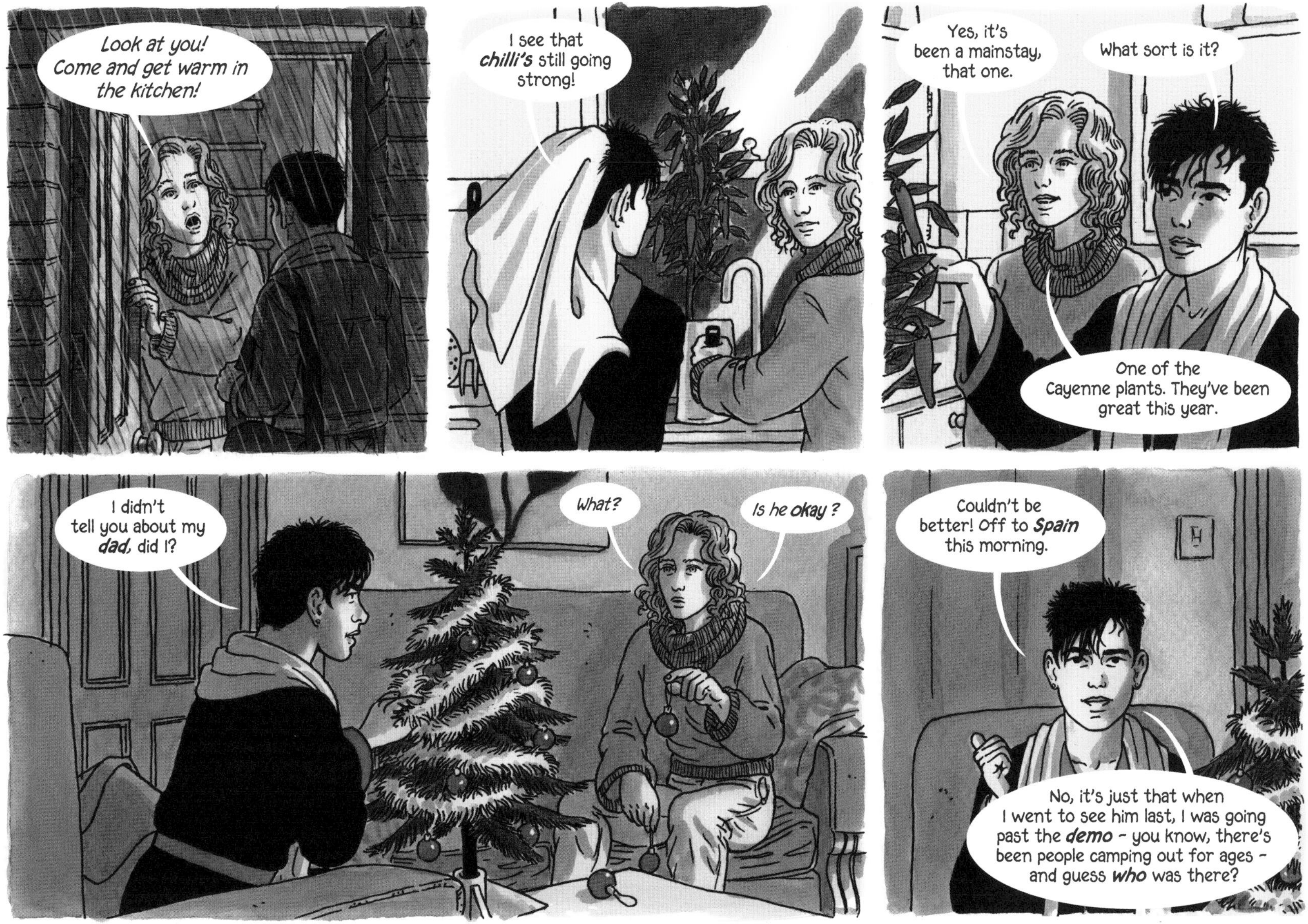
Look at you! Come and get warm in the kitchen!
I see that chilli's still going strong!
Yes, it's been a mainstay, that one.
What sort is it?
One of the Cayenne plants. They've been great this year.
I didn't tell you about my dad, did I?
What?
Is he okay?
Couldn't be better! Off to Spain this morning.
No, it's just that when I went to see him last, I was going past the demo - you know, there's been people camping out for ages - and guess who was there?

Signs: ANTI-CARBON PRO-SCIENCE / SAVE OUR WATER N... / "SAFE FRACKING" IS A FAIRY TALE / NO TO FRACKING / YOU CAN'T DRINK MONEY / SAVE OUR WATER NO FRACKING / THEY GET RICH YOU GET CANCER

Signs: OUR WATER NO RACKING / T RICH GET CER

My *dad!*

Woah. You know the government's not working when *granddad* starts to riot!

He's not my granddad.

Well, *you know.*

Cheers!

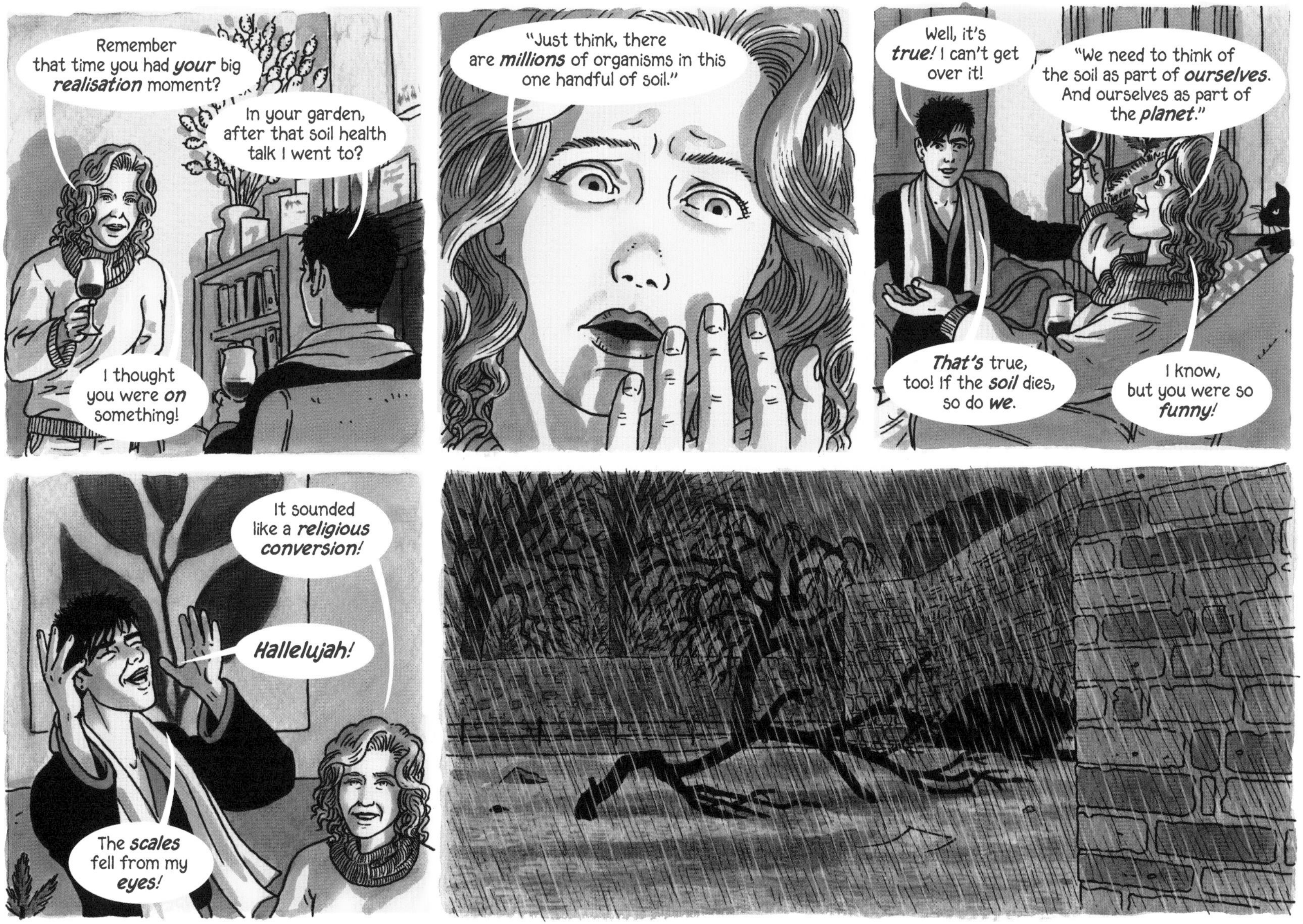
Remember that time you had your big realisation moment?
In your garden, after that soil health talk I went to?
I thought you were on something!
"Just think, there are millions of organisms in this one handful of soil."
Well, it's true! I can't get over it!
"We need to think of the soil as part of ourselves. And ourselves as part of the planet."
That's true, too! If the soil dies, so do we.
I know, but you were so funny!
It sounded like a religious conversion!
Hallelujah!
The scales fell from my eyes!

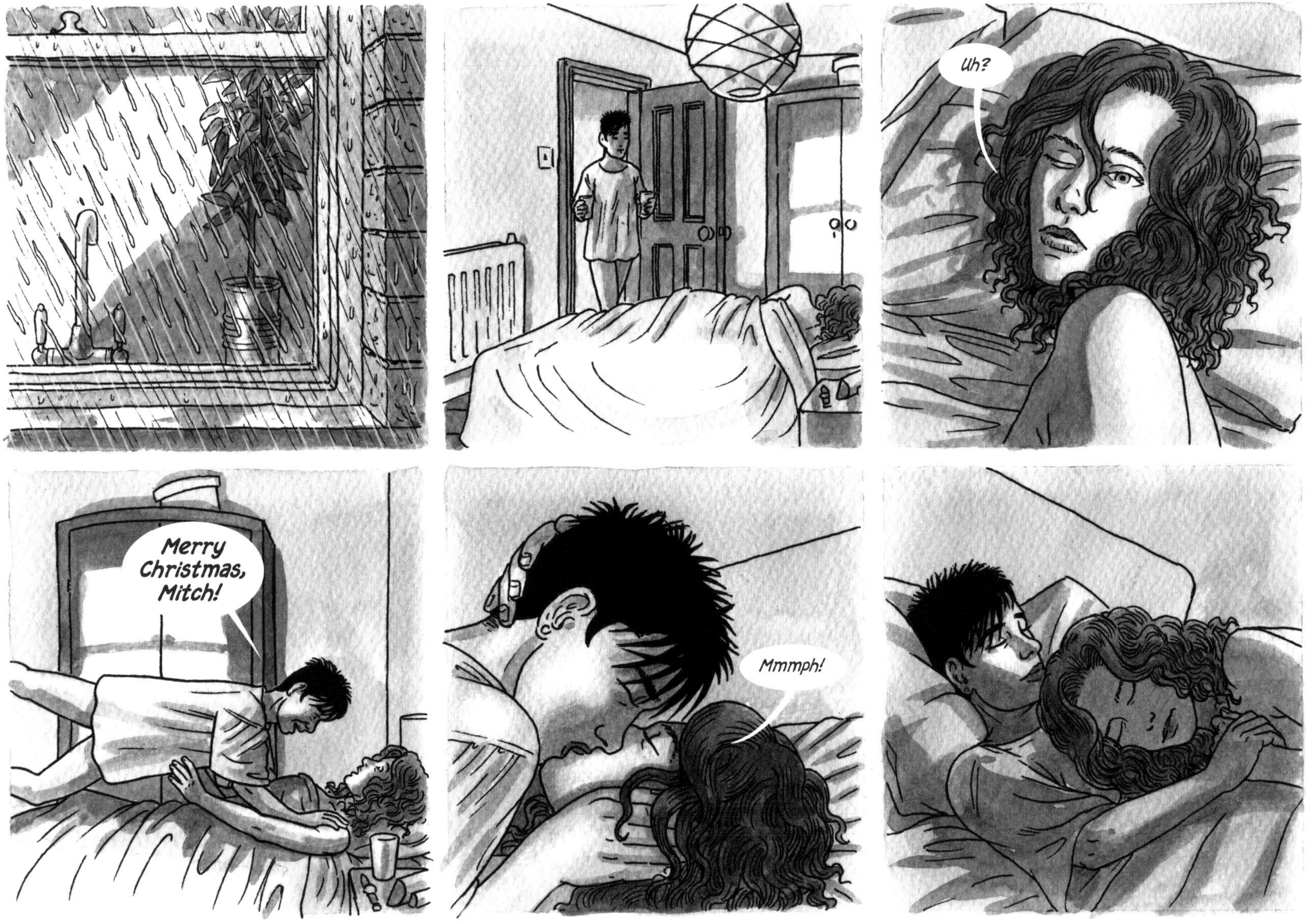
Uh?
Merry Christmas, Mitch!
Mmmph!

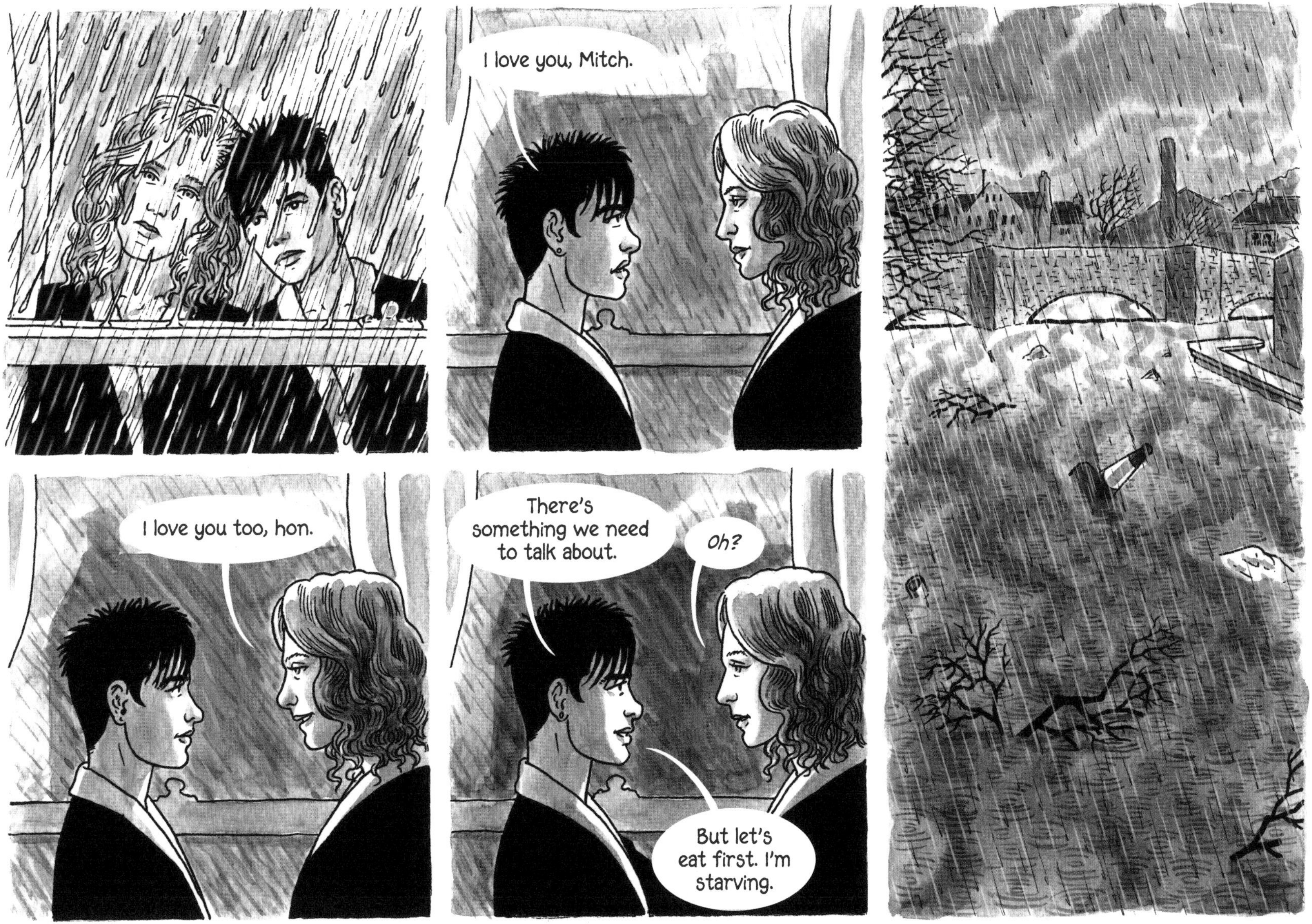
I love you, Mitch.
I love you too, hon.
There's something we need to talk about.
Oh?
But let's eat first. I'm starving.

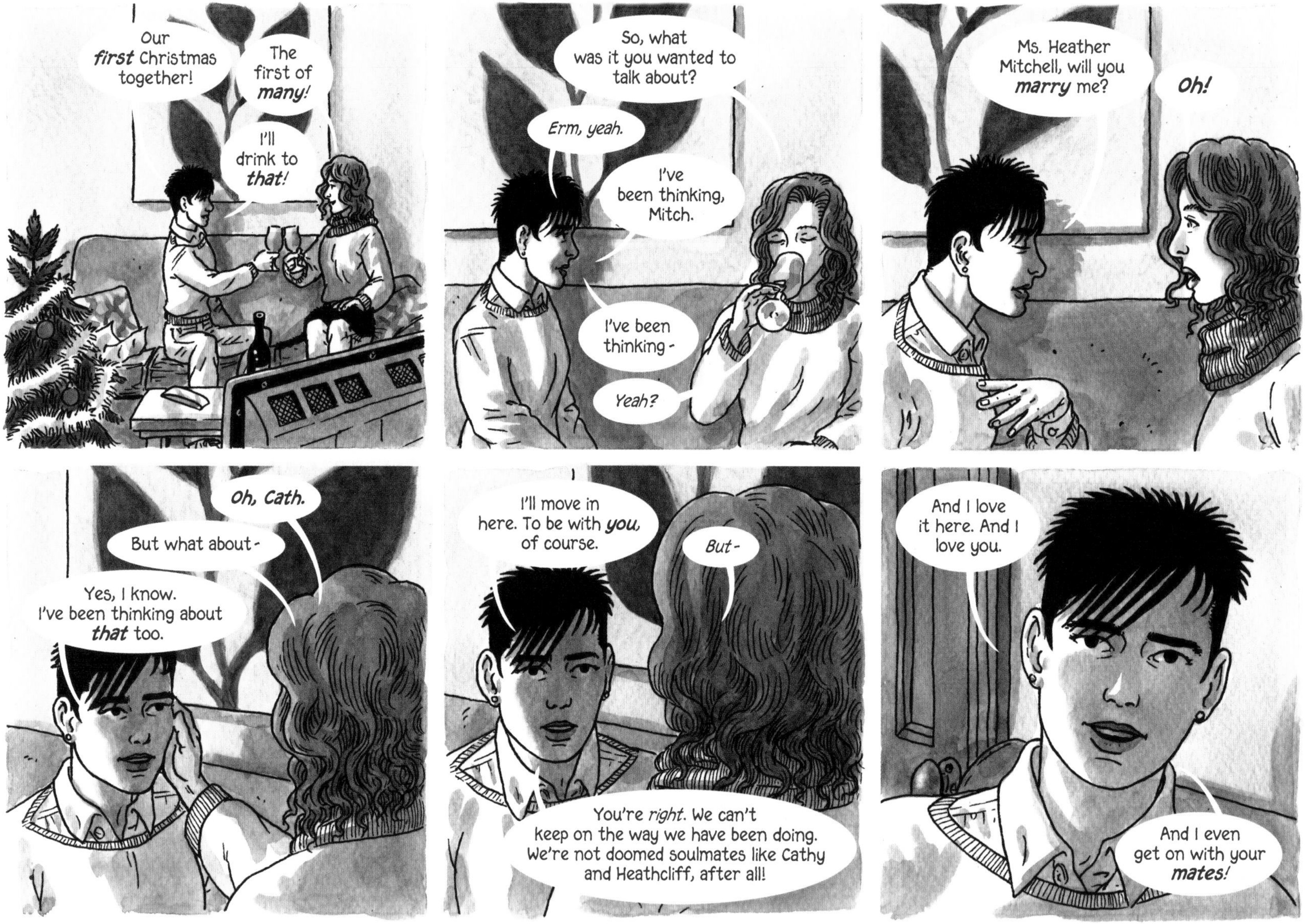
Our *first* Christmas together!
The first of *many!*
I'll drink to *that!*
So, what was it you wanted to talk about?
Erm, yeah.
I've been thinking, Mitch.
I've been thinking -
Yeah?
Ms. Heather Mitchell, will you *marry* me?
Oh!
Oh, Cath.
But what about -
Yes, I know. I've been thinking about *that* too.
I'll move in here. To be with *you*, of course.
But -
You're *right*. We can't keep on the way we have been doing. We're not doomed soulmates like Cathy and Heathcliff, after all!
And I love it here. And I love you.
And I even get on with your *mates!*

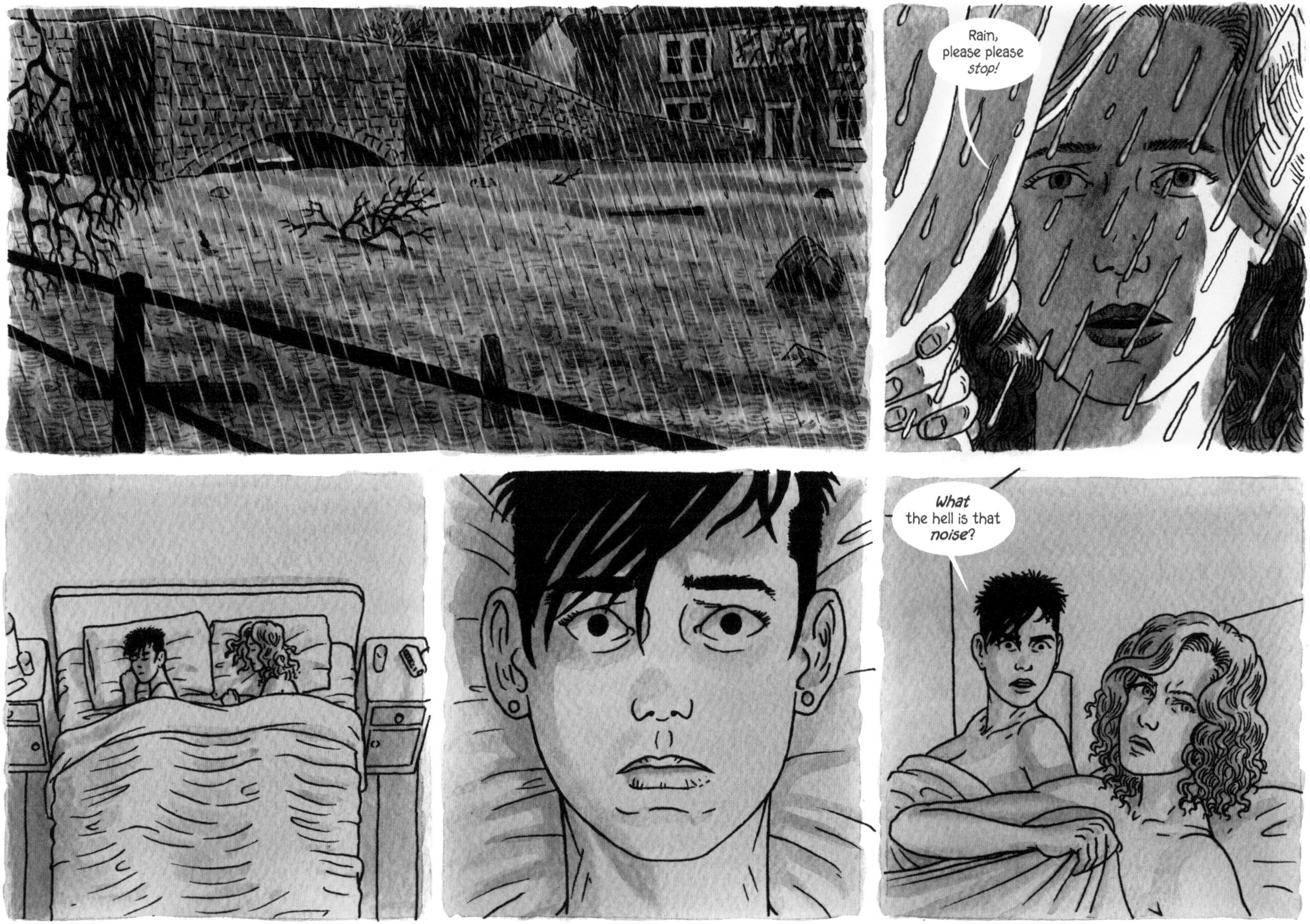
Rain, please please *stop!*
What the hell is that *noise*?

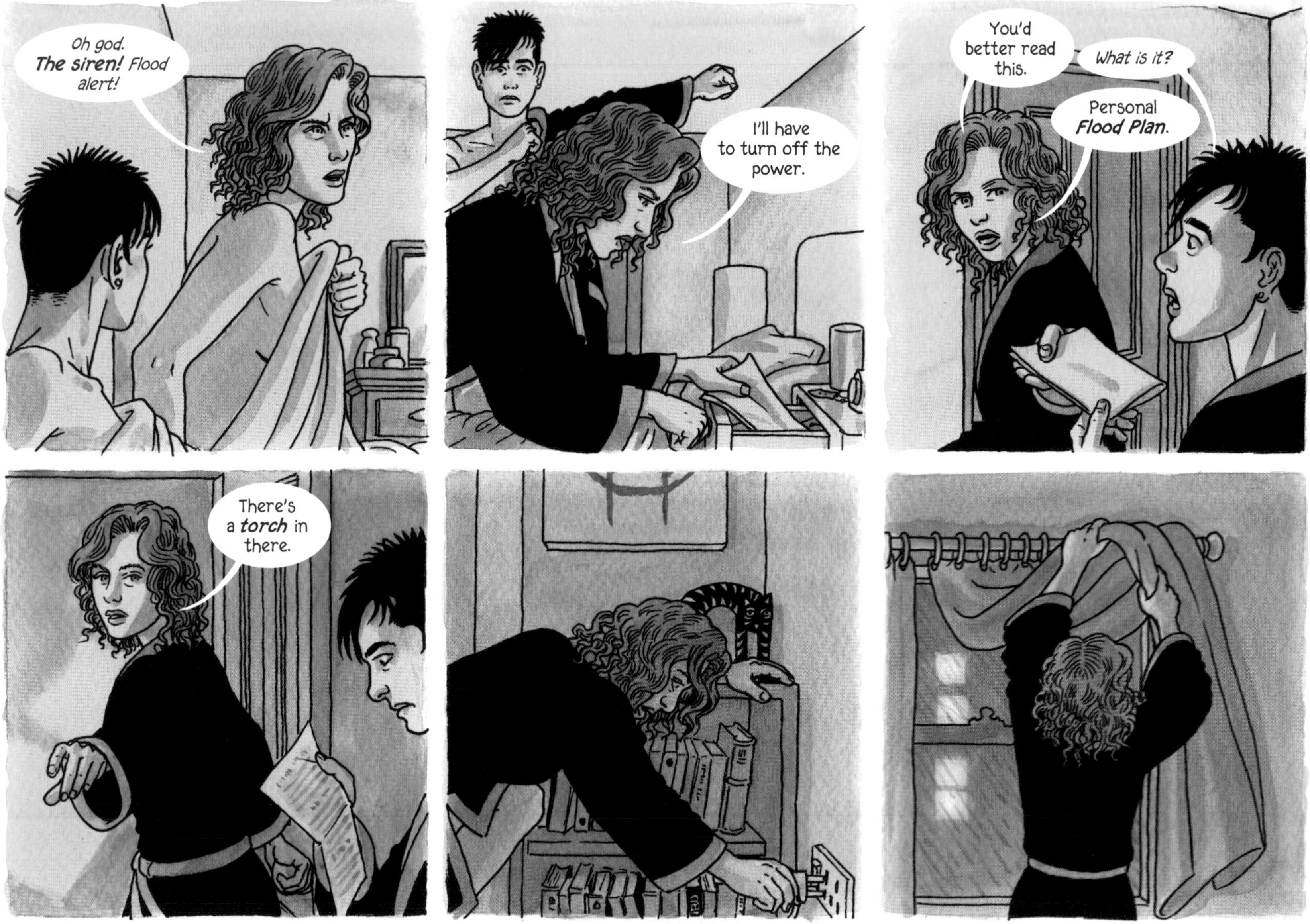
Oh god. **The siren!** Flood alert!
I'll have to turn off the power.
You'd better read this.
What is it?
Personal **Flood Plan**.
There's a **torch** in there.

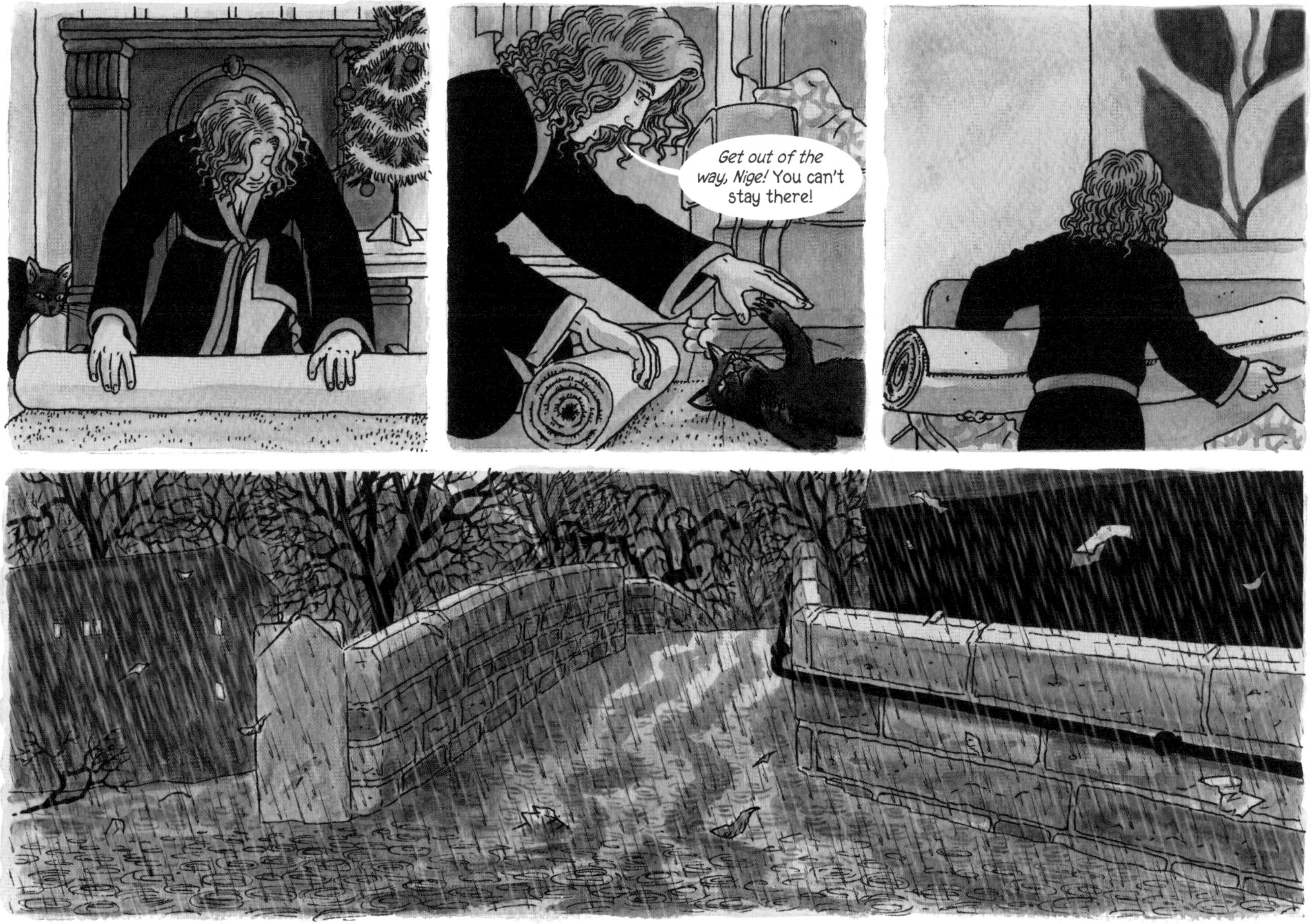
Get out of the way, Nige! You can't stay there!

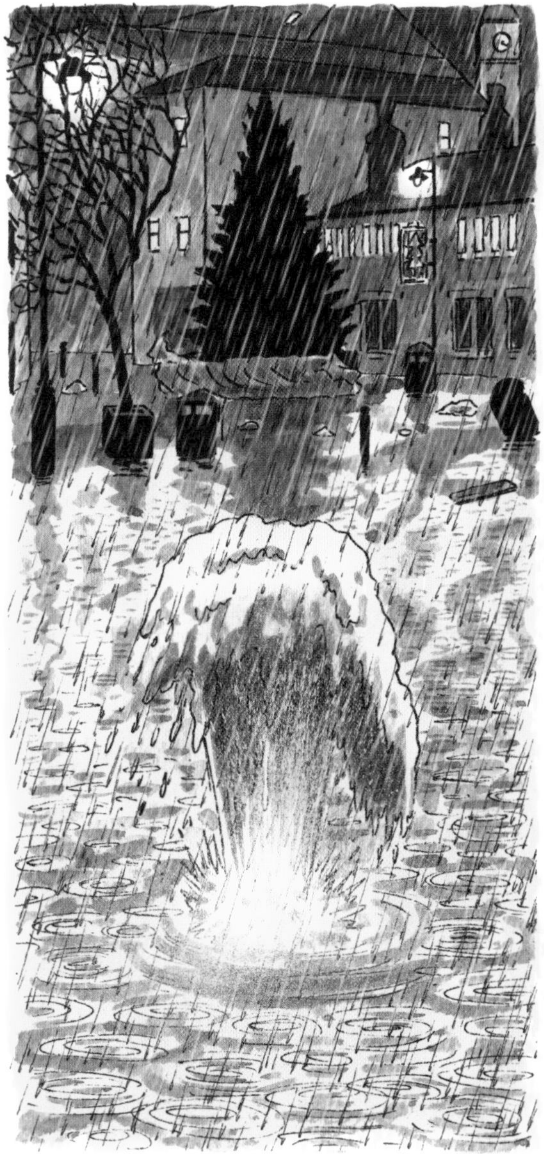

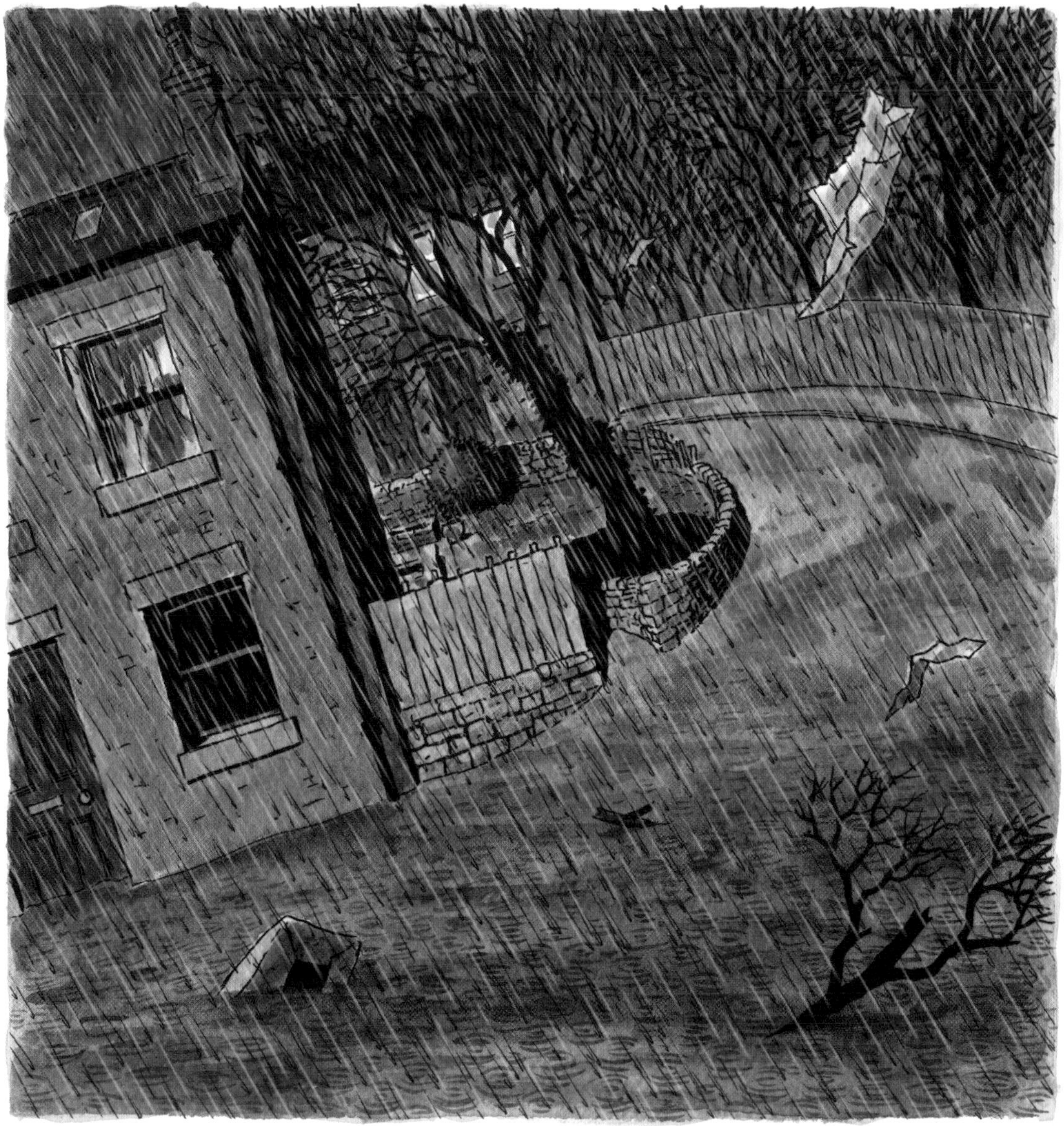

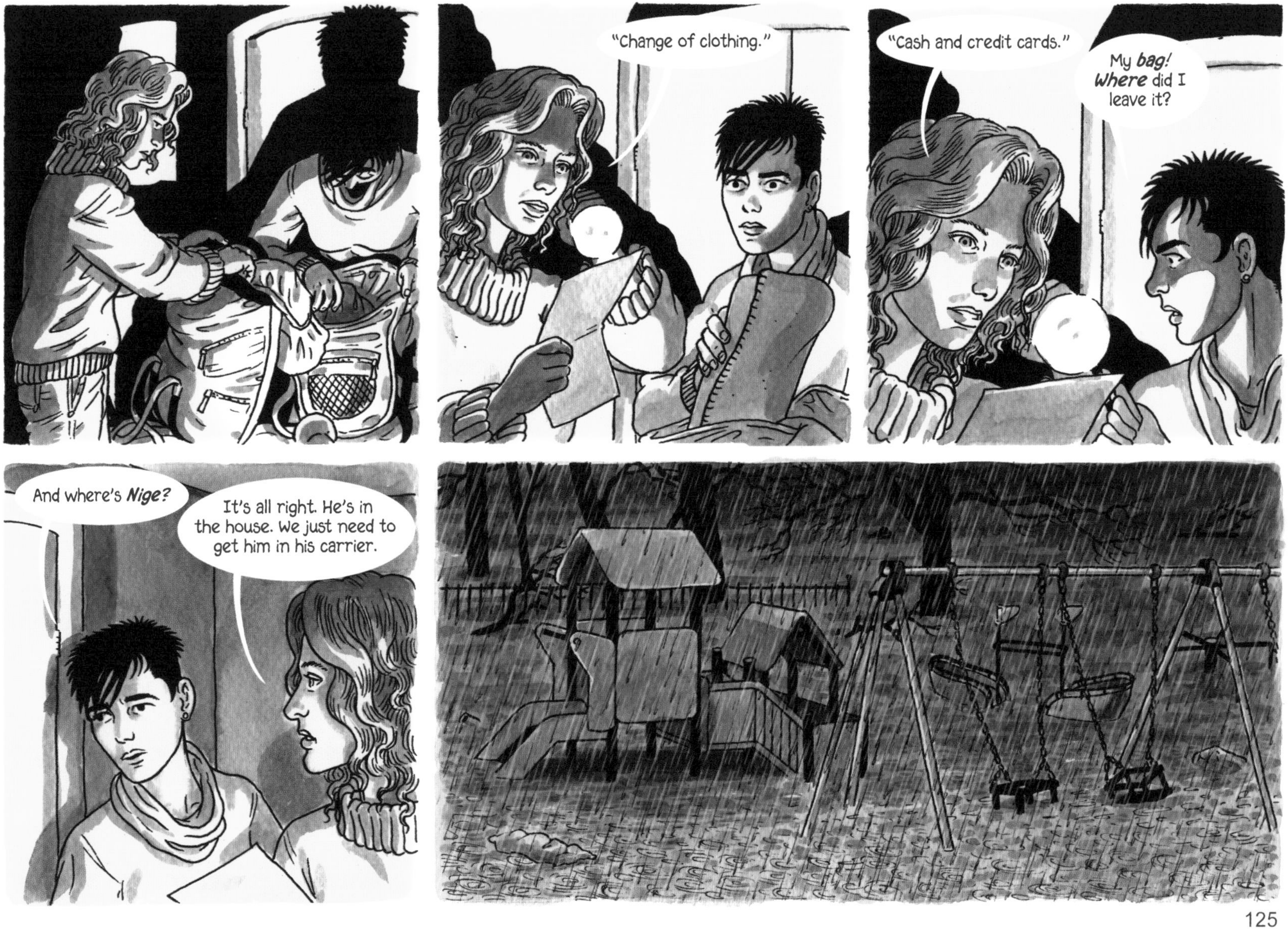
"Change of clothing."
"Cash and credit cards."
My *bag!* *Where* did I leave it?
And where's *Nige?*
It's all right. He's in the house. We just need to get him in his carrier.

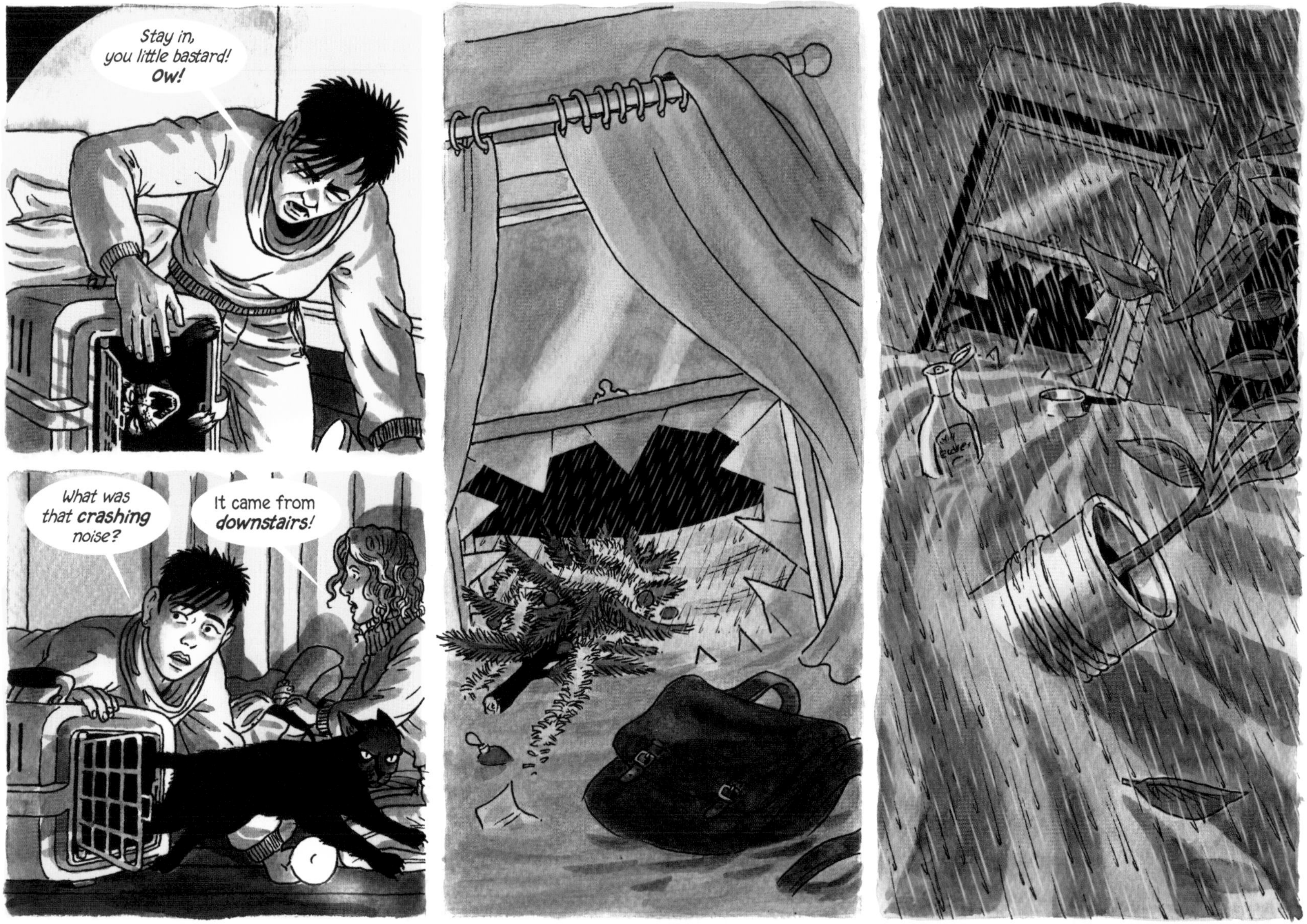
Stay in, you little bastard! **Ow!**
What was that **crashing** noise?
It came from **downstairs!**

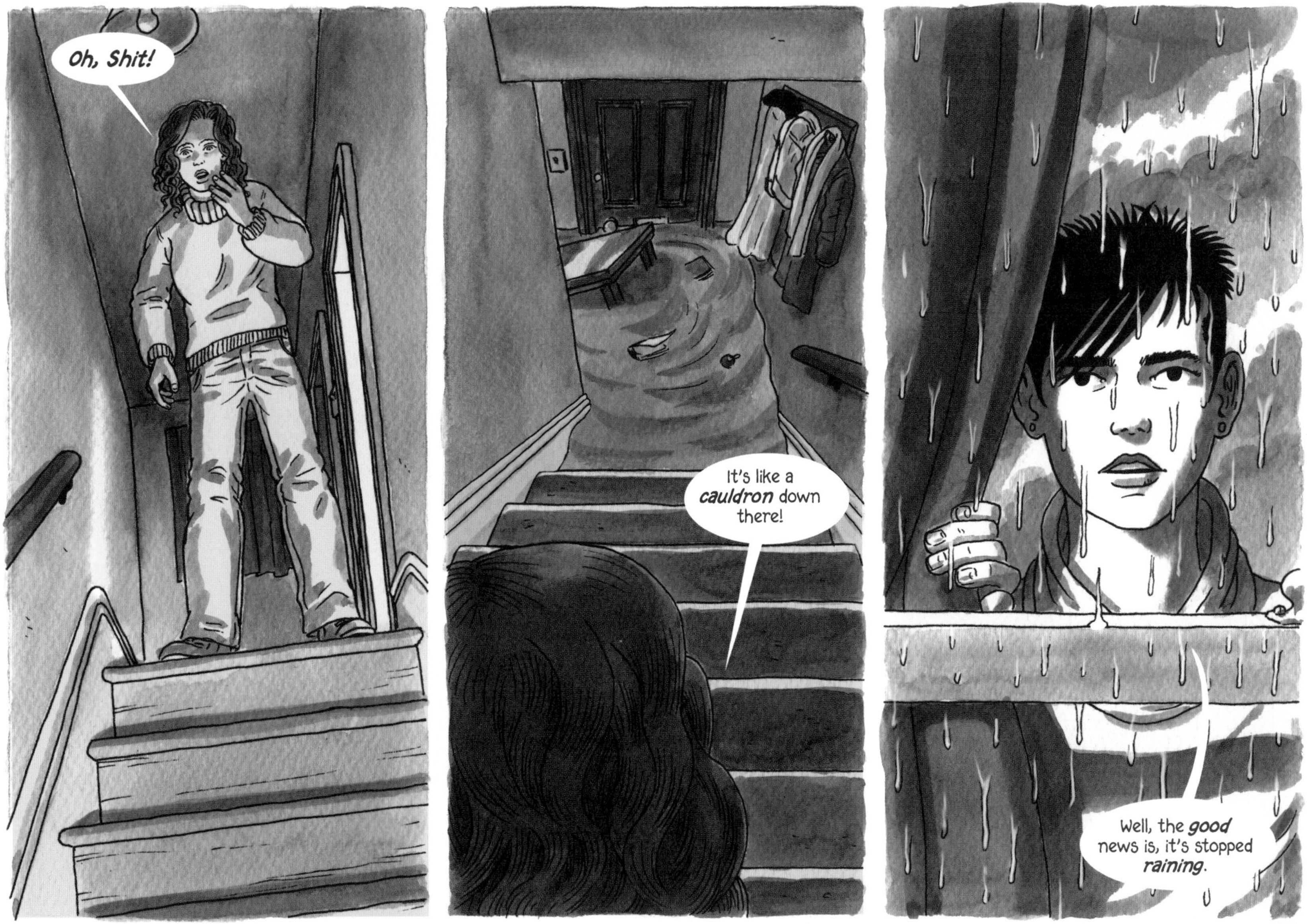
Oh, Shit!
It's like a cauldron down there!
Well, the good news is, it's stopped raining.

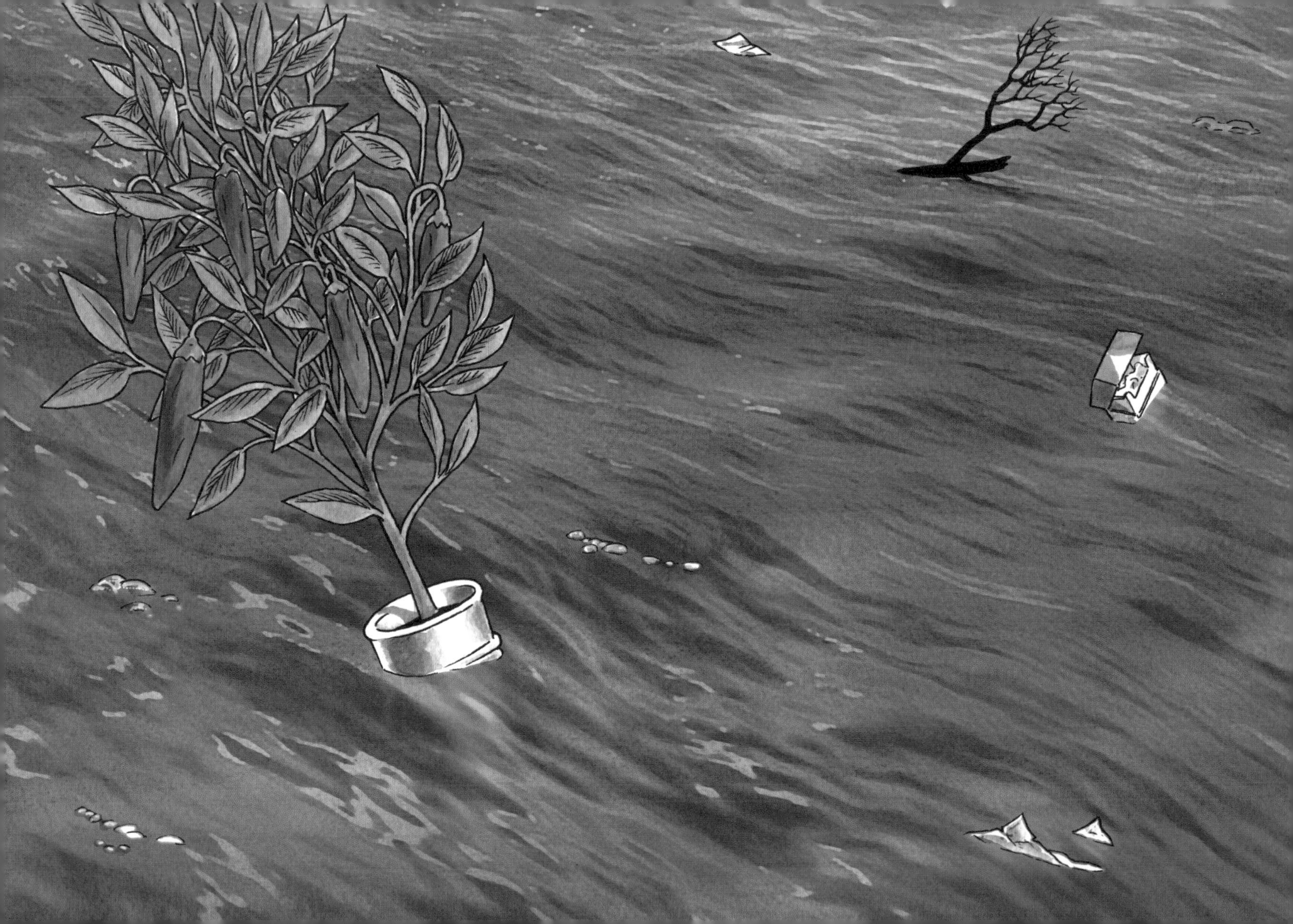

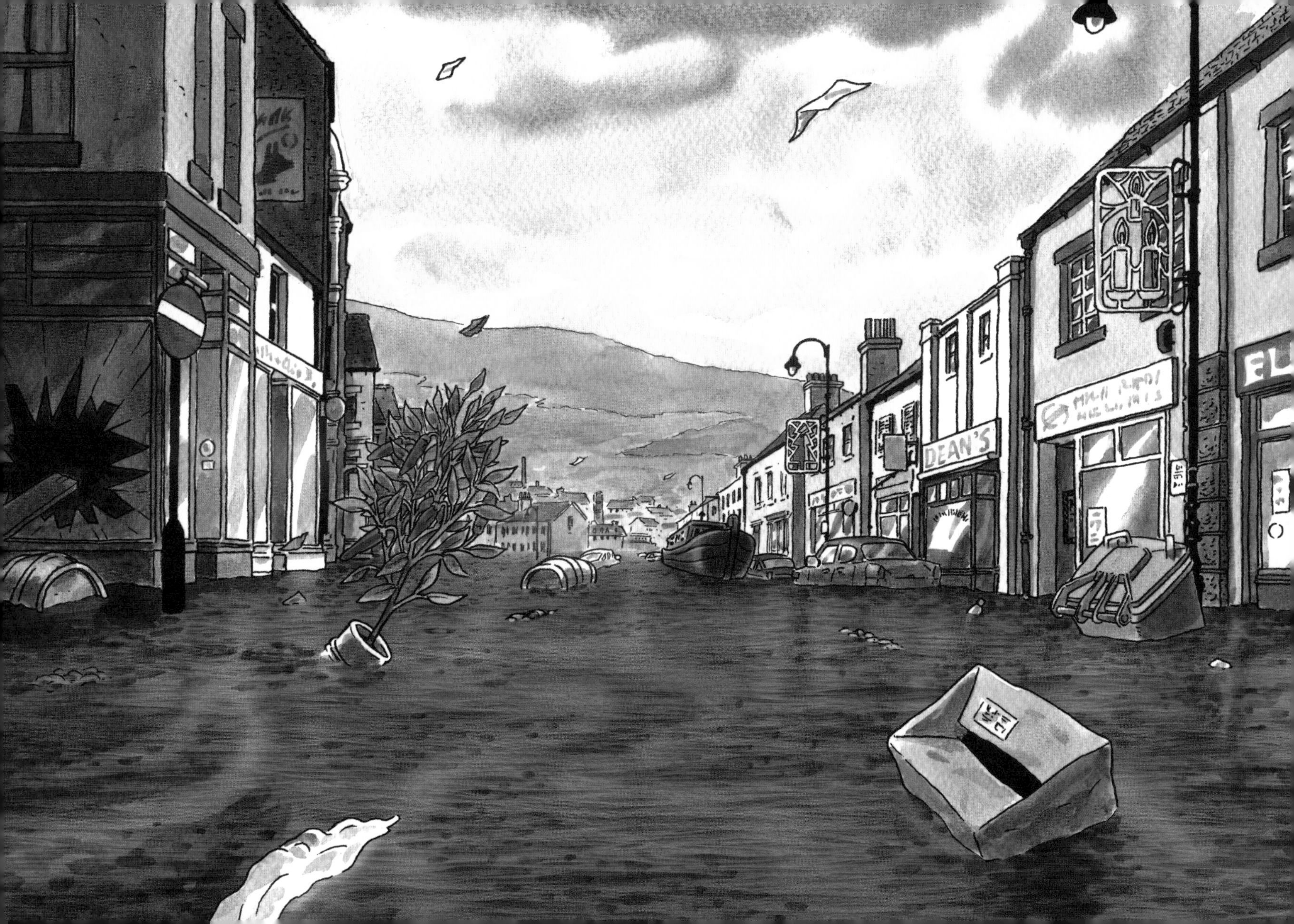
DEAN'S

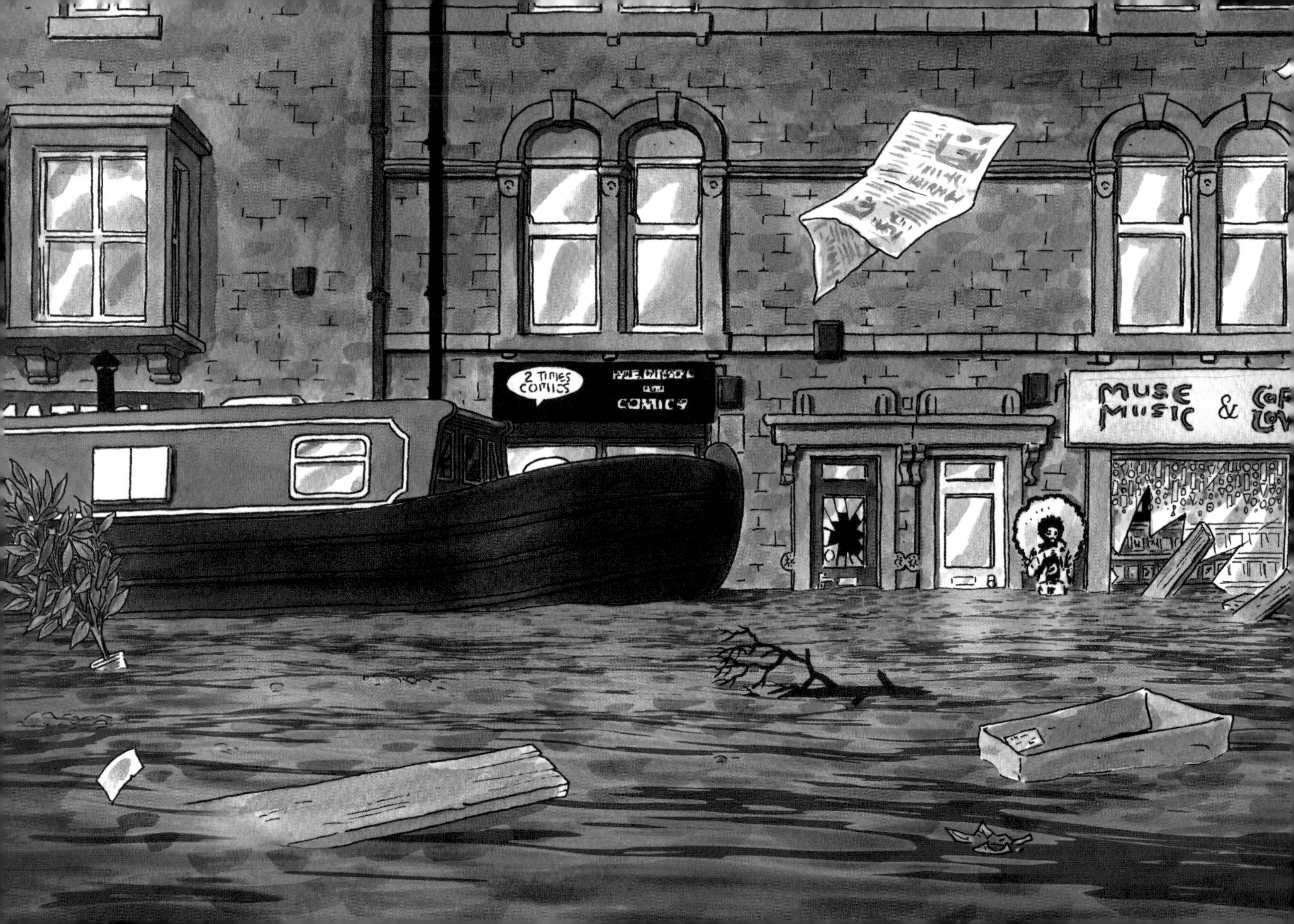
2 TIMES COMICS
MUSE MUSIC &

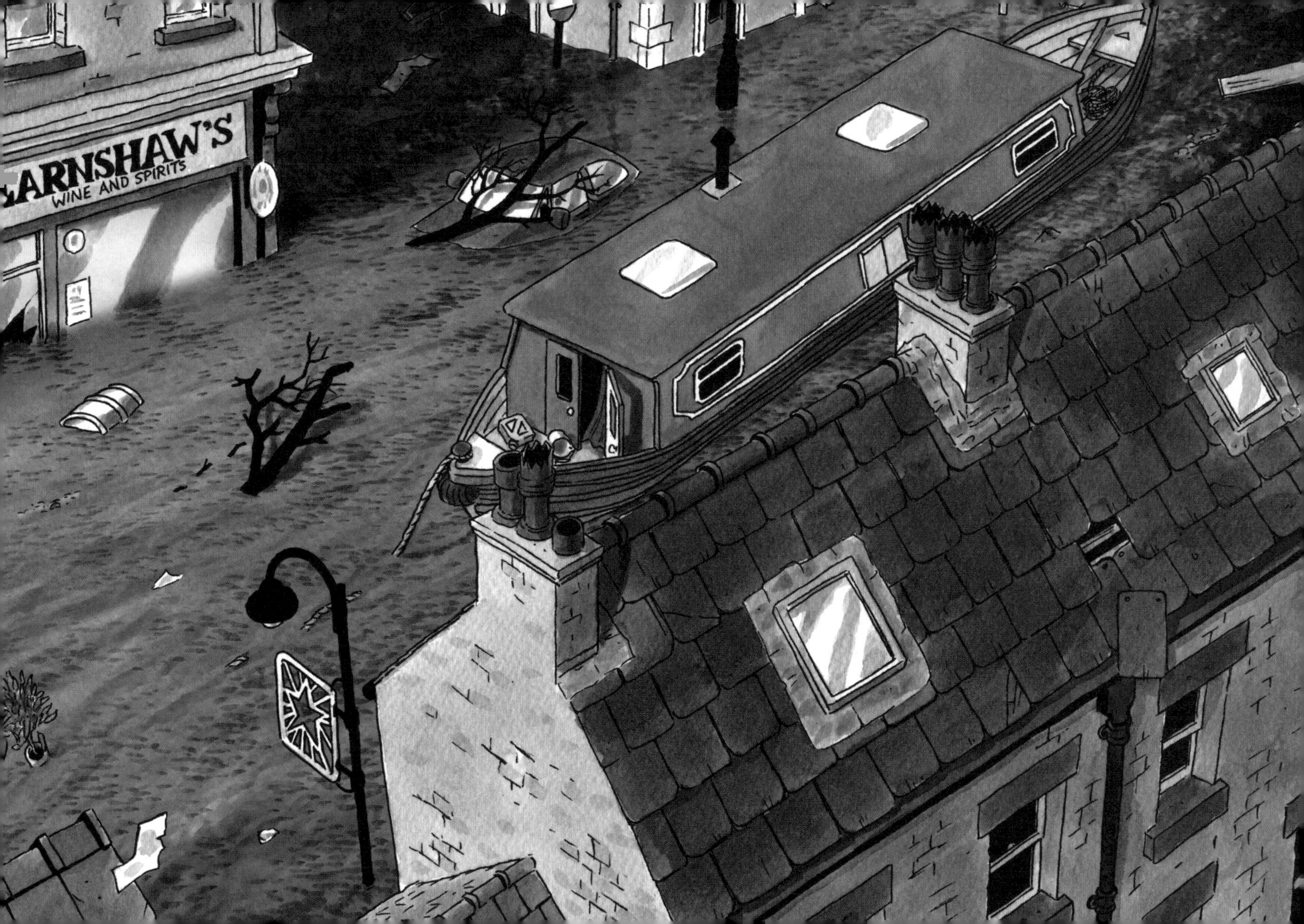

EARNSHAW'S
WINE AND SPIRITS

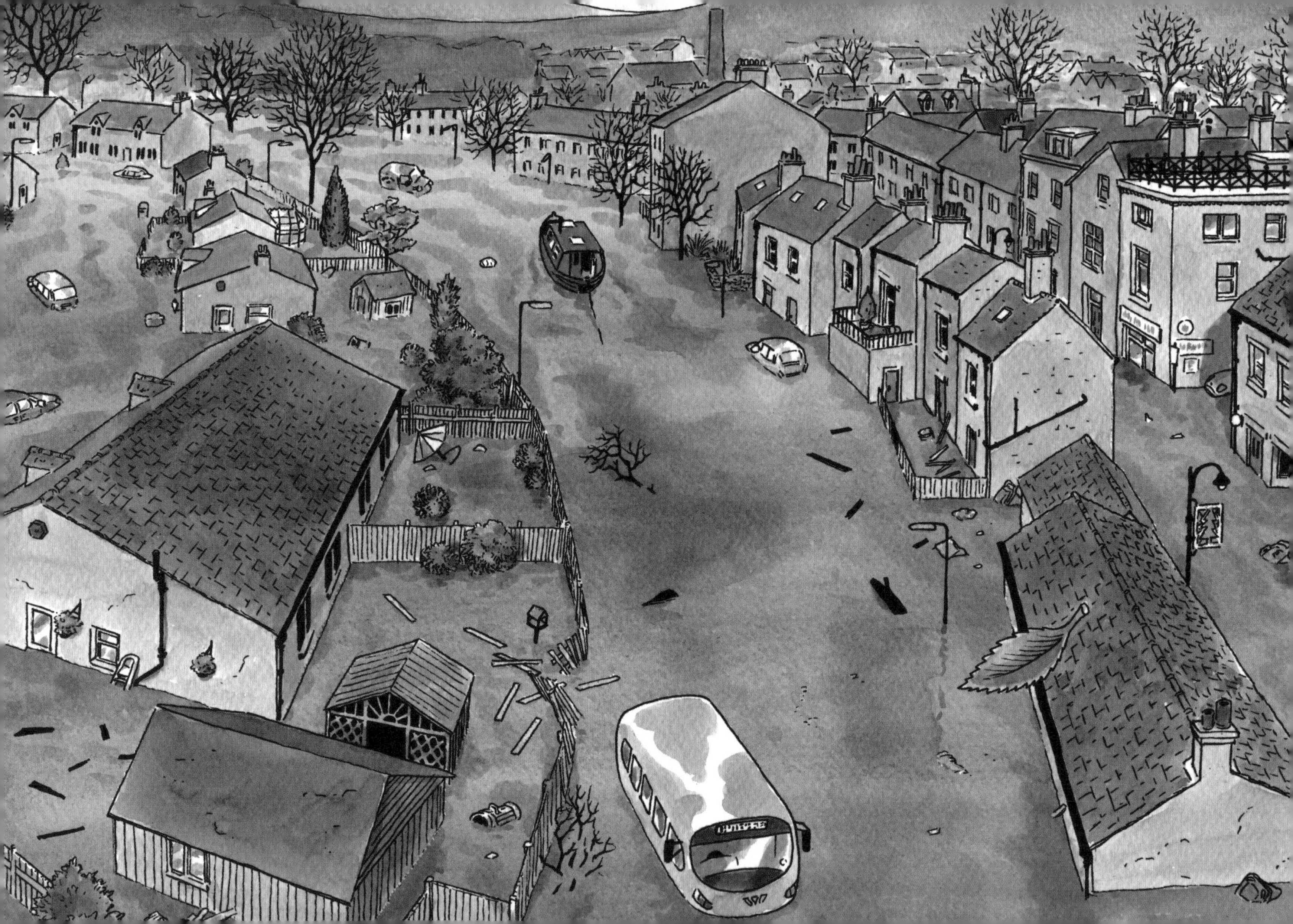

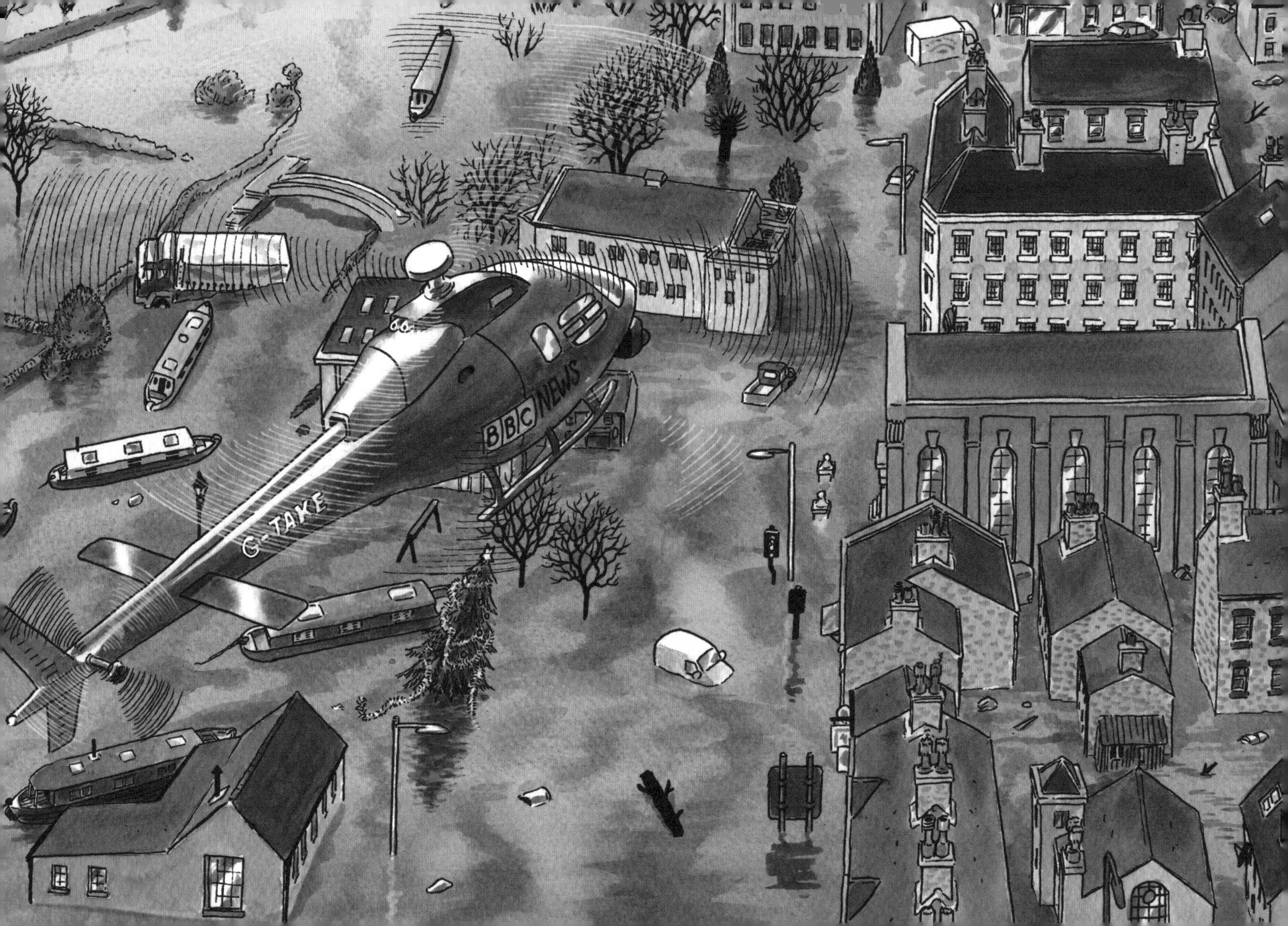
BBC NEWS
G-TAKE

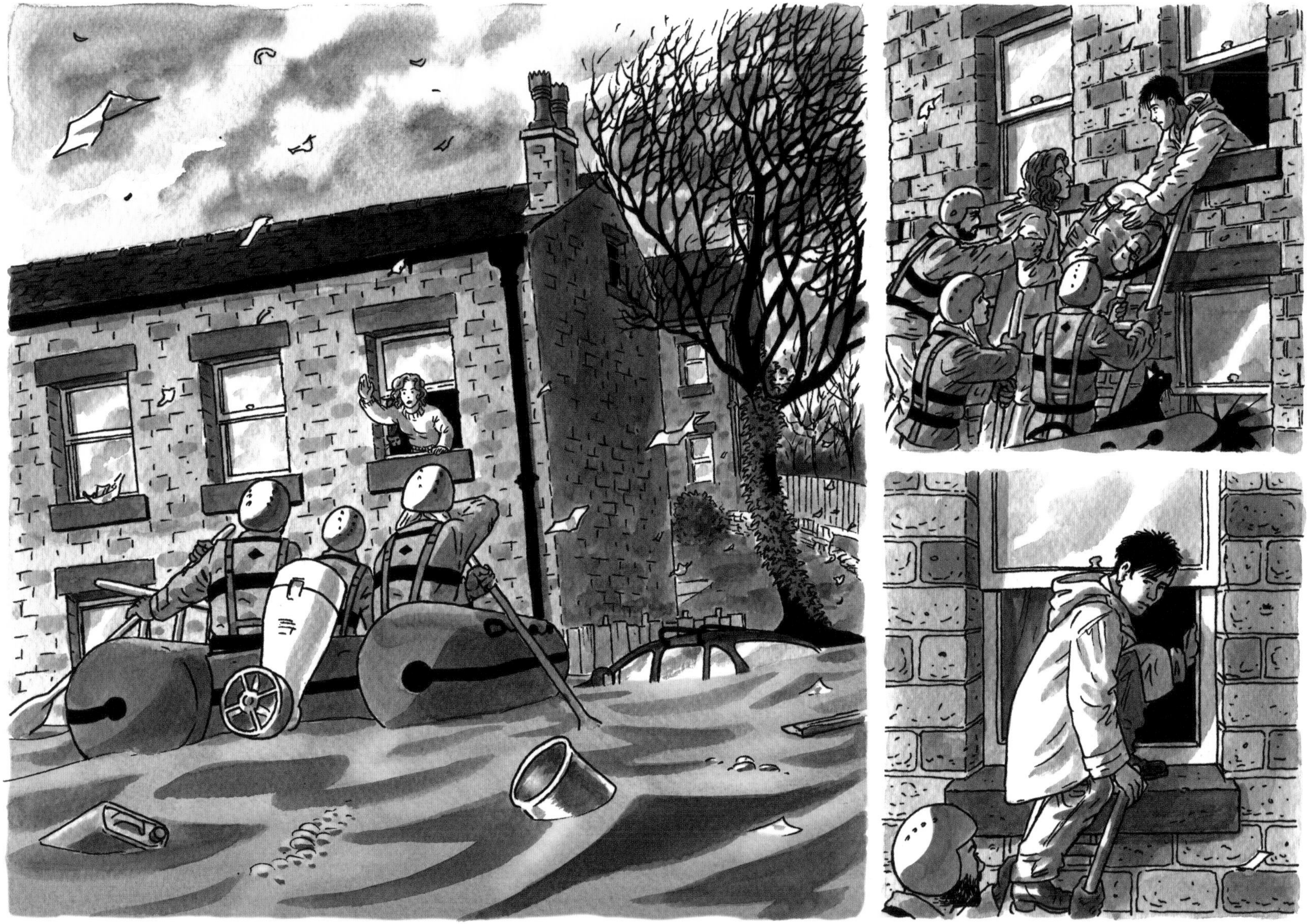

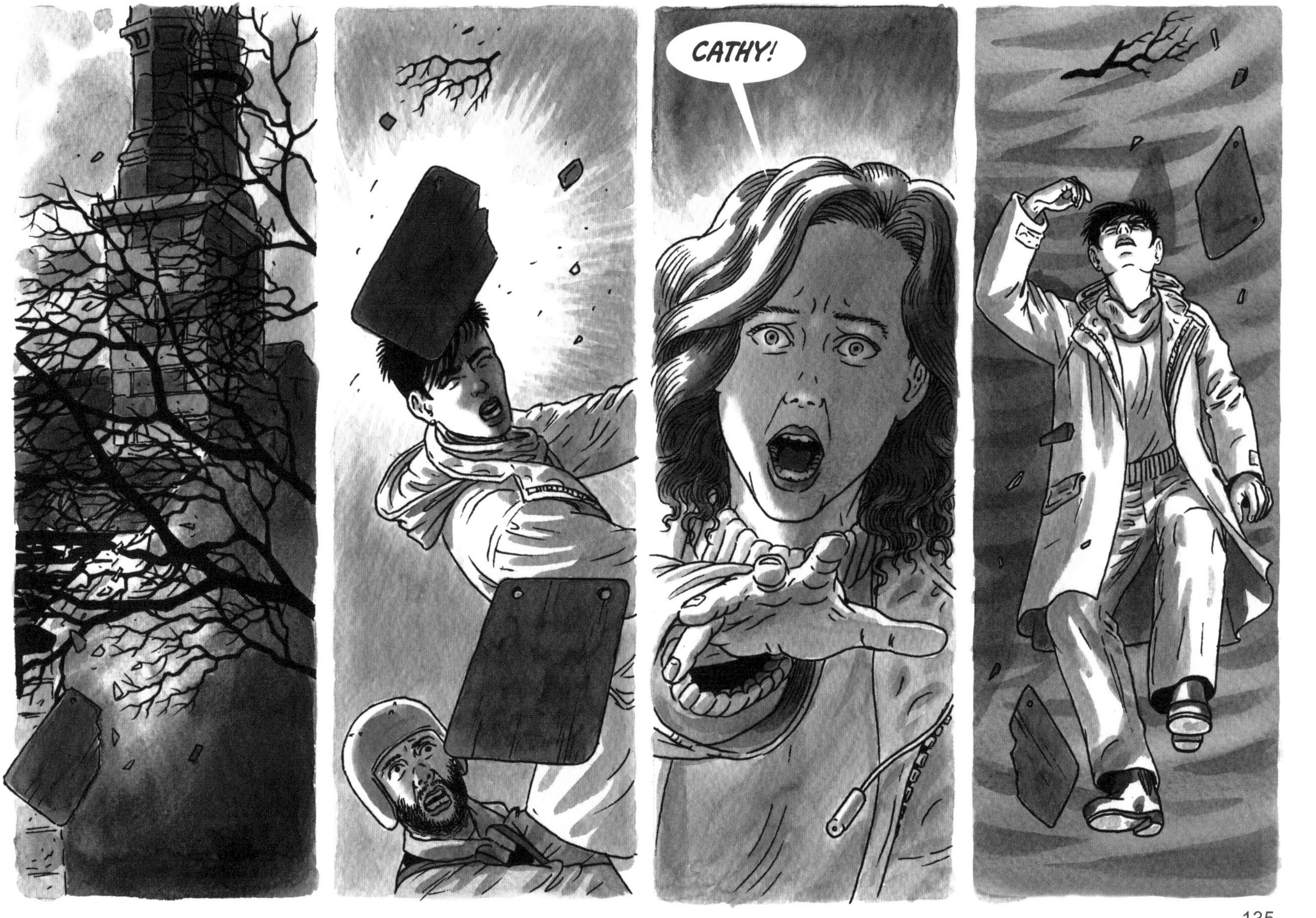
CATHY!

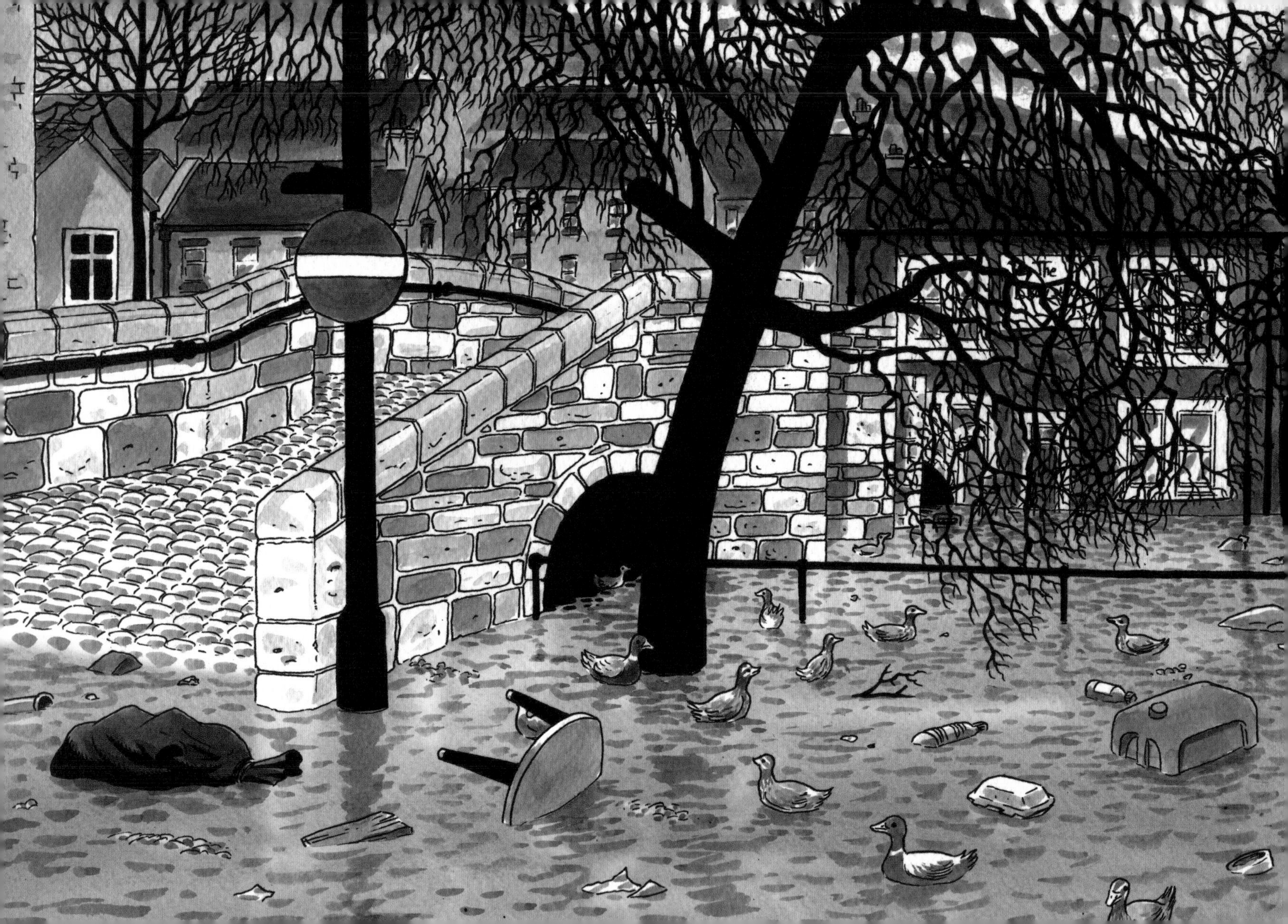
The

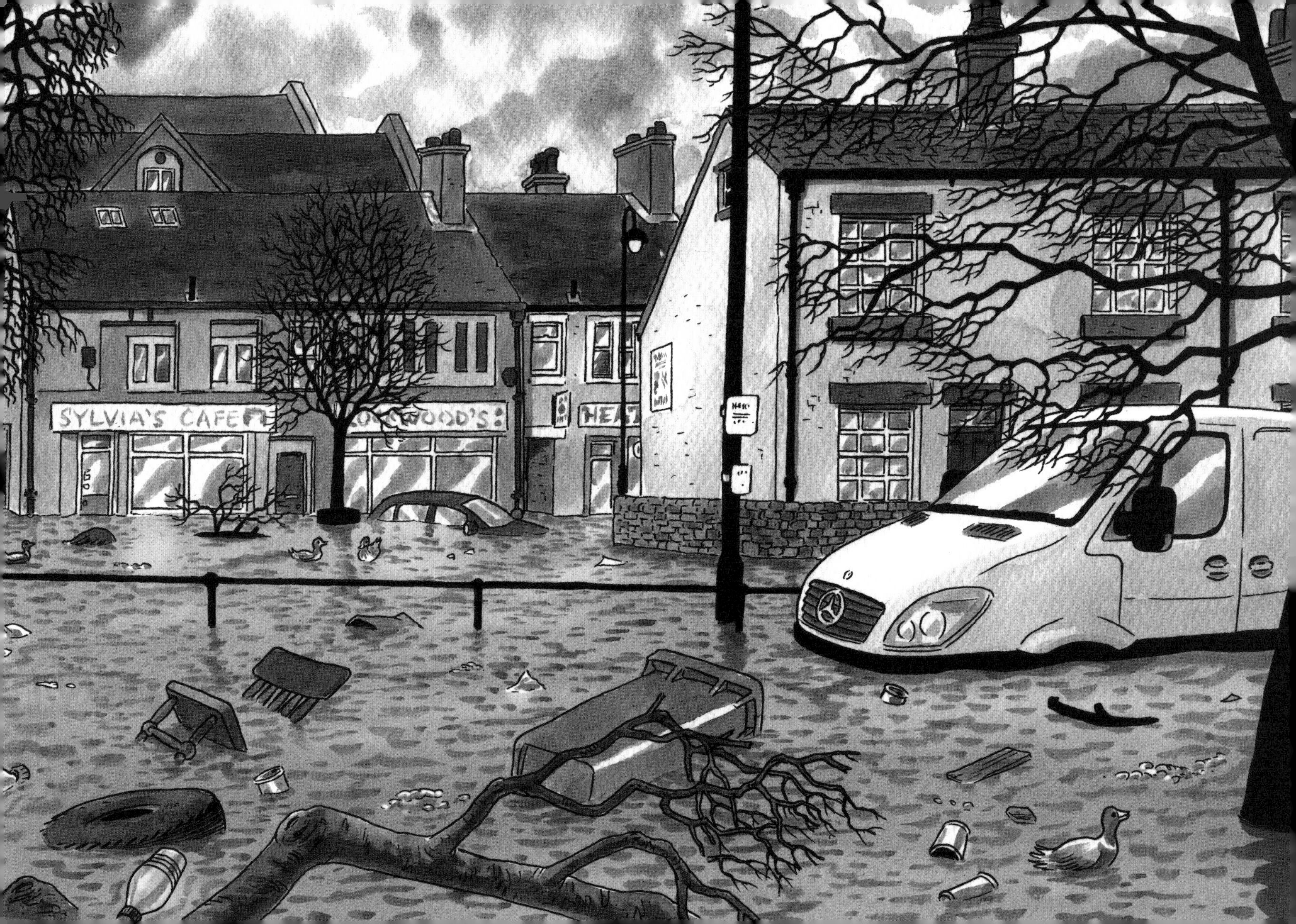
SYLVIA'S CAFE

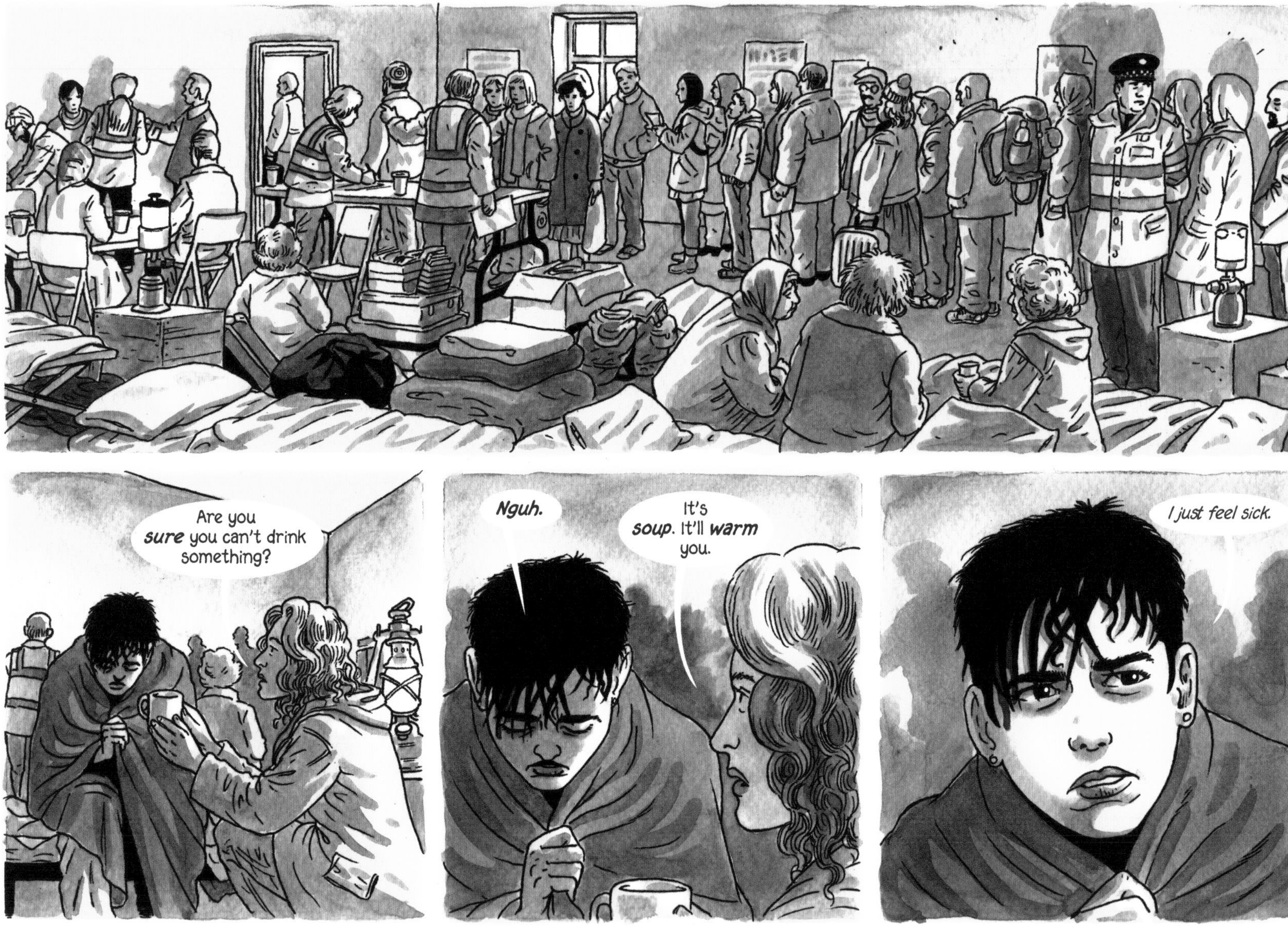
Are you sure you can't drink something?
Nguh.
It's soup. It'll warm you.
I just feel sick.

Oh, *Cath*, you must have caught something from that foul water.

Did you *swallow* some of it?

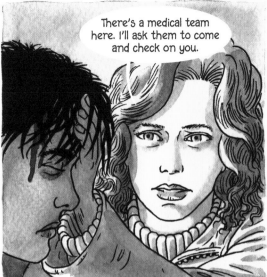

There's a medical team here. I'll ask them to come and check on you.

Ey up, fancy a *samosa,* love?

Ooh! I'd *love* one!

How about your friend?

Er, not just *now*.

Bit *poorly,* is she?

Here. She'll be dehydrated.

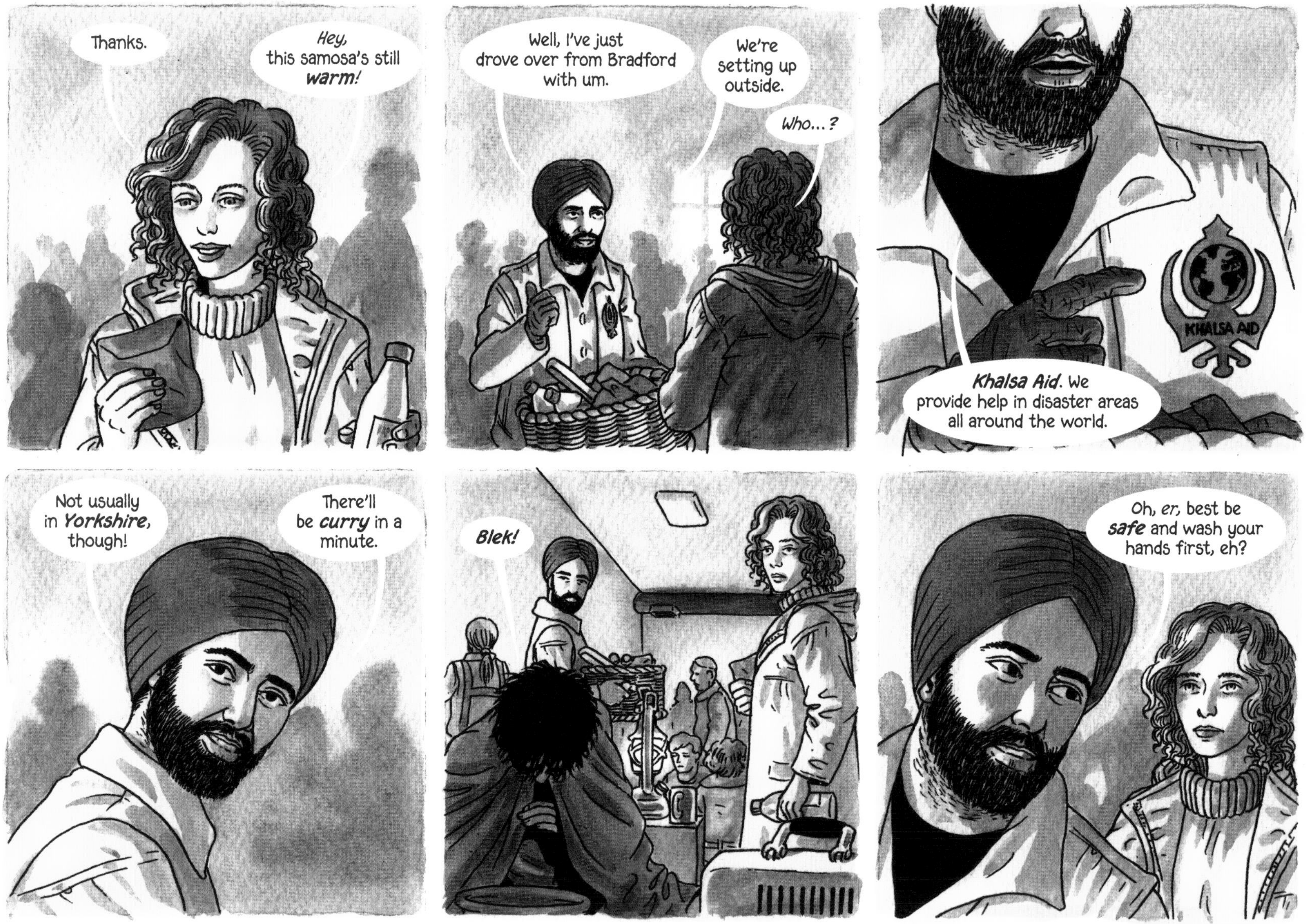
Thanks.
Hey, this samosa's still warm!
Well, I've just drove over from Bradford with um.
We're setting up outside.
Who...?
KHALSA AID
Khalsa Aid. We provide help in disaster areas all around the world.
Not usually in Yorkshire, though!
There'll be curry in a minute.
Blek!
Oh, er, best be safe and wash your hands first, eh?

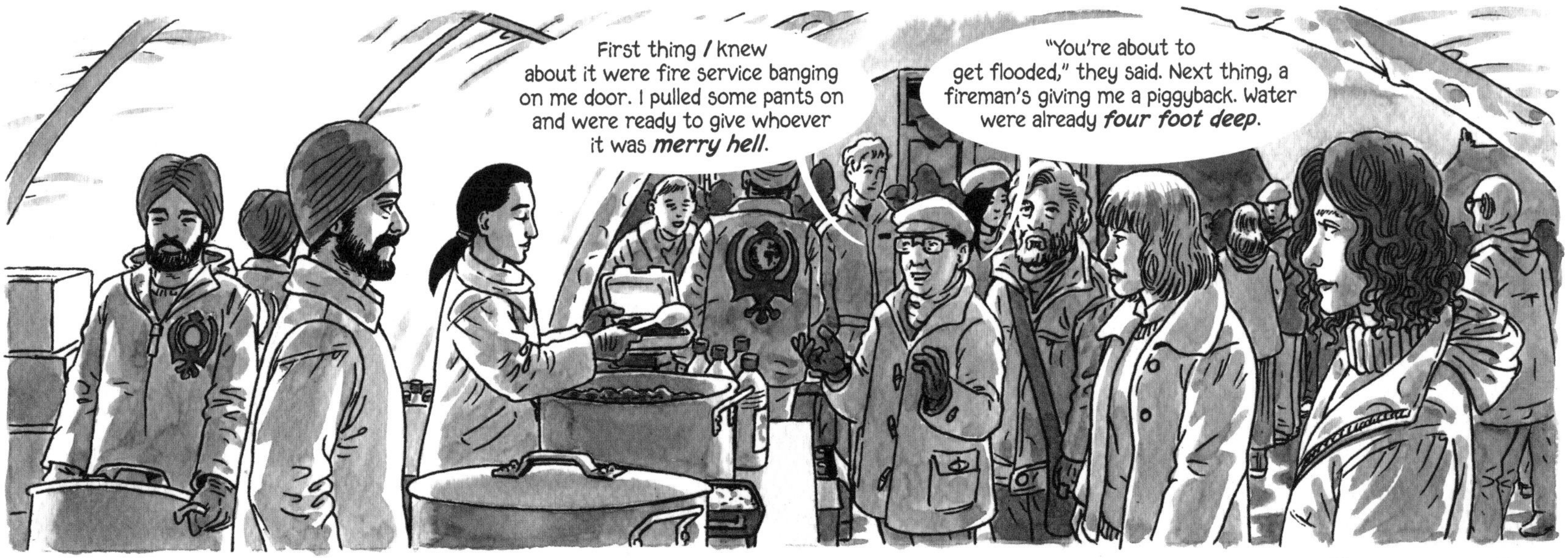
First thing I knew about it were fire service banging on me door. I pulled some pants on and were ready to give whoever it was merry hell.
"You're about to get flooded," they said. Next thing, a fireman's giving me a piggyback. Water were already four foot deep.

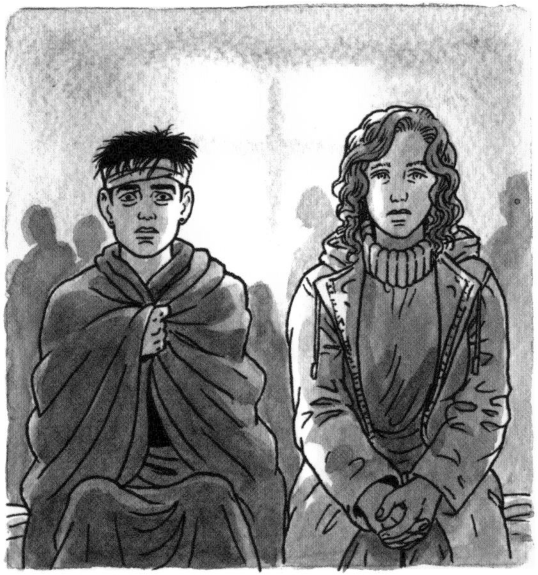

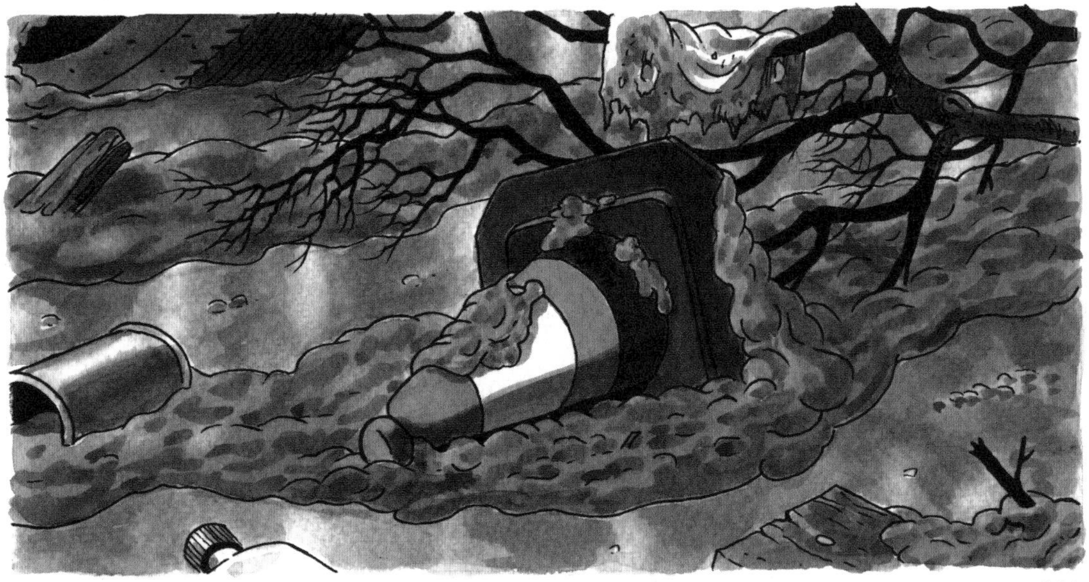

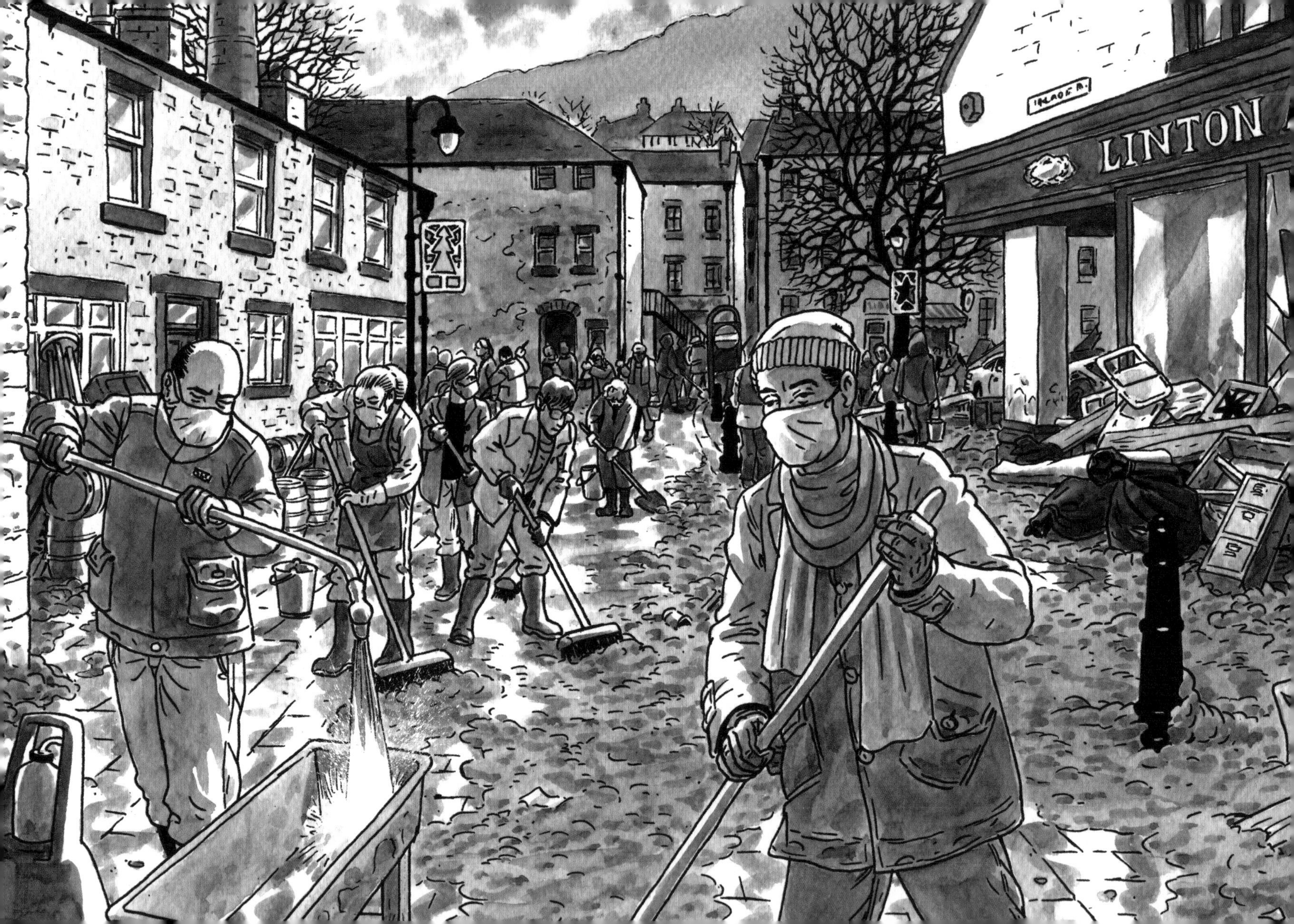
LINTON

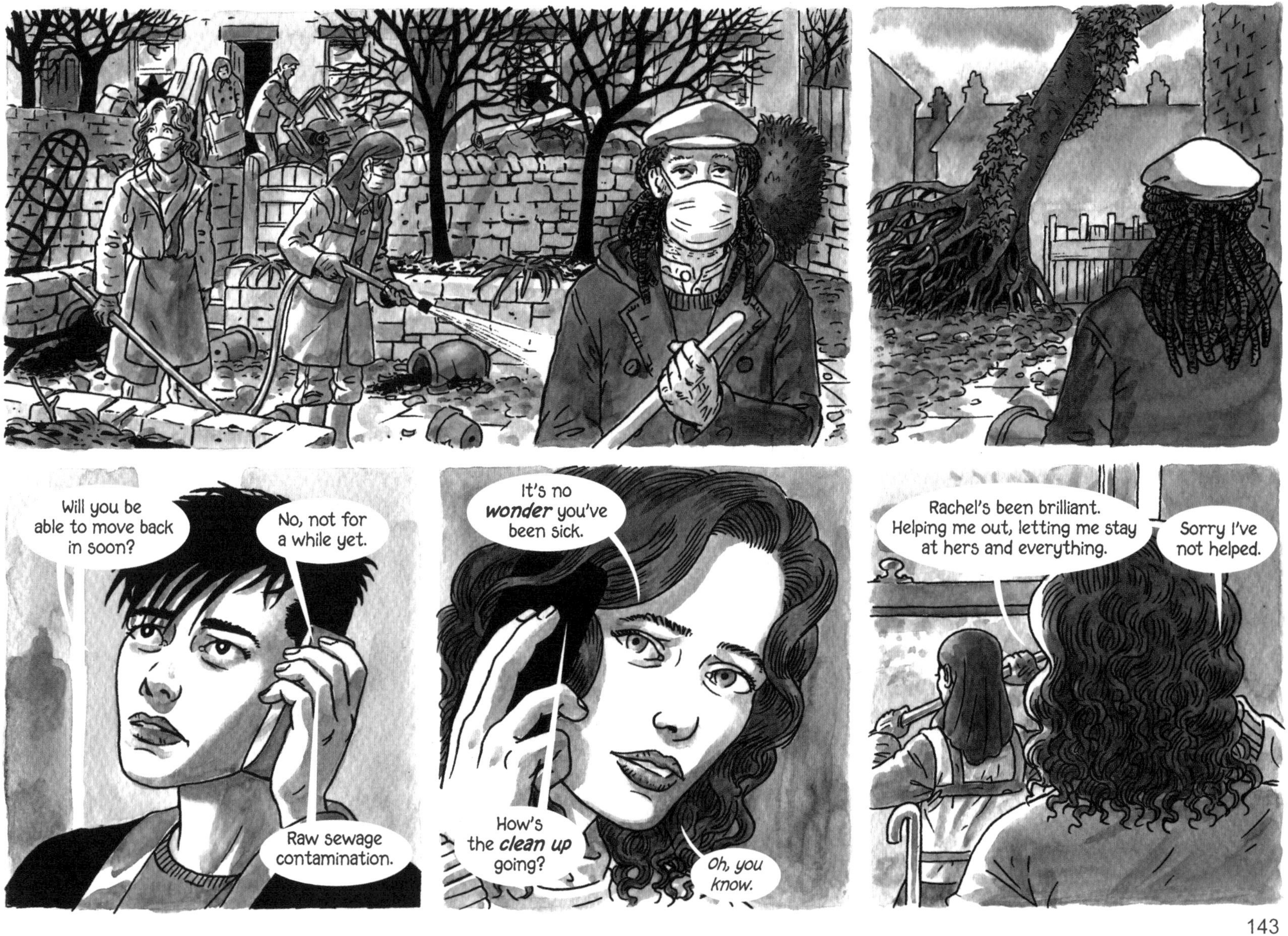
Will you be able to move back in soon?
No, not for a while yet.
Raw sewage contamination.
It's no **wonder** you've been sick.
How's the **clean up** going?
Oh, you know.
Rachel's been brilliant. Helping me out, letting me stay at hers and everything.
Sorry I've not helped.

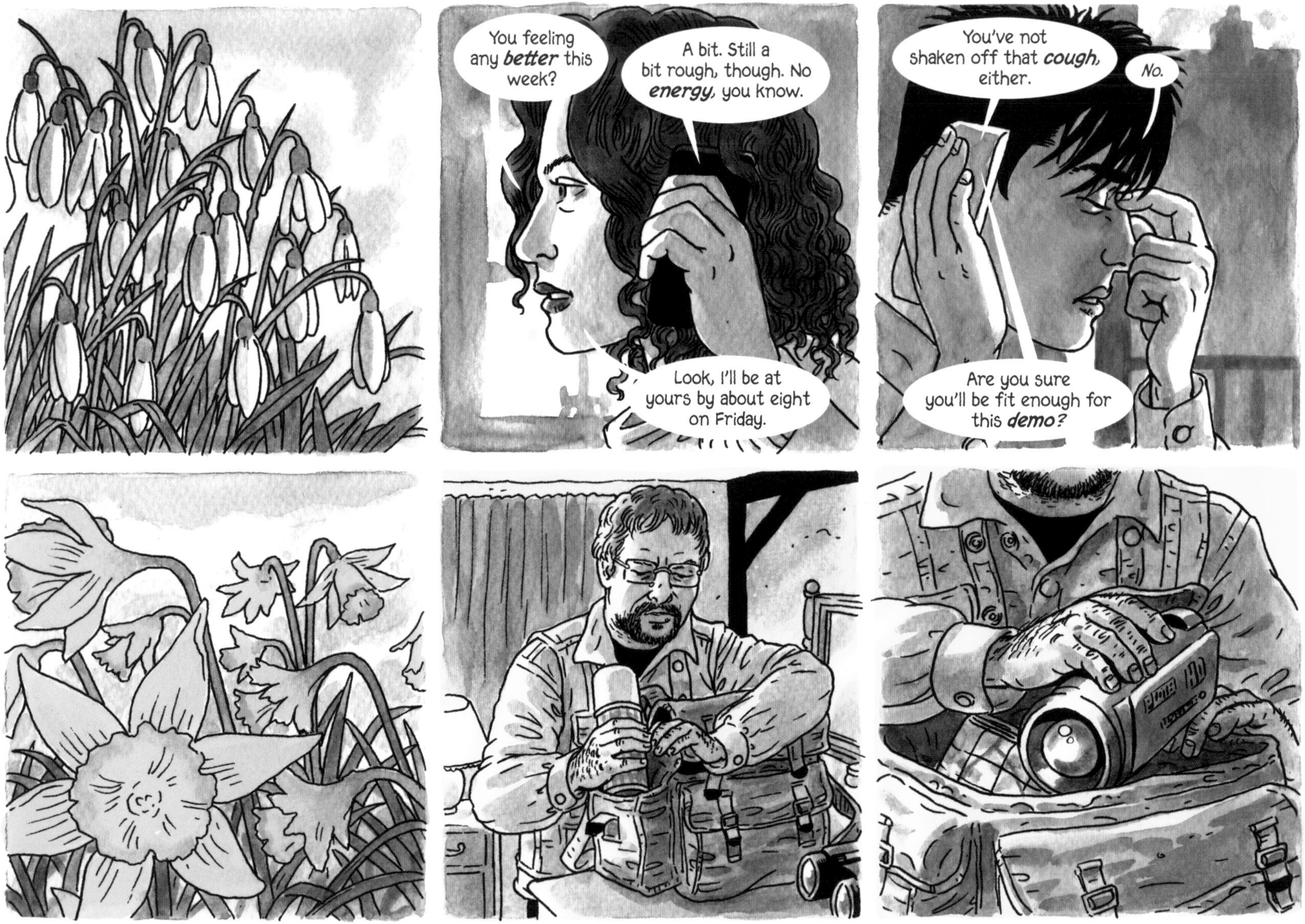
You feeling any *better* this week?
A bit. Still a bit rough, though. No *energy,* you know.
Look, I'll be at yours by about eight on Friday.
You've not shaken off that *cough,* either.
No.
Are you sure you'll be fit enough for this *demo?*

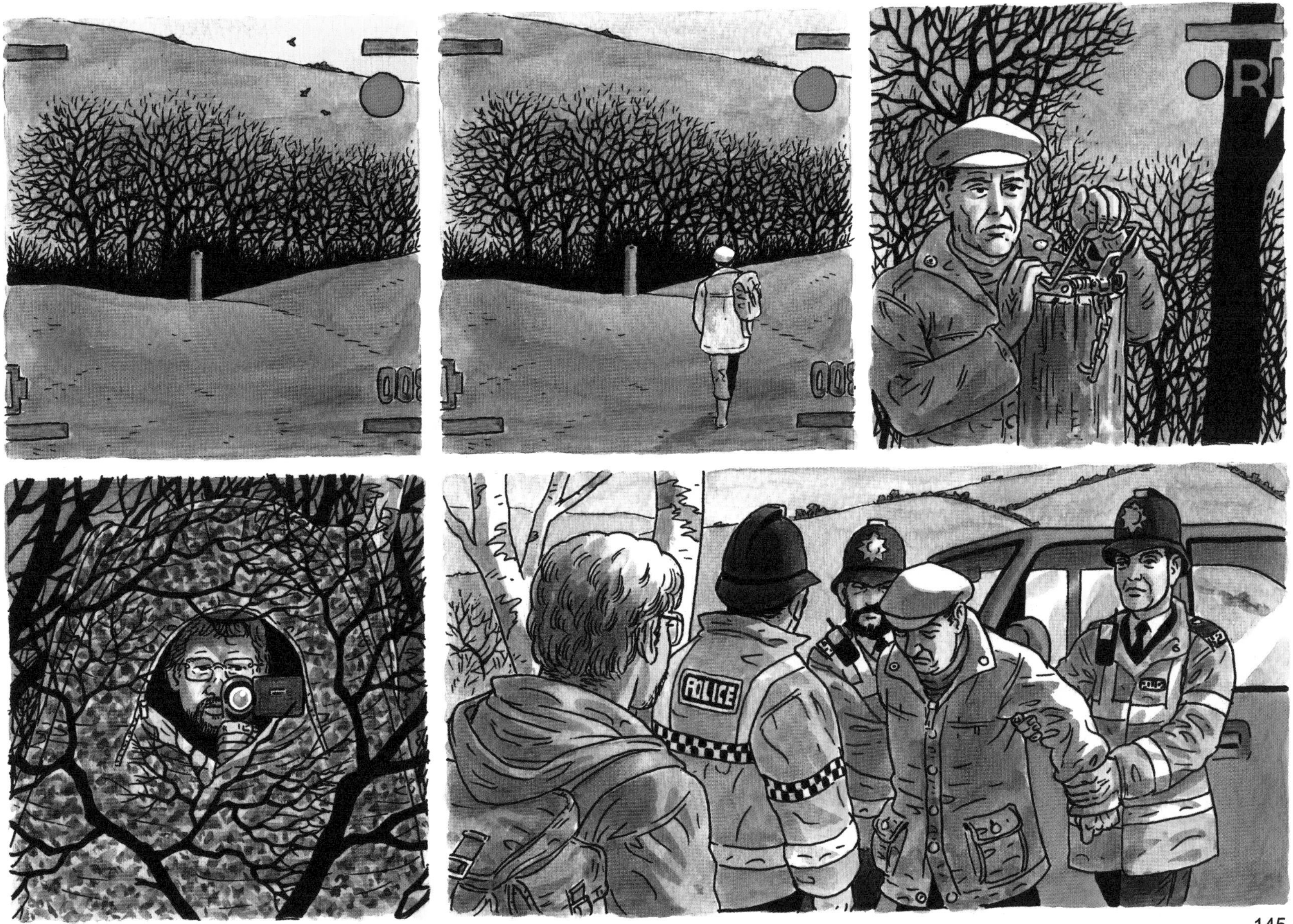
POLICE

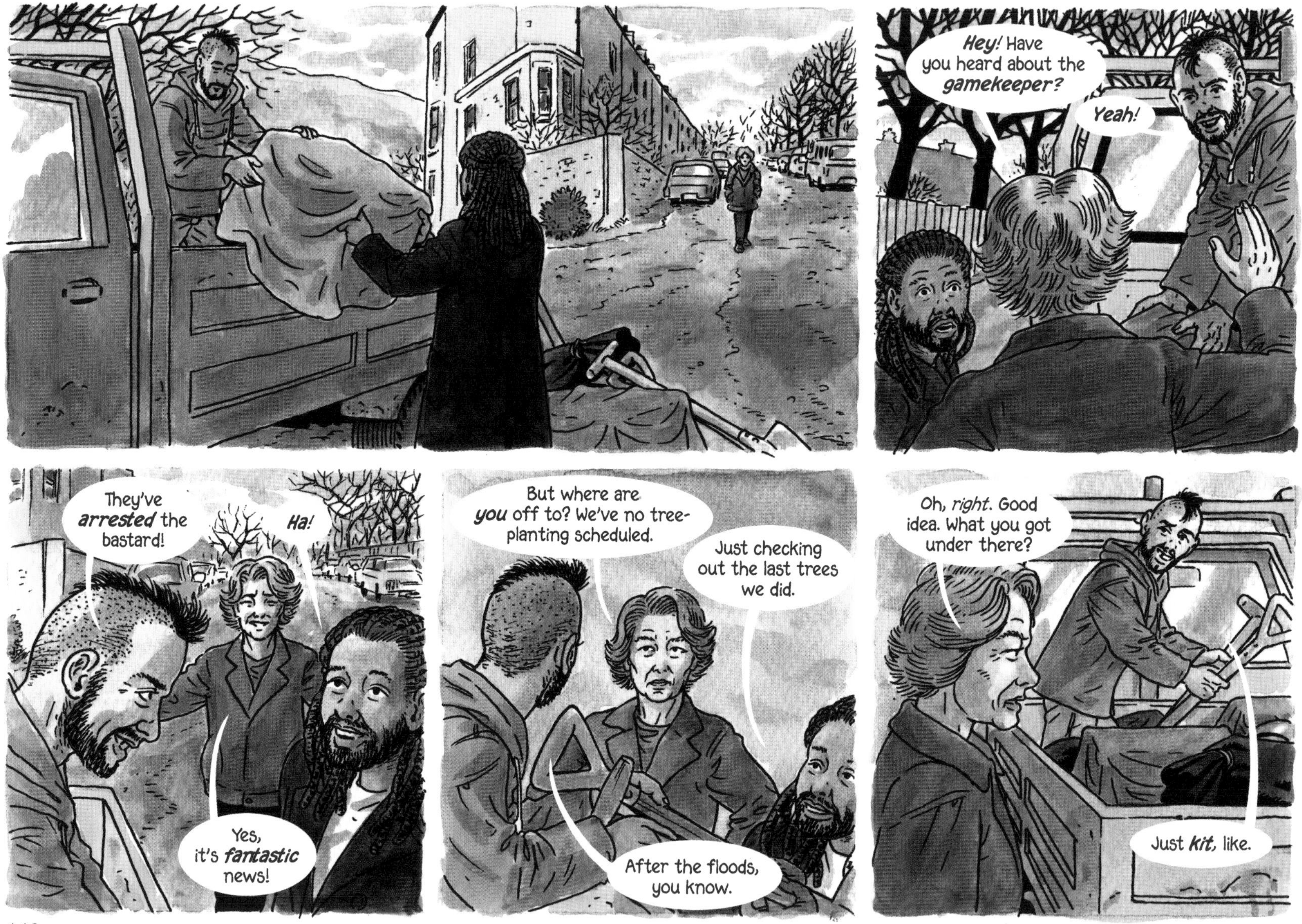

Hey! Have you heard about the gamekeeper?
Yeah!
They've arrested the bastard!
Ha!
Yes, it's fantastic news!
But where are you off to? We've no tree-planting scheduled.
Just checking out the last trees we did.
After the floods, you know.
Oh, right. Good idea. What you got under there?
Just kit, like.

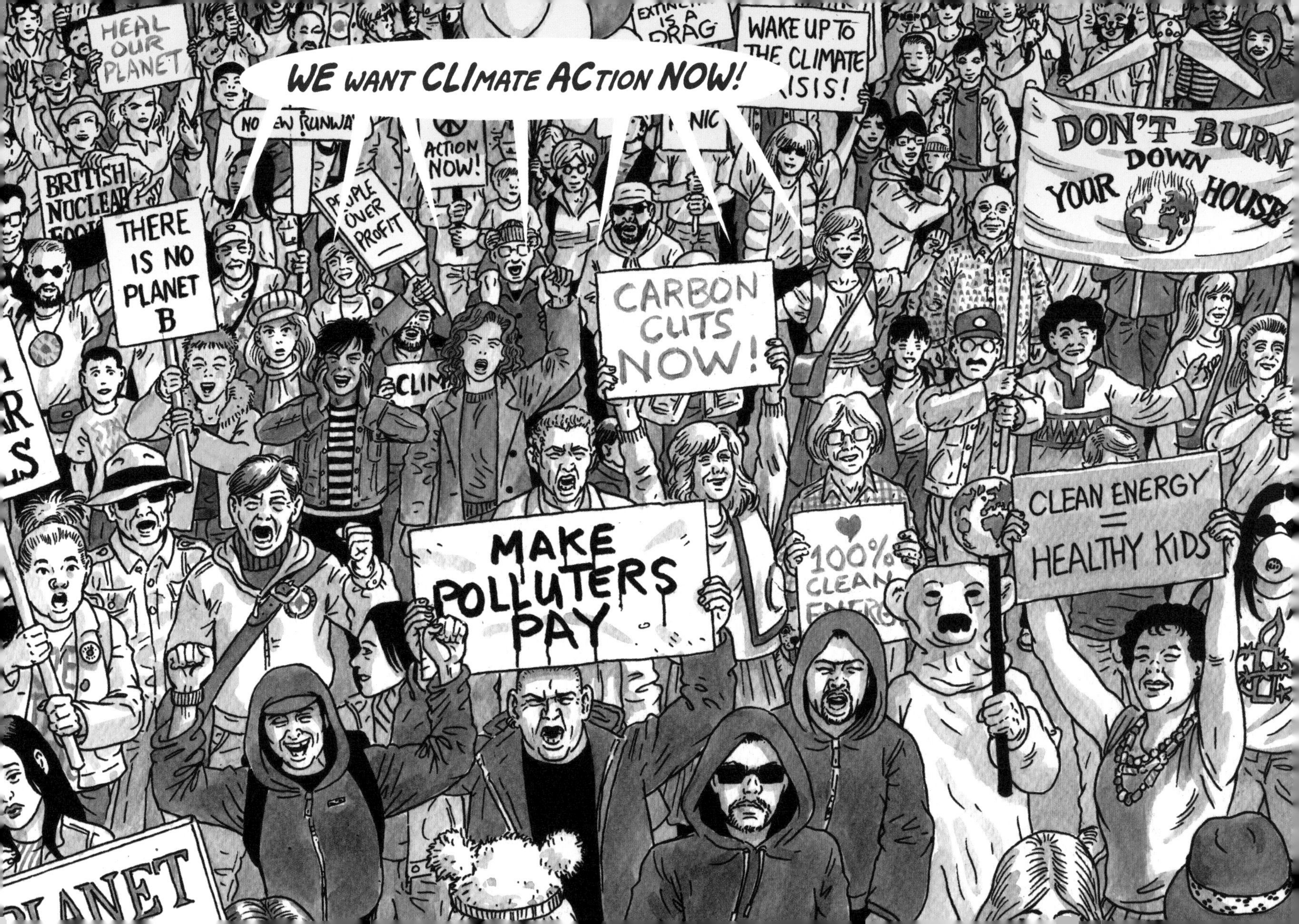

WE WANT CLIMATE ACTION NOW!
HEAL OUR PLANET
WAKE UP TO THE CLIMATE CRISIS!
BRITISH NUCLEAR
THERE IS NO PLANET B
PEOPLE OVER PROFIT
ACTION NOW!
DON'T BURN DOWN YOUR HOUSE
CARBON CUTS NOW!
CLEAN ENERGY = HEALTHY KIDS
MAKE POLLUTERS PAY
100% CLEAN
PLANET

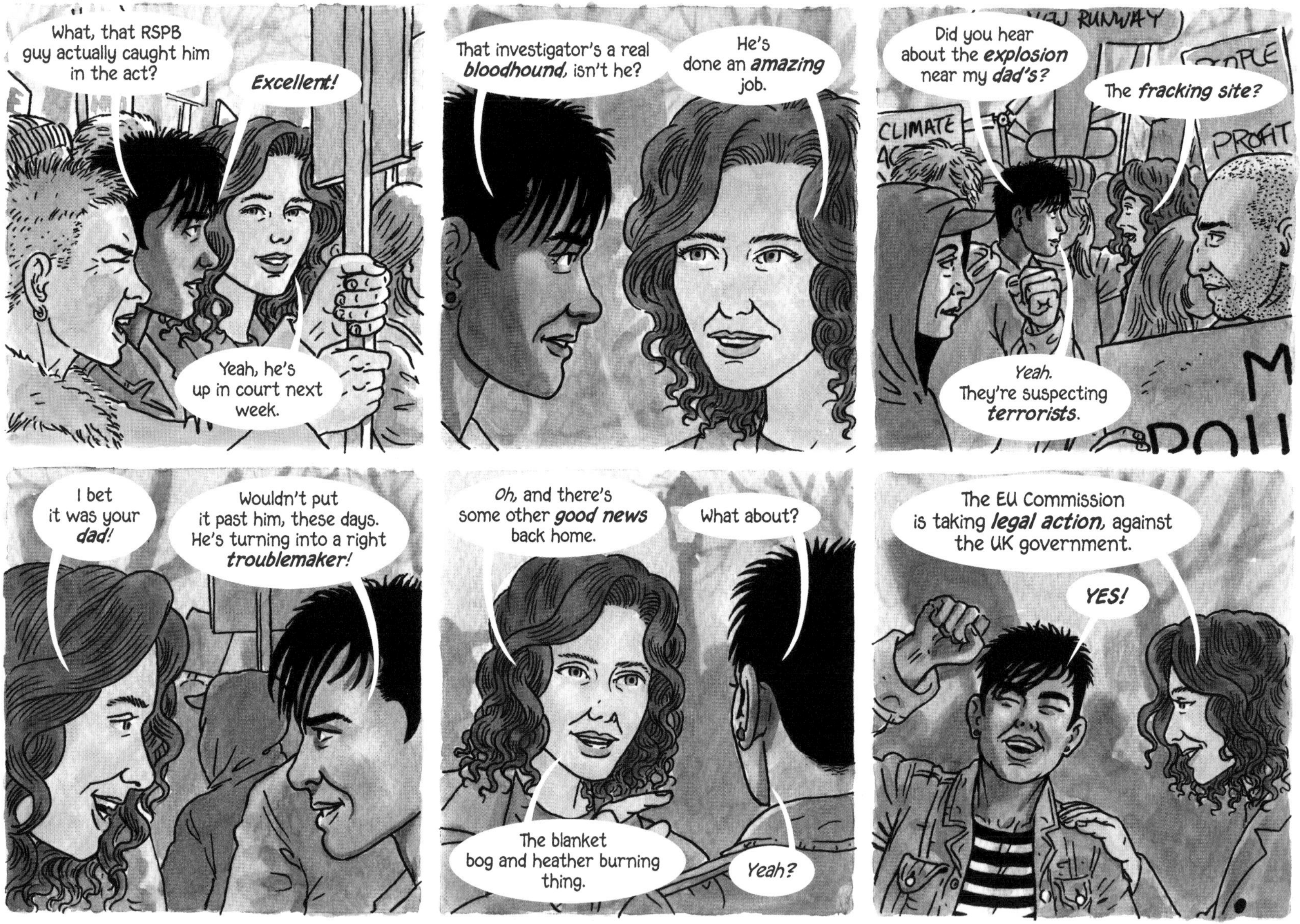
What, that RSPB guy actually caught him in the act?
Excellent!
Yeah, he's up in court next week.
That investigator's a real bloodhound, isn't he?
He's done an amazing job.
Did you hear about the explosion near my dad's?
The fracking site?
Yeah. They're suspecting terrorists.
NEW RUNWAY
PEOPLE
CLIMATE
PROFIT
I bet it was your dad!
Wouldn't put it past him, these days. He's turning into a right troublemaker!
Oh, and there's some other good news back home.
What about?
The blanket bog and heather burning thing.
Yeah?
The EU Commission is taking legal action, against the UK government.
YES!

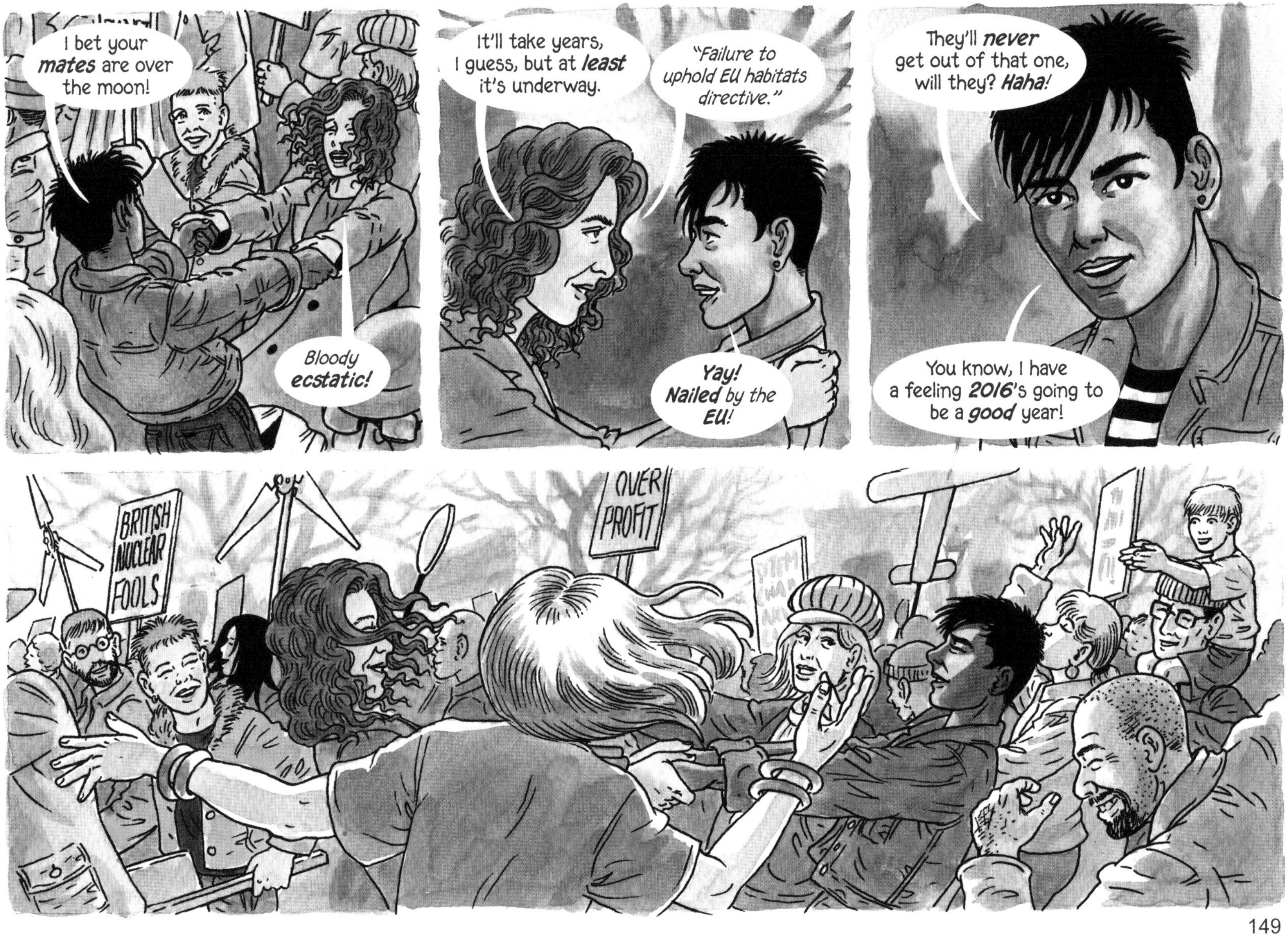

I bet your *mates* are over the moon!
Bloody *ecstatic!*
It'll take years, I guess, but at *least* it's underway.
"Failure to uphold EU habitats directive."
Yay! Nailed by the *EU!*
They'll *never* get out of that one, will they? *Haha!*
You know, I have a feeling *2016*'s going to be a *good* year!
BRITISH NUCLEAR FOOLS
OVER PROFIT

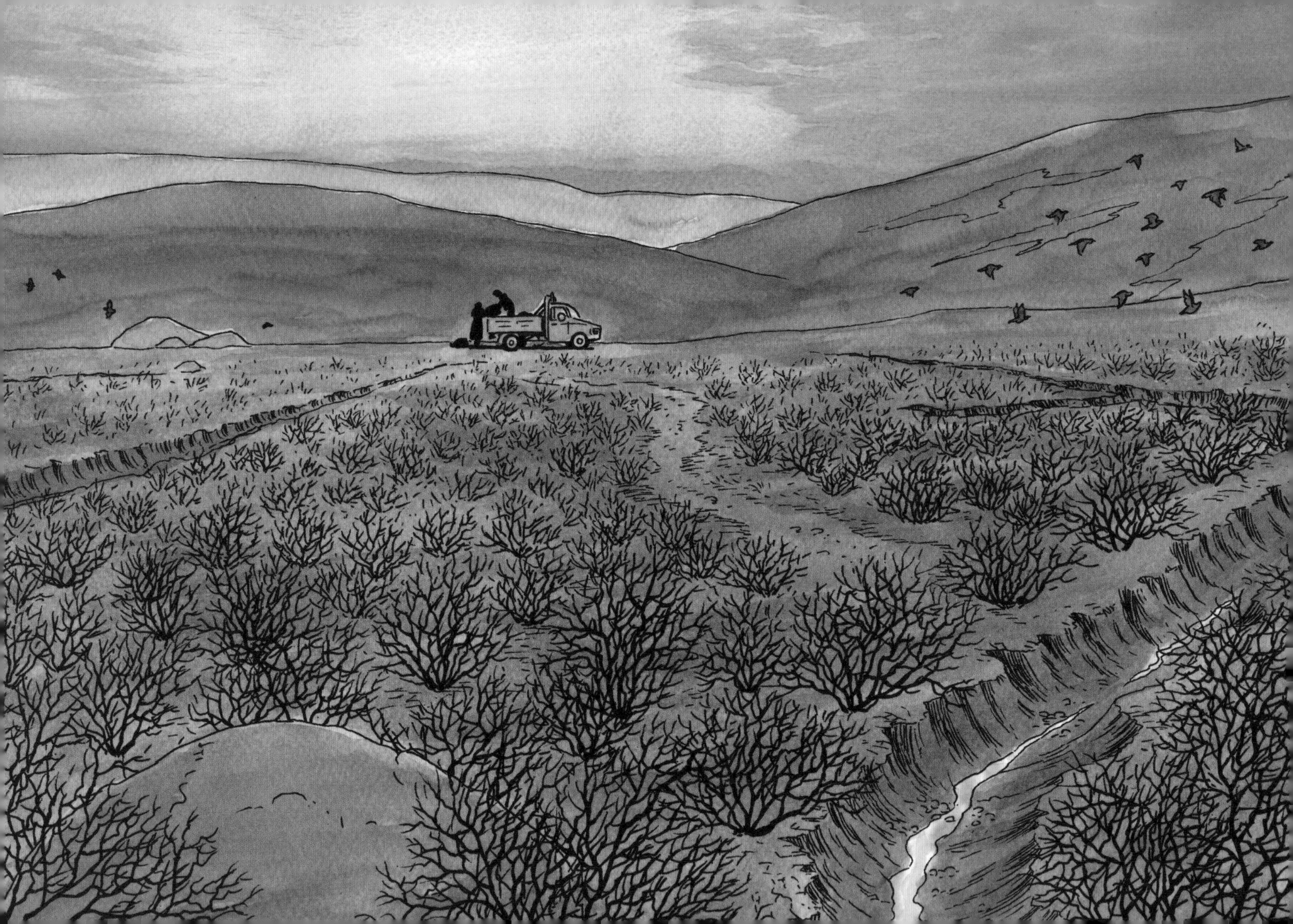

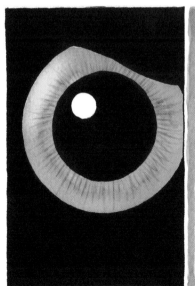

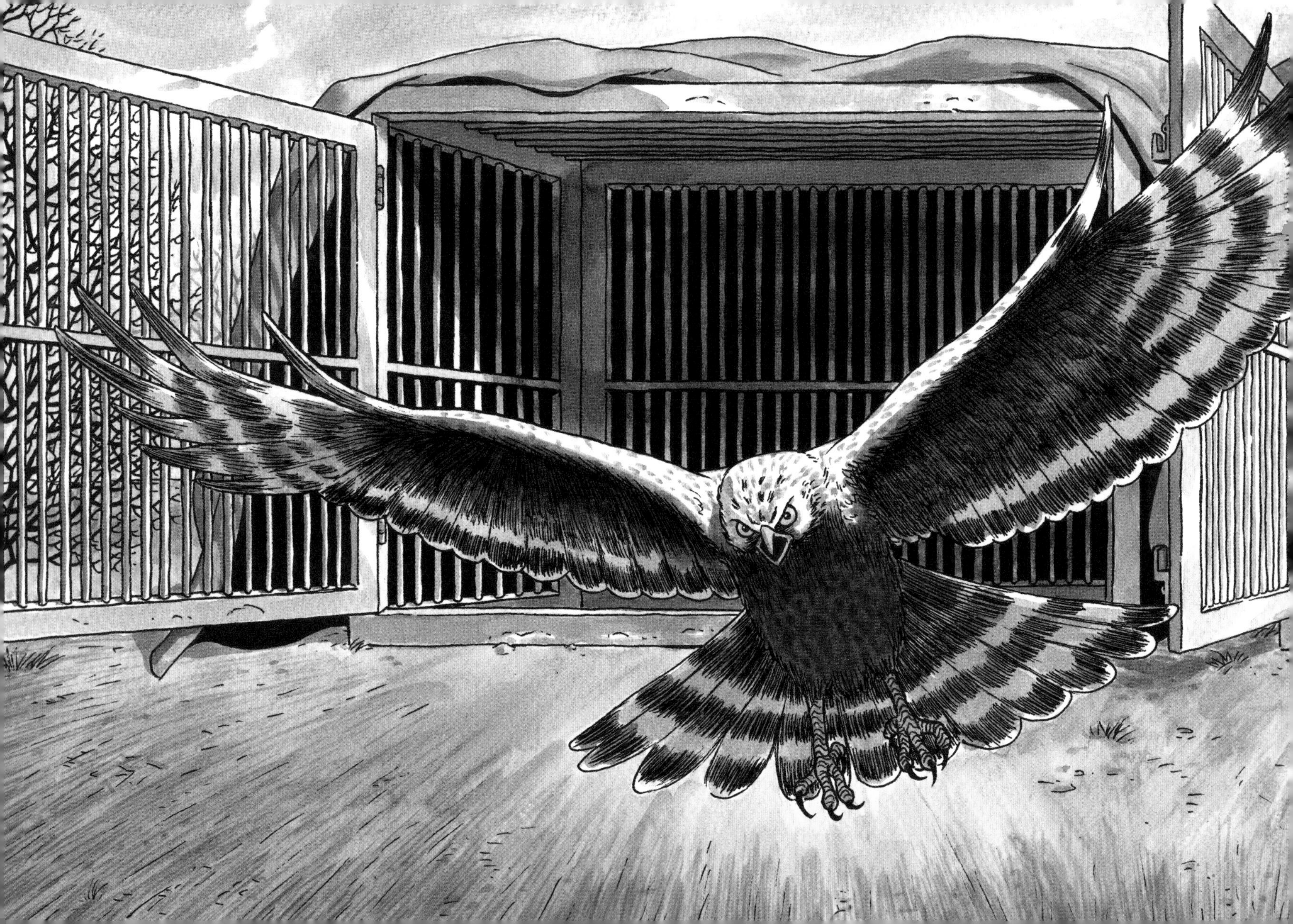

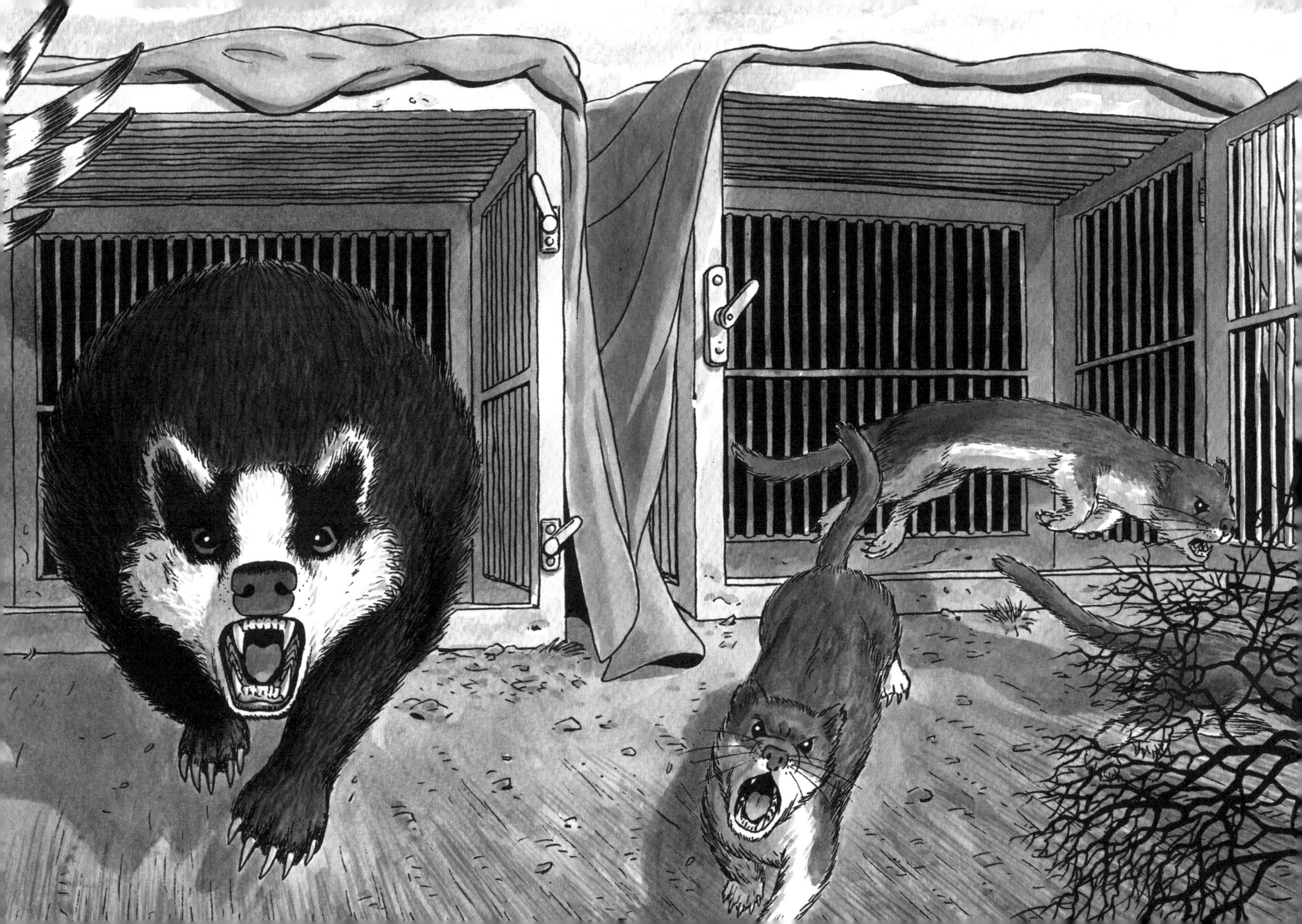

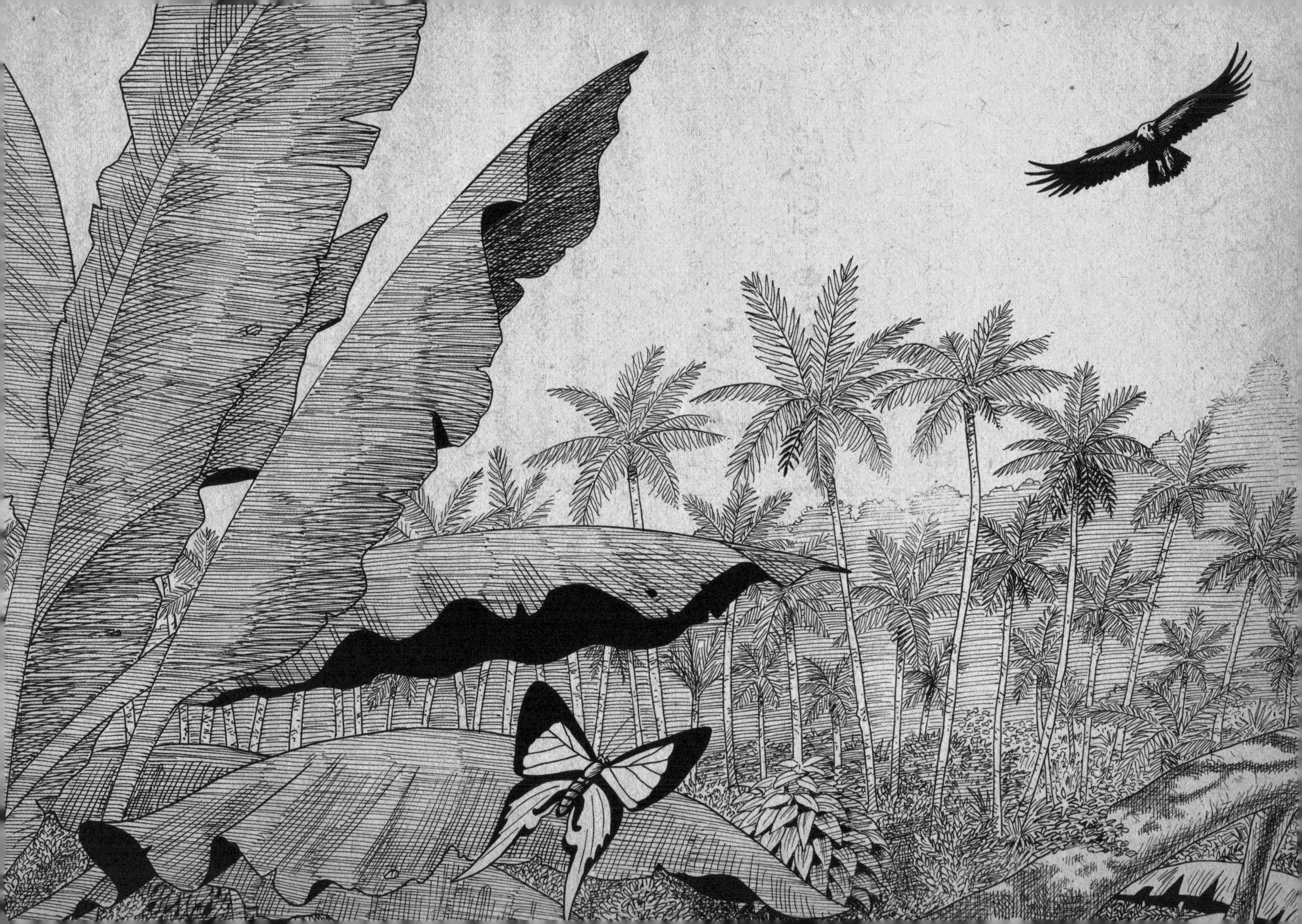

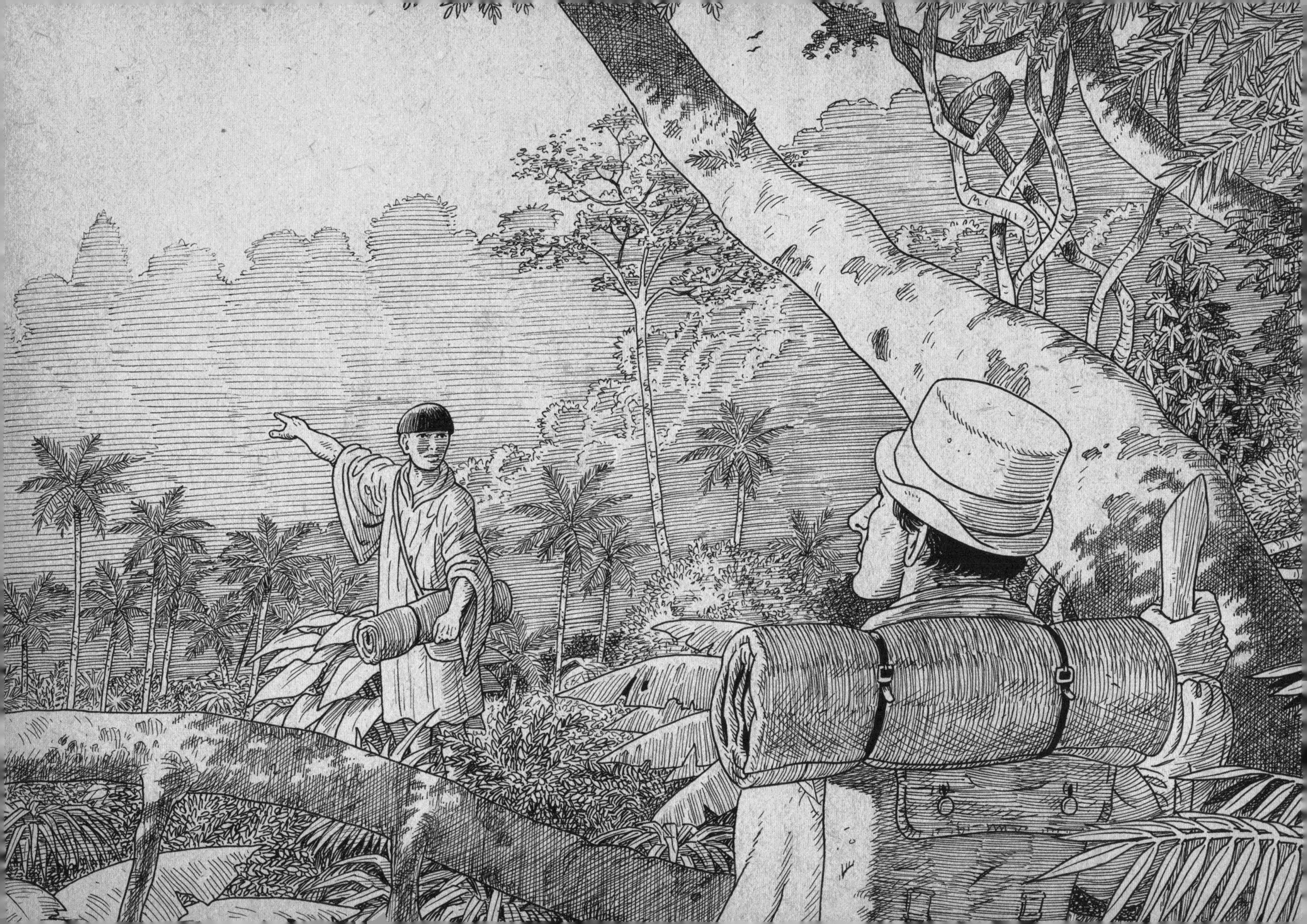

SOURCES AND WELLSPRINGS

The idea of bookending this story with Humboldt's travel journal from 1799–1804 emerged while we were at the Edinburgh International Book Festival in 2016, promoting *The Red Virgin and the Vision of Utopia*. I went along to a talk by Andrea Wulf about her new publication, *The Invention of Nature*, her biography of Alexander von Humboldt. I was captivated.

Humboldt, I learned, was the first scientist to reflect on our human impact on the environment. As Wulf says, when Humboldt identified the three ways in which the human species was affecting the climate, "he named deforestation, ruthless irrigation and, perhaps most prophetically, the 'great masses of steam and gas' produced in the industrial centers. No one but Humboldt had looked at the relationship between humankind and nature like this before." He was thinking ecologically, though the term itself was coined later by Ernst Haeckel. In his time, Humboldt's influence was extraordinary, though acceptance of his ideas was selective. His predictions about human-induced climate change—which he first made as early as 1800—were dismissed as far-fetched. Yet he was a major influence. Evolutionary theorist Charles Darwin names Humboldt as the inspiration for his voyage on the *Beagle*, which eventually led to the publication of his extraordinary *Origin of Species*. The Romantic poetry of Wordsworth and Coleridge is infused with Humboldt's concept of nature and the cosmos. He inspired the emergence of environmentalism, begun by luminaries such as Henry Thoreau and Haeckel. He seemed like a fitting addition to my present-day environmental story.

As for our little tale, its characters and events are fictitious, but the idea was triggered by the devastating flooding that hit the north of England on Boxing Day in 2015. I began working on the book on the first of January 2016, when the flood waters had barely subsided. You can watch accounts of the Yorkshire floods on YouTube; for example, "Waving not Drowning—How Hebden Bridge and Mytholmroyd fought back after the Boxing Day floods." My brother Mike is an avid fell-walker in neighboring Derbyshire. When I told him about the story I was working on, he immediately sent me a copy of *Inglorious: Conflict in the Uplands*—the book Aaron's reading from as he

Ashworth, Sally. "How Hebden Bridge flood volunteers 'became an anchor' for victims," *The Guardian*, 11 January 2016.

Avery, Mark. *Inglorious: Conflict in the Uplands*. London: Bloomsbury, 2015.

Cocker, Mark. *Our Place: Can We Save Britain's Wildlife Before It Is Too Late?* London: Jonathan Cape, 2018.

Humboldt, Alexander von. *Personal Narrative of Travels to the Equinoctial Regions of the New Continent During the Years 1799-1804* vol 4. London: Longman, Hurst, Rees, and Orme.

Monbiot, George. "A Storm of Ignorance," *The Guardian*, 8 December 2015.

Monbiot, George. "Going Downhill Fast," *The Guardian*, 30 December 2015.

Monbiot, George. "Meet the Conservationists Who Believe That Burning Is Good For Wildlife," *The Guardian*, 14 January 2016.

Wulf, Andrea. *The Invention of Nature: The Adventures of Alexander von Humboldt, The Lost Hero of Science*. London: John Murray, 2016.

recounts to Cath the exploits of avian mass murderer Lord Walshingham. The book's author, the indefatigable Mark Avery, is a former Conservation Director for the Royal Society for the Protection of Birds and now a wildlife blogger and tireless campaigner against driven grouse shooting and the illegal killing of wildlife. His book greatly enhanced my understanding of the struggle going on over our upland regions, where I'd chosen to set my story.

Rain centers on one relatively small example of moorland ownership by an elite group that impacts catastrophically on the unlanded majority living in the valley below. But, as the fictitious Rachel says, "There's a million other valleys need saving." They need saving not just for the sake of their human inhabitants, but for the insects and plants, birds and mammals, and all the other inhabitants large and small that we share this planet with—our non-human fellow earthlings. (The nature writer Mark Cocker disarmingly calls them "the more-than-human," displaying a modesty about humanity that is most unusual in our species.)

Instead of being despoilers, rapists of this planet of which we're a sentient part, we need to learn how to be its custodians. That means learning to think ecologically:

Ecological thinking entails that we see ourselves *within* nature and that we understand how everything we do has ecological consequences. We can, in truth, never escape nature . . . We live on a planet where life is only to be found in about a fifteen-mile deep veneer that is wrapped around the surface of the Earth. As far as we have been able to establish in the last 4,000 years, this is the only planet that bears life. We spend our days among the greatest event in all the galaxies. (Cocker 2018, pp291–2)

We need to know that we're part of this living, breathing, awesomely beautiful planet. And that we're stardust.

Mary Talbot
November 2018

OTHER KEY RESOURCES WERE THE WEBSITES OF THE FOLLOWING ORGANIZATIONS, CAMPAIGNS, AND FORUMS:

Bronte Country (www.bronte-country.com)
Campaign Against Climate Change (www.campaigncc.org)
Countryside Alliance (www.countrysidealiance.org)
Darwin Online (www.darwin-online.org.uk)
Friends of the Earth (www.foe.co.uk)
Game and Wildlife Conservation Trust (www.gwct)
Global Soil Biodiversity Initiative (www.globalsoilbiodiversity.org)
Hebden Bridge Web (www.hebdenbridge.co.uk)

Moorland Association (www.moorlandassociation.org)
National Flood Forum (www.bluepages.org.uk)
Natural England (www.gov.uk/government/organisations/natural-england)
Royal Society for the Protection of Birds (www.rspb.org.uk)
Soil Association (www.soilassociation.org)
Upper Calder Valley Plain Speaker (www.energyroyd.org.uk)
Woodland Trust (www.woodlandtrust.org)

MARY M TALBOT

Now a freelance writer, Mary Talbot is an internationally acclaimed scholar of gender and language who previously held academic posts for over twenty-five years and has published extensively in her field. Her first graphic novel, *Dotter of her Father's Eyes* (with Bryan Talbot), won the 2012 Costa Biography Award. Her second and third, *Sally Heathcote, Suffragette* (with Kate Charlesworth and Bryan Talbot) and *The Red Virgin and the Vision of Utopia* (with Bryan Talbot), both bring a strong narrative approach to complex historical material. She has also collaborated with Kate Charlesworth on a chapter for the dystopian SF graphic novel *IDP: 2043*, with Alwyn Talbot on a short strip for *Cross: A Political Satire Anthology*, and with Kate and Bryan again for *Here I Stand*, an Amnesty International anthology. In 2018, Mary and Bryan contributed a four-page strip to the anthology *Traces of the Great War*.

BRYAN TALBOT

Winner of many comic awards, including an Eisner award, Le Prix SNCF, and several Eagles, Bryan Talbot has been working in the medium for forty years. He's produced underground and alternative comics, notably *Brainstorm!*, SF and superhero stories such as *Judge Dredd, Nemesis the Warlock, Teknophage,* and *Batman: Legends of the Dark Knight*. He's worked on DC Vertigo titles, including *Hellblazer, Sandman,* and *Fables,* and created the graphic novels *The Adventures of Luther Arkwright, Heart of Empire, The Tale of One Bad Rat, Alice in Sunderland, Cherubs!* (with Mark Stafford), and *Metronome*. He is published in over twenty countries and is a frequent guest at international comic festivals. He has been awarded honorary doctorates in both Arts and Letters and was recently elected a Fellow of the Royal Society of Literature. Apart from his work with Mary, in the last eight years he's written and drawn the twice Hugo-nominated *Grandville* series of five anthropomorphic detective thrillers.

Mary and Bryan Talbot are founder patrons of the Lakes International Comic Art Festival.

www.mary-talbot.co.uk
www.bryan-talbot.com

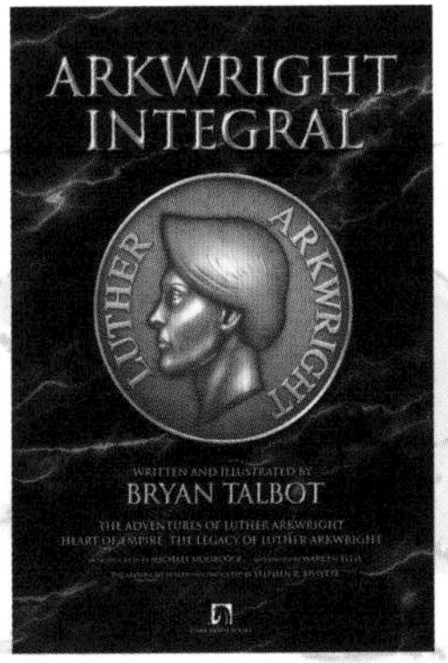
ARKWRIGHT INTEGRAL
LUTHER ARKWRIGHT
WRITTEN AND ILLUSTRATED BY
BRYAN TALBOT
THE ADVENTURES OF LUTHER ARKWRIGHT
HEART OF EMPIRE: THE LEGACY OF LUTHER ARKWRIGHT

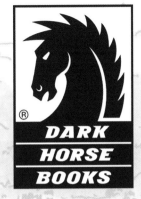

DARK HORSE BOOKS

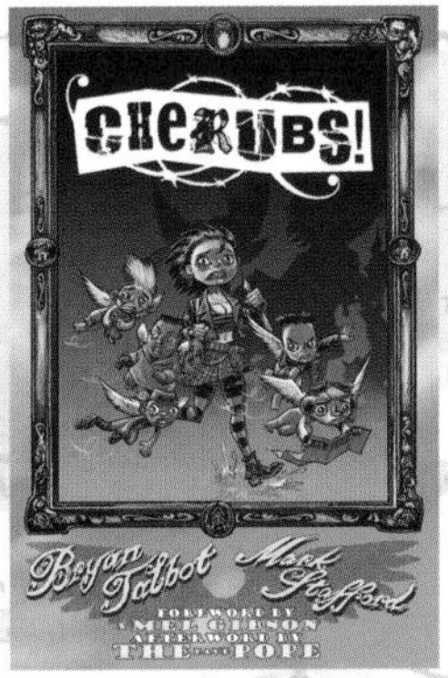
CHERUBS!
Bryan Talbot
Mark Stafford

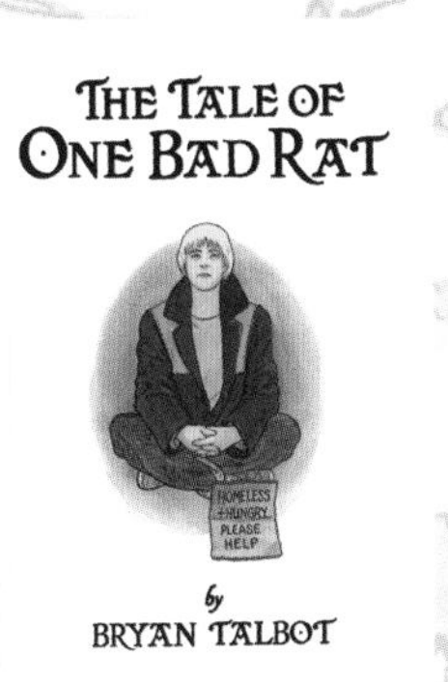
THE TALE OF
ONE BAD RAT
HOMELESS + HUNGRY PLEASE HELP
by
BRYAN TALBOT

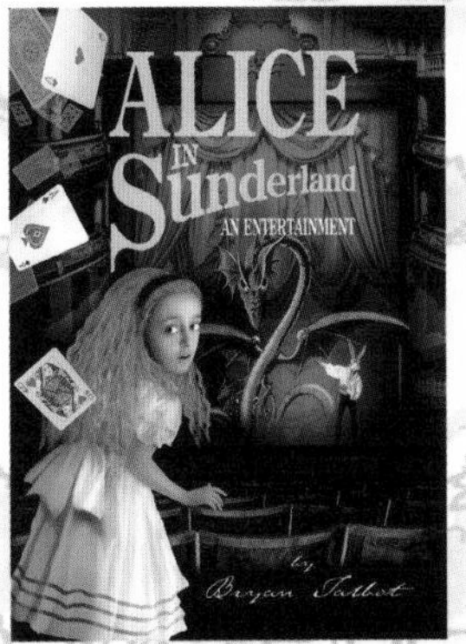
ALICE IN Sunderland
AN ENTERTAINMENT
by Bryan Talbot

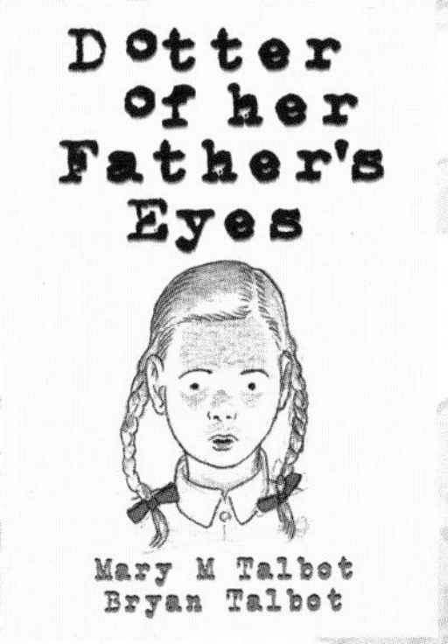
Dotter of her Father's Eyes
Mary M Talbot
Bryan Talbot

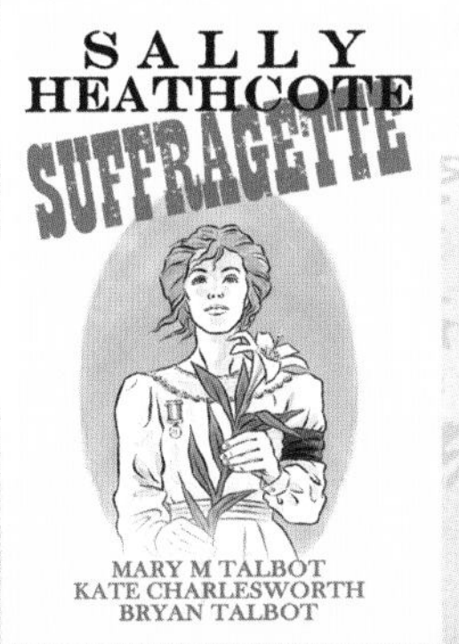
SALLY HEATHCOTE
SUFFRAGETTE
MARY M TALBOT
KATE CHARLESWORTH
BRYAN TALBOT

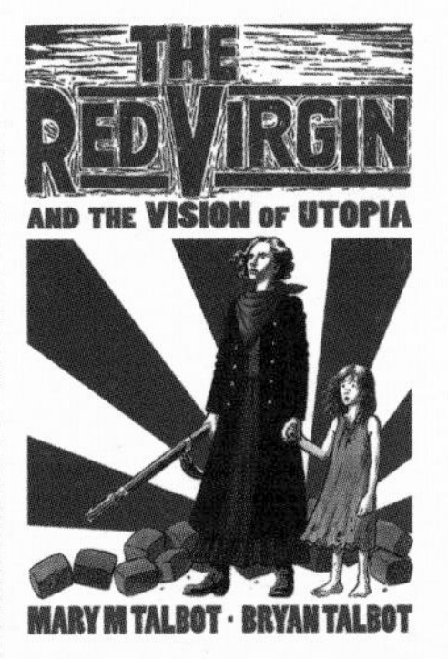
THE RED VIRGIN
AND THE VISION OF UTOPIA
MARY M TALBOT · BRYAN TALBOT

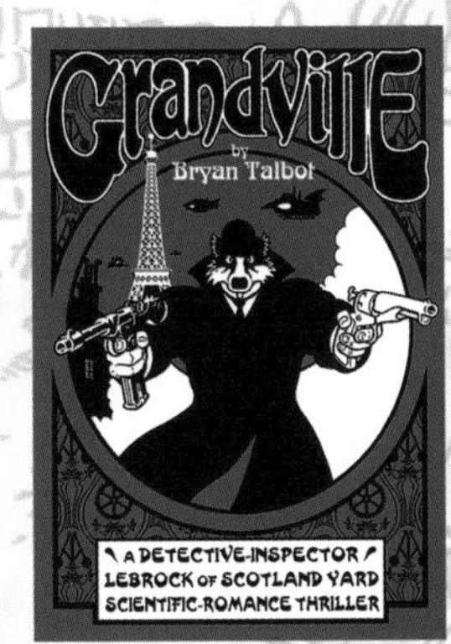
Grandville
by Bryan Talbot
A DETECTIVE-INSPECTOR LEBROCK OF SCOTLAND YARD SCIENTIFIC-ROMANCE THRILLER

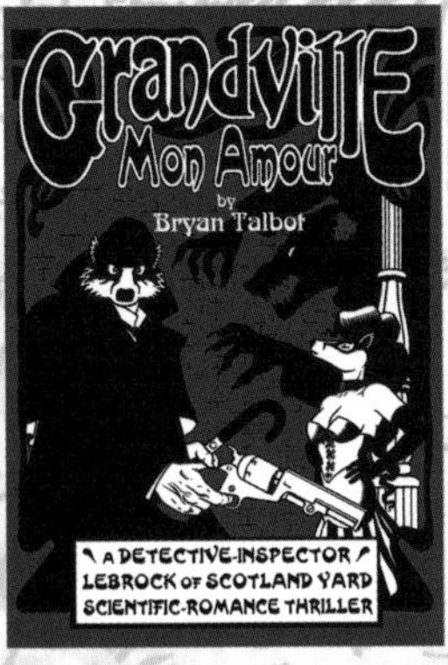
Grandville
Mon Amour
by Bryan Talbot
A DETECTIVE-INSPECTOR LEBROCK OF SCOTLAND YARD SCIENTIFIC-ROMANCE THRILLER

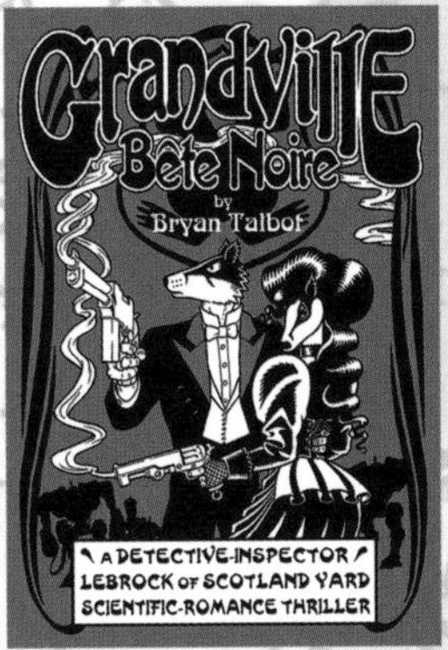
Grandville
Bête Noire
by Bryan Talbot
A DETECTIVE-INSPECTOR LEBROCK OF SCOTLAND YARD SCIENTIFIC-ROMANCE THRILLER

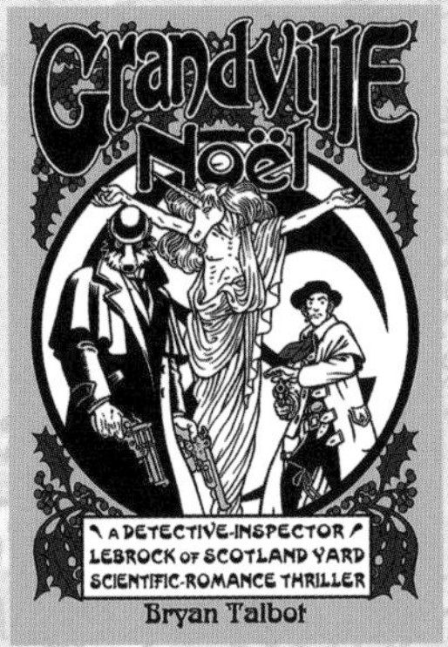
Grandville
Noël
A DETECTIVE-INSPECTOR LEBROCK OF SCOTLAND YARD SCIENTIFIC-ROMANCE THRILLER
Bryan Talbot

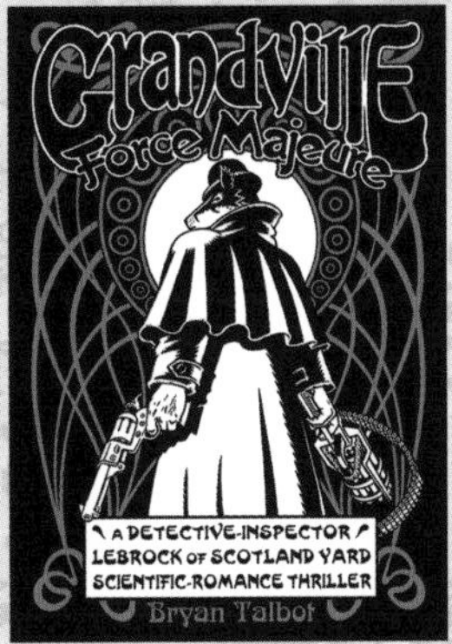
Grandville
Force Majeure
A DETECTIVE-INSPECTOR LEBROCK OF SCOTLAND YARD SCIENTIFIC-ROMANCE THRILLER
Bryan Talbot

publication design **BRYAN TALBOT** with **PATRICK SATTERFIELD**

president and publisher **MIKE RICHARDSON**

U.S. editor **CHRIS WARNER**

U.S. assistant editor **KONNER KNUDSEN**

digital art technician **CHRIS HORN**

R A I N

Dark Horse Books
A division of Dark Horse Comics LLC
10956 S.E. Main Street • Milwaukie OR 97222

DarkHorse.com

To find a comics shop in your area: comicshoplocator.com

First edition: October 2019 • ISBN 978-1-50671-520-9

1 3 5 7 9 10 8 6 4 2

Printed in China

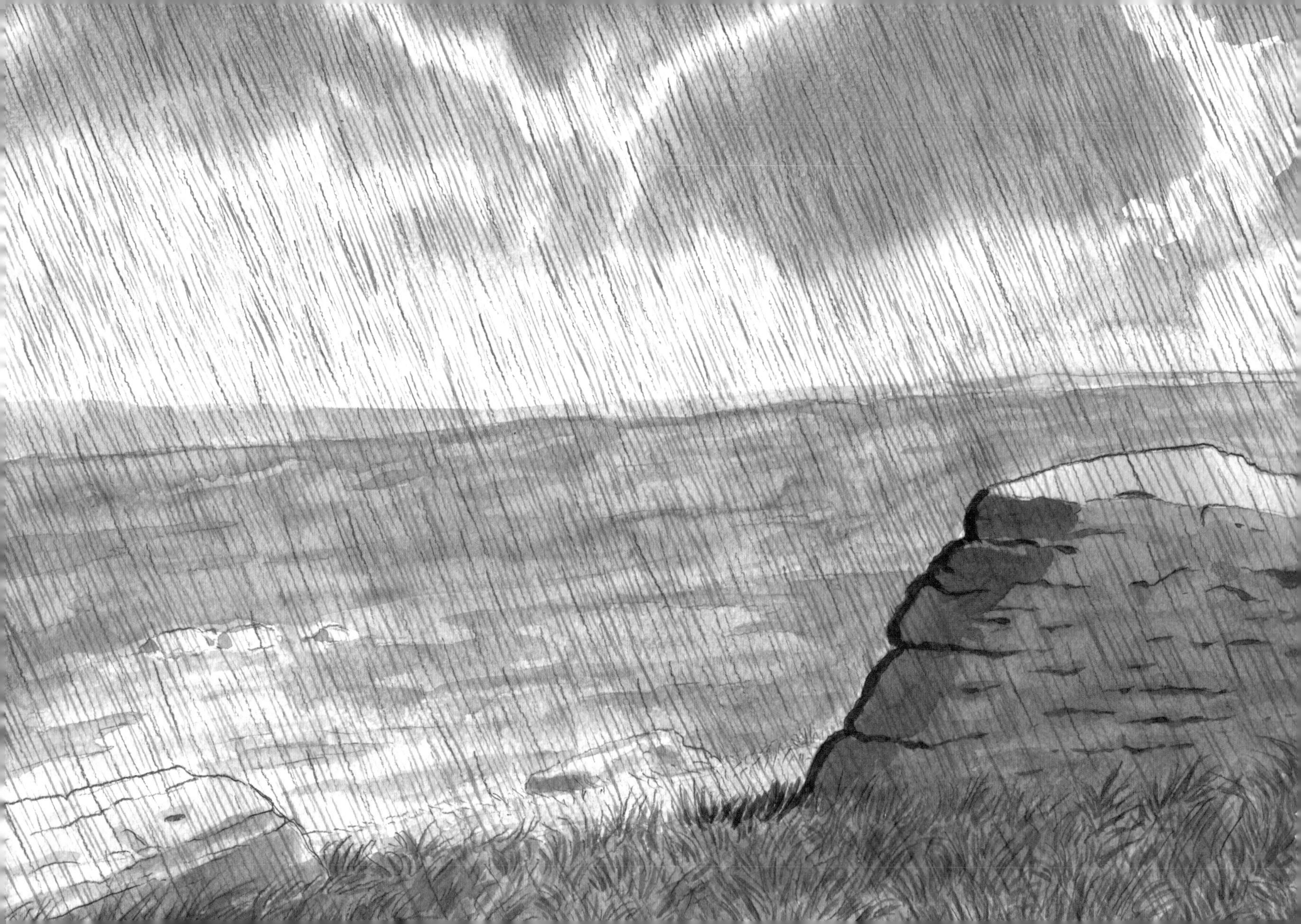